WORKING WITH
WITH
PC WORKS

WORKING WITH
PC WORKS

MICHAEL L. SLOAN

Scott, Foresman and Company
Glenview, Illinois   London

Cover photo: Courtesy of International Business Machines Corporation.

Trademark notices appear on the page following the Acknowledgments.

Library of Congress Cataloging-in-Publication Data

Sloan, Michael L.
    Working with PC Works / Michael L. Sloan
        p.   c.m.
    Includes index.
    1. Microsoft Works (Computer program)   2. Business—Data
processing.   I. Title.
    HF5548.4.M53S56   1989
    005.36′9—dc19   89-4152
                                                                          CIP

1 2 3 4 5 6 MVN 94 93 92 91 90 89

ISBN 0-673-38192-7

Notice of Liability

The information in this book is distributed on an "As Is" basis, without warranty. Neither the author nor Scott, Foresman and Company shall have any liability to customer or any other person or entity with respect to any liability, loss, or damage caused or alleged to be caused directly or indirectly by the programs contained herein. This includes, but is not limited to, interruption of service, loss of data, loss of business or anticipatory profits, or consequential damages from the use of the programs.

Scott, Foresman professional books are available for bulk sales at quantity discounts. For information, please contact Marketing Manager, Professional Books Group, Scott, Foresman and Company, 1900 East Lake Avenue, Glenview, IL 60025.

ACKNOWLEDGMENTS

I would like to thank the following people and organizations for their help during the writing and editing of this book:

Amy Davis of Scott, Foresman and Company

Chuck Maddox, for his invaluable assistance in preparing the artwork of this book for publication

The advertising firm of Rundell and Sloan, Ltd.

Claudia Sloan, my partner, helpmate, and wife

The entire staff of Farnsworth Computer Center of Aurora, IL

This book is dedicated to the students, faculty, and staff of the Illinois Mathematics and Science Academy.

CONTENTS

INTRODUCTION

Welcome to *Working with PC Works*. Throughout the course of this book, you'll be learning how to use the many features and functions of Microsoft's new program, *Works*. Rather than just giving you a list of those features and the commands that activate them, I have presented several practical examples in the form of projects. That way, you can see not only *how* to use a particular feature (such as tabs in the word processor), but also *why* you would want to use the feature (perhaps to align a column of numbers).

The book is divided into eight chapters. Chapter 1 was written primarily for persons who have had relatively little experience using their computers. It discusses how to use the keyboard, how to create data disks, and what equipment you'll need to use the *Works* program. Chapter 1 also talks about several common features in *Works*: executing commands, using a mouse, starting and quitting the program, etc. If you've had your PC for a while, and you're familiar with these features, feel free to skim Chapter 1 or skip it altogether.

Chapter 2 deals with the first major function of *Works*, the word processor. Chapter 3 explains *Works'* database function, while Chapter 4 talks about the spreadsheet and all the features and commands that make it such a powerful analytical tool. The only spreadsheet feature that isn't discussed in Chapter 4 is *Works'* ability to draw a chart from the data in a spreadsheet; this is the subject of Chapter 5.

Data communication, the last of the four applications comprising *Works,* is covered in Chapter 6. Here, in the process of performing the chapter project, you (with your PC) will be able to talk over the telephone to an electronic bulletin board system that I have set up especially for your use with *Works.*

Chapter 7 deals with transferring data between the various applications (word processor, database, etc.). And Chapter 8 offers tips and techniques for getting the most out of *Works.*

While each chapter is pretty much self-contained, I recommend that you read them and perform the projects in sequence. The exercises in Chapters 6 and 7 use files and documents that you create in earlier chapters. Speaking of exercises, I urge you to *do* each one as you read it in the book so that you'll be able to compare your results with the diagrams that accompany the text.

I hope you enjoy reading this book as much as I enjoyed writing it. Good luck, and happy computing.

Chapter 1
PC WORKS, YOUR COMPUTER, AND YOU

System Requirements for *Works*
You and Your Computer
Using *Works* for the First Time
An Approach to Learning *Works*

Your personal computer (PC) is a truly marvelous creation. Unimaginably complex, it is nonetheless easy to operate. But your PC is just a big paperweight without instructions telling it what to do. These instructions are called computer programs, and this book was written to aid you in using one particular PC program, Microsoft *Works*.

Works is really four separate programs—a word processor, a database, a spreadsheet, and a data communications tool—all rolled into one package. Each of these four applications is discussed in a chapter. (I gave the charting capabilities of the spreadsheet their own chapter.)

Chapter 1, though, was written specifically for persons who are unfamiliar with the operation of their PC and are using *Works* for the first time. It describes the individual components of your computer system (memory, printers, keyboard, mouse, etc.) and how to use some of the general features of *Works*, such as pull-down menus. If you are an experienced PC user, feel free to skip most of this chapter. I would like you to read the section *Commanding Works* before you proceed to Chapter 2.

SYSTEM REQUIREMENTS FOR *WORKS*

As you probably know, there are many models of IBM (or MS-DOS) personal computers—original PCs, XTs, ATs, PS/2s, etc.—each with its own unique features. Microsoft *Works* was written to be used with any IBM PC, XT, or AT, PS/2, or any computer that is 100% compatible with these IBM models.

To use *Works*, your computer system must meet certain minimum requirements. This is true for all computer programs, but the specific requirements vary from one program to the next.

Memory

Your computer has two kinds of memory, read only memory (called ROM) and random access memory (called RAM). ROM is used to hold permanent instructions for your PC. These instructions are literally "burned" into the integrated circuit (IC) ROM chips and ensure that your computer will know how to do certain tasks the moment you turn it on. For example, the ROM tells your PC how to begin reading information from disks and how to display information on the screen.

The other kind of memory, RAM, is where your PC stores all of the instructions for a particular application, such as Microsoft *Works*. It also stores the documents you are currently working on. Memory is measured in units called *bytes*. And one byte of memory can hold (or store) one character of information. The letter "A," the number "6," the symbol "?," even the space between two words are all characters, and each occupies one byte of RAM storage.

Works requires that your computer have at least 384K (K is an abbreviation for kilo, meaning "thousand") bytes of RAM. Since RAM is used to keep both program instructions and your own documents while you're creating or modifying them, all 384K of memory isn't available for your documents. What happens if your word processor document, or database, or spreadsheet grows to be larger than available RAM? Well, *Works* keeps as large a portion of your document as it can in your computer's RAM. The remainder is kept on disk (see the discussion on disk drives below).

≡ Disk Drives

The disk drive is the component in your computer system that allows you to permanently store the documents you create with Microsoft *Works* onto round magnetic disks. Think of a disk drive as a device for copying information either from RAM onto those disks, or from the disks into RAM. Whichever way you transfer the information, the original version stays put. What I mean is that when you save a document you've created with *Works* onto a *data* disk (see *Formatting a Data Disk*, below), the document is still in the computer (in RAM) for you to add to or modify. If you do make further modifications, you have to save this new version to the disk. Otherwise, any modifications will be lost when you turn off the computer.

Similarly, when you load a document from a data disk into your computer, the document remains on the disk, unchanged. Only the act of saving will alter the version of your document on the data disk.

Types of Drives

There are currently three types of disk drives. Two of them use 5¼-inch disks (sometimes called "floppy" disks) and differ only in the amount of data they can store on the disk. One type can store 360K bytes (disk storage is measured in bytes, too). The other 5¼-inch disk drive can store 1200K bytes (or 1.2 megabytes) of data.

The third type of disk drive uses a smaller, 3½-inch disk that can store up to 720K bytes. The size of the data disk your computer system uses determines the maximum size document you can create in *Works*.

Hard Disk Drives

Several manufacturers make what are called hard disk drives. (The term *hard* is used because the disks are rigid instead of flexible.) The advantages of a hard disk are increased storage and ease of operation. Typical hard disks can hold up to 20 megabytes of data, or more. (*Note*: A 20 megabyte hard disk can store the equivalent of more than 55 360K disks.) Using a hard disk eliminates the need for shuffling disks in and out of your disk drives and generally improves *Works'* performance. If you can afford one, I'd recommend adding a hard disk drive to your computer system.

Microsoft *Works* requires your computer system to have two 5¼-inch disk drives, or one 3½-inch disk drive, or a hard disk drive.

☰ The Operating System

Your computer needs to know how to communicate with its disk drives: how to format a blank disk (see below), how to write data to a disk, how to read data from a disk, and so forth. Your computer doesn't know how to do any of these things when you first turn it on. The computer instructions for these operations form what is called the disk operating system, or DOS.

If your computer system doesn't include a hard disk drive, you have to place a DOS system disk in drive A each time you turn on your PC. With a hard disk, DOS is placed on the hard disk, and the computer is instructed to look there for it. The process of loading DOS into a computer is called "booting" the computer.

You might wonder why DOS isn't made a permanent part of your computer. Why, for example, isn't DOS burned into ROM (see above) so that it wouldn't have to be loaded from a disk each time the PC is turned on? The answer is that DOS commands and features are constantly being improved. New versions of DOS are released, often several times per year. The versions are numbered, and if you want to see which version of DOS you have, just start up your computer.

At the DOS prompt (A:> or C:>), type the command **VER** and press Enter . When I type **VER**, my PC responds:

IBM Personal Computer DOS Version 3.10

Programs are written with a particular version of DOS in mind. They're guaranteed to work properly with that DOS version and will usually work with any newer versions. Microsoft *Works* will work with any version of DOS designated as 2.0 or higher.

☰ Formatting a Data Disk

Whether or not your computer system includes a hard disk, you will want to save your *Works* documents to 3½- or 5¼-inch disks. Hard disk drive owners may wonder why they would want to use floppy disks at all. The answer is: to avoid catastrophe. Experienced computer users know this, but if you are new to computing, read these words and believe them with all your heart. Everything breaks. And this includes your hard disk drive. When your hard disk "crashes" (*when*, not *if*), you will probably lose everything you've stored on it—programs *and* documents. After your drive is repaired or replaced, restoring the programs to the hard disk is an easy task. After all, you still have the original program disks. But what about your documents? All that work, all that creativity, gone!

To prevent this disaster, everybody keeps copies of documents on disks. This is called "backing up" your data. So, hard disk or not, you'll have to create (or *format*) some data disks. If you don't have a hard disk, you'll also need to format at least two other disks, one to contain a copy of the *Works* program (created by *Works*' Setup utility) and the other to be a copy of *Works*' Spell/Help disk (created by copying all the files from the original Spell/Help disk onto one of your formatted disks).

Formatting (sometimes called initializing) a disk is a simple process, but you might wonder why you have to do it at all. The reason is that disk manufacturers make 3½- and 5¼-inch disks for a variety of different computers. For example, IBM PCs and Apple IIs both use the same 5¼-inch disks. Each type of computer organizes data on the disk a different way. When you format a disk, the computer arranges (formats) the available storage space on the disk in its own special way. And because each type of computer uses a different arrangement

of data on the disk, manufacturers ship the disks completely
unformatted. A disk has to be formatted only once. In fact, if you
reformat a disk, any data that had been stored on the disk is destroyed.

If you have a hard disk drive, the formatting utility will be on
the hard drive. All you have to do to format a blank disk is to place
the disk in Drive A, close the drive door, type

FORMAT A:/V

press (Enter), and follow the instructions that appear on your screen.

If you don't have a hard disk drive, place your DOS boot disk
in drive A, place a blank disk in drive B, type

FORMAT B:/V

press (Enter), and follow the instructions that appear on your screen.

Here's a general rule for formatting disks: The letter (A or B)
following the **FORMAT** command represents the drive that contains
the disk you intend to format. Always specify the drive that has the
disk to be formatted (FORMAT A: or FORMAT B:).

After the disk has been formatted, DOS will ask you for a volume
name for the disk (that's because you added "/V" to the **FORMAT**
command). Type **DATA** and press (Enter). DOS will tell you the
number of bytes of storage available on the newly formatted disk and
then ask you if you want to format another disk. Type either **y** for
yes or **n** for no, and that's all there is to formatting a disk. (*Note*:
If your computer system doesn't include a hard disk drive, you'll want
to format two more disks named, perhaps, Program and Spellhelp.)

☰ Printers

While *Works* doesn't require that your computer system include a
printer, you'll almost certainly want to print out your documents. *Works*
will work with an incredible variety of printers. Part of the process
of setting up *Works* is identifying the printer(s) you intend to use.

Printers come in a variety of types, with a multitude of features
and options. Dot matrix printers, for example, form characters by
printing small, closely spaced dots. The better ones offer "near letter
quality" text and the ability to print graphics, such as the graphs and
charts you can create with *Works*.

Impact printers form characters the same way a typewriter does: one whole character at a single stroke. Their text quality is usually excellent, but they are incapable of printing graphics.

Ink jet printers "spray" dots of ink on paper in the form of characters. Some models produce quite good graphics (ask to see a demonstration). They are usually quieter in operation than either impact or dot matrix printers, and their one drawback is that they cannot print multiple-part forms.

Thermal printers "burn" dots onto thermally sensitive paper. I must admit a bias against thermal printers. I don't like the feel of the special thermal paper. Most of the current models do a reasonably good job on text and graphics, but these printers also cannot print multiple-part forms.

Laser printers are becoming increasingly more popular, though they're still rather expensive when compared with dot matrix printers. All laser printers can produce excellent letter quality text and superior graphics, and the better ones feature near publication quality. Laser printers are exceptionally quiet in operation.

Your printer choice depends on your printing needs and your budget, but you might also want to look at the list of *Works*-supported printers in the *Works* Setup utility to make sure that your printer will be supported.

What does it mean to be "supported"? Most printers are capable of producing text in a variety of styles, for example, *italicized*, or underlined, or **boldfaced**. Some can print text in different sizes and can even change the *font* or design of the characters they print. To activate these features, your printer has to receive special instructions or commands from *Works*. And *Works* only knows the commands for the printers listed in the Setup program.

☰ Modems

The word *modem* is made up from two words: *mod*ulator and *dem*odulator. The purpose of owning a modem is to allow your computer to talk to other computers over the telephone. To do this, the ones and zeros that make up computer data have to be converted (modulated) into tones that can be carried by telephone lines. At the other end of the line, these tones have to be translated back (demodulated) into ones and zeros. Modems perform this modulating/demodulating process.

The data communication section of *Works* was developed so that you could send and receive documents to and from other computers. If the other computer is in the same room as your PC, you can just connect the two computers together with a cable. (Your local computer dealer can provide you with such a cable.) If the other computer is some distance away, you're going to have to use the telephone, and that means you'll need a modem.

You can use any modem, so long as it is 100% Hayes compatible. The engineers at Hayes Microcomputer Products, Inc., have developed a series of commands for their modems (similar to the printer commands described above) that have become an industry standard. *Works* knows these modem commands and assumes that your modem will understand them.

YOU AND YOUR COMPUTER

Before you start up Microsoft *Works*, there are a few things you should know about your computer.

The Keyboard

If you've used a typewriter, your PC's keyboard should be somewhat familiar. There are, however, a few extra keys whose functions you should be aware of. The (Shift) key behaves in exactly the same way as on a typewriter. If it's held down while other keys are being typed, letter keys produce capital letters and other keys produce the symbol printed on the upper part of the key cap. For example, pressing (Shift) (4) yields a $ character.

The (Caps Lock) key acts like a two-position switch. Press it once and it locks in its Caps Lock position, and usually a lamp will light on your keyboard indicating Caps Lock is in effect. If you press (Caps Lock) again, it returns to its normal position. When Caps Lock mode is in effect, pressing any of the letter keys will produce capital letters. However, the number keys and symbol keys are unaffected by Caps Lock.

Over on the keypad, there's a key labeled (Num Lock) that behaves in a way similar to (Caps Lock). Each number key on the keypad serves a dual purpose. Normally, if you *don't* invoke (Num Lock), the number keys on the keypad serve as cursor control keys (see the section below on scrolling through a list). When you press (Num Lock), these keys are changed to ordinary number keys, similar to those at the top of the main keyboard. If you were entering a large amount of numerical data, you'd probably want to use the keypad in Num Lock mode. Most of the time, though, you'll want to use these keys for cursor control. (*Note:* On most keyboards, a lamp lights when Num Lock mode is in effect.)

The (Control) key is used the same way as the (Shift) key is used. You hold it down while you type some other letter, number, or symbol key. The effect you get depends on the program. For example, holding down the (Control) key while pressing the letter (B) in the *Works* word processor changes selected plain text to boldface. (*Note:* The Control key is sometimes labeled **Ctrl**.)

The (Alt) key is usually found just to the left (and sometimes to the right) of the space bar. In *Works*, (Alt) is used primarily to select commands and options from *pull-down menus* and *dialog boxes*. (More about these in a moment.)

You'll use the (Esc) key a lot in *Works*. Any time you change your mind and decide that you don't want to execute a command you've chosen from the menu, you can usually press (Esc) to cancel the command.

There are 10 (or on some PCs, 12) so-called Function Keys, labeled (F1), (F2), etc. These keys perform certain specific tasks depending on the program you're running. In *Works*, for example, pressing (F1) displays a list of help topics.

One more comment about your keyboard. Every key is a "repeating" key. This means that if you hold down any key for more than half a second, you'll get a lot of those characters. You are encouraged to develop a light touch at the keyboard.

☰ The Mouse

One of the unique features of Microsoft *Works* is its use of the mouse. While using the mouse is optional, many operations, especially those involving pull-down menus, are easier with a mouse than with the keyboard. The mouse rolls along the surface of your desk or table and, as it rolls, its motion is translated into movement of a block-shaped cursor on your screen. On the top of the mouse is a button that you are supposed to press whenever you want to select something on the screen—a process called *point and click*. What this means is that you roll the mouse around until the mouse cursor is pointing at the object of your attention and then press and release (click) the mouse button.

You are also encouraged to develop a light touch with the mouse button. (*Note: Works* is designed to use Microsoft's MS-Mouse, though other mouse types may work. Also, your mouse may have more than one button on it. If so, *Works* will look at only one of the buttons and ignore the other[s].)

Microsoft has taken advantage of the mouse in the design of *Works*. Instead of requiring you to memorize a list of commands for their programs, they have placed these commands in what are called *pull-down menus*. The names of the menus are displayed across the top of the screen on the menu bar. To select a command from a menu, you point at the menu name, then press and hold down the mouse button. When you do this, the list of commands under the menu title is "pulled down" (that's why it's called a pull-down menu). Now, still holding down the mouse button, you move (drag) the mouse so that the cursor moves down the list of commands and stops at the command you want. Only then do you release the mouse button.

If you don't have a mouse, menu selection involves pressing the [Alt] key along with other keys to choose the menu command you want. Let's try it.

≡ USING *WORKS* FOR THE FIRST TIME

I'm going to assume that you've already installed and configured *Works* for your computer. You've run the Setup utility and indicated whether you're going to run *Works* from disks or from a hard disk drive. You've chosen the kind of video interface card and screen you have, and identified your printer from the Setup list as both the text printer *and* the chart printer. If you're using separate printers for text and graphics, you should have identified one printer as the text printer and the other as the chart printer.

If you're running *Works* from a hard disk drive, you should install both Spell and Help utilities. Installing the *Works* tutorial is optional, but you may find some of its exercises useful. Without a hard disk, you should create a copy of *Works*' Spell/Help disk for your day-to-day use. (*Note*: You should never use original disks for anything except making copies.)

If you own an MS-Mouse, you should select the "Copy mouse program to DOS disk" option in Setup. If your computer system doesn't include a hard disk drive, Setup will prompt you to insert your DOS disk. It will then copy a file called MOUSE.SYS to your disk and add a command ("device=MOUSE.SYS") to the file called CON-FIG.SYS. (It will create the file, CONFIG.SYS, if it doesn't already exist.) If you are running *Works* from a hard disk, these changes will be made to your hard disk's root directory. (*Note:* The MOUSE.SYS file is read by your computer only when it first starts up. So if you want *Works* to know that you are going to use a mouse, you have to restart your computer after you've finished using the *Works* Setup program.)

≡ Starting *Works*

"Boot" your PC. If you're running *Works* from disks, place the copy of the *Works* program disk (created by the Setup program) into drive A, type **WORKS**, and press [Enter] . If you're running *Works* from a hard disk drive, change to the subdirectory containing *Works* (probably also called WORKS) by typing **CD WORKS** and pressing [Enter]. Then type **WORKS** and press [Enter] to start the program.

After a few moments, your screen will light up and show you the *Works* NEW dialog box (more about dialog boxes in a moment). Figure 1-1 shows this dialog box.

The term *dialog box* refers to any screen that presents you with information and expects you to respond in some way. The response may be to make a choice from a displayed list or to type something such as the name for a new document.

Figure 1-1   The NEW dialog box

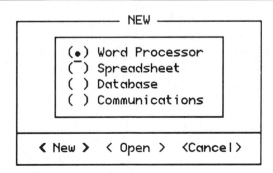

Across the top of your screen you'll see two menu titles, File and Window, on what *Works* calls its menu bar. The dialog box is below the menu bar.

The NEW dialog box serves two purposes. First, you can use it to select (open) a document you had previously created and saved to a data disk. Second, you can tell *Works* to create a brand new document. But we're not going to take either of these options because I just wanted you to practice menu command selection using either the keyboard or the mouse.

Before you can use the commands contained in the menu bar, you have to get rid of (close) the dialog box. This is easy. If you have a mouse, slide it until the mouse cursor (it looks like a small rectangular box) points to the word <**Cancel**> in the dialog box. Then click the mouse button. If you don't have a mouse, just press the (Esc) key. Either way, the dialog box disappears.

☰ Commanding *Works*

Now let's try selecting a command from a menu. Each word on the menu bar represents a list or *menu* of *Works* commands. Let's select one of the commands that comprise the File menu. Command selection involves two steps. First, you select the menu containing the command you want, and second, you choose the command itself from the menu list. Again, I'll show you how to choose a menu command using either the mouse or the keyboard.

If you have a mouse, use it to place the mouse cursor on the word File in the menu bar. Press and continue to hold down the mouse button.

If you're using the keyboard, hold down the (Alt) key, and type (F) (Figure 1-2). (*Note*: Throughout the book, I'll place a plus symbol [+] between two keystrokes if you should hold down the first key while you type the second, e.g., (Alt) + (F) .)

Now let's choose a command from the File menu. The first command in the list, **New...**, will redisplay the NEW dialog box. If you have a mouse, drag the mouse cursor down the File menu until you reach the first command, **New...**, and the command lights up (or *highlights*), indicating that it's selected. Then release the mouse button.

Without a mouse, when you pressed (Alt) + (F) the first command in the menu, **New...**, was automatically highlighted. So, to select it, just press (Enter) . (*Note*: If you wanted to select any other command

Figure 1-2 The File menu

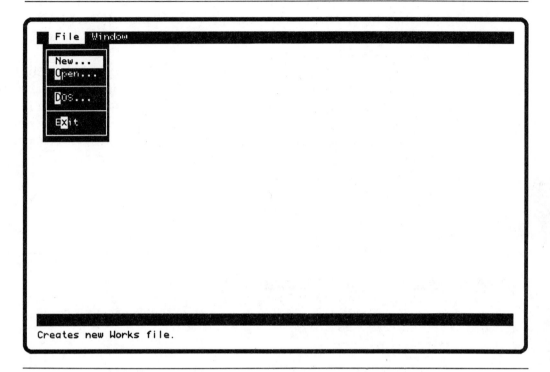

in the File menu, you could either use the down-arrow [⬇] key on the keypad to highlight the command you wanted, then press `Enter`, or you could type the letter in the command that appears brighter than the others—**N** for **New...**, **x** for **Exit**, etc.)

Whether you use the mouse method or the keyboard method to select the **New...** command, the result is the same. The NEW dialog box is displayed (Figure 1-1). (*Note*: If you pull down a menu and decide you don't want to select any of its commands, you can "roll it up" by either pressing `Esc` or pointing the mouse cursor at some other spot on the screen and clicking the mouse button.)

☰ The Help Index

Dispose of the dialog box again either by "clicking" on the word **Cancel** or by pressing the `Esc` key, and let's choose another command. Pull down the Window menu, either by pointing to it with the mouse and holding down the mouse button or by typing `Alt` + `W` .

The Window menu provides access to *Works'* on-screen help system, the *Works* tutorial, a special SETTINGS dialog box, and any documents you may have opened or created during your current *Works* session. Let's look at the Help Index. Select this command by either dragging the mouse cursor or by pressing (Enter).

If you've installed *Works* on your hard disk along with its help files (part of the Setup procedure), *Works* will display its Help Index immediately (Figure 1-3). If you're running *Works* from disks, you'll see a message on your screen prompting you to replace the *Works* Program disk with the copy of the Spell/Help disk you created earlier. Do this, and press (Enter). Now everybody's screen should display the HELP - INDEX dialog box shown in Figure 1-3.

Figure 1-3   The Help Index

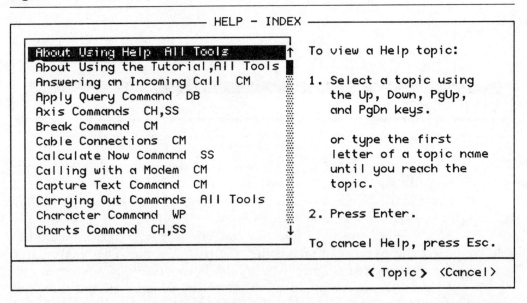

This dialog box presents a "scrollable" list of help topics. To browse through the list, you can use the ⬆ and ⬇ keys on your keypad that scroll the list by one topic, up or down. If you hold down either arrow key, you can scroll through the list rapidly. Another way of scrolling through the list is to press (PgUp) or (PgDn). These keys scroll the list one screen's worth of topics, up or down. You can even jump to the end of the list by pressing (End), or back to the beginning by pressing (Home). When you first display the dialog box, the first topic in the list is highlighted. By using the various keypad keys, you can highlight the topic you want. In fact, if you know the topic you want, you can type the first letter of the topic's name, and the list will automatically scroll to topics beginning with that letter.

If you have a mouse, you can use it to scroll through the list instead of using the keypad. Running down the right side of the topics list is a thin bar called a *scroll bar.* The scroll bar can be used in several ways. If you point the mouse cursor at the down arrow (↓) at the bottom of the scroll bar, each time you click the mouse button the list will scroll by one topic toward the end of the list. Holding down the mouse button while pointing at the ↓ achieves the same effect as holding down the ⌞↓⌟ key on the keypad. Clicking on the ↑ at the top of the scroll bar scrolls the list the other way.

Somewhere between the two arrows on the scroll bar you'll see a small dark block (▮) called the *elevator.* The position of the elevator along the scroll bar indicates the section of the list currently being shown. In other words, if the elevator is halfway down the scroll bar, you're looking at topics halfway through the list. If you place the mouse cursor below the elevator on the scroll bar and click the mouse button, the topics will scroll by one screenful toward the end of the list. Clicking above the elevator scrolls the list the other way. You can also use your mouse to drag the elevator to a different position on the scroll bar. For example, if you drag the elevator to the bottom of the scroll bar and release the mouse button, you'll see the end of the topics list.

Use either the keypad or the mouse to select the topic **Exit Command All Tools**. If you have a mouse, point the mouse cursor at this topic and click *twice.* From the keypad, highlight the topic using the arrow keys, then press ⌞Enter⌟. Figure 1-4 shows the help screen for this topic.

Some help topics contain several pages of information. You can tell by looking at the title line of the help screen. At the end of the title you'll see **(page 1 of 1)**. If this topic had extended over several pages, this line might have read **(page 1 of 3)**. Pressing ⌞PgDn⌟ advances to the next page, if there is one. Pressing ⌞PgUp⌟ lets you back up a page.

When you've finished reading the help page(s), you can take one of three actions. You can press ⌞Enter⌟ (or click on the word **Index**) to return to the Help Index. You can type ⌞L⌟, the first letter in the word **Lesson** (or click on the word), to show a tutorial lesson about the help topic. Or you can press ⌞Esc⌟ (or click on the word **Cancel**) to leave the Help Index and return to *Works.*

Figure 1-4 Help for the **Exit** command

```
 ┌──────────── Exit Command  All Tools  (page 1 of 1) ────────────┐
 │                                                                │
 │ Use the Exit command when you are finished using Works.        │
 │                                                                │
 │ To exit Works:                                                 │
 │                                                                │
 │ ▌ From the File menu, choose the Exit command.                 │
 │                                                                │
 │   If you haven't saved an open file, or haven't saved since you│
 │   made changes, Works asks if you want to save your changes.   │
 │                                                                │
 │   ▌ Choose Yes to save your changes.                           │
 │                                                                │
 │   ▌ Choose No to lose your changes.                            │
 │                                                                │
 │   ▌ Press Esc to cancel Exit.                                  │
 │                                                                │
 ├────────────────────────────────────────────────────────────────┤
 │  Next♦PgDn  Back♦PgUp          < Index >  <Lesson>  <Cancel>   │
 └────────────────────────────────────────────────────────────────┘
```

Let's take the third option. Press (Esc) and let me show you a shortcut in using the Help feature. Suppose you wanted help with the **Close** command in the File menu. Pull down the File menu, and highlight the **Close** command. But instead of pressing (Enter), press function key (F1). *Works* displays its help screens for the highlighted command.

Press (Esc), and let's execute one more command from the File menu. (*Note*: If you're running *Works* from disks, you'll see a message asking you to place the *Works* program disk back into drive A.)

☰ Quitting *Works*

Pull down the File menu again by typing (Alt) + (F). (Use this keyboard method even if you have a mouse.)

Look closely at the pulled-down menu (Figure 1-2). Can you see that one letter in each command appears brighter than the other letters? Usually it's the first letter in the command, but in the last command, **Exit**, it's the second letter, **x**. *Works* emphasizes these letters to indicate that you can select any of the commands just by typing the brightened letter. You could, for example, redisplay the NEW dialog box by typing

n after you had pulled down the File menu. Right now, though, I'd like you to quit *Works* by typing **x** for the **Exit** command. This quits *Works* and returns you to the DOS prompt.

Note: You should always use the **Exit** command when you're through with *Works*. I know it's easier to just turn off your PC, but don't do it. When you finish a *Works* session, use the **Exit** command.

AN APPROACH TO LEARNING *WORKS*

There are several approaches to learning how to use a microcomputer software package. Before I started to write this book, I considered several of them. I decided to incorporate the commands and features of *Works* into a series of projects (word processing projects, database projects, and so forth). So, rather than just reading about a bunch of commands and seeing brief descriptions of their functions, you'll discover various *Works* commands and features in the course of completing a particular project. It is for this reason that I have not included with this book a disk containing the examples discussed in the chapters that follow. I want you to construct each of the projects from the beginning, so that when you begin creating your own projects, you'll have the experience of starting from scratch.

As you perform each step in the projects that comprise the following chapters, you'll see a picture of how the display screen looked while I was performing that step. And when you've completed the projects for a particular application, you will have used all the program commands for that application and observed their effects.

And now, on to word processing.

Chapter **2**
THE WORD
PROCESSOR

It's tempting to start this chapter by asking "What is word processing?" But word processing is a task with which we are all familiar. We're used to organizing sentences into written paragraphs, indenting the first sentence of a paragraph, correcting our mistakes, and moving a phrase from one part of a document to another. If you've used a typewriter, you've even, on occasion, chosen to "format" a document by double spacing.

So, what's so different about using a computer for word processing? The difference is that the computer can do automatically many of the tasks you would do manually. A good computer word processing program, for example, will automatically indent your paragraphs for you. It will double space without your having to press the Enter key twice at the end of each line. And, most important, it will let you compose "on screen," making corrections as you go. Then, when you have your document exactly the way you want it, the program will print it out. It will even number the pages automatically.

Terrific, you say, but how does it work? That's what you're going to find out in this chapter.

PROJECT 1: THE STORE MEMO

Let's suppose you are the president of a successful (naturally) computer retail store, the Miracle Computer Store. You want to distribute a memo to all members of your staff telling them about a recent marketing survey.

Creating a New Document

So let's begin. Boot your PC and start the *Works* program. (See Chapter 1 for a detailed description of starting *Works*.) Be sure you have an initialized data disk available. You'll want to save your documents as soon as you type them in. If you haven't created a data disk yet, see the section on making a data disk in Chapter 1. (*Note*: If your computer has a hard disk drive, insert the data disk into drive A after you've started *Works*. Otherwise, the *Works* program disk will be in drive A and your data disk should be in drive B.)

A few seconds after you've typed **WORKS** from the DOS prompt, you'll see the *Works* NEW dialog box (Figure 2-1). (There's a discussion of dialog boxes in Chapter 1, too.) To create a new, blank word processor document, just press Enter .

Figure 2-1   The NEW dialog box

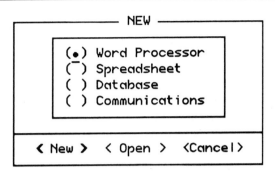

Figure 2-2 shows the new word processor window. (*Note*: Everything you see in Microsoft *Works* is considered to be in a window—a word processor window, a database window, and so on.)

☰ Examining the Word Processor Window

Before you actually begin this project, let's discuss some of the visible features of the computer screen you're looking at. At the top of the screen is the menu bar with seven menus (File, Edit, Print, Select, Format, Options, and Window). Everything below the menu bar is the word processor window.

The Ruler
Directly below the menu bar is the ruler. The ruler displays paragraph margins, indents, and tabs and is quite a bit longer than its apparent length of about 7½ inches. The space available for you to type your document is really much larger than you think it is. Not only is it taller than the height of the screen, but it's also wider. In fact, a word processor document can be up to 22 inches wide. Now you can understand why the screen is called a window. Since you couldn't possibly see the entire document on the screen at one time, *Works* provides you with a window (about 7½ inches wide by 5 inches tall) to examine any part of the total document.

Symbols
Works displays three symbols directly below the ruler. The >> symbol represents the start of a new page and is called the page break marker.

Figure 2-2   *Works'* word processor window

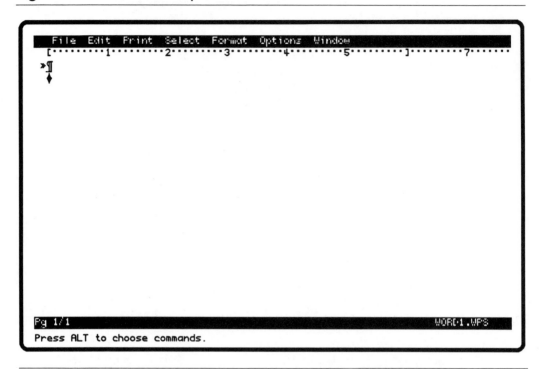

The blinking underline (__) is the *text cursor*. It shows where the next character typed will appear. The *Works* manual calls this simply the *cursor* so, to avoid confusion, I'll call it the cursor, too. The diamond-shaped symbol (◆) below the cursor is the end mark. It always appears below the last line of your document.

You may also see a paragraph symbol (¶) just above the cursor. If you do, the *Works* feature **Show All Characters** is in effect. I find this feature distracting. If you agree and you'd like to turn off **Show All Characters**, here's how. Pull down the Options menu (see Chapter 1 for a description of pull-down menus) either with your mouse or by typing Alt + O. The **Show All Characters** command will have a small mark (•) just to the left of the command indicating that the feature is active. Select the command, and the ¶ symbol will disappear.

Status and Message Lines

The status line appears highlighted and is the next-to-the-bottom line on the word processor screen. It displays the current page number, the total number of pages in the document, character formats (such as bold or italic) if any are applied to the character above the cursor, and the document name. By default, *Works* assigns the name WORD1.WPS to your first word processor document. You'll change this name the first time you save the document to disk.

The status line also indicates whether Caps Lock (CL) or Num Lock (NL) features are in effect. If you see "CL" on the status line, press (Caps Lock) to cancel the feature. Similarly, press (Num Lock) if you see "NL" on the status line.

The message line is the last line on your screen and is common to all four *Works* applications. It prompts you to do certain things or suggests actions that you can take.

Scroll Bars—Mouse Users Only

If you're using a mouse with *Works*, look at the bottom and along the right edge of the window and you'll see scroll bars. (See Chapter 1 for a description of how to use scroll bars.) Let's try using the horizontal scroll bar. (Nonmouse users will have to sit this exercise out.) Point your mouse cursor at the *right*-pointing arrow on the horizontal scroll bar and click once. It looks as if the ruler has moved to the left. Actually, the ruler is fixed. By clicking the right scroll arrow, you've shifted the window to the right. The scroll bars—the horizontal one you've just used, and the vertical scroll bar that's along the right edge of the window—provide the means for moving your window to see any part of your document. Without a mouse, you'll use the keypad keys to move the window around your document.

☰ Typing the Document

Figure 2-3 shows the content of your store memo. I'd like you to type it into the blank word processor window. I know it's rather long, but the features I want to demonstrate require a document this long. And yes, I know there are spelling and other errors in the memo. I put them there so that you could practice using *Works'* spelling checker, so please type the memo exactly as it appears.

As you begin typing the paragraphs of the memo, remember this rule: Press the (Enter) *only* at the end of paragraphs, *not* at the end of each line. If you've used a typewriter, you're probably used to hitting the (Enter) after each line. Break yourself of this habit—you'll see why in just a minute.

Here are some hints as you type. The cursor indicates where characters will appear (where they will be inserted) when you type. Right now, the cursor is at the upper-left corner of the window. As

Figure 2-3 Text for Project 1

```
December 1


To: All Employees of Miracle Computer Store
From: J.P. Smithson, President
Subject: Review of Store Policies


As we move into the final weeks of the holliday season, it
is important for all of us to keep in mind the basic and
essential goal of MCS. We are in business to make money. We
must never lose sight of that goal. But making money means
more than just pushing boxes out the door.

As you know, MCS hired a marketing firm to perform a study
on our customers last month. We wanted to find out what
brought our customers into our store for the first time,
whether they bought anything from us, whether they were
satisfied with what they bought, and how they were treated.
The results of the study proved very interesting and I want
to share some of them with you.

The study showed that over 60% of the people who came into
our store in November were first-time customers. And over
half of them came in because our store was recommended to
them. The rest of those first-time customers came in for a
variety of reasons -- just passing by, saw our ad in the
local paper, picked us out of the phone book, etc.

But it is the customers who came in because we were
recommended that I want to talk about. I want to
congratulate and to thank each of you for your individual
efforts. A good reputation does not happen by accident. It
is built over time with perceived care and consideration.

In the coming weeks, we can expect to see a substantial
increase in store traffic. How large an increase is
anybody's guess, but if last year's holiday season is any
guide, look out! This increase in traffic will inevidably
increase the demands on your time. Try to keep in mind that
no matter how many times you've heard and answered a
particular question, that question is unique for the
customer who asks it. Remember to always be polite, but
remember also that we are here to sell and service computers
and related products. I know these two concepts may
sometimes conflict, but I trust in your professionalism to
treat our customers the way each of us would like to be
treated.

One final thought, don't forget to encourage customers who
purchase computer systems to buy our 1-year service
contract. These service contracts serve two purposes. They
provide protection to our customers against unexpected
repair costs, and they generate additional revenue to the
the store. As an incentive, I am offering a bonus of $10 for
each service contract sold this month.

Happy holidays, and remember our motto at the Miracle
Computer Store, "If it's a good computer, it's a miracle."
```

you type, characters appear immediately above the cursor, and the cursor moves to the right. As you finish each line (or if you press (Enter)), the cursor automatically moves to the beginning of the next line.

Notice that as you complete typing the second line of the first paragraph, *Works* automatically moves the word "essential" to the next line because it was too long to fit on the line above. This feature of moving the whole word to the beginning of the next line is called *word wraparound*.

Unless you're a much better typist than I am, you'll probably make one or two (or more) mistakes as you type the document. If you see a mistake and you want to correct it by erasing the error and retyping, move the cursor just to the *right* of the characters you want to erase by using the arrow keys on the keypad (or by pointing the mouse there and clicking). Press the (Backspace) key once for each character you want to erase. Then type the correct character(s). Don't forget to return the cursor to the end of your document so that you can finish typing the memo. (*Note: Works* gives you other ways of correcting mistakes, and we'll discuss them in a moment.)

To leave blank lines, just press the (Enter) key. (There are two blank lines between the date and the heading, two more between the heading and the first paragraph, and single blank lines between succeeding paragraphs.)

Continue typing the rest of the memo. Remember, press (Enter) only at the end of each paragraph. (*Note*: You'll actually need to press it *twice* at the end of each paragraph, if you want to leave a blank line between paragraphs.

As you finish the second paragraph, your *Works* window will begin to scroll downward. Don't worry. You're not losing any text. *Works* is just moving the window to show you a different (lower) section of the available work space so that you can continue to see what you're typing.

The Page Break

As you get near the end of the memo, you'll see a >> symbol appear (Figure 2-4) along the left edge of the text. The >> indicates where the second page will begin when you print out the memo. Ignore the page break marker for now.

≡ Saving the Document

Before you do anything else, you should save your document. To save your document, pull down the File menu ((Alt) + (F)) and select the **Save** command. Figure 2-5 shows the SAVE AS dialog box that appears when you use the **Save** command for the first time with a new document.

Figure 2-4 Notice the page break marker

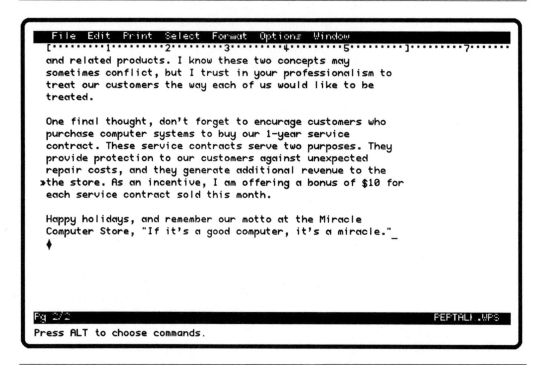

Saving is a simple process. First, though, make sure you've inserted your formatted DATA disk in a disk drive (A or B). This drive letter should appear in the dialog box after the words **Current Path**: (e.g., **Current Path: A:**). If the drive containing your DATA disk isn't listed as the current path, here's what to do. Type (Alt) + (O) to move the cursor into the **Other Drives & Directories** section of the dialog box. Then, use the (↓) key to highlight the drive that has your Data disk, and press (Enter).

Once the correct disk drive has been selected, type (Alt) + (N) to move the cursor into the **File Name** portion of the dialog box. For this project, let's name the document PEPTALK. So, type **PEPTALK**, and press (Enter).

Works copies the document from your PC's memory to your Data disk. The dialog box disappears, and if you look at the status line on your screen, you'll see that the document's name has been changed from WORD1.WPS to PEPTALK.WPS (or whatever you've called it). *Works* appends the extension ".WPS" to all of its word processor documents.

Figure 2-5 The SAVE AS dialog box

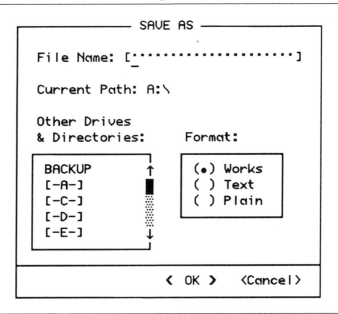

A word about document names. The names you give to your documents must be "legitimate" DOS file names, from 1 to 8 characters long. The characters should be letters and/or numbers but not symbols. Spaces are not allowed. You can, if you wish, add your own three-letter extension to your file name, but I advise against it. *Works* differentiates the four kinds of documents (word processor, spreadsheet, etc.) by the file name extension that it supplies automatically: ".WPS" for word processor files, ".WKS" for spreadsheets, ".WCM" for communication documents, and ".WDB" for databases.

☰ Editing the Document

Now that you've typed in and saved the memo, let's use some of the word processor features *Works* makes available. You've already seen one way of correcting text in your document, using the (Backspace) to delete characters and then retyping. Here's a slightly different method.

Suppose you wanted to change the words "move into" to "approach" in the first paragraph. You'll have to be able to see the first paragraph before you can edit it. Press (Control) + (Home) to scroll the window and move the cursor to the beginning of your document.

In fact, before you do any editing, let's learn how to move the cursor to where you want it.

Cursor Movement

You already know that you can use the arrow keys to move the cursor. (←) and (→) move the cursor, respectively, left and right one character. If you want to move the cursor several characters left or right, you can press the key several times or you can hold down the key and let your computer's repeat key feature zip the cursor around.

But suppose you wanted to move the cursor to the beginning of the next word. You can do this by using (Control) with an arrow key. Try it! (Control) + (→) moves the cursor one word to the right; (Control) + (←) moves it one word to the left.

Similarly, while (↓) and (↑) move the cursor, respectively, up or down by one line, pressing (Control) + (↓) moves it down to the beginning of the next *paragraph*. (Control) + (↑) moves the cursor to the beginning of the previous paragraph.

(PgUp) and (PgDn), used by themselves, scroll the window up or down by one screen each time they're pressed. But if you type (Control) + (PgDn), you'll move the cursor to the bottom line on the screen *without* scrolling the window. Typing (Control) + (PgUp) moves the cursor to the top of the screen, also without scrolling the window.

(Home) and (End) each have two cursor movement functions. Used by themselves, (Home) moves the cursor to the beginning of the line, (End) moves it to the end of the line. If you type (Control) + (Home), though, you'll move the cursor to the very beginning of the document. And, as you might expect, typing (Control) + (End) moves it to the end of the entire document.

Replacing Text

Now let's make that text correction. Move the cursor so that it's under the "m" in "move" in the first paragraph. You want to replace the words "move into" with the word "approach." You could delete the two words by using (Backspace) and then typing the new word, but I said I was going to show you a different method of correcting text, a method called text replacement.

You're going to replace some text in your document with other text, so the first step is to tell *Works* which text you intend to replace. You do this by *highlighting* the text. There are two general methods of highlighting. One uses the (Shift) key, the other uses function key (F8).

With the (Shift) key method, you place the cursor at the beginning of the text you want to highlight (you've already done this). Then, you hold down either (Shift) key and use the cursor movement keys on the keypad to highlight the amount of text you wish. In this example, you could hold down (Shift) while typing (Control) + ⊝ twice to highlight the words "move into," then release the (Shift) (Figure 2-6).

Figure 2-6   Highlight the text you want to replace

```
 File  Edit  Print  Select  Format  Options  Window
[··········1··········2··········3··········4··········5··········]··········7······
»December 1


To: All Employees of Miracle Computer Store
From: J.P. Smithson, President
Subject: Review of Store Policies


As we  move into the final weeks of the holliday season, it
is important for all of us to keep in mind the basic and
essential goal of MCS. We are in business to make money. We
must never lose sight of that goal. But making money means
more than just pushing boxes out the door.

As you know, MCS hired a marketing firm to perform a study
on our customers last month. We wanted to find out what
brought our customers into our store for the first time,
whether they bought anything from us, whether they were
satisfied with what they bought, and how they were treated.
The results of the study proved very interesting and I want
to share some of them with you.
Pg 1/2                                               PEPTALI .WPS
Press ALT to choose commands.
```

To "unhighlight" text, move the cursor without using (Shift), or press (Esc).

The second method of highlighting text uses the extend key, (F8). With the cursor positioned under the "m" in "move," press (F8). The word EXTEND will appear on the status line. Now, type (Control) + ⊝ twice, and the two words "move into" will be highlighted.

Once you have highlighted the text, *anything* you type will replace what is highlighted. With the words "move into" highlighted, type the word **approach** and add a space to separate it from the next word in the document (Figure 2-7). (*Note*: When you use (Control) + ⊝ with either

Figure 2-7 Typing the new word replaces the highlighted text

```
 File  Edit  Print  Select  Format  Options  Window
[········1·········2·········3·········4·········5·········]·········7·······
»December 1


To: All Employees of Miracle Computer Store
From: J.P. Smithson, President
Subject: Review of Store Policies


As we approach the final weeks of the holliday season, it is
important for all of us to keep in mind the basic and
essential goal of.MCS. We are in business to make money. We
must never lose sight of that goal. But making money means
more than just pushing boxes out the door.

As you know, MCS hired a marketing firm to perform a study
on our customers last month. We wanted to find out what
brought our customers into our store for the first time,
whether they bought anything from us, whether they were
satisfied with what they bought, and how they were treated.
The results of the study proved very interesting and I want
to share some of them with you.
Pg 1/2                                              PEPTALI .WPS
Press ALT to choose commands.
```

(Shift) or (F8) to highlight a word, the space after the word is highlighted, too.)

Here is a variation on the above method that will save you some time when you're replacing (or deleting) a single word. Suppose, in the second paragraph, you wanted to change "perform" to "conduct." If you want to highlight a single word, move the cursor to any letter in the word and press (F8) twice. Notice that not only the whole word but also the space after the word is highlighted. Now you can type the word **conduct** (don't forget to type the space after the word).

(*Note*: Mouse users can use the "click and drag" method to highlight text.)

Deleting text

Works provides two methods for deleting text altogether. First, with either method, you have to highlight the text you want to delete. Then, you can either press the (Del) key on the keypad or select **Delete** from the Edit menu.

A Summary of Highlighting Techniques

Most of the changes you'll make to a document require that you first select (highlight) the text you want to change. You've learned two ways of highlighting so far: using ⌨Shift⌨ and using ⌨F8⌨ .

⌨Shift⌨ can be used with any of the cursor movement keys to highlight any amount of text. But ⌨F8⌨ is designed to highlight specific amounts of text, depending on how many times you press it.

The first time you press ⌨F8⌨ , the word EXTEND appears on the status line; from then on, moving the cursor extends the highlighted text from the original position of the cursor. This is exactly like holding down the ⌨Shift⌨ except that you don't have to hold down ⌨F8⌨ . In fact, if you want to stop highlighting text, you have to press ⌨Esc⌨ .

But ⌨F8⌨ can do much more than just act like the ⌨Shift⌨ key. If you press ⌨F8⌨ a second time, the word containing the cursor is highlighted. Press it a third time, and the sentence containing the cursor is highlighted. A fourth press, and the whole paragraph containing the cursor is highlighted. And if you press ⌨F8⌨ five times, the entire document is highlighted.

(*Note*: There may be times when you'd like to highlight two or more portions of text that are *not* adjacent. Don't bother trying. *Works* doesn't allow it. You must do each separately.)

≡ Recovering from Mistakes

If you've been following the project step by step (and I hope you have), you'll remember a caution I gave you earlier about highlighted text. Let me repeat it. Once you have highlighted some text, any character you type on the keyboard will immediately replace the highlighted text. Allow me to demonstrate this to you and, at the same time, show you how to recover from the error.

The Undo Command

Press ⌨F8⌨ five times to select the entire document. While the entire document is highlighted, hit the space bar (or any other character on the keyboard), and then don't do anything else for a moment. (Trust me, do it.)

All the highlighted text has been replaced by the single character you typed. All that work, gone forever. Well, not quite. Pull down the Edit menu, and look at the first command, **Undo**. **Undo** was designed to be used in this kind of situation. Select the **Undo** command, and watch all of your memo return. (*Note*: You can execute the **Undo** command by pressing (Alt) + (Backspace) instead of using the Edit menu.)

Undo has saved me from disaster more than once, but it only works if you select it *immediately* after you make the mistake. (Remember, to cancel highlighting, press (Esc) and move the cursor.)

Resaving Your Document

If your document becomes so messed up that **Undo** can't help, the only way to recover is to revert to the last version of the document you saved. This is the best argument I know for saving your work often. (*Comment*: My electric power company has an annoying habit of interrupting power for a few seconds every week or so. If this happens to you while your computer is running, everything in its memory will be lost. So I strongly recommend that you resave your document every five minutes or so. That way you'll never lose more than five minutes' worth of work.)

Resaving a file is easy. Just select **Save** from the File menu. *Works* automatically replaces the file on your Data disk with the current version in your PC.

≡ Spell Checking

One of your first editing tasks for any document should be to check for spelling errors. *Works* has a built-in spelling checker, and this part of the project will show you how to use it.

When you ask *Works* to spell check your document, it looks to see if you have highlighted any text. If you have, only the highlighted text is checked. If no text is highlighted, the search begins at the current cursor location. So if you want to check the entire document, you should move the cursor to the top. Do this by typing (Control) + (Home). Then, pull down the Options menu ((Alt) + (O)) and select **Check Spelling**. (*Note*: If you are running *Works* from disks, you'll see a message on the screen asking you to remove the Program disk and insert the Spell/Help disk.)

Works begins to compare each word in your document with its own dictionary. In this document, the first word it brings to your attention is the name "Smithson." The CHECK SPELLING dialog box is displayed (Figure 2-8) so that you can tell *Works* what action to take.

The word "Smithson" isn't misspelled; it just isn't in *Works'* dictionary. You can tell *Works* to do one of three things. First, you could press (Alt) + (I) and *Works* would **Ignore** this instance of the word. Second, you could press (Alt) + (A) and *Works* would **Add** "Smithson" to your personal dictionary. *Works* would "know" the

Figure 2-8   The CHECK SPELLING dialog box

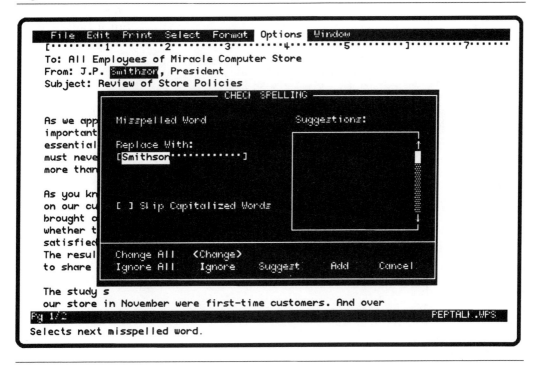

word the next time it occurs in this, or any other, document. The third option, **Ignore All**, tells *Works* to ignore all instances of the word while you're editing this particular document. Let's take this option by pressing (Alt) + (G).

Works continues checking the memo, and next pauses at the word "holliday." This word really is misspelled, and there are two actions you can take. Within the dialog box, the word "holliday" appears highlighted in the **Replace With**: text box. If you think you know the correct spelling, you can type it into the text box and then select the **Change** option. Let's try it. Type **holiday**, and then press (Enter) (or (Alt) + (C)). *Works* changes "holliday" into "holiday."

Works next finds "inevidably." If you're not sure how to spell this word, press (Alt) + (S) and *Works* will suggest some possible words (Figure 2-9).

When you take the **Suggest** option, *Works* displays one or more possible choices in the **Suggestions**: list box. The words are arranged in the order of their likelihood of being the correct choice. That's why

Figure 2-9   Suggestions from the Spell Checker

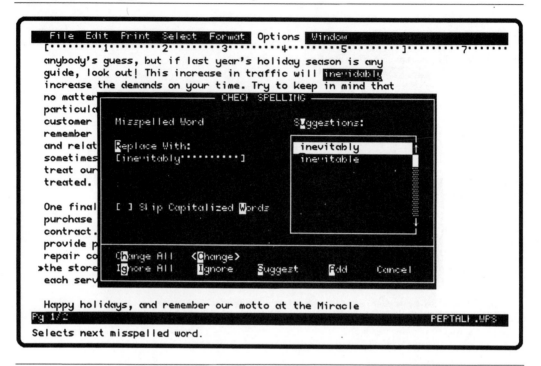

the first choice in the list is highlighted and placed in the **Replace With**: text box. Pressing Enter (or Alt + C) accepts the highlighted word as the replacement. If you want one of the other choices in the list box, use ↓ or ↑ to select the word you want, then press Enter.

Another option, if you think you've misspelled the word more than once in the document, is to take the **Change All** option, Alt + H. *Works* will search your entire document replacing instances of the misspelled word with your choice from the **Suggestions**: list box.

If you didn't like any of the suggested words, you could press Alt + R to move the highlight back to the text box and type your own word.

The first of the two suggested words in the list box is the one you want, so highlight it and press Enter. (*Note*: If *Works* can't find any words to suggest when you press Alt + S, the list box will remain empty and the original word will remain highlighted in the **Replace With**: text box.)

Continue checking the memo. The last error that *Works'* spelling checker finds isn't a spelling error; it's a doubled word ("the the"). This is a frequent typing mistake. Figure 2-10 shows the dialog box as *Works* asks if it should replace the two words with a single word. Press ⟨Enter⟩ to accept. (*Note: Works* will also check for improper capitalization.)

Figure 2-10   The Spell Checker catches doubled words, too

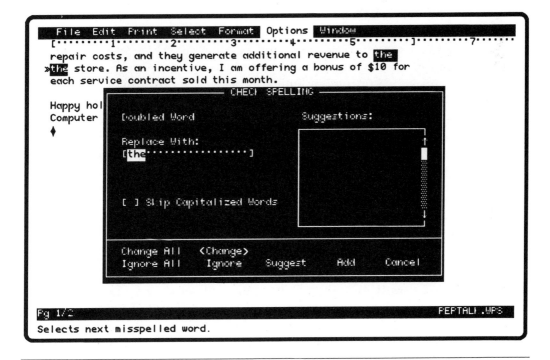

There are two other spell checking features of which you should be aware. First, once you've replaced a word, *Works* will automatically suggest your replacement if it finds another instance of the misspelled word. Of course, if you've taken the **Change All** option, *Works* won't find another instance of the misspelled word. Second, if you want *Works* to ignore capitalized words as it checks for spelling errors, press ⟨Alt⟩ + Ⓦ when the CHECK SPELLING dialog box is displayed. (*Note*: The two Check Spelling options, **Ignore All** and **Change All**, are available only in *Works* version 1.05 or later.)

When the entire document has been checked, *Works* will display a message saying: **Check Spelling finished.** Press ⎣Enter⎦. Resave your document by selecting **Save** from the File menu, and let's continue editing your memo.

≡ Cutting and Pasting

Now that you've saved the current version of your memo (you have, haven't you?), let's mess up the document and then revert to the saved version.

The expression "cutting and pasting" refers to an old-fashioned technique of moving text from one place in a document to another. This involved cutting out sentences or paragraphs from a printed copy of the document with a scissors or razor blade and then gluing or pasting the portion of text at some other location on the page.

With *Works*, you can cut and paste electronically. So put away your scissors and paste pot, and let's see how it's done. Suppose you wanted to move the first paragraph of your memo to a point just above the next-to-the-last paragraph (the one beginning "One final thought").

Before you can move any text, you must first select it. Place the cursor somewhere in the first paragraph. Then press ⎣F8⎦ four times to highlight the whole paragraph. Press the ⎣↓⎦ once, to highlight the blank line separating the first and second paragraphs, too (Figure 2-11).

Next, pull down the Edit menu and select the **Move** command. The text remains highlighted, but the word MOVE appears on the status line.

The next step is to move the cursor to the location where you want to paste the text. Scroll down to the paragraph beginning "One final thought," and place the cursor at the beginning of this paragraph. Now press ⎣Enter⎦, and the text you highlighted automatically moves to its new location (Figure 2-12). Amazing, isn't it?

Cutting and pasting is an extremely useful technique for editing your documents. Try experimenting with the **Move** command. Move phrases, sentences, and paragraphs from one place to another in your document. Don't worry about messing up your memo; we're going to throw away this version and revert to the version you saved earlier as soon as you're through cutting and pasting. Here is a brief summary of the cut and paste process.

Figure 2-11 Highlight the text you wish to move

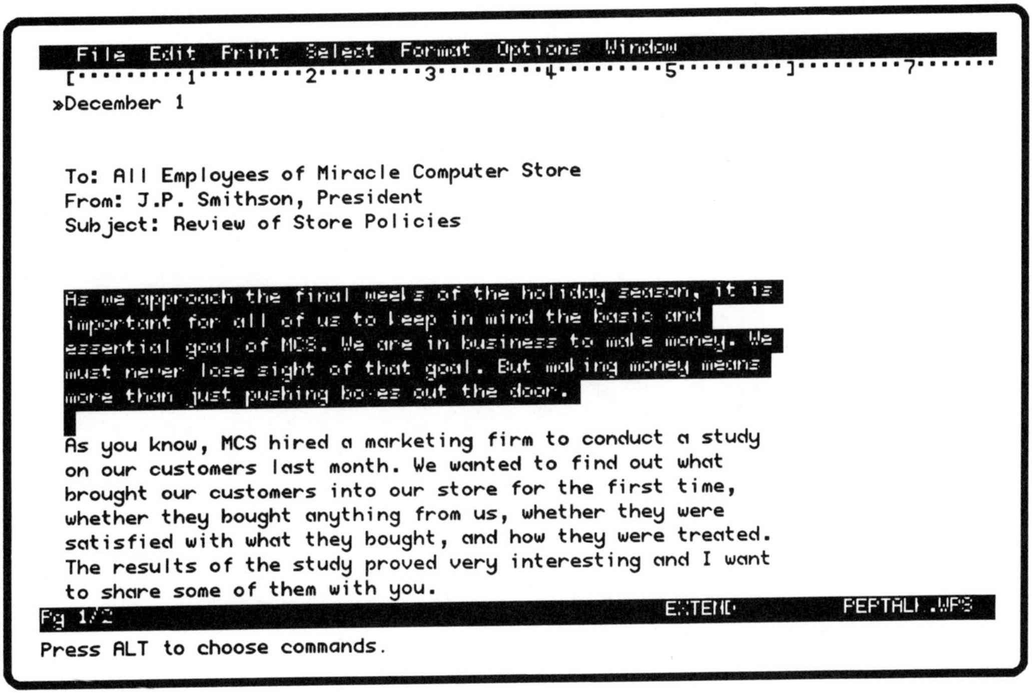

```
   File  Edit  Print  Select  Format  Options  Window
[·········1·········2·········3·········4·········5·········]·········7·······
»December 1


To: All Employees of Miracle Computer Store
From: J.P. Smithson, President
Subject: Review of Store Policies

As we approach the final weeks of the holiday season, it is
important for all of us to keep in mind the basic and
essential goal of MCS. We are in business to make money. We
must never lose sight of that goal. But making money means
more than just pushing boxes out the door.

As you know, MCS hired a marketing firm to conduct a study
on our customers last month. We wanted to find out what
brought our customers into our store for the first time,
whether they bought anything from us, whether they were
satisfied with what they bought, and how they were treated.
The results of the study proved very interesting and I want
to share some of them with you.
Pg 1/2                                    EXTEND        PERTALK.WPS
Press ALT to choose commands.
```

- ■ Select the text
- ■ Choose **Move**
- ■ Move the cursor
- ■ Press (Enter)

(*Note*: Instead of selecting **Move** from the Edit menu, you can press (F3).)

Move vs. Copy

The two Edit menu commands **Move** and **Copy** behave similarly. Both move selected (highlighted) text to another location in your document. The difference between the commands is that **Move** removes the selected text from its original location in your document, while **Copy** leaves the text alone. You can execute the **Copy** command by pressing (Shift) + (F3) instead of using the Edit menu.

Figure 2-12   Completing the move

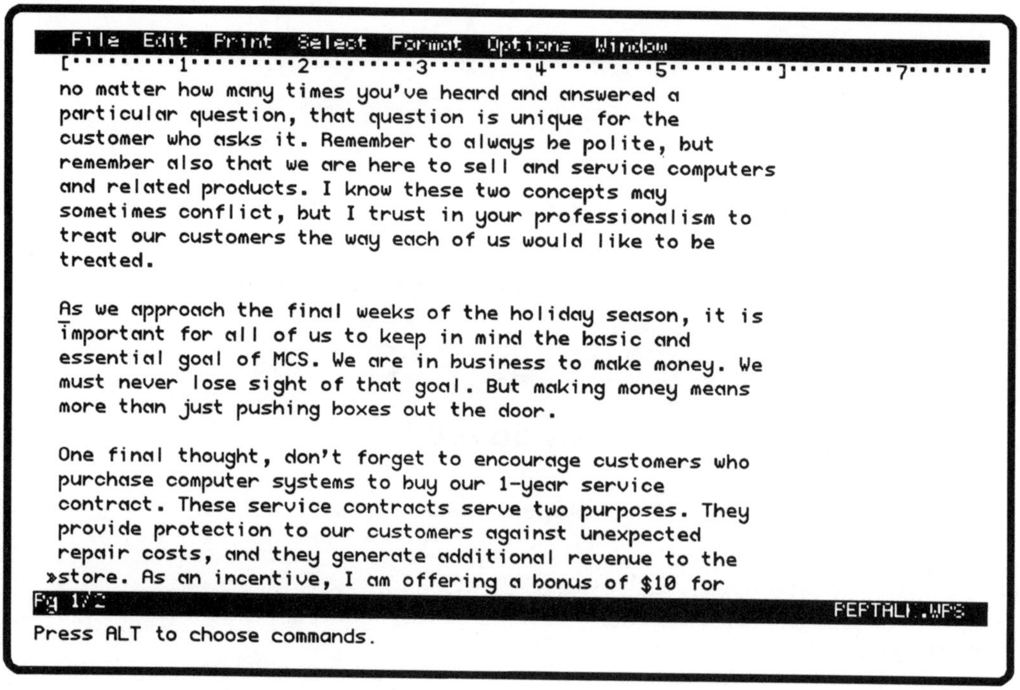

```
 File  Edit  Print  Select  Format  Options  Window
[·········1·········2·········3·········4·········5·········]·········7······
no matter how many times you've heard and answered a
particular question, that question is unique for the
customer who asks it. Remember to always be polite, but
remember also that we are here to sell and service computers
and related products. I know these two concepts may
sometimes conflict, but I trust in your professionalism to
treat our customers the way each of us would like to be
treated.

As we approach the final weeks of the holiday season, it is
important for all of us to keep in mind the basic and
essential goal of MCS. We are in business to make money. We
must never lose sight of that goal. But making money means
more than just pushing boxes out the door.

One final thought, don't forget to encourage customers who
purchase computer systems to buy our 1-year service
contract. These service contracts serve two purposes. They
provide protection to our customers against unexpected
repair costs, and they generate additional revenue to the
»store. As an incentive, I am offering a bonus of $10 for
Pg 1/2                                              PEPTALK.WPS
Press ALT to choose commands.
```

☰ Reverting to an Earlier Version

Now that you've thoroughly messed up your memo, let's throw this version away and bring back the last saved version.

Throwing away a Document

Pull down the File menu and select the **Close** command. *Works* immediately beeps once and displays an alert box (Figure 2-13). You are about to throw away a document that has been changed since the last time it was saved, and *Works* wants to know if you *really* want to throw it away without saving the changes. The three options are to cancel the command, <**Cancel**>, by pressing (Esc), *not* to save the changes, <**No**>, and to save the changes, <**Yes**>. You don't want to save these changes, so press (Alt) + (N) for No. *Works* throws away the document and clears the screen.

Figure 2-13   Do you really want to throw this document away without saving it?

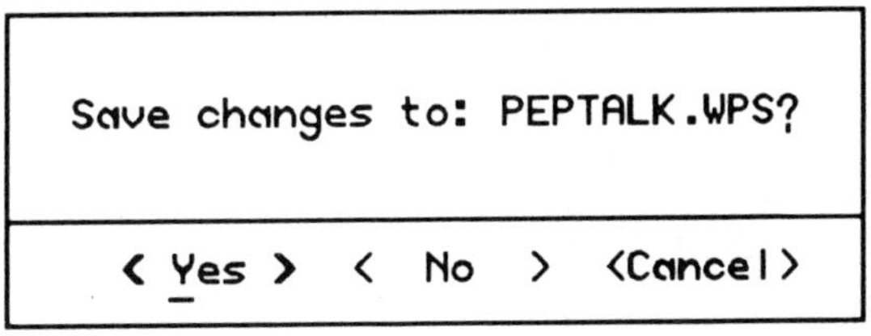

```
+---------------------------------------------+
|                                             |
|    Save changes to: PEPTALK.WPS?            |
|                                             |
+---------------------------------------------+
|                                             |
|    < Yes >   <  No  >   <Cancel>            |
|                                             |
+---------------------------------------------+
```

Opening a Previously Saved Document

To read in (or *open*) a previously saved *Works* document, pull down the File menu and select **Open**. *Works* displays its OPEN dialog box. Figure 2-14 shows this dialog box with your memo, PEPTALK.WPS, listed. (*Note:* If you have a *two-drive* system, and you don't see your memo listed, press (Alt) + (O) and use the (↓) to select the drive containing your Data disk. Then press (Enter).)

Press (Alt) + (F) to move the cursor to the **Files in:** list box. Then use the (↓) to select the PEPTALK.WPS file. Press (Enter). *Works* copies the document from the disk into your PC and displays it on your screen.

Saving More Than One Version of a Document

You might wonder if you can save several versions of the same document. You can. All you have to do is give each version a different name. The **Save As** command from the File menu is used for this purpose. If you choose **Save As**, *Works* will display its SAVE AS dialog box (Figure 2-5). Choose a different name for the document (for example, PEPTALK1), press (Enter), and *Works* will save the current version of the document without erasing the previous version from the disk. (*Note:* When you actually do this, you'll notice that the name of your document as displayed on the status line will change to the name you gave the new version. When you later select the **Save** command, it's this new version that will be updated on your data disk. In other words, the document whose name appears on the status line is the one that's updated when you save.)

Figure 2-14 The OPEN dialog box

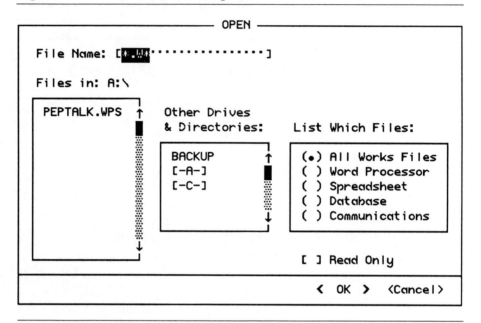

≡ Global Search and Replace (Find and Change)

If you pull down the Select menu, you'll see three commands: **Go To**, **Search**, and **Replace**. Two of these, **Search** and **Go To**, are used to move the cursor to a particular word or location in your document, while **Replace** provides yet another means of editing your work.

Go To

One way of moving quickly through your document is with the **Go To** command. Do you remember those >> symbols *Works* uses to indicate the start of a new page? Well, **Go To** allows you to scroll the window to any of these page break indicators.

Pull down the Select menu ((Alt) + (S)) and choose **Go To**. Figure 2-15 shows the resulting dialog box. Type **2** in the **Page Number** text box and press (Enter) . *Works* scrolls the window and moves the cursor to the beginning of page 2.

Figure 2-15 The GO TO dialog box

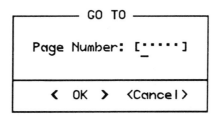

If you type a nonexistent page number and press (Enter), *Works* will display an alert message advising you of the incorrect choice. (*Note:* Instead of choosing **Go To** from the Select menu, you can press (F5).)

Search

The **Search** command allows you to search for a particular word or phrase within your document. It's especially useful when you have large documents, but let's demonstrate it with your memo. Because **Search** begins looking from the current cursor location, press (Control) + (Home) to move the cursor to the beginning of the memo.

Now, pull down the Select menu and choose **Search** (Figure 2-16). The dialog box provides you with a **Search For**: text box in which to type the word or phrase you want to locate. Type **mcs** (in lower case), and press (Enter). *Works* finds the first instance of "mcs."

Figure 2-16 The SEARCH dialog box

```
┌──────────── SEARCH ────────────────┐
│                                     │
│  Search For: [··················]   │
│                                     │
│  [ ] Match Whole Word               │
│  [ ] Match Upper/Lower Case         │
│                                     │
├─────────────────────────────────────┤
│            < OK >   <Cancel>        │
└─────────────────────────────────────┘
```

If you want to find the next occurrence, you could display the dialog box again and press (Enter), but there's a much easier technique. Just press (F7) . Each time you press (F7), *Works* finds the next occurrence of "mcs." After *Works* has shown you the last occurrence of "mcs," pressing (F7) will display another dialog box (Figure 2-17) telling you that *Works* couldn't find another instance of "mcs." Press (Enter) to acknowledge the message.

Figure 2-17   The last occurrence has been found

```
┌─────────────────────────────────────────┐
│                                         │
│     Search For text not found.          │
│                                         │
├─────────────────────────────────────────┤
│                          ‹  OK  ›        │
└─────────────────────────────────────────┘
```

Press (Control) + (Home) and then select the **Search** command again so that we can talk about the two options **Match Whole Word** and **Match Upper/Lower Case**. The **Match Whole Word** option does just what it says. Suppose, for example, you were trying to find the word "any." Normally, **Search** will show you not only every instance of "any," but also "anything," "anybody's," and even "many." In other words, it shows you every instance of the three letters "any." If you check the **Match Whole Word** option (by pressing (Alt) + (M)), **Search** will only locate occurrences of the whole word "any" in your document.

The other option, **Match Upper/Lower Case**, makes **Search** case sensitive. Let's go back to the previous example and use **Search** to look for "mcs," but this time check the **Match Upper/Lower Case** option by typing (Alt) + (U). **Search** won't show any occurrences of "mcs," and you'll see a dialog box telling you that "mcs" was not found. Press (Enter) to acknowledge the message.

Replace

Replace performs a process called global search and replacement. It allows you to replace one word or phrase in your memo with another, not just once, but as many times as the original word or phrase occurs in the entire document (globally).

Options in **Replace** allow you to specify whether you want to replace all the instances at once or approve each change separately. Let's see how it works.

As with **Search**, **Replace** starts from the cursor location. So move the cursor to the beginning of your memo, pull down the Select menu, and choose **Replace**. The dialog box for **Replace** (Figure 2-18) has a text box for typing in what you want to replace (**Search For:**), as well as one for the replacement text (**Replace With:**).

Figure 2-18 The REPLACE dialog box

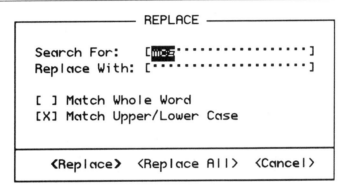

Suppose you wanted to replace every instance of "MCS" with "the Miracle Computer Store." In the area labeled **Search For:**, type **MCS**, and *don't* press (Enter). Press (Tab) after you've typed "MCS" to move the cursor to the second text box, labeled **Replace With:**. Here, type **the Miracle Computer Store** and, again, don't press (Enter). Notice that as you type "the Miracle Computer Store," the text scrolls within the text box.

Below the text boxes, you'll see the same two options you saw in the SEARCH dialog box: **Match Whole Word** and **Match Upper/Lower Case**. They operate here in the same manner. If there isn't an "X" in the box next to **Match Upper/Lower Case**, select this feature by typing (Alt) + (U).

At the bottom of the dialog box are three options. The last, **<Cancel>**, gets you out of **Replace** without changing anything. (Remember, you cancel a dialog box by pressing (Esc).)

The second option, **<Replace All>**, does just what it says. With the choices you have made for **Search For:** and **Replace With:**, choosing

<Replace All> will change every instance of "MCS" into "the Miracle Computer Store." Press (Alt) + (A).

After all the changes have been made, you'll see a message telling you that 2 changes have been made. Press (Enter) to acknowledge the message.

Before we look at the other option in the REPLACE dialog box, scroll the window to the top of the document and position the cursor at the beginning of the memo by typing (Control) + (Home). This ensures that the search process will start from the beginning of the memo, rather than from some point in the middle. Now choose **Replace** again from the Select menu. The **Replace** option at the bottom of the dialog box allows you to make the changes selectively throughout your document.

Suppose you wanted to change occurrences of the word "computer" to "microcomputer" in your memo. You wouldn't want to use the <Replace All> option because you would want to leave some instances of "computer" unchanged (such as those in Miracle Computer Store).

Type **computer** in the **Search For**: text box, press (Tab), and type **microcomputer** in the **Replace With**: text box. Remember not to press (Enter). Deselect the **Match Upper/Lower Case** feature by pressing (Alt) + (U). Notice that the brackets around the <**Replace**> option are brighter compared with the other two options. If you press (Enter), you will have achieved the same effect as typing (Alt) + (R). Press (Enter) and look at Figure 2-19.

Works highlights the first example of "computer" in your memo. Since you don't want to replace this particular "computer," press (N). Again the instance of "computer" is within the name of the store, so you don't want to change it. The third time, "computer" is still being used as part of the store name, but the fourth instance *is* one we want to replace. Notice that the actual word in the text is "computers" and that the "s" isn't highlighted. That's because *Works* is just looking for the word "computer." To change "computers" into "microcomputers," type (Y). Another instance of "computer" is found, and we want to change it, also. Again type (Y). Keep looking for other instances of "computer" to change by typing either (Y) or (N) until you see a dialog box telling you that no more occurrences can be found. When you see this message, press (Enter).

This is a good time to save your memo again.

Figure 2-19 *Works* asks you to confirm the replacement

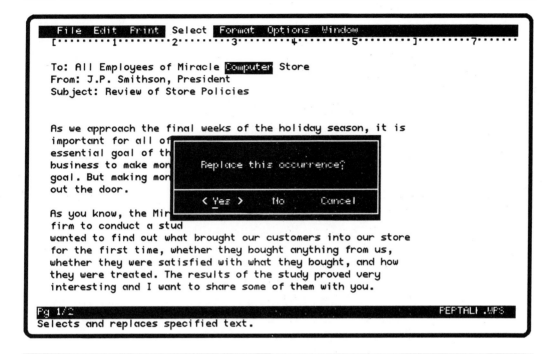

≡ Paragraph Formatting

Let's distinguish between two terms: *editing* and *formatting*. *Editing* means to alter the content of a document by correcting mistakes, adding or deleting text, etc. *Formatting* means to alter the appearance of the document—the layout of its paragraphs (indents, alignments, line spacing, etc.), the typeface of its characters (type font, size, emphasis), the location of page breaks, the addition of page headers and/or footers, and so forth. *Works* provides a variety of commands for formatting your documents.

Paragraph Indents and First Line Indent

If you look at the ruler, you'll see what looks like a left bracket symbol, [, at the 0-inch mark, and a right bracket symbol,], at the 6-inch mark. The [symbol marks the paragraph's left indent. The] symbol marks the paragraph's right indent. Two questions immediately come to mind: *Which paragraph's indents does the ruler describe?* and *What's an indent?*

The answer to the first question is that the ruler describes the paragraph containing the cursor. The second question requires a bit more than just a one-line explanation.

If you look at the ruler, you'll see that each paragraph in your memo begins at the 0-inch mark on the ruler. But when you print the document (which you'll do in a little while), the text isn't printed at the left edge of the paper. Left and right *margins* are set in the LAYOUT dialog box (you'll use this dialog box shortly). Typically, the left margin is set to 1.3 inches, which means that if a paragraph in your document begins at 0 inches, measured on the ruler, it will *print* 1.3 inches from the left edge of the paper.

That's why the term *indent* is used to describe a paragraph's ruler settings. Left and right ruler indents are relative, respectively, to left and right margin values.

To see the effect of indenting, move the cursor into the first multiple line paragraph (the one beginning "As we approach"). The ruler affects whole paragraphs, and each paragraph can have its own ruler settings.

Pull down the Format menu ((Alt) + (T)) and select the **Paragraph** command. When you first enter the PARAGRAPH dialog box (Figure 2-20), the text box for **Left Indent**: is selected. You can move the cursor to other parts of the dialog box by pressing (Tab), or (Shift) + (Tab), or by pressing (Alt) along with the brightened letter in each feature's name (e.g., (Alt) + (G) for **Right Indent**).

Let's set the left indent to .5 inches. Select the text box for **Left Indent**: if you've moved the cursor, type **.5**, and press (Enter) to accept the formatting change. Figure 2-21 shows the result. Notice that the [symbol in the ruler has moved to the .5-inch mark.

Display the PARAGRAPH dialog box again. **1st Line Indent**: controls the position of the beginning of the paragraph's first line *relative to the left indent*. Set **1st Line Indent**: to .5 inch, press (Enter), and see that the paragraph's first line is indented half an inch relative to the remaining lines. A new symbol, ¦, representing the location of the first line indent, appears on the ruler at the 1-inch mark.

Figure 2-20   The PARAGRAPH dialog box

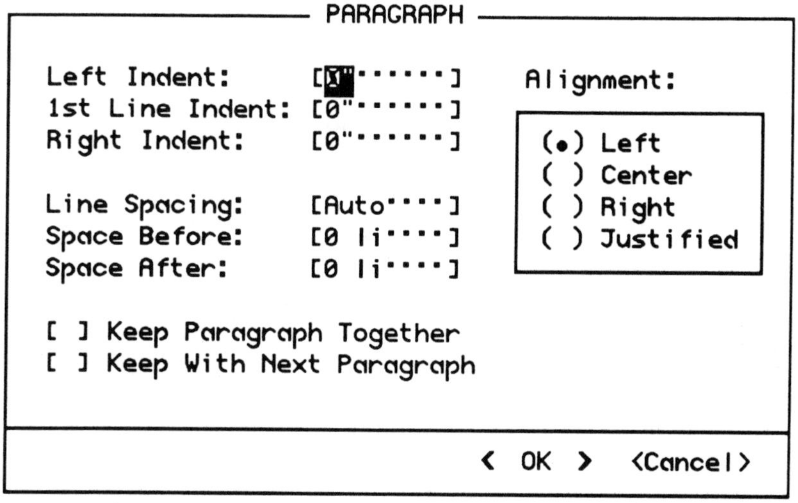

```
┌──────────────────── PARAGRAPH ────────────────────┐
│                                                    │
│   Left Indent:      [0"·······]    Alignment:      │
│   1st Line Indent:  [0"·······]                    │
│   Right Indent:     [0"·······]   ┌──────────────┐ │
│                                   │ (•) Left     │ │
│                                   │ ( ) Center   │ │
│   Line Spacing:     [Auto····]    │ ( ) Right    │ │
│   Space Before:     [0 li····]    │ ( ) Justified│ │
│   Space After:      [0 li····]    └──────────────┘ │
│                                                    │
│   [ ] Keep Paragraph Together                      │
│   [ ] Keep With Next Paragraph                     │
│                                                    │
│                                                    │
│                          ‹  OK  ›   ‹Cancel›       │
└────────────────────────────────────────────────────┘
```

**Figure 2-21   Only the paragraph containing the cursor is affected
                by format changes**

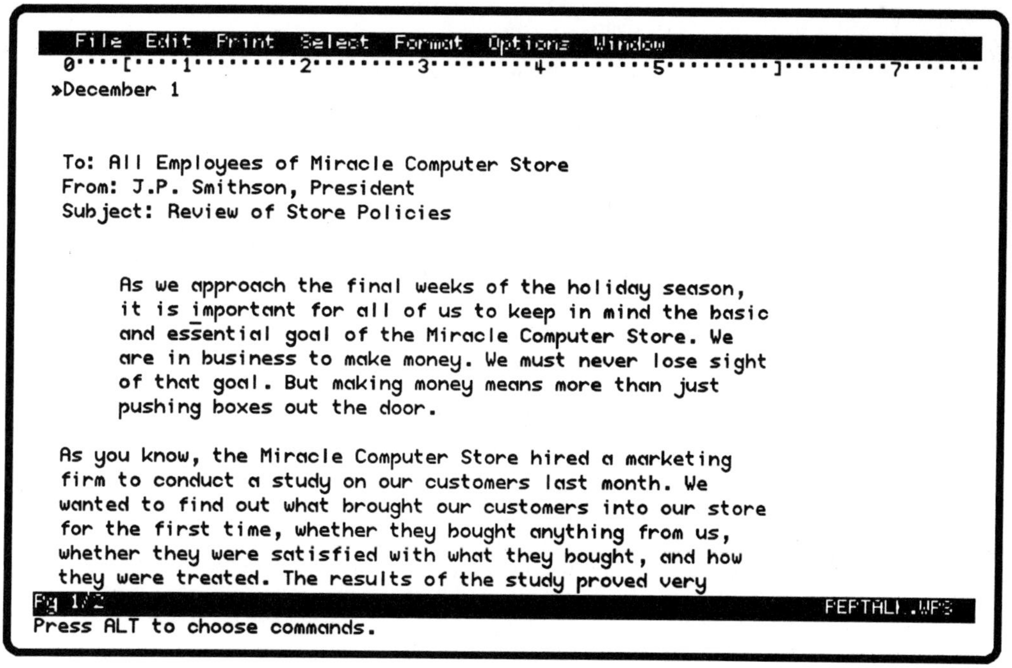

```
┌──────────────────────────────────────────────────────────┐
│  File  Edit  Print  Select  Format  Options  Window        │
│  0····[····1·········2·········3·········4·········5·········]·········7····· │
│  »December 1                                               │
│                                                            │
│  To: All Employees of Miracle Computer Store              │
│  From: J.P. Smithson, President                            │
│  Subject: Review of Store Policies                         │
│                                                            │
│       As we approach the final weeks of the holiday season,│
│       it is important for all of us to keep in mind the basic│
│       and essential goal of the Miracle Computer Store. We │
│       are in business to make money. We must never lose sight│
│       of that goal. But making money means more than just  │
│       pushing boxes out the door.                          │
│                                                            │
│  As you know, the Miracle Computer Store hired a marketing │
│  firm to conduct a study on our customers last month. We   │
│  wanted to find out what brought our customers into our store│
│  for the first time, whether they bought anything from us, │
│  whether they were satisfied with what they bought, and how│
│  they were treated. The results of the study proved very   │
│  Pg 1/2                                      PERTALI.WPS   │
│  Press ALT to choose commands.                             │
└──────────────────────────────────────────────────────────┘
```

The first line indent does not always have to be to the right of the left indent. Display the PARAGRAPH dialog box, and change **1st Line Indent:** to -.5 inch. Press [Enter] and compare your screen to Figure 2-22. Giving the first line indent a negative value is the technique for creating what are called *hanging* paragraphs. You'll see an even better example in the next project.

Figure 2-22 Use a negative value for 1st Line Indent to create a hanging paragraph

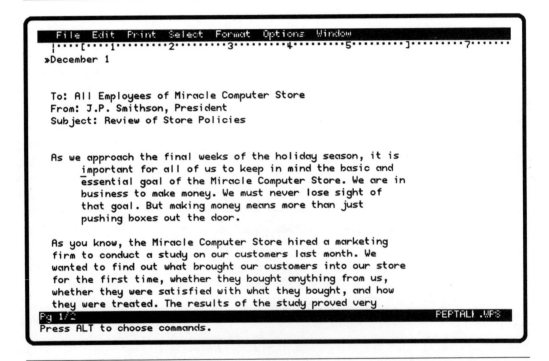

Values for the right indent are relative to the right margin (set in the LAYOUT dialog box). Therefore, setting **Right Indent:** to 1 inch means to indent the right edge of the paragraph 1 inch to the *left* of the right margin. Change **Right Indent:** in the PARAGRAPH dialog box to 1 inch, and see that this affects all the lines in the selected paragraph.

Before you proceed to the next section, change the left, right and first line indents to their original value of 0.

Spacing

Works provides three types of paragraph spacing control: Line Spacing, Space Before, and Space After. All three spacing options work on whole paragraphs. To illustrate the three types of spacing, place the cursor in the second multiple-line paragraph (the one beginning "As you know").

You can choose either of two standard line spacing values directly from the Format menu: **Single Space** or **Double Space**. But if you want triple spacing or 1½ line spacing, you'll need the PARAGRAPH dialog box. Select the **Paragraph** command from the Format menu, and refer to Figure 2-20.

The default value (the value *Works* chooses for new documents) for Line Spacing is **Auto,** and for most printers Auto spacing is the same as single spacing. (See the section on fonts later in this chapter.) Press (Alt) + (S) to move the cursor to the **Line Spacing**: text box. Type a value of **1.5,** and press (Enter). Notice that the paragraph containing the cursor appears to be double-spaced. That's because your computer's monitor can't display lines of text with 1½ line spacing. But when you *print* the document, your printer will space the lines correctly.

If you don't specify a unit (such as inches) when you enter a spacing value, *Works* assumes the value is in lines. You can, however, enter values in a variety of different units by adding the unit abbreviation to the value—"in" for inches, "cm" for centimeters, "pts" for points, etc. By the way, one line is ⅙ of an inch. (*Note:* See the section on *Measurement Units* in Chapter 8.) Values may be entered in fractions of lines (or other units) expressed as decimals.

Display the PARAGRAPH dialog box again, and let's see what the other two spacing options do. Change the value of Line Spacing back to Auto, (Tab) to **Space Before:,** and type a value of 1. Press (Enter), and see that *Works* has inserted one extra line of space between the paragraph containing the cursor and the one above (before) it (Figure 2-23).

Redisplay the dialog box, change **Space Before:** back to 0, and type a value of **1** for **Space After:** This time when you press (Enter), *Works* inserts an extra blank line between the paragraph containing the cursor and the one below (after) it.

You can use Space Before or Space After to place a blank line between paragraphs rather than pressing (Enter) twice after each paragraph. As with Line Spacing, both Space Before and Space After can

Figure 2-23 Change Space Before from 0 to 1 line

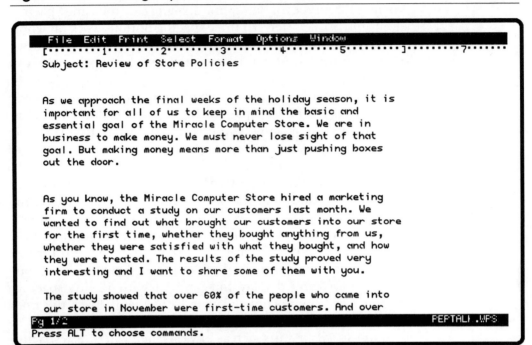

```
 File  Edit  Print  Select  Format  Options  Window
[··········1·········2·········3·········4·········5·········]·········7·······
Subject: Review of Store Policies


As we approach the final weeks of the holiday season, it is
important for all of us to keep in mind the basic and
essential goal of the Miracle Computer Store. We are in
business to make money. We must never lose sight of that
goal. But making money means more than just pushing boxes
out the door.


As you know, the Miracle Computer Store hired a marketing
firm to conduct a study on our customers last month. We
wanted to find out what brought our customers into our store
for the first time, whether they bought anything from us,
whether they were satisfied with what they bought, and how
they were treated. The results of the study proved very
interesting and I want to share some of them with you.


The study showed that over 60% of the people who came into
our store in November were first-time customers. And over
Pg 1/2                                              PEPTALI .WPS
Press ALT to choose commands.
```

accept values in tenths of inches. When you're through experimenting with different spacing values, set Line Spacing back to Auto, and the other two spacing options to 0.

Alignment

The term *alignment* describes the position of lines of text relative to the left and right indents. If you look at the ruler, it should show the left indent at 0 and the right indent at 6 inches.

The *Works* word processor has four types of alignment: Left, Centered, Right, and Justified. Alignment always refers to paragraphs, and you'll remember that a paragraph ends when you press Enter. To *Works*, the date line and the three lines of the heading are each separate paragraphs. Let's see how the various forms of alignment work.

Place the cursor anywhere on the date line. Formatting commands only affect selected paragraphs. The location of the cursor tells *Works* which paragraph to alter. (*Note*: If you wanted to format more than one paragraph at a time, you would have to highlight all of them.) Suppose you wanted the date line to be centered, that is, printed halfway between the left and right indents. You might think you'd have to type a bunch of spaces in front of the line, but it's much easier than that. All you have to do is pull down the Format menu and choose **Center** (or press Control + C). *Works* immediately centers the line between the left and right indents (Figure 2-24).

Figure 2-24   Center alignment

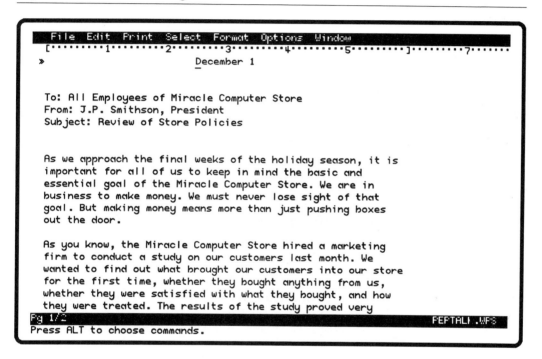

If you want the date right aligned, that is, printed flush with the right margin, press Control + R (Figure 2-25).

One of the most striking formatting effects is created with the **Justified** command. This command is only effective with multiple-line paragraphs, so move the cursor to somewhere in the first paragraph in the body of the memo (the one that starts "As we approach"). Now choose **Justified** from the Format menu (or press Control + J). All the lines of the paragraph, except the last one, spread out to fill the entire space between the left and right margins (Figure 2-26).

You'll probably want to justify all the paragraphs in your memo. The easiest way to do this is to press F8 five times, then select the **Justified** command. (*Note*: Don't forget to deselect the text by pressing an arrow key.)

Figure 2-25   Right alignment

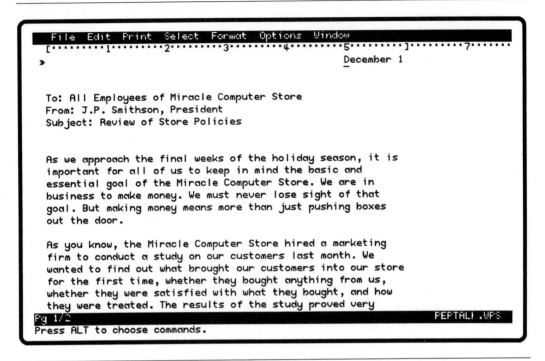

The only drawback to this method is that the date line's format has also been changed. But that's easily corrected. Move the cursor back to the date line and choose the center or right alignment.

Displaying the Ruler

All this time, *Works* has displayed a ruler at the top of the window. You might wonder if the ruler has to be displayed all the time. The answer is no. You can hide the ruler with the **Show Ruler** command in the Format menu. Each time you select this command, the ruler will be hidden if it was displayed, or vice versa.

Tabs

Look at Figure 2-27. See how the words following "To:," "From:," and "Subject:" are aligned. This effect uses the Tab feature and requires two steps.

First, highlight the three lines of text. Next, pull down the Format menu and select **Tabs**. Figure 2-28 shows the TABS dialog box. (*Note:*

Figure 2-26   Justified alignment

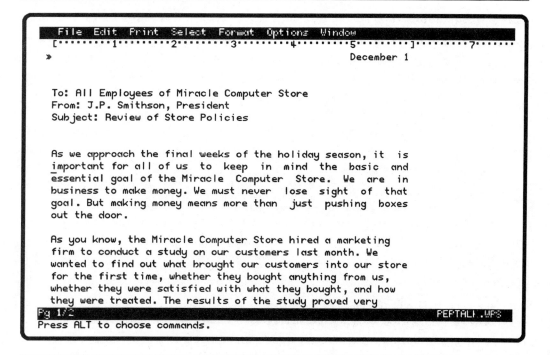

If your version of the *Works* program is earlier than 1.05, your TABS dialog box will look and perform differently from the one described here.)

Let's set a tab for the three selected lines at 1 inch. Press (Alt) + (P) to move the cursor to the **Position:** text box. Type 1 to insert a tab stop at 1 inch. Then, press (Alt) + (S) to set the tab stop. Notice that a listing of your tab stop appears in the **Tabs:** list box. Press (Esc) to close the dialog box, and look at the ruler.

A tab indicator, L, will appear on the ruler. The L represents a left-aligned tab marker. *Works* supplies four types of tabs—Left, Center, Right, and Decimal—but I'll wait until the next project to discuss the other tab types.

Here's an important thing to remember. You can only set tabs in paragraphs that were highlighted at the time the tab was set. This is true for any and all paragraph formatting changes. If you want a formatting change to affect the entire document, for example, you must select the entire document first, before you make the change.

Figure 2-27 Aligning text with tabs

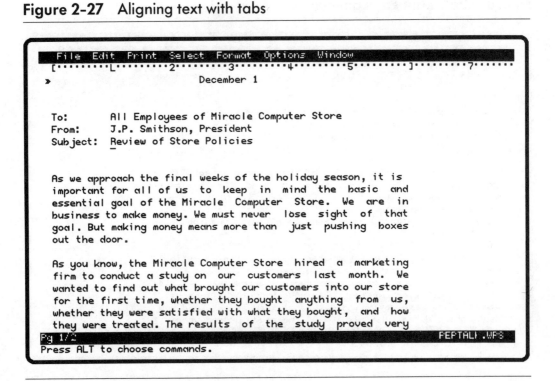

Figure 2-28 The TABS dialog box

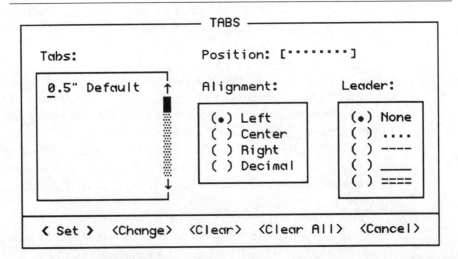

Now that you've set a tab for those three lines in your memo, press an arrow key to deselect the text. (*Note*: You *must* unhighlight the text before you do the second step.) Move the cursor to the space after the colon (:), and press the (Del) to delete the space. Then press the (Tab) to insert a tab character. Do the same thing in the other two lines. Now compare your screen with Figure 2-27.

Let's review the Tab setting procedure once more. First you highlight the appropriate section of text and add one or more Tabs to the ruler. Then you deselect the text and type Tab characters where you need them.

Once you insert a tab marker in the ruler, it can be moved to a different location or removed entirely. Remember, first select the text you want the change to affect. With the text selected, you can display the TABS dialog box. To remove a tab stop from the ruler, highlight the tab value in the **Tabs**: list box, and press (Alt) + (C) .

If you want to *move* a tab stop, first select the paragraph that uses the tab stop. Then, display the TABS dialog box, and highlight the tab stop in the list box. Next, press (Alt) + (P), and type the new location into the **Position**: text box. Press (Alt) + (H) to accept the change, and close the dialog box by pressing (Esc).

Tab characters in your document can be deleted in the same manner as any other character. But first, it helps if you can see them. Pull down the Options menu ((Alt) + (O)) and select **Show All Characters**. Now, in addition to all of the standard characters you typed, you can see paragraph symbols (¶), tab symbols (→), even the spaces between words (small dots). If you want to remove a typed tab character from your document, place the cursor under the →, and press (Del). You can hide these special symbols by selecting **Show All Characters** again.

Even when no tab markers are visible on the ruler, adding a tab character to your text *will* have an effect. *Works* supplies automatic tab markers on the ruler every half inch. I know you can't see them; they're invisible. When you insert your own tabs on the ruler, your tabs override *Works*' tabs.

≡ Character Formatting

Works supplies several forms of character formatting. You can add emphasis such as underlining, italics, and boldface to your text. You can subscript and superscript. You can even select different fonts and sizes, if your printer supports this feature.

Adding Emphasis

The first five commands in the Format menu allow you to emphasize your text in a variety of ways. I say variety because a particular text passage may be altered by a single character format command or by several commands acting together. As an example, suppose you wanted to make one sentence in the first paragraph stand out—the one that reads, "We are in business to make money." One way to emphasize this passage is to display it underlined.

Highlight the text by placing the cursor somewhere in the sentence and pressing (F8) three times. Then pull down the Format menu and select **Underline** (or press (Control) + (U)). Deselect the text by moving the cursor. It doesn't look underlined, does it? *Works* doesn't display character emphasis on your screen. Instead, it "brightens" the text and indicates on the status line which emphasis has been applied. Move the cursor to any character in the emphasized sentence, and look at the status line. You should see the letter U indicating that the character above the cursor will be printed underlined.

If you want more emphasis on that sentence, you might try adding bold formatting. Highlight the sentence again and select **Bold** from the Format menu (or press (Control) + (B)). Now you should see both a B and a U on the status line.

Subscripting and Superscripting

Subscript and superscript are used for numbering footnotes and for typing chemical and mathematical formulae. For example, in the formula for sulfuric acid, H_2SO_4, the numbers 2 and 4 were placed below the normal line by highlighting them, one at a time, and using the **Subscript** command. The mathematical expression, $Ax^2 + Bx + C = 0$, shows the effect of the **Superscript** command on the number 2.

Both commands are available from the CHARACTER dialog box (see below), or by pressing (Control) + (=) for subscript or (Control) + (Shift) + (=) for superscript formatting. (*Note*: You can remove character formatting by choosing **Plain Text** from the Format menu or by pressing (Control) + (Spacebar).)

Fonts and Sizes

The term *font* refers to the overall design of the characters that are printed on paper. *Works* can only display one font on your screen, but your printer may be capable of printing in several fonts. This is particularly true of laser printers, but even some dot matrix printers can print in more than one font.

The CHARACTER dialog box shows the fonts available for your printer. (Remember, you told *Works* which printer you were using when you originally configured the program with the Setup utility.) If you listed more than one text printer when you used Setup, you can choose the printer you want with the **Select Text Printer** command in the Print menu. Selecting this command displays a dialog box listing all the printers you chose in Setup (Figure 2-29). Use arrow keys to select the printer you want, then press (Enter).

Figure 2-29   The SELECT TEXT PRINTER dialog box

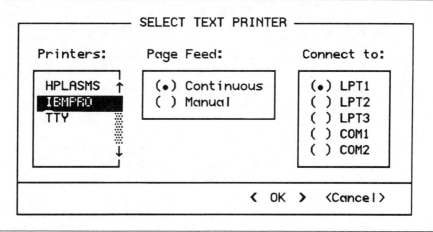

As with any other formatting, you must first highlight the text before you can change its font and/or size. Display the CHARACTER dialog box by selecting **Character** from the Format menu (Figure 2-30). The **Fonts:** list box shows the fonts available for the printer you selected. Press (Alt) + (F) to move the cursor into the **Fonts:** list box.

As you scroll through the fonts (assuming there is more than one font listed), watch the **Sizes:** list box. Each font will come in one or more sizes. Pressing (Alt) + (S) (or (Tab)) moves the cursor to the **Sizes:** list box. The size values can be a bit misleading. In general, the higher the number, the larger the text will be printed. But "larger" means different things to different printers.

For dot matrix printers, all characters are printed with the same height, so larger font sizes correspond to *wider* text. The dialog box

Figure 2-30   The CHARACTER dialog box for the IBM ProPrinter

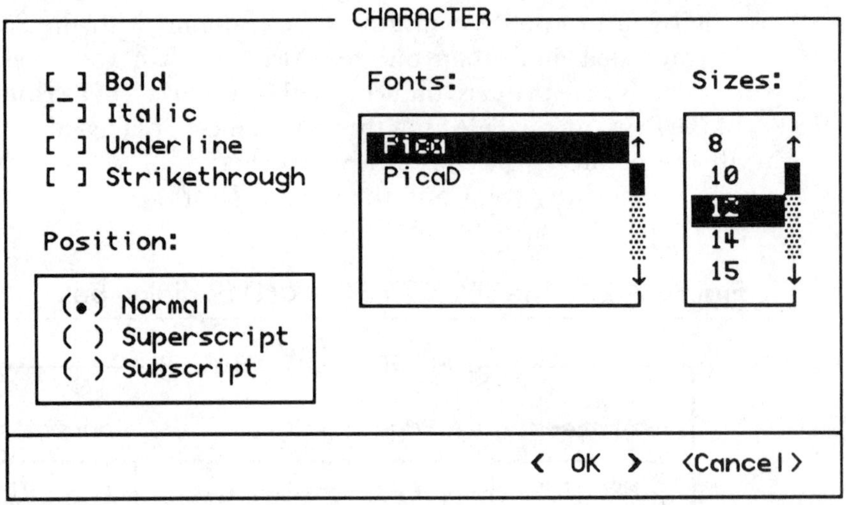

```
┌──────────────────── CHARACTER ────────────────────┐
│                                                    │
│    [ ] Bold              Fonts:          Sizes:    │
│    [ ] Italic                                      │
│    [ ] Underline        ┌──────────┐↑   ┌────┐↑    │
│    [ ] Strikethrough    │ Pica     │    │ 8  │     │
│                         │ PicaD    │    │ 10 │     │
│    Position:            │          │    │ 12 │     │
│                         │          │    │ 14 │     │
│    ┌──────────────────┐ │          │↓   │ 15 │↓    │
│    │ (•) Normal       │ └──────────┘    └────┘     │
│    │ ( ) Superscript  │                            │
│    │ ( ) Subscript    │                            │
│    └──────────────────┘                            │
│                                                    │
├────────────────────────────────────────────────── │
│                         ‹  OK  ›     ‹Cancel›      │
└────────────────────────────────────────────────────┘
```

in Figure 2-30 lists fonts and sizes for an IBM Proprinter. Figure
2-31 shows a printout of the six sizes for Pica font (the **Sizes**: list
box scrolls to reveal the sixth size). As you can see, the six lines
are the same height and differ only in the width of their characters.

Laser printers, on the other hand, are capable of printing text
of various heights as well as widths. Figure 2-32 shows the
CHARACTER dialog box for a Hewlett-Packard LaserJet printer. The
four sizes for Times Roman font (8, 10, 12, and 14) represent the actual
height of the characters, measured in *points*. (*Note*: There are 72 points
to the inch.) Figure 2-33 shows the four different font sizes. It also
shows the same four sizes in Helvetica font. Notice the difference between
the two fonts.

Forcing a Page Break

You're going to print this document in a minute, but before you do,
there's one more formatting change I'd like you to make. Scroll down
to the paragraph beginning "In the coming weeks" and notice that
a page break occurs in the middle of this paragraph (there's a >> symbol

Figure 2-31 For dot matrix printers, different point sizes result in different width text

---

```
This line is printed in Pica 8

This line is printed in Pica 10

This line is printed in Pica 12

This line is printed in Pica 14

This line is printed in Pica 15

This line is printed
in Pica 16
```

Figure 2-32 The CHARACTER dialog box for the HP LaserJet printer

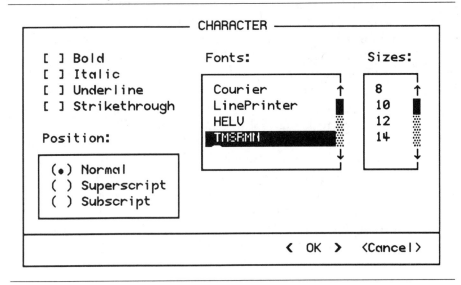

Figure 2-33 On a laser printer, different point sizes result in an overall change in character size

This line is printed in Times Roman 8

This line is printed in Times Roman 10

This line is printed in Times Roman 12

This line is printed in Times Roman 14

This line is printed in Helvetica 8

This line is printed in Helvetica 10

This line is printed in Helvetica 12

This line is printed in Helvetica 14

in the left margin of the screen, about halfway through the paragraph). While it's not wrong to split a paragraph between pages, your documents will be easier to read if you avoid splitting paragraphs.

If you want to force *Works* to start a new page at the beginning of this paragraph, move the cursor to the beginning of the paragraph and press (Control) + (Enter). *Works* will indicate the page break by drawing a dotted line across the page and will automatically recalculate the page breaks that follow. Let's try it.

Place the cursor at the beginning of the "One final thought..." paragraph and press (Control) + (Enter). Figure 2-34 shows the result. Now, when you print the document, the entire paragraph (and the remainder of the memo) will be on the second page.

If you want to remove a page break, just place the cursor directly on the dotted line, and press (Del). (*Note:* You can't remove the page breaks that *Works* inserts in your document, only those you put in.)

☰ Printing Your Document

Actually, printing a document is quite simple. But there are a few things you ought to do before you print. (*Note*: These cautions are

Figure 2-34   Inserting your own page break

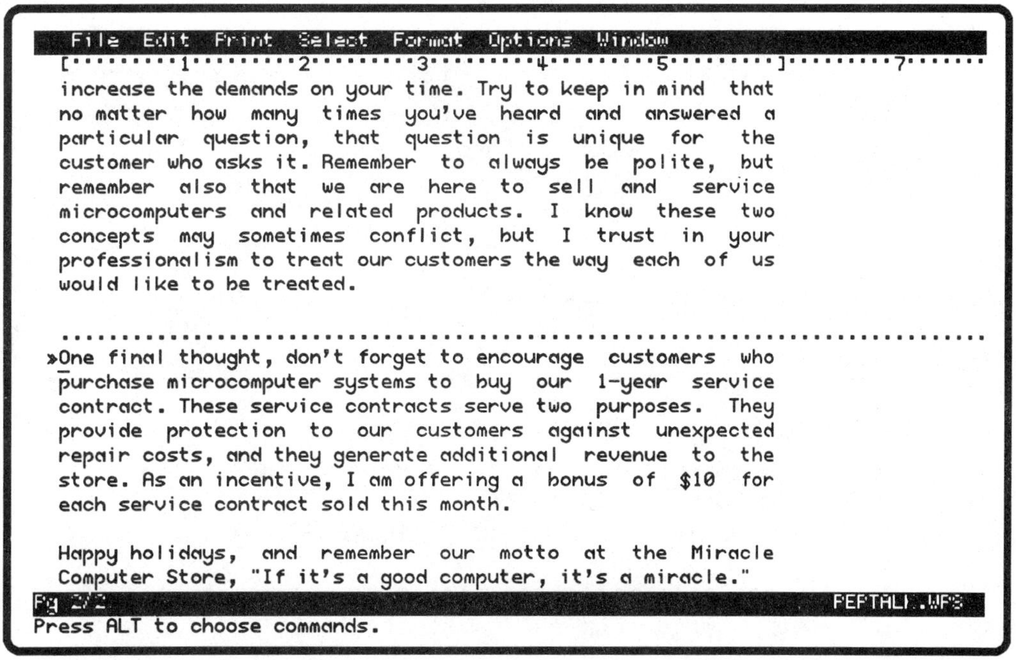

```
┌──────────────────────────────────────────────────────────────┐
│ ▐ File Edit Print Select Format Options Window               ▌ │
│ [········1·········2·········3·········4·········5·········]·········7······ │
│  increase the demands on your time. Try to keep in mind  that  │
│  no matter  how  many  times  you've  heard  and  answered  a  │
│  particular  question,  that  question  is  unique  for   the  │
│  customer who asks it. Remember  to  always  be  polite,  but  │
│  remember  also  that  we  are  here  to  sell  and   service  │
│  microcomputers  and  related  products.  I  know  these  two  │
│  concepts  may  sometimes  conflict,  but  I  trust  in  your  │
│  professionalism to treat our customers the way  each  of  us  │
│  would like to be treated.                                     │
│                                                                │
│  ·····························································  │
│ »One final thought, don't forget to encourage  customers  who │
│  purchase microcomputer systems to  buy  our  1-year  service  │
│  contract. These service contracts serve two  purposes.  They  │
│  provide  protection  to  our  customers  against  unexpected  │
│  repair costs, and they generate additional  revenue  to  the  │
│  store. As an incentive, I am offering a  bonus  of  $10  for  │
│  each service contract sold this month.                        │
│                                                                │
│  Happy holidays,  and  remember  our  motto  at  the  Miracle  │
│  Computer Store, "If it's a good computer, it's a miracle."    │
│ Pg 2/2                                            PEPTALK.WPS  │
│ Press ALT to choose commands.                                  │
└──────────────────────────────────────────────────────────────┘
```

valid for *all* programs, not just *Works*.) First, remember *always* to save your document before attempting to print. Why, you ask? Because if your printer should malfunction, it could cause your PC to freeze or lock up. This situation does not happen often; in fact, you may never experience it. But one such incident is one too many. A frozen or "hung" computer can only be restarted by turning it off, thus losing all data stored in it (in other words, your document). If you save your document *before* you try to print it, and you *do* experience a problem, all you have to do is to turn off the computer, wait a few seconds, turn it back on, load the *Works* program, and then load your document. Nothing is lost except a couple of minutes.

Second, look at your printer. Check that it is turned on, that it's connected to your computer, and that there is paper in the printer.

Third, make sure that the printer you've connected to your computer is the one you've selected in the SELECT TEXT PRINTER dialog box. If you're not sure, display this dialog box by choosing **Select Text Printer** from the Print menu, and make the appropriate selection.

OK. You've saved your memo, and you've checked out your printer. It's connected to your PC, it's turned on, and there's paper in it.

Print Layout

Pull down the Print menu and select **Layout**. The LAYOUT dialog box (Figure 2-35) allows you to make certain choices regarding the appearance of your document when it's printed. The first section of the dialog box allows you to set values for the four page margins: Top, Bottom, Left, and Right.

Figure 2-35   The LAYOUT dialog box

```
┌──────────────────────── LAYOUT ────────────────────────┐
│                                                         │
│   Top Margin:     [1"······]    Page Length:  [11"·····]│
│   Bottom Margin: [1"······]    Page Width:   [8.5"····]│
│   Left Margin:    [1.3"·····]                           │
│   Right Margin:   [1.2"·····]    1st Page Number: [1·····]│
│                                                         │
│   Header: [··············································]│
│   Footer: [Page - &p································]     │
│                                                         │
│   [ ] No Header on 1st Page    Header Margin: [0.5"····]│
│   [ ] No Footer on 1st Page    Footer Margin: [0.5"····]│
│                                                         │
├─────────────────────────────────────────────────────────┤
│                              ‹ OK ›   ‹Cancel›          │
└─────────────────────────────────────────────────────────┘
```

I again want to distinguish the margins in the LAYOUT dialog box from the Left and Right Indents shown on the ruler. The indents on the ruler are adjustable for each individual paragraph in your document. But *all* the ruler values are relative values. Zero on the ruler means to print the text at the Left Margin value specified in LAYOUT. This means that if the Left Margin were set to 1.3 inches (its default value), text with a zero Left Indent on the ruler would be printed starting 1.3 inches from the left edge of the paper.

Works automatically sets the Left Margin to 1.3 inches and the Right Margin to 1.2 inches, leaving you with 6 inches of "printable" space with standard 8½-inch wide paper.

Top and Bottom Page Margins do what you would expect. Their default values are each 1 inch. While you're free to change them, don't decrease these values below half an inch if you intend to include a Header or Footer (see below).

All four margins default to the measurement unit selected in the SETTINGS dialog box—inches (*Works'* default choice), centimeters, points, 10 pitch, or 12 pitch.

The two paper size values, Page Length and Page Width, tell *Works* the size of your printer's paper. *Works* chooses default values of 11 inches for Page Length and 8.5 inches for Page Width, but you can change them to match the paper you're using. As with the values for margins, paper size values may be expressed in fractions of inches (or other units of measure), expressed as decimals. The combination of Page Length and Top and Bottom Margins determines where page breaks are placed in your document. (See a discussion of page breaks earlier in this chapter.)

Text on page = Page Length − (Top Margin + Bottom Margin)

And Page Width, combined with Left and Right Margin values, determines the maximum text width (and the location of the Right Indent on the ruler).

Text Width = Page Width − (Left Margin + Right Margin)

If you decide to number the pages of your document, the value in the **1st Page Number**: text box determines the starting page number. Close the LAYOUT dialog box (by pressing ⌈Enter⌋).

Note: I've intentionally put off discussing headers and footers at this point. I'll come back to them after you've printed the document.

Continuous vs. Manual Feed

Display the SELECT TEXT PRINTER dialog box (Figure 2-29) by selecting the option from the Print menu. The default value for **Page Feed**: is Continuous (⌈Alt⌋ + ⌈O⌋), and if you're using continuous form paper, you should accept this option. If you're feeding separate sheets of paper (e.g., letterhead) into your printer, select Manual Page Feed by typing ⌈Alt⌋ + ⌈A⌋. Then, close the dialog box by pressing ⌈Enter⌋ .

The Print Command

Let's print the document. Pull down the Print menu again and select the **Print** command. The PRINT dialog box, shown in Figure 2-36, provides four additional options.

Figure 2-36 The PRINT dialog box

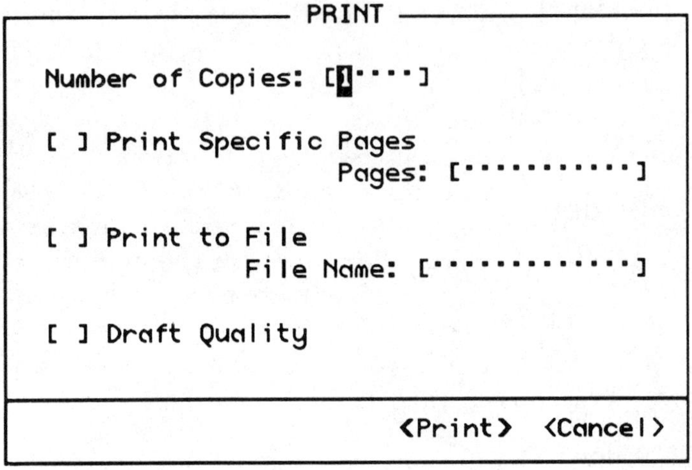

```
┌──────────────────────── PRINT ────────────────────────┐
│                                                        │
│   Number of Copies: [▌····]                           │
│                                                        │
│   [ ] Print Specific Pages                            │
│                    Pages: [···········]               │
│                                                        │
│   [ ] Print to File                                   │
│                File Name: [············]              │
│                                                        │
│   [ ] Draft Quality                                   │
│                                                        │
├────────────────────────────────────────────────────────┤
│                              <Print>   <Cancel>        │
└────────────────────────────────────────────────────────┘
```

The **Number of Copies**: option lets you print any number of copies of your document with a single **Print** command. Leave the number of copies set to 1.

The **Print Specific Pages** option allows you to choose to print some of the pages in your document instead of all of them. To print only page 2, for example, you would type (Alt) + (S) to select this option, then type (Alt) + (G) to move the cursor to the **Pages**: text box, and type **2** to indicate the single page you wanted to print. (*Note*: You can print noncontiguous pages, such as 3, 7, and 10, by separating the page numbers by commas. And you can specify a range of pages by separating the first and last pages in the range by a colon. For example, typing **3,5:8,12** into the **Pages**: text box would result in pages 3, 5, 6, 7, 8, and 12 being printed.) Since you want to print the entire memo, though, ignore this option for the moment.

The **Print to File** option lets you print your document to a text file on disk. This is useful if you want to read your word processor document using a different word processor program (see Chapter 8).

The **Draft Quality** option ((Alt) + (D)) prints the document ignoring all character formatting—bold, underline, etc. Printing in draft quality is faster than normal printing, but for now don't select draft quality printing.

Press (Enter) to accept the values in the PRINT dialog box. *Works* may take several seconds to prepare your document for printing. Shortly, though, your printer should begin printing your two-page memo. Notice that the second printed page began with the text that appeared just after the Page Break marker on your screen. (*Note*: If you've selected the Manual Feed option, *Works* will prompt you to insert a sheet of paper for each page of your document. You must press (Enter) to continue printing.)

Header and Footer

Let's go back and discuss the remaining options in the LAYOUT dialog box. Pull down the Print menu and select **Layout** again.

The two options **Header**: and **Footer**: allow you to type a single line of text and have it printed at the top (Header) or at the bottom (Footer) of each page in your document. There are several special features of the Header and Footer options that we'll talk about in a moment, but don't lose sight of the purpose of Header and Footer: to insert a single line of text at the top and/or bottom of each page of your document. (*Note*: *Works* allows you to insert multiple-line headers and/ or footers in your documents using the **Headers & Footers** command in the Options menu. See Chapter 8 for more information.)

Since headers and footers work exactly the same way (except for their position on the page), I'll only talk about the Header. But everything that's said about the Header pertains to the Footer as well. Unfortunately, you can't see the effect of adding a Header (or Footer) on your computer screen. Headers and Footers only become visible when you print your document. You're going to be printing your memo several times to see the results of using various Header features, so have a good supply of paper handy.

Works supplies a default Footer for every new document, "Page - &P." So that you can concentrate on just the Header, let's delete the default Footer. Press (Alt) + (F) to select it; then press (Del) to delete it.

Let's try a simple Header first. Press (Alt) + (H) to move the cursor to the **Header**: text box. Type **December Memo** and press (Enter). Choose the **Print** command from the Print menu and press (Enter). Notice that the words you typed in the **Header**: text box appear centered at the top of both pages of your memo.

Suppose you wanted the Header to be at the left margin of the paper instead of centered at the top of each page. Display the LAYOUT dialog box, press (Alt) + (H) to highlight the **Header**: text box, then press (Home) so that the cursor is at the beginning of the Header. *Works* has several special commands for customizing the Header (Table 2-1). Three of them control the placement of text along the Header line. &L causes text to be printed starting at the Left Margin of the Header; &C centers the text between the Left and Right Margins; &R aligns the Header with the Right Margin.

Table 2-1   Header/Footer formatting commands

Header/Footer Feature	Command
Left align header/footer text	&L
Center header/footer text	&C
Right align header/footer text	&R
Print page number	&P
Print file name	&F
Print current date	&D
Print current time	&T
Print one ampersand (&)	&&

Let's try some of these commands. With the cursor in front of the word "December," type **&L** (so that the Header reads "&LDecember Memo"), press (Enter), and print the memo again. It works, doesn't it? Feel free to replace &L with &R and see that the Header is shifted all the way to the right.

Page Numbers in the Header

By far the most frequent use of the Header (or Footer) is for displaying page numbers. *Works* will automatically number your pages for you. Here's what you have to do. Choose **Layout**, highlight the Header text, and press the (Del) key to erase it. (That's how you completely eliminate a Header from your document.) Type **&R-&P-**. The &R will position the page number at the right of the Header line. &P is the command for generating page numbers, starting with 1 (the default value in the **1st Page Number:** text box). The two dashes are for show; they make the page number stand out. Press (Enter), print the document, and see that each page of your memo is now numbered.

Other header commands allow the current date and time, as well as the name of your document, to be included in the header. You can even have part of the header printed at the left, part in the center, and the rest at the right. So, for a final Header example, get the LAYOUT dialog box, erase the old Header, and type in this Header: **&L&T&C&F&R-&P-**. I know it seems complicated, but look back at Table 2-1 and it should start making sense. &L prints what follows at the left margin. &T prints the current time. &C centers the document title (generated by &F), while &R makes the page number, &P, flanked by dashes, appear at the right edge of the Header.

Figure 2-37 shows the final version of the memo.

Figure 2-37   Final version of PEPTALK

```
2:51 PM                    PEPTALK.WPS                      -1-


                           December 1


To:        All Employees of Miracle Computer Store
From:      J.P. Smithson, President
Subject:   Review of Store Policies


As we approach the final weeks of the holiday season, it is
important for all of us to keep in mind the basic and
essential goal of the Miracle Computer Store. We are in
business to make money. We must never lose sight of that
goal. But making money means more than just pushing boxes
out the door.

As you know, the Miracle Computer Store hired a marketing
firm to conduct a study on our customers last month. We
wanted to find out what brought our customers into our store
for the first time, whether they bought anything from us,
whether they were satisfied with what they bought, and how
they were treated. The results of the study proved very
interesting and I want to share some of them with you.

The study showed that over 60% of the people who came into
our store in November were first-time customers. And over
half of them came in because our store was recommended to
them. The rest of those first-time customers came in for a
variety of reasons -- just passing by, saw our ad in the
local paper, picked us out of the phone book, etc.

But it is the customers who came in because we were
recommended that I want to talk about. I want to
congratulate and to thank each of you for your individual
efforts. A good reputation does not happen by accident. It
is built over time with perceived care and consideration.

In the coming weeks, we can expect to see a substantial
increase in store traffic. How large an increase is
anybody's guess, but if last year's holiday season is any
guide, look out! This increase in traffic will inevitably
increase the demands on your time. Try to keep in mind that
no matter how many times you've heard and answered a
particular question, that question is unique for the
customer who asks it. Remember to always be polite, but
remember also that we are here to sell and service
microcomputers and related products. I know these two
concepts may sometimes conflict, but I trust in your
professionalism to treat our customers the way each of us
would like to be treated.
```

Figure 2-37   (Continued)

```
2:51 PM                    PEPTALK.WPS                   -2-


One final thought, don't forget to encourage customers who
purchase microcomputer systems to buy our 1-year service
contract. These service contracts serve two purposes. They
provide protection to our customers against unexpected
repair costs, and they generate additional revenue to the
store. As an incentive, I am offering a bonus of $10 for
each service contract sold this month.

Happy holidays, and remember our motto at the Miracle
Computer Store, "If it's a good computer, it's a miracle."
```

Most of the time, you won't want to print the header at the top of the first page. The option **No Header on 1st Page** (Alt + N) suppresses the printing of the Header for the first page of your document. Alt + O does the same thing for the Footer.

By default, *Works* prints the Header 0.5 inches from the top of the page (and the footer 0.5 inches from the bottom of the page). You can change these values with Alt + M and Alt + A, but be sure that the values you choose for Header Margin and Footer Margin are *less* than the values specified for Top Margin and Bottom Margin, respectively.

This completes the description of all the LAYOUT options. In fact, you've experienced and used the majority of *Works*' word processor commands. The next project will give you further practice with these commands and introduce most of the remaining new ones. (*Note*: The commands used for merging a word processor document with database information will be discussed in Chapter 7.)

PROJECT 2: THE SCHOOL BID PROPOSAL

Our second word processor project is a response to a bid request from a local high school for microcomputer equipment. The school has asked you and several of your competitors to propose a package of equipment and support services. Figure 2-38 shows your response letter.

The purpose of this project is to reinforce some of the skills from the previous project and to introduce the remaining new word processor commands and features. I decided to show you the letter in its final form right at the beginning of the project so that you could see it develop, step by step, toward a known result. As you can see in Figure 2-38, there are two areas in which special formatting techniques are needed: the list of equipment and the three hanging paragraphs describing support services.

Begin your document by typing the date, inside address, salutation, and first paragraph.

The word "Equipment" has been modified in two ways: emphasis and justification. After you have typed the word, press (Enter) twice so that "Equipment" has a blank line above and below it.

Go back and highlight the entire word "Equipment." Select **Bold** and **Center** from the Format menu. Now move the cursor two lines below "Equipment" to the line that will contain the column headings for your table (Qty, Description, etc.).

This is a good place to save your document. Give your document the name "PROPOSAL."

≡ Formatting a Table

When you include a table in a word processor document, think of it as being composed of two parts. The first part is the first line of the table. It contains the column headings. Column headings identify the information that appears below them. The data or list of items you type below the column headings comprises the second part of the table. Each of these parts is formatted separately.

Column Headings

Type **Qty** (an abbreviation for Quantity), and press the (Tab) key. Similarly, type the remaining three column headings (Description, Cost, and Extension) separated by tab characters (Figure 2-39). *Don't* press

Figure 2-38 The finished letter for Project 2

```
December 8

Ms. Catherine Streeter
Director of Instructional Computing
Glen Grove Central High School
601 Circle Drive
Glen Grove, Illinois 60138

Dear Ms. Streeter:

In response to your school's request for proposals for
computer equipment for a microcomputer laboratory, Miracle
Computer Store proposes the following equipment and support
services.

                          Equipment

Qty    Description                    Cost      Extension
 30    Hewlett Packard Vectra CS      925.00    27,750.00
 30    Packard Bell Monochrome Monitor 79.00     2,370.00
 30    DOS 3.2                         83.50     1,905.00
  6    Panasonic 1092 Printer         350.00     2,100.00
  6    Printer Cable                   15.00        90.00
 30    Microsoft Works                149.95     4,498.50

       TOTAL                                   $38,713.50

                     Support   Services

The above total price of $38,713.50 includes the following
support services.

        ■    Miracle Computer Store will install, connect,
             and test all equipment specified in this
             proposal.

        ■    Miracle Computer Store will provide six hours
             of training on the operation of the equipment
             for one or two members of your staff.

        ■    Telephone support from one of our educational
             consultants is available for three months
             following the date of installation at no
             additional cost.

Thank you for giving us the opportunity to bid on your new
computer lab.

Sincerely,


J.P. Smithson, President
```

Figure 2-39 Insert tab characters between the column headings

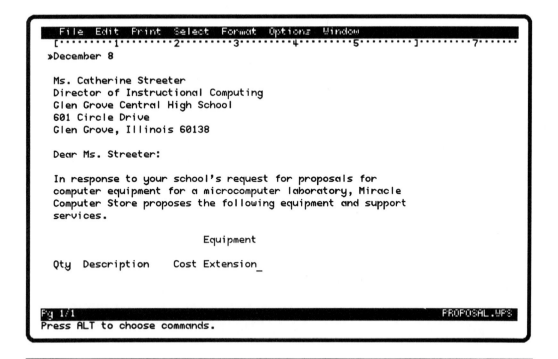

```
 File  Edit  Print  Select  Format  Options  Window
[·········1·········2·········3·········4·········5·········]·········7······
»December 8

Ms. Catherine Streeter
Director of Instructional Computing
Glen Grove Central High School
601 Circle Drive
Glen Grove, Illinois 60138

Dear Ms. Streeter:

In response to your school's request for proposals for
computer equipment for a microcomputer laboratory, Miracle
Computer Store proposes the following equipment and support
services.

                         Equipment

Qty  Description    Cost Extension_



Pg 1/1                                                    PROPOSAL.WPS
Press ALT to choose commands.
```

Enter at the end of the line yet. You must leave the cursor on the line for which you intend to set tab stops.

Each time you pressed Tab, the cursor advanced a few spaces to the right. *Works* supplies default tab stops every half inch, so when you press the Tab key, the cursor aligned with the next half-inch mark on the ruler. When you place your own tab stops on the ruler (which you're about to do), they override *Works'* default tab stops.

Let's insert tab stops at 0.7, 4, and 5 inches on the ruler (you only need *three* tab stops because the first column heading will begin at the left indent). The text following the first tab character you typed (Description) will align with the first tab stop. The text following the second tab character you typed will align with the second tab stop, and so forth. To insert the tab stops, pull down the Format menu and select **Tabs**. Figure 2-28 shows the TABS dialog box.

Press Alt + P to move the cursor to the **Position:** text box, then type **0.7**, and press Alt + S to set the tab stop. Use the same procedure to insert a second tab stop at 4 inches, and a third tab stop at 5 inches. The **Tabs**: list box should show *Works'* default tab stop, plus your three tab stops.

If you make a mistake, use the method described in the previous project to remove the incorrect tab stop. You can remove all the tab stops (except for *Works'* default tabs) by pressing $\boxed{\text{Alt}}$ + $\boxed{\text{A}}$. (*Note:* If your version of the *Works* program is earlier than 1.05, your procedure for setting tab stops will be somewhat different from the method described here. See your computer dealer, or contact Microsoft for an update.)

Close the TABS dialog box by pressing $\boxed{\text{Esc}}$. Figure 2-40 shows all three tab stops inserted into the ruler and their effect on the line you had highlighted. Note the position of the tab stops (Ls) on the ruler and the corresponding alignment of the words in the heading line.

Figure 2-40   Three tab stops have been added to the ruler

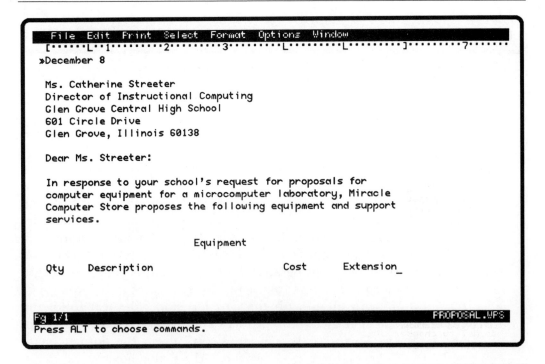

Displaying Tab Characters

Normally, you can't see tab characters you type when you press (Tab), any more than you can see end-of-paragraph characters when you press (Enter). But *Works* has a special display mode that lets you see these special characters. Pull down the Options menu and select **Show All Characters** (Figure 2-41). Look at your document and see that a small arrow (→) appears at each place you pressed (Tab). Also, a paragraph symbol (¶) appears at each place you pressed (Enter).

The **Show All Characters** feature helps you to see where you've inserted tab and other characters. If you find these characters distracting, you can hide them by selecting **Show All Characters** again.

Press (Enter) to move the cursor to the next line, and notice that all the tab stops you set in the ruler are still there. Even though you begin a new paragraph when you press (Enter), *Works* continues to use the same ruler settings from the preceding paragraph. However,

Figure 2-41   Using the **Show All Characters** command

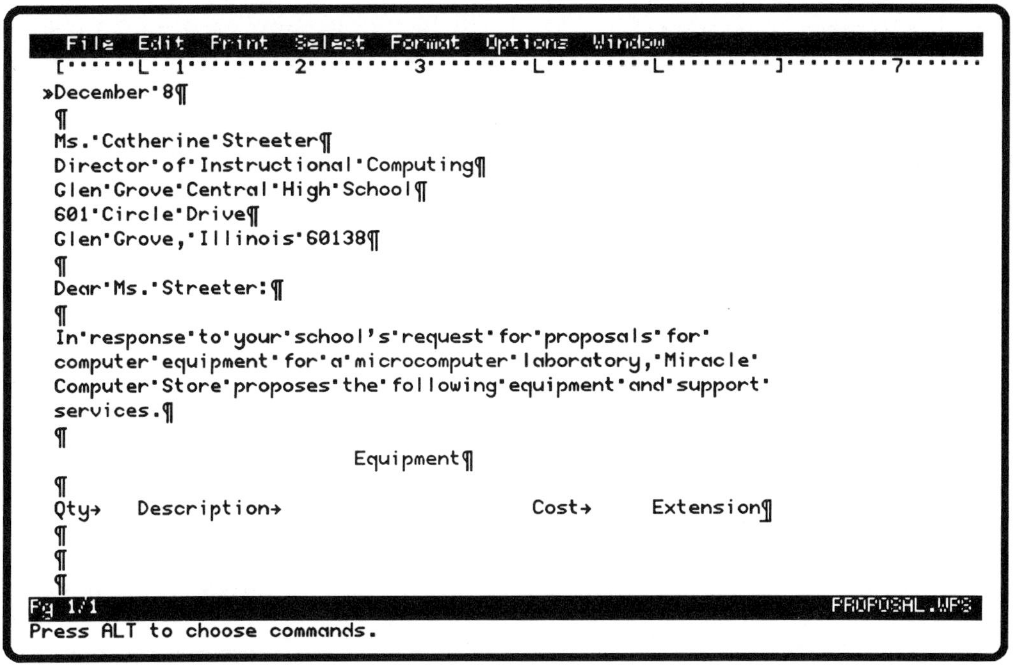

```
  File  Edit  Print  Select  Format  Options  Window
[·····L··1·········2·········3·········L·········L·······]·········7·······
»December·8¶
 ¶
Ms.·Catherine·Streeter¶
Director·of·Instructional·Computing¶
Glen·Grove·Central·High·School¶
601·Circle·Drive¶
Glen·Grove,·Illinois·60138¶
 ¶
Dear·Ms.·Streeter:¶
 ¶
In·response·to·your·school's·request·for·proposals·for·
computer·equipment·for·a·microcomputer·laboratory,·Miracle·
Computer·Store·proposes·the·following·equipment·and·support·
services.¶
 ¶
                       Equipment¶
 ¶
Qty→   Description→                     Cost→   Extension¶
 ¶
 ¶
 ¶
Pg 1/1                                              PROPOSAL.WPS
Press ALT to choose commands.
```

changing the ruler does *not* affect the ruler settings for *previously* written paragraphs. Prove this to yourself by moving the cursor to any of the paragraphs above the table heading line, and see that there are no tab stops in the ruler for these paragraphs. Then, return the cursor to the line below the heading, and let's fill in the table.

Right-Aligned Tab Stop

First, let's add one more tab stop for the quantity values. Display the TABS dialog box. Enter a Position value of 0.3 inches, but before you set the tab stop, press Alt + R. *Works* supplies four types of tab stops: Left, Center, Right, and Decimal. Pressing Alt + R chooses a right-aligned tab stop. The different types of tab stops determine *how* text that follows the typed tab character aligns with the tab stop. With a left-aligned tab stop, the *left* edge of the text aligns with the tab stop. With a right-aligned tab stop, the *right* edge of the text aligns with the tab stop. (*Note*: There's a separate section on using different types of tab stops and tab *leaders* in Chapter 8.)

Why do you want to use a right-aligned tab stop for the first column of your table? So that the numerical Quantity values will align properly. Without a right-aligned tab stop, the Quantity, 6, would appear directly under the 3 in 30. With the right-aligned tab stop, the 6 will align under the 0 in 30.

Press Alt + S to set the right-aligned tab stop at 0.3 inches, close the dialog box, and let's complete the table. Figure 2-42 shows the current ruler for the body of the table.

Now, for each of the four entries on the line, press Tab and type the entry. At the end of each line, press Enter .

Type all six lines, and notice that the columns for Cost and Extension don't line up properly (Figure 2-43). That's because the tab stops for these columns are the ones you set for the heading line. They're left-aligned, and for a column of numbers with decimal points, you need to use a *decimal*-aligned tab stop.

You need to replace the left-aligned tab stops at 4 and 5 inches with decimal-aligned tab stops. And you need to do this for all six lines of the table. Therefore, before you do anything else, you must highlight all six lines so that the tab changes you make will affect the entire table (except for the heading line).

Move the cursor to the first line under the table heading, and press F8 three times to highlight the entire line. Then, press ⬇ five times to highlight the rest of the table.

Figure 2-42   Add a right-aligned tab stop at 0.3 inches

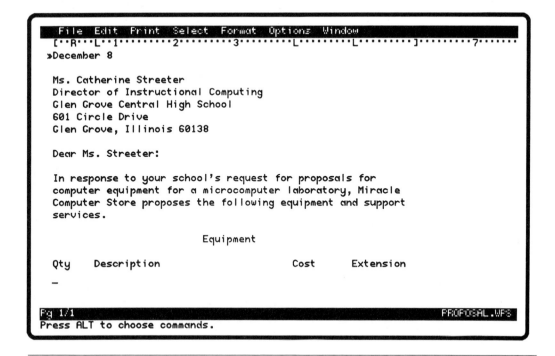

```
 File  Edit  Print  Select  Format  Options  Window
[··R···L··1··········2··········3··········L··········L··········]·········7······
»December 8

Ms. Catherine Streeter
Director of Instructional Computing
Glen Grove Central High School
601 Circle Drive
Glen Grove, Illinois 60138

Dear Ms. Streeter:

In response to your school's request for proposals for
computer equipment for a microcomputer laboratory, Miracle
Computer Store proposes the following equipment and support
services.

                          Equipment

Qty    Description                   Cost      Extension
 ─

Pg 1/1                                                  PROPOSAL.WPS
Press ALT to choose commands.
```

Display the TABS dialog box. You want to replace the left-aligned tab stop at 4 inches with a decimal-aligned tab stop at 4.3 inches. To do this, highlight the 4-inch tab stop in the list box. Press (Alt) + (P) to move the cursor, and enter 4.3 in the **Position:** text box. Press (Alt) + (I) to make this a decimal-aligned tab stop, and press (Alt) + (H) to accept the changes you made. Note the change in the *list box* when you press (Alt) + (H).

Perform the same procedure on the 5-inch tab stop to change it to decimal-aligned at 5.6 inches. When you've finished changing both tab stops, and the list box reflects those changes, press (Esc) to close the dialog box.

Figure 2-44 shows the result.

Now the Cost and Extension numbers line up. Notice that the decimal points of the numbers line up with the decimal tab stops in the ruler.

Figure 2-43   The values for Cost and Extension don't line up

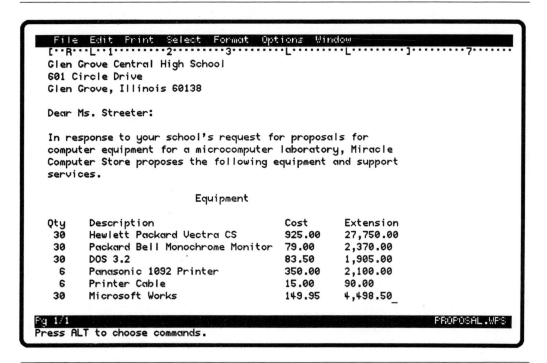

```
   File  Edit  Print  Select  Format  Options  Window
[··R··L··1·········2·········3·········L·········L·········]········7·······
Glen Grove Central High School
601 Circle Drive
Glen Grove, Illinois 60138

Dear Ms. Streeter:

In response to your school's request for proposals for
computer equipment for a microcomputer laboratory, Miracle
Computer Store proposes the following equipment and support
services.

                        Equipment

Qty    Description                     Cost      Extension
 30    Hewlett Packard Vectra CS       925.00    27,750.00
 30    Packard Bell Monochrome Monitor 79.00     2,370.00
 30    DOS 3.2                         83.50     1,905.00
  6    Panasonic 1092 Printer          350.00    2,100.00
  6    Printer Cable                   15.00     90.00
 30    Microsoft Works                 149.95    4,498.50_

Pg 1/1                                              PROPOSAL.WPS
Press ALT to choose commands.
```

Unhighlight the text, move the cursor to the end of the last line in the table, and press (Enter) twice to leave a blank line between the last item and the total. For the Total line in the table, press (Tab) twice before you type the word "TOTAL" so that it lines up with the descriptions. Press (Tab) twice more, then type the value of $38,713.50 and compare your table with the one in Figure 2-45.

I almost forgot. Go back and highlight the entire column headings line. Choose the **Underline** command from the Format menu. Now, compare it with Figure 2-45.

Continuing with the Letter

Once you have the table looking the way you want it to look, save your document again. Place the cursor at the end of the table, and press (Enter) twice to leave a blank line. Let's remove all the tab stops from the ruler. You won't need them for the rest of the letter. Display the TABS dialog box, and choose <**Clear All**> by pressing (Alt) + (A). This removes all the tab stops from the paragraph (a blank line, in this case) containing the cursor, but has no effect on the table.

Figure 2-44   Using decimal tab stops aligns the numbers

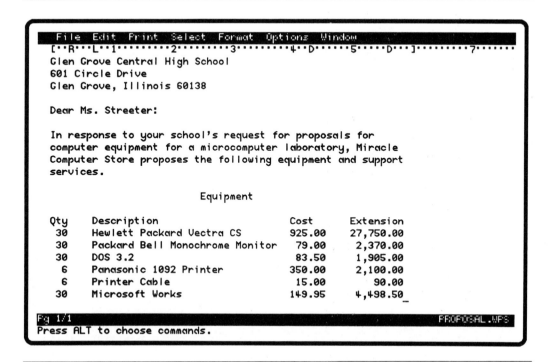

Remember, modifications to the ruler *only* affect paragraphs that were selected (either by being highlighted or by containing the cursor) when the ruler change was made. Close the dialog box by pressing (Esc).

Now, type **Support Services**. Press (Enter) twice to leave a blank line. Then go back and highlight "Support Services." Format it as bold, and center it. Instead of using the Format menu, take a shortcut by typing (Control) + (B) to bold and (Control) + (C) to center. Move the cursor two lines below "Support Services," type the next sentence, and skip a line.

☰ Hanging Paragraphs

Before you format the next three paragraphs as hanging paragraphs, look at Figure 2-46. You're probably wondering how to type those ■ symbols. It's simple. Just hold down (Alt) and type (2)(2)(3) *on the keypad*. When you release (Alt), the ■ symbol will appear. (*Note*:

Figure 2-45 The TOTAL line uses the same format as previous lines

```
 File  Edit  Print  Select  Format  Options  Window
[··R··L··1·······2·······3·······4··D······5····D··]·······7······
Glen Grove, Illinois 60138

Dear Ms. Streeter:

In response to your school's request for proposals for
computer equipment for a microcomputer laboratory, Miracle
Computer Store proposes the following equipment and support
services.

                    Equipment

Qty    Description                Cost      Extension
 30    Hewlett Packard Vectra CS  925.00    27,750.00
 30    Packard Bell Monochrome Monitor  79.00   2,370.00
 30    DOS 3.2                     83.50     1,905.00
  6    Panasonic 1092 Printer     350.00     2,100.00
  6    Printer Cable               15.00        90.00
 30    Microsoft Works            149.95     4,498.50

       TOTAL                               $38,713.50_

Pg 1/1                                            PROPOSAL.WPS
Press ALT to choose commands.
```

See the *Alternate Characters* section in Chapter 8 to learn how to type other "hidden" symbols.)

Formatting a Hanging Paragraph

Before you begin typing the hanging paragraphs, let's change the paragraph formatting. Be sure the cursor is two lines below the last sentence ("The above total price"). Then, pull down the Format menu and select the **Paragraph** command.

Change the Left Indent to 1 inch, the 1st Line Indent to -.5 inches, and Space After to 1 line. Remember that you can move the cursor from one option to the next by pressing (Tab). When you've made all three changes to the PARAGRAPH dialog box, press (Enter).

For each of the three hanging paragraphs, type a ■ symbol (see above), press (Tab), and type the remainder of the paragraph. Notice that the second and succeeding lines of the hanging paragraphs begin where the first line of text begins, while the ■ symbol "hangs" off

Figure 2-44 Using decimal tab stops aligns the numbers

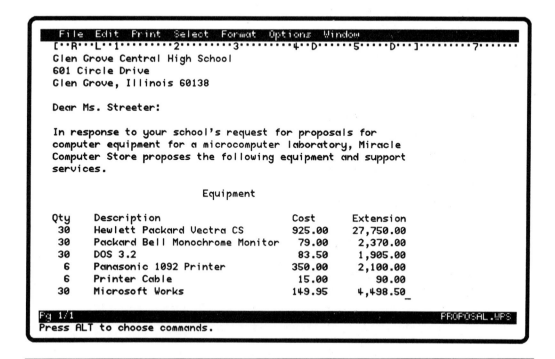

```
 File  Edit  Print  Select  Format  Options  Window
[··R···L··1·········2·········3·········4··D·····5·····D··]·········7······
Glen Grove Central High School
601 Circle Drive
Glen Grove, Illinois 60138

Dear Ms. Streeter:

In response to your school's request for proposals for
computer equipment for a microcomputer laboratory, Miracle
Computer Store proposes the following equipment and support
services.

                    Equipment

Qty    Description                     Cost      Extension
30     Hewlett Packard Vectra CS       925.00    27,750.00
30     Packard Bell Monochrome Monitor  79.00     2,370.00
30     DOS 3.2                          83.50     1,905.00
 6     Panasonic 1092 Printer          350.00     2,100.00
 6     Printer Cable                    15.00        90.00
30     Microsoft Works                 149.95     4,498.50

Pg 1/1                                                     PROPOSAL.WPS
Press ALT to choose commands.
```

Remember, modifications to the ruler *only* affect paragraphs that were selected (either by being highlighted or by containing the cursor) when the ruler change was made. Close the dialog box by pressing (Esc).

Now, type **Support Services**. Press (Enter) twice to leave a blank line. Then go back and highlight "Support Services." Format it as bold, and center it. Instead of using the Format menu, take a shortcut by typing (Control) + (B) to bold and (Control) + (C) to center. Move the cursor two lines below "Support Services," type the next sentence, and skip a line.

≡ Hanging Paragraphs

Before you format the next three paragraphs as hanging paragraphs, look at Figure 2-46. You're probably wondering how to type those ■ symbols. It's simple. Just hold down (Alt) and type (2) (2) (3) *on the keypad*. When you release (Alt), the ■ symbol will appear. (*Note:*

Figure 2-45 The TOTAL line uses the same format as previous lines

```
 File  Edit  Print  Select  Format  Options  Window                    .
[··R··L··1·········2·········3·········4··D·····5····D··]··········7······
Glen Grove, Illinois 60138

Dear Ms. Streeter:

In response to your school's request for proposals for
computer equipment for a microcomputer laboratory, Miracle
Computer Store proposes the following equipment and support
services.

                    Equipment

Qty    Description                     Cost     Extension
 30    Hewlett Packard Vectra CS      925.00    27,750.00
 30    Packard Bell Monochrome Monitor 79.00     2,370.00
 30    DOS 3.2                         83.50     1,905.00
  6    Panasonic 1092 Printer         350.00     2,100.00
  6    Printer Cable                   15.00        90.00
 30    Microsoft Works                149.95     4,498.50

       TOTAL                                   $38,713.50_

Pg 1/1                                             PROPOSAL.WPS
Press ALT to choose commands.
```

See the *Alternate Characters* section in Chapter 8 to learn how to type other "hidden" symbols.)

Formatting a Hanging Paragraph

Before you begin typing the hanging paragraphs, let's change the paragraph formatting. Be sure the cursor is two lines below the last sentence ("The above total price"). Then, pull down the Format menu and select the **Paragraph** command.

Change the Left Indent to 1 inch, the 1st Line Indent to -.5 inches, and Space After to 1 line. Remember that you can move the cursor from one option to the next by pressing (Tab). When you've made all three changes to the PARAGRAPH dialog box, press (Enter).

For each of the three hanging paragraphs, type a ■ symbol (see above), press (Tab), and type the remainder of the paragraph. Notice that the second and succeeding lines of the hanging paragraphs begin where the first line of text begins, while the ■ symbol "hangs" off

Figure 2-46 Formatting hanging paragraphs

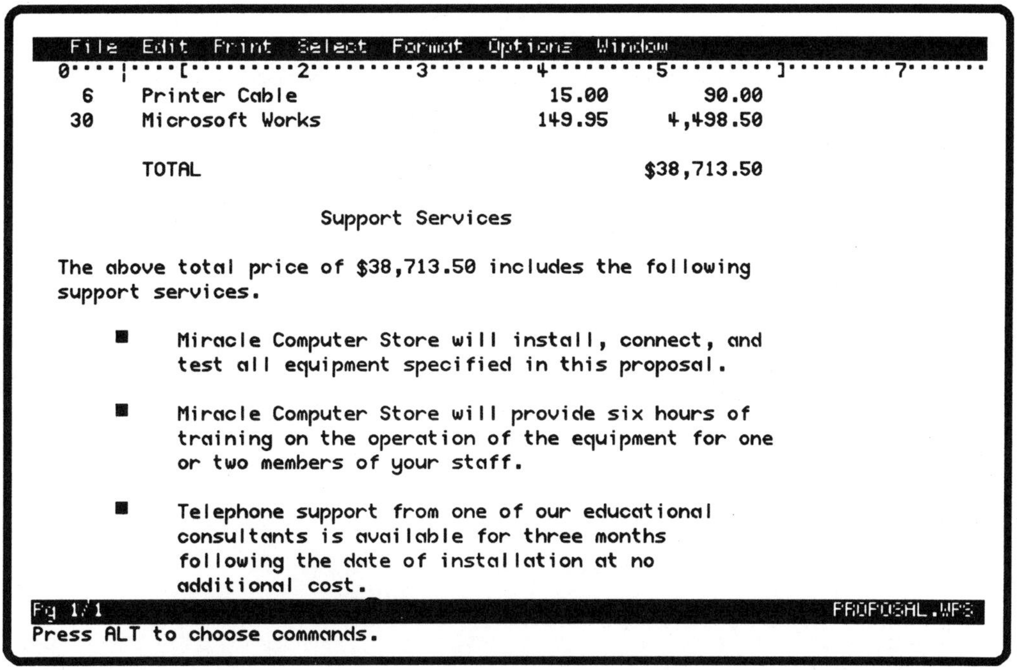

```
 File  Edit  Print  Select  Format  Options  Window
0····¡····[········2·········3·········4·········5·········]·········7······
   6      Printer Cable                  15.00        90.00
  30      Microsoft Works               149.95     4,498.50

          TOTAL                                    $38,713.50

                      Support Services

The above total price of $38,713.50 includes the following
support services.

     ▪    Miracle Computer Store will install, connect, and
          test all equipment specified in this proposal.

     ▪    Miracle Computer Store will provide six hours of
          training on the operation of the equipment for one
          or two members of your staff.

     ▪    Telephone support from one of our educational
          consultants is available for three months
          following the date of installation at no
          additional cost.

Pg 1/1                                              PROPOSAL.WPS
Press ALT to choose commands.
```

to the left of the paragraph. The choice of the symbol is arbitrary. Any symbol will hang the same way. Notice also that as you press (Enter) at the end of the hanging paragraph, *Works* automatically leaves an extra line between paragraphs. That's because you changed Space After from 0 to 1 line.

After you've typed the last hanging paragraph and pressed (Enter), display the PARAGRAPH dialog box and change the Left and 1st Line Indents to 0 inches. Leave the Space After value as it is. Close the dialog box and type the rest of the letter.

Let's make two more format changes so that the hanging paragraphs really stand out. Move the cursor to the first hanging paragraph, and display the PARAGRAPH dialog box again. Enter a value of 0.5 for the Right Indent, and press (Alt) + (J) to change the alignment to Justified. Close the dialog box, and compare your screen to Figure 2-47.

Figure 2-47   Change the right indent and alignment of the first hanging paragraph

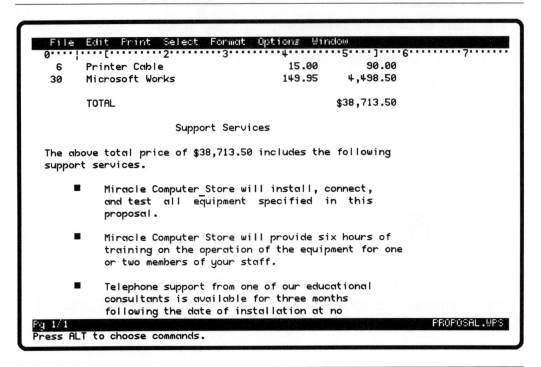

```
 File  Edit  Print  Select  Format  Options  Window
0 · · · · | · · · · [ · · · · · · · · 2 · · · · · · · · · 3 · · · · · · · · · 4 · · · · · · · · · 5 · · · · ] · · · · 6 · · · · · · · · · 7 · · · · · ·
    6      Printer Cable                   15.00       90.00
   30      Microsoft Works                149.95     4,498.50

           TOTAL                                    $38,713.50

                      Support Services

The above total price of $38,713.50 includes the following
support services.

     ■    Miracle Computer_Store will install, connect,
          and test all equipment specified in this
          proposal.

     ■    Miracle Computer Store will provide six hours of
          training on the operation of the equipment for one
          or two members of your staff.

     ■    Telephone support from one of our educational
          consultants is available for three months
          following the date of installation at no
```
```
Pg 1/1                                                             PROPOSAL.WPS
Press ALT to choose commands.
```

Copying Formats

That looks pretty good. Let's format the other two hanging paragraphs the same way. You could make the same format changes using the PARAGRAPH dialog box for each of the other hanging paragraphs, but there's an easier procedure. With the cursor still within the first hanging paragraph (now correctly formatted), pull down the Edit menu, and select **Copy Special**. This command copies all of the selected paragraph's formatting characteristics—Indents, Tabs, Alignment, and Spacing—to a place in your computer's memory. Once you have copied a paragraph's format, you can paste that format onto other paragraphs.

Move the cursor to the second hanging paragraph. Highlight this paragraph *and* the following one. Then press (Enter). *Works* displays its COPY SPECIAL dialog box (Figure 2-48), asking you whether you want to copy character formats (its default choice) or paragraph formats.

Figure 2-48 Copying paragraph formatting

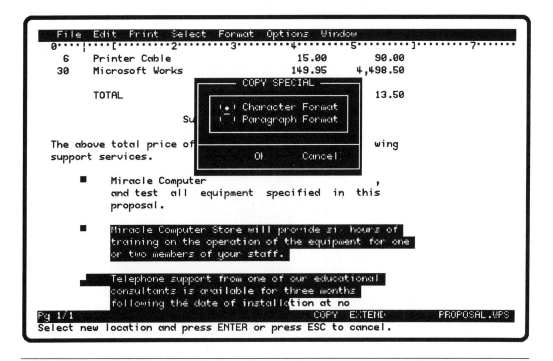

Choose Paragraph Format by pressing ⬇, then press ⎡Enter⎤. Unhighlight the text, and see that all three hanging paragraphs are formatted identically (at least they should be).

The only other reformatting you need to do is to change the alignment of all the paragraphs in the letter (except the ones you've centered) to Justified. Use the ⎡Control⎤ + ⎡J⎤ shortcut to justify each paragraph, and notice that single-line paragraphs are unaffected by justification. Now your letter should look exactly like the one in Figure 2-39. Save this final version, but before you print it, display the LAYOUT dialog box and delete the default Footer. There's little point in printing a page number at the bottom of a one-page document. Now, print it.

(*Note*: Some printers may not print alternate characters correctly due to differences between the printer's and the computer's alternate character sets. If your printer doesn't print the ■ symbol, refer to Chapter 8 and Appendix A and try other characters.)

☰ Final Comments

This finishes the second word processor project, but your work has just started. The only way to become familiar with the commands and features of any program is to use them, repeatedly. There is no substitute for practice. Make up your own projects, and use as many of the commands as you can. Don't think you have to memorize all the word processor commands. *Works* provides an on-screen help feature to jog your memory.

Help

If you can't remember how to use a particular feature, pull down the Window menu, and select **Help Index**. *Works* displays an index of help topics (Figure 2-49). You can scroll through the index until you find a topic that relates to your question. See Chapter 1 for more information on using *Works'* Help Index.

Figure 2-49 Help is available from within *Works*

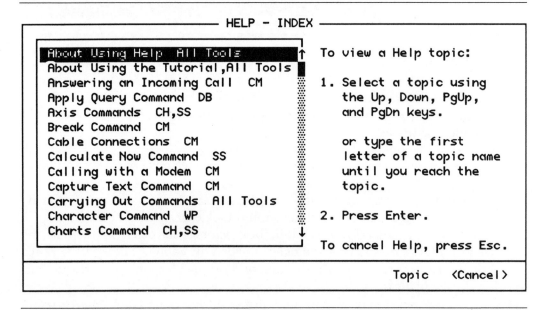

Chapter **3**
THE DATABASE

The database application is a tool for making lists: lists of people, lists of equipment, lists of just about anything. For example, as owner of the Miracle Computer Store, you'd probably want to keep a list of all your customers and the equipment they bought from you. You might also want to track the activity of your service department staff so that you can see how much of their time was spent actually repairing customers' equipment. These are the two projects you'll be doing in this chapter.

PROJECT 3: THE CUSTOMER LIST

Before you begin creating the customer list database, stop and think about the information you want to include for each customer. Yes, you can change your mind later and modify the database by adding or deleting information. But a few minutes spent planning your database *before* you create it can save spending significantly more time later on.

So, what information are you going to include for each customer in your database? Obviously, the customer's name, but do you want to type the entire name as a single entry, or have separate entries for first and last name? *Works* builds a database with *fields*. Each field is set up to contain a particular piece of information. You can either set up one field that contains the entire name, or two fields (one containing the first and the other the last name).

What's the advantage of setting up two fields for the name? The purpose of creating this database is to enable you to retrieve information about your customers. If you wanted to see the information about a certain customer, you'd probably search the database looking for the customer's last name. So having the last name in a separate field is a good idea.

What other information might you want to include? Address, telephone number, equipment purchased, date purchased, whether an extended warranty was purchased, and the salesperson's name are all reasonable items. The choice of what to include depends on how you intend to use the database. Table 3-1 shows a list of the fields for your customer database. (Ignore the numbers following the field names for the moment.) Notice that City, State, and Zip are each given a separate field. You might want to use your customer database to generate a bulk mailing. With a separate field for Zip, you'll be able to arrange your customers in zip code order. (You'll see how to sort the data later in the exercise.)

One of *Works*' unique features is the ability to combine data (e.g., names and addresses) from a database with a letter in the word processor to produce personalized form letters. That project will be covered in Chapter

Table 3-1   Fields for customer database

First Name	(32)
Last Name	(31)
Address	(70)
City	(31)
State	(9)
Zip	(11)
Phone	(19)
Computer System	(50)
Warranty	(11)
Date Purchased	(29)
Salesperson	(37)

7. The customer database you're about to create now is the one that will be used in Chapter 7.

☰ Creating the Database

Begin by telling *Works* that you want to create a new database document. If you've not booted the program yet, do so, and you'll see the *Works* NEW dialog box. Use the ⬇ to select the database application, and then press ⌨Enter. (*Note*: If you're already in the *Works* program, choose **New** from the File menu, and then follow the above procedure.) Figure 3-1 shows the new database's Form Design window.

Creating Fields
The Form Design window lets you create the fields that comprise your database. Creating fields is easy. All you have to do is type the name of the field, followed by a colon (:). The only restriction on the field name is that it cannot be more than 15 characters long.

You could type each field on its own separate line so that the fields in the Form Design screen looked like the list in Table 3-1. But *Works* allows you to position the fields anywhere on the screen. In fact, if your database contained so many fields that they couldn't all fit within one screen, you could spread them out over as many as eight Form Design screens. Pressing ⌨PgDn and ⌨PgUp moves the window from screen to screen.

For this project, one Form Design screen should suffice. Let's place the first field at the beginning of the third line. Use ⬇ to move the cursor

88   WORKING WITH *PC WORKS*

Figure 3-1   The Form Design window

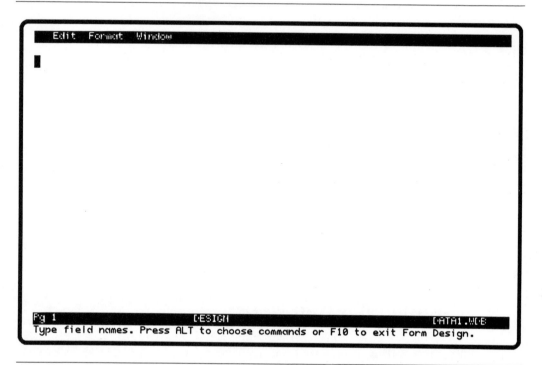

down two lines, and type the first field name on the list, **First Name**, followed by a colon (Figure 3-2). Notice that as you type, the characters appear just under the menu bar rather than on the form itself. Press (Enter), and the field name appears on the Form Design screen, at the cursor location. Look closely, and you'll see a thin underline following the field name (Figure 3-2). This line defines the space into which you'll enter actual data. (*Note*: You'll probably need to adjust the width of the data entry area, but leave it at its default width of 10 spaces for now.)

If you don't see a line following the field name on your Form Design screen, you forgot to add a colon to the field name. To correct this, leave the text highlighted, press (Del), retype the field name *with the colon*, and press (Enter).

Move the cursor about halfway across the screen on the same line, and type the second field name, **Last Name**, also followed by a colon. Press (Enter).

Figure 3-2   Be sure to add a colon to the end of the field name

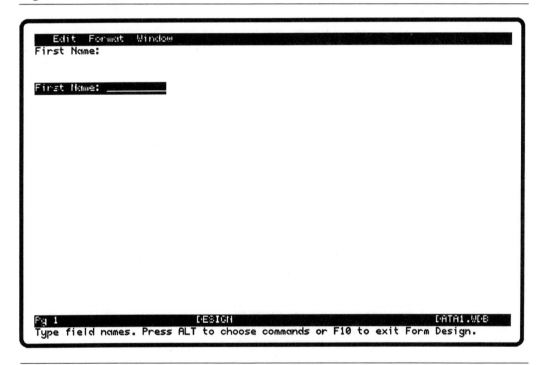

Look at Figure 3-3, and type the remaining fields listed in Table 3-1 so that they appear in about the same location on your Form Design screen.

Editing the Form Design Screen

Once you've placed a field name on the screen, you might wonder if you can move it to a different location. Yes, you can.

To move a field name, first highlight it. Then, press ⌐F3⌐ (or select **Move** from the Edit menu). Next, use the arrow keys to move the cursor to a different spot on the screen. And finally, press ⌐Enter⌐.

If you want to change the name of a field, just highlight it, type the new name (*remember the colon*) and press ⌐Enter⌐. If you want to change a character or two, you can edit the field name instead of retyping it. Just highlight the name and press ⌐F2⌐. Then you can move the cursor and edit the name as you would any text.

Figure 3-3 A sample form design

```
┌─────────────────────────────────────────────────────────────┐
│  Edit  Format  Window                                         │
│                                                               │
│                                                               │
│  First Name: _____        Last Name: _____          │
│  Address: _____                                          │
│  City: _____              State: _____  Zip: _____ │
│                                Phone: _____              │
│                                                               │
│                                                               │
│  Computer System: _____                    Wty: _____ │
│                                                               │
│  Date Purchased: _____    Salesperson: _____        │
│  █                                                            │
│                                                               │
│ Fg 1                        DESIGN                  DATA1.WDB │
│ Type field names. Press ALT to choose commands or F10 to exit Form Design. │
└─────────────────────────────────────────────────────────────┘
```

You can add ordinary text to your form design screen to improve its readability. For example, you might place a title at the top of the screen, and draw a line to separate demographic from sales fields (Figure 3-4).

To add text to your Form Design screen, place the cursor where you want the text to appear, type the text, and press (Enter). As long as you *don't* type a colon at the end, *Works* will treat what you type as ordinary text rather than as a field name. (*Note*: If for some reason you want to type a line of text that ends with a colon, type a quote ["] as the first character.)

Extending the Data Entry Cell

I mentioned earlier that the length of the underline following the field name determines the space available for entering data. Let's discuss this a bit more.

Figure 3-4 Add text to the form to improve its readability

```
 Edit  Format  Window
"Miracle Computer Store Customer List
                    Miracle Computer Store Customer List

 First Name: _____         Last Name: _____

 Address: _____

 City: _____      State: _____    Zip: _____

                       Phone: _____

~~~~~~~~~~~~~~~~~~~~~~~~~~~~~~~~~~~~~~~~~~~~~~~~~~~~~~~~~~~~~~~~~~~~~~~~~~~~~

 Computer System: _____                        Wty: _____


 Date Purchased: _____    Salesperson: _____




Pg 1                 DESIGN                              DATA1.WDB
Type field names. Press ALT to choose commands or F10 to exit Form Design.
```

Look at the First Name field, for example. By default, *Works* sets up a data entry *cell* 10 spaces wide. Does this mean that you can enter only first names of 10 or fewer characters? No. You can enter any amount of data for any field, but if, in this example, you typed a first name that had more than 10 characters, only the first 10 characters would be displayed on the screen. Let me show you what I mean. Press (F10) to exit the Form Design screen and enter the Form Entry screen. (Notice the word FORM on the status line.)

Press (PgUp) to move the cursor to the first field on the screen, First Name. Type the name **Christopher**, and press (Tab). See? Only the first 10 letters of "Christopher" are displayed.

Even though *Works* remembers the whole name, it would be nice to be able to *see* all of it. So, let's go back to the Form Design screen and widen the data entry cells for each of the fields. Pull down the Options menu, and select **Define Form**.

Move the cursor to highlight the First Name field. Then, pull down the Format menu and select **Width**. Figure 3-5 shows the WIDTH dialog box.

The value 22 represents the total width of the field name (including the colon and the following space), plus the data entry cell. Let's add 10 more spaces to the cell. Type **32** into the **Width**: text box, and press (Enter). The line following First Name has been lengthened, and if you press (F10), you'll see that all of Christopher is now displayed.

Figure 3-5   The WIDTH dialog box

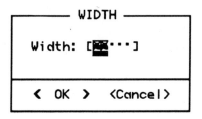

Return to the Form Design screen (by selecting **Define Form** from the Format menu), refer to Figure 3-6, and lengthen (or shorten) the data entry cells for each of the remaining fields. Use Figure 3-6 as a model, but don't feel that you have to duplicate it exactly. If you want to use the same values I used, the numbers following the field names in Table 3-1 represent the field widths (you probably guessed that already).

Field Types

Before you begin entering data into your database, there is one field whose field *type* you must change. *Works* allows you to specify the format of data you intend to enter into each field. While all fields can accept both text and numbers, by default numerical entries are displayed unformatted. The Format menu contains seven numerical formats (in addition to General), and since you'll be entering dates into the Date Purchased field, you need to choose Time/Date format for this field. (Why? So that later you can sort the customer list *chronologically*, by Date Purchased.)

Changing a field's type is easy. First, highlight the Date Purchased field. Then, pull down the Format menu to see a list of all the field

Figure 3-6 Choose widths to match the expected data

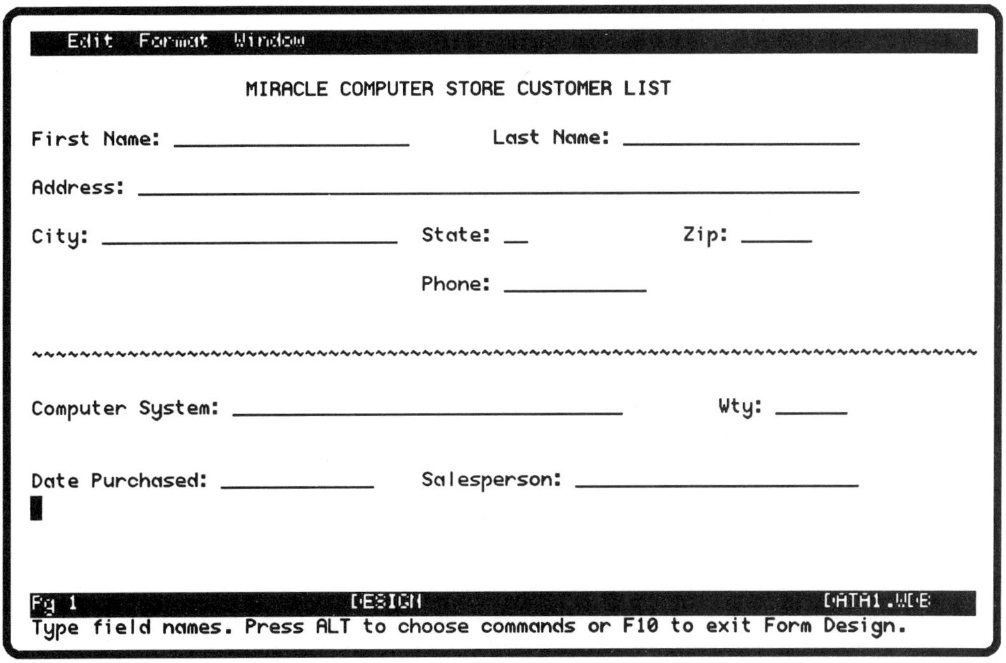

```
┌──────────────────────────────────────────────────────────────┐
│  Edit  Format  Window                                          │
│              MIRACLE COMPUTER STORE CUSTOMER LIST              │
│                                                                │
│  First Name: _____    Last Name: _____ │
│                                                                │
│  Address: _____ │
│                                                                │
│  City: _____    State: __      Zip: _____       │
│                                                                │
│                              Phone: _____                │
│                                                                │
│  ~~~~~~~~~~~~~~~~~~~~~~~~~~~~~~~~~~~~~~~~~~~~~~~~~~~~~~~~~~~~~~~~ │
│                                                                │
│  Computer System: _____     Wty: _____      │
│                                                                │
│  Date Purchased: _____    Salesperson: _____ │
│  ▌                                                             │
│                                                                │
│ Pg 1                      DESIGN                    DATA1.WDB   │
│ Type field names. Press ALT to choose commands or F10 to exit Form Design. │
└──────────────────────────────────────────────────────────────┘
```

data types. Select **Time/Date**, and *Works* will display its TIME/DATE dialog box (Figure 3-7).

Works provides four date and two time formats. Press (Alt) + (M) to select Month, Day, Year format, and notice that as you make this selection a choice of two Date displays (Short or Long) becomes available. The default value is Short, which means that dates will appear in the form: 10/27/89. This same date in Long format would appear as: Oct. 27, 1989. Press (Alt) + (L) to select Long display.

Note: If you had selected either of the two time formats (Hour, Minute, Second or Hour, Minute), *Works* would have given you the choice of 24 Hour or 12 Hour display. Press (Enter) to accept your selections.

Before you exit from the Form Design screen, look at the status line. The word DESIGN indicates that this is the Form Design screen. Now, press (F10), and see that the status line shows the word FORM, indicating that this is the Form screen for data entry.

You couldn't save the database while you were in the Form Design screen. So, before you do anything else, save your database to your

Figure 3-7   The TIME/DATE dialog box

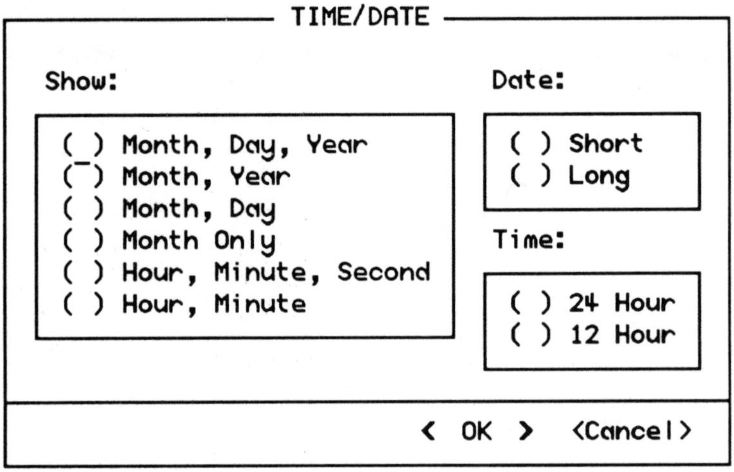

```
 ──────────────────────── TIME/DATE ────────────────────────
┌──────────────────────────────────────────────────────────┐
│                                                            │
│   Show:                              Date:                 │
│  ┌──────────────────────────────┐  ┌────────────────────┐ │
│  │ ( ) Month, Day, Year         │  │ ( ) Short          │ │
│  │ (‾) Month, Year              │  │ ( ) Long           │ │
│  │ ( ) Month, Day               │  └────────────────────┘ │
│  │ ( ) Month Only               │   Time:                 │
│  │ ( ) Hour, Minute, Second     │  ┌────────────────────┐ │
│  │ ( ) Hour, Minute             │  │ ( ) 24 Hour        │ │
│  └──────────────────────────────┘  │ ( ) 12 Hour        │ │
│                                     └────────────────────┘ │
│  ────────────────────────────────────────────────────────  │
│                              <  OK  >    <Cancel>          │
└──────────────────────────────────────────────────────────┘
```

data disk. Call it CUSTOMER. (*Note*: Refer to the section in Chapter 2 on saving documents if you need help.)

☰ Entering Data

It's time to enter some data into your database. You can invent your own data if you'd like, but I have provided a list of ten sets of data for you to work with (Table 3-2). By the way, *Works* and most other database programs refer to a set of data (name, address, phone, etc.) as a *record*. Think of your database as consisting of a number of records (one for each customer). Each record is composed of entries, one entry for each field. And each field holds a particular type of data (Text, Date, etc.).

The Status Line

Press (PgUp) to move the cursor to the first field to highlight it, and look at the status line (Figure 3-8). The "1" at the extreme left indicates that you are working with record number 1, the first record. If this value is anything other than 1, press (Control) + (PgUp) to move the window to record 1. The next item on the status line is the field name that's currently selected (highlighted).

This is followed by two numbers separated by a slash (1/1). The first number tells you how many records are currently being displayed.

Table 3-2 Data for customer database

First Name	Last Name	Address	City	State	Zip	Phone	Computer System	Warranty	Date Purchased	Salesperson
Susan	Larson	324 Elm St.	Oak Park	IL	60199	555-4784	HP Vectra	Y	4/19/88	Brown
Chuck	Maddox	1344 W. Archer	Maywood	IL	60198	555-0878	Compaq 386	N	5/14/88	Phillips
LuAnn	Smith	749 First Ave.	Bellewood	IL	60194	555-6831	Apple IIGS	Y	5/19/88	Brown
Merre Lynn	Hare	54 Third Ave.	Bellewood	IL	60194	555-8462	Macintosh II	N	6/15/88	Smithson
David	Barr	1212 Wood Drive	Deer Park	IL	60195	555-9804	Apple IIc	N	7/18/88	Phillips
Valerie	Popeck	649 Pinetree Ct.	Maywood	IL	60198	555-0048	Apple IIGS	N	10/9/88	Brown
Ogden	Spruill	2214 Orchard	Oak Park	IL	60199	555-8336	Macintosh SE	Y	10/18/88	Phillips
Dave	Workman	1417 East End	Bellewood	IL	60194	555-3070	HP Vectra	N	11/3/88	Brown
Sue	Eddins	314 Euclid Circle	La Grange	IL	60193	555-2718	Apple IIc	Y	11/5/88	Brown
Rosemary	Semenchuk	914 Cherry Lane	Oak Park	IL	60199	555-5653	Macintosh II	N	11/25/88	Phillips

Figure 3-8 The Form window

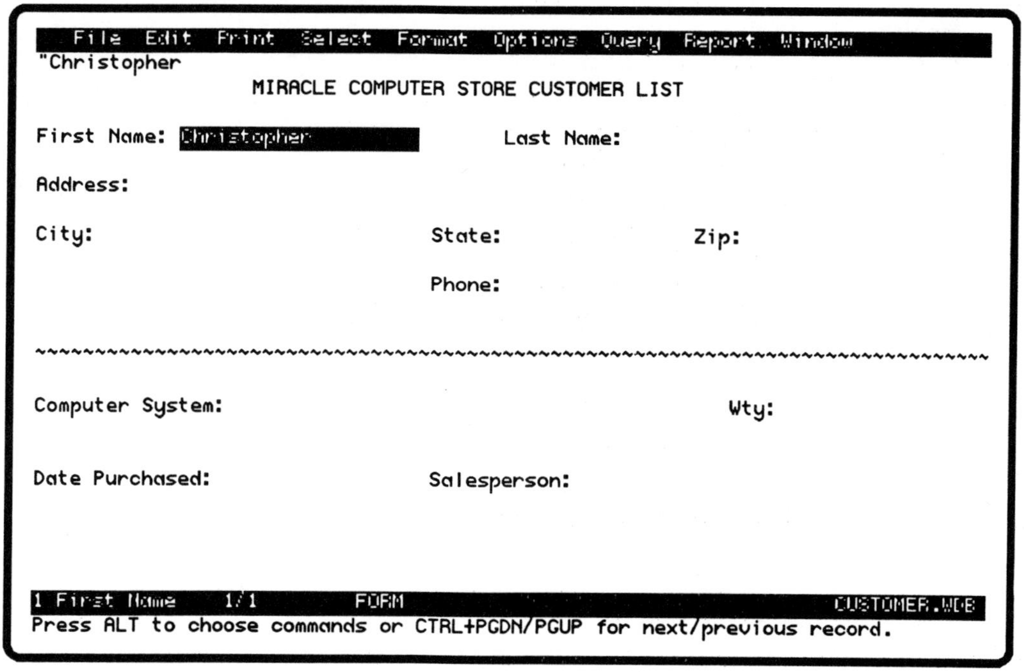

The second number shows the total number of records in your database file. (*Note: Works* allows up to 4,096 records per file.)

The remaining information on the status line you've seen before. The word FORM tells you which screen you're working on. And the last item on the status line is the name of your file.

Now, look at the line immediately below the menu bar (called the *formula bar*). If you've been following along on your own computer (you have, haven't you?), you'll have the name "Christopher" both in the data entry cell and on the Formula bar. Type **Susan**, and "Christopher" is immediately replaced on the formula bar. Press (Tab), and "Susan" replaces "Christopher" on the form as well (Figure 3-9).

Figure 3-9   Enter the First Name for record 1

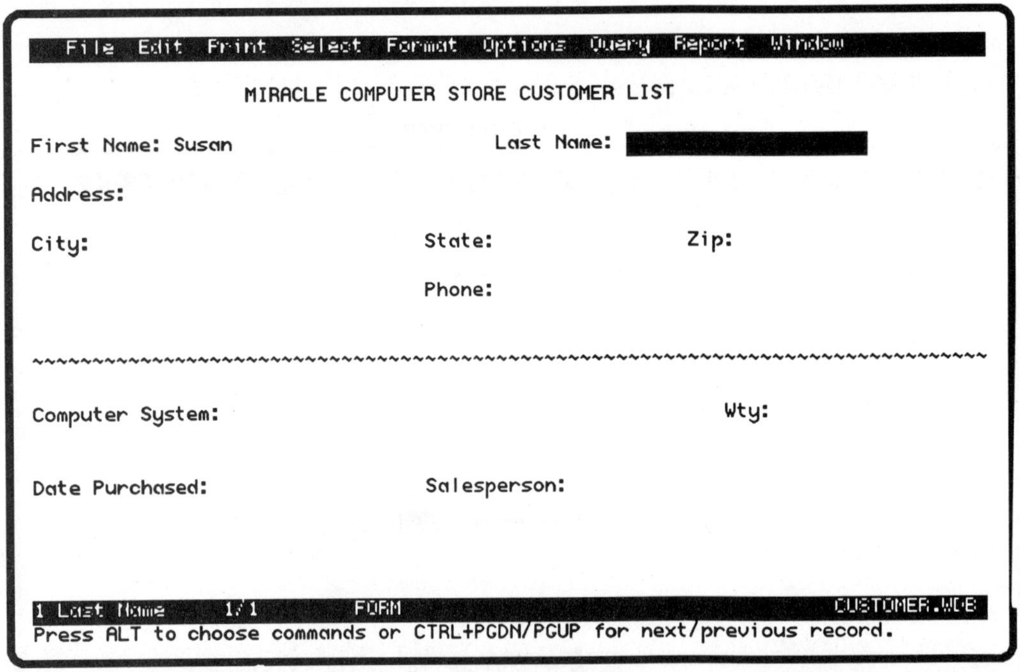

```
 File  Edit  Print  Select  Format  Options  Query  Report  Window
                   MIRACLE COMPUTER STORE CUSTOMER LIST

 First Name: Susan              Last Name:

 Address:

 City:                    State:            Zip:

                          Phone:

 ~~~~~~~~~~~~~~~~~~~~~~~~~~~~~~~~~~~~~~~~~~~~~~~~~~~~~~~~~~~~~~~~~~

 Computer System:                                  Wty:


 Date Purchased:          Salesperson:




 1 Last Name      1/1          FORM                   CUSTOMER.WDB
 Press ALT to choose commands or CTRL+PGDN/PGUP for next/previous record.
```

As you've seen, data you type appears first on the formula bar. Only after you press (Tab) is the entry inserted into the form. Pressing (Tab) accomplishes something else, too. It moves the cursor to the next field—to the right if there is a field to the right, otherwise to the next field below. If you had pressed (Enter) instead of (Tab), your data would still have been inserted into the record, but the cursor would have remained at the same field. You can also use the arrow keys to move the cursor around the form. I've found that for most data entry, it's faster to press (Tab) after each entry.

Let's continue filling out the first record. With the Last Name field highlighted, type **Larson** and press (Tab). Continue typing the remaining fields of the record, pressing (Tab) after each entry (Figure 3-10). Notice that when you typed "4/19/88," *Works* inserted "Apr. 19, 1988" into the form. That's because you changed the Date Purchased format to Date with Long display. (*Note*: If the year of the date entry is the same as the present year, you don't have to type it. *Works* will supply it automatically from your computer's internal clock.)

Figure 3-10   Complete the entries for record 1

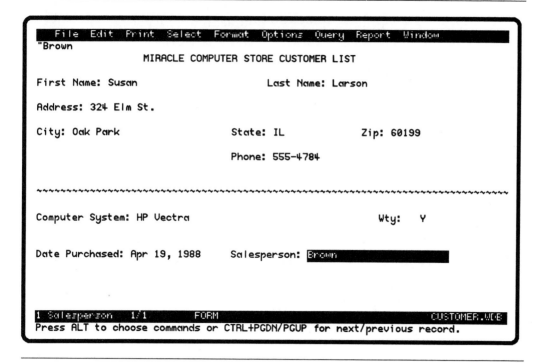

Viewing Other Records

When you press (Tab) after the last field, Salesperson, all the field entries will "disappear" and the first field, First Name, will be highlighted. Don't worry; your entries haven't been thrown away. Look at the record counter (at the left end of the status line). It now reads "2." When you pressed the Tab key after the last field entry, *Works* automatically presented you with a new, blank record. If you want to see record 1's entries, press (↑) or (Control) + (PgUp).

Return to record 2 by pressing [Control] + [PgDn], and begin entering the next set of data from Table 3-2. When you get to the State field, pause a moment, and don't type "IL."

Notice that all ten of the customers in Table 3-2 live in Illinois. In other words, the entry for State remains unchanged from one record to the next. *Works* allows you to copy the entry for any field from the previous record. With the State field selected, press [Control] + ['] to copy the contents of the State field from the previous record onto the formula bar. Then press [Tab] to accept the entry. Enter the remaining fields for record 2.

Continue adding records until you've typed all ten. Then resave the database. (I know it's a lot of typing, but it's hard to show the effect of a sorting feature, for example, if your database only has one record.)

More Formatting

In a moment, you're going to change to a different way of displaying the data you've just typed in. But before you do, let's look at some of the other formatting features for the Form display. Press [Control] + [Home] to flip back to the first record. Then, move the cursor to the Last Name field.

Pull down the Format menu and look at the choices. Most of the format commands apply to numerical data only, but the last command, **Style**, works with all data types, including text. Select the **Style** command. Figure 3-11 shows the STYLE dialog box.

Figure 3-11   The STYLE dialog box

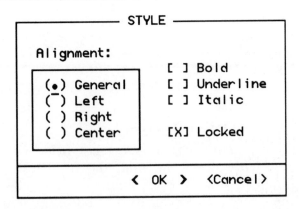

Suppose you wanted all of the Last Name entries to appear in bold. Just press (Alt) + (B), close the dialog box by pressing (Enter), and presto! All the last names are in bold. You can use the STYLE dialog box to add italic and underline emphasis, too, but don't expect to see these effects on your screen. *Works* indicates bold, underline, and/or italic by displaying the data at twice the brightness of unemphasized text. The true effects are seen only when you print out the database.

You can cancel the bold effect by selecting it again in the STYLE dialog box so that the "X" disappears from the box next to Bold. Then, close the dialog box and move the cursor back to the First Name field.

☰ Manipulating the Data

All this time, you've been looking at one of the two views *Works* provides for displaying database records, the Form view. This view displays all of the fields (or at least one screenfull) for one particular record.

The List Display

Pull down the Options menu and select **View List.** Figure 3-12 shows the result. Each field in your database is a column in the List display, but right now only seven fields are showing. You see these seven fields for all ten of the records you typed; in fact, the List view can show you up to 20 records at a time.

Your view is not limited to the first seven fields in your database. You can see the other fields by using (→) or (←) to scroll right or left. You can see any seven adjacent fields this way.

But you can adjust the List display with more than just the arrow keys. *Works* chooses an arbitrary width (10 characters) for each of the columns in the List display, but you can widen or narrow the width of any column as you please. The technique is the same one you used to change the size of the data cell in the Form display.

Suppose you wanted to widen the First Name column from 10 to 12 characters. To do this, place the cursor in the First Name column, pull down the Format menu, and select **Width.** Enter 12 in the text box, press (Enter), and the column changes to the new width.

Figure 3-12 The List window shows the first seven fields

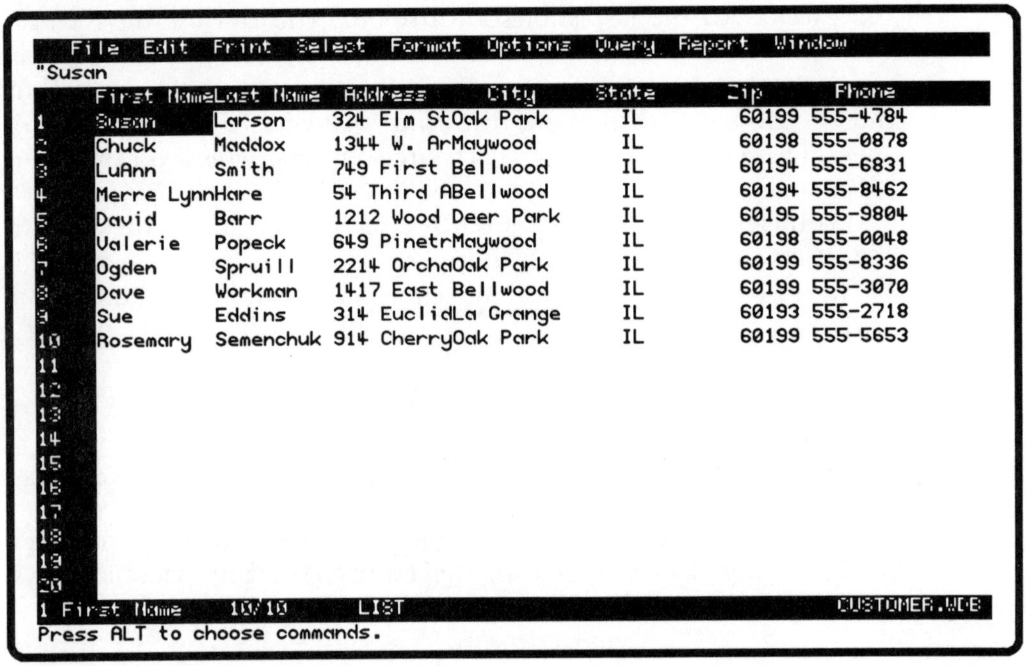

```
 File  Edit  Print  Select  Format  Options  Query  Report  Window
"Susan
      First NameLast Name  Address      City       State      Zip     Phone
1    Susan     Larson     324 Elm StOak Park        IL      60199 555-4784
2    Chuck     Maddox     1344 W. ArMaywood         IL      60198 555-0878
3    LuAnn     Smith      749 First Bellwood        IL      60194 555-6831
4    Merre LynnHare       54 Third ABellwood        IL      60194 555-8462
5    David     Barr       1212 Wood Deer Park       IL      60195 555-9804
6    Valerie   Popeck     649 PinetrMaywood         IL      60198 555-0048
7    Ogden     Spruill    2214 OrchaOak Park        IL      60199 555-8336
8    Dave      Workman    1417 East Bellwood        IL      60199 555-3070
9    Sue       Eddins     314 EuclidLa Grange       IL      60193 555-2718
10   Rosemary  Semenchuk  914 CherryOak Park        IL      60199 555-5653
11
12
13
14
15
16
17
18
19
20
1 First Name      10/10          LIST                         CUSTOMER.WDB
Press ALT to choose commands.
```

Works allows column widths from 0 to 79 characters, but don't use a value of zero. If you do, the column will become a *hidden* column and disappear. (*Note*: If you do this by mistake, you can use the **Go To** command, explained below, to move the cursor to the hidden field, and then change the width to some value greater than zero.)

Go ahead and adjust the width of the remaining columns. The smaller you make them, the more columns (and therefore the more data) you'll be able to see on the screen at one time. You won't want to make them too narrow, or some of the data you entered won't be displayed. One field you'll have to widen is the Date Purchased field. Ten characters is too narrow for the long date format. So, rather than truncate the year, *Works* fills the 10 spaces with # symbols. Change the width to 14, and the dates will be displayed.

Rearranging Columns

Works arranges the columns in the List window in the order in which they were first created. But you can display the fields in any order you wish. Suppose you wanted the customer's last name to be the leftmost column. Here's what you do.

First, place the cursor on any piece of data in the Last Name field, and choose **Field** from the Select menu. This action highlights the entire column. Next, press (F3) (or select **Move** from the Edit menu). Then, move the cursor to the First Name field, and press (Enter). (*Note*: If your version of *Works* is earlier than 1.05, you'll have to highlight the First Name column before you press (Enter).) Unhighlight the Last Name column by pressing (Esc). Figure 3-13 shows the result.

Figure 3-13   Moving a field to a different position

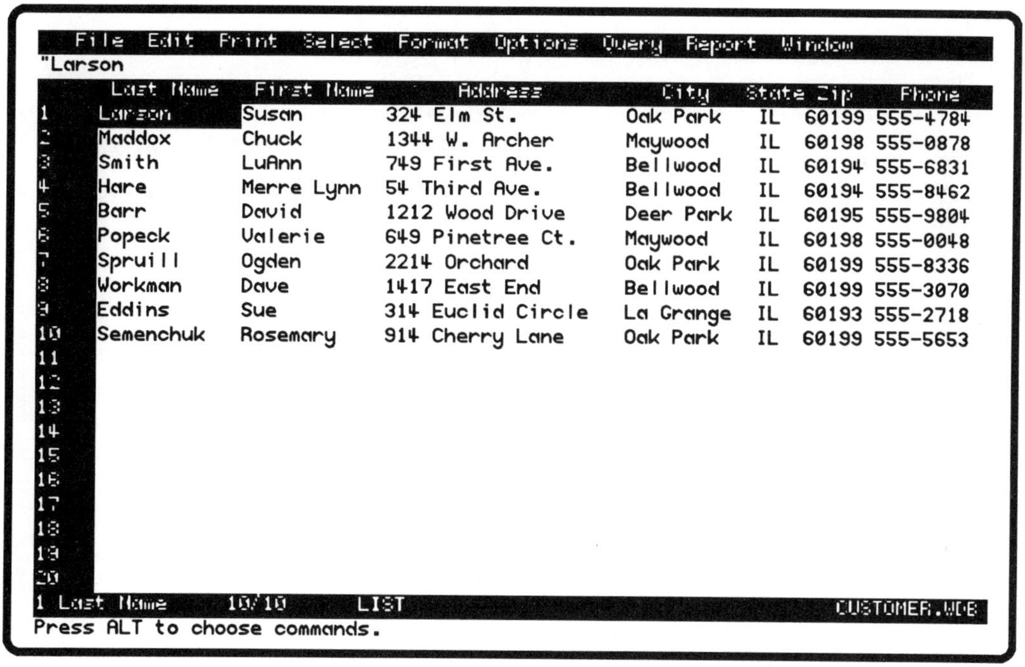

For practice, move the First Name field back to the first column position. (*Note*: With my version of *Works*, 1.05, columns may be moved only to the left. This will probably have been corrected in a later version by the time you read this.)

Dividing the Window

There is one other way you can change the List display. *Works* allows you to divide the window into as many as four "panes." Pull down the Options menu and select **Split**. *Works* displays two lines: a horizontal one across the top where field names are usually displayed, and a vertical one between the row numbers and the first column. Your arrow keys will move these lines into the data display area. And when you press (Enter) , the area will be divided into two or four panes.

Why would you want to do this? Suppose you wanted to see the Date Purchased information for your customers. Even after narrowing the fields, you still wouldn't be able to see both the customer's names and the date purchased on the screen at the same time. But with two panes, you can set one of them to display the First and Last Name, and the other to display the Date Purchased (Figure 3-14).

Figure 3-14 Use the split bar to divide the window

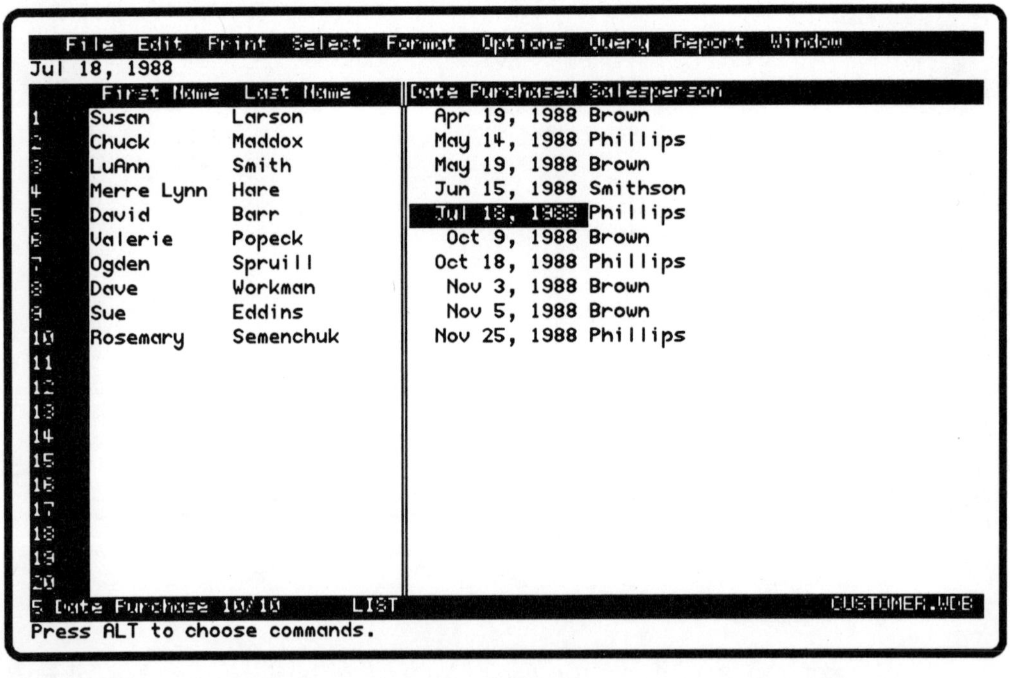

To do this, select **Split** from the Options menu. Leave the horizontal split line at the top (or return it there if you've moved it), and move the vertical split line about one-third of the way across the screen. Press (Enter) .

Pressing (F6) moves the cursor between panes. In the left pane, scroll until you see the First Name and Last Name fields. Press (F6) to move the cursor to the right pane, and scroll until you see the Date Purchased field. Compare your screen with Figure 3-14.

(*Note*: When you have divided your window vertically into two panes, they will scroll vertically together.)

The other split bar is used to divide the window so that you can see two groups of records on your screen at one time. Each pane can be independently scrolled vertically, but the two panes will be scrolled together horizontally. I know this sounds complicated, but experiment with the two split lines, both separately and together, and then reread this section. This is one feature you have to use to understand. Now, return the horizontal and vertical split lines to their original positions (top and far left, respectively).

A Second Look at Data Formatting

Scroll horizontally until you can see the Warranty column. For display purposes, those Ys and Ns might look better if they were centered in the column. Highlight one of the entries under Warranty to select it. Then choose **Style** from the Format menu (Figure 3-11).

Press (Alt) + (C) to change the alignment of the Warranty data from Left to Center. Before leaving the STYLE dialog box, notice that you can set three style formats for the field data. You can display all the data for Warranty (or any other field) in bold, italics, or underline. Press (Alt) + (B), and then press (Enter) (Figure 3-15). Warranty data appears both centered and in boldface. If you decide you don't want the boldface effect, select **Style** again. Press (Alt) + (B) to remove the check mark, and press (Enter).

By the way, the field that **Style** affects must be determined *before* you choose the command. You have to highlight a data entry in the selected field, and *then* choose **Style**. For practice, center the entries in the State field.

Changing the Field Name

Because field names are used as column headings in the List display, you may decide that you want to change one or more of them. For example, you might decide that if you changed "Warranty" to "Wty," you could narrow the column without chopping off the field name.

To change the name of the Warranty field, highlight one of the Warranty entries. Choose **Name** from the Edit menu (Figure 3-16). In the **Name**: text box, the field name Warranty is already highlighted. Type **Wty** and press (Enter). Now you can narrow Wty's column width as shown in Figure 3-17.

Figure 3-15 Center the Warranty entries and make them bold

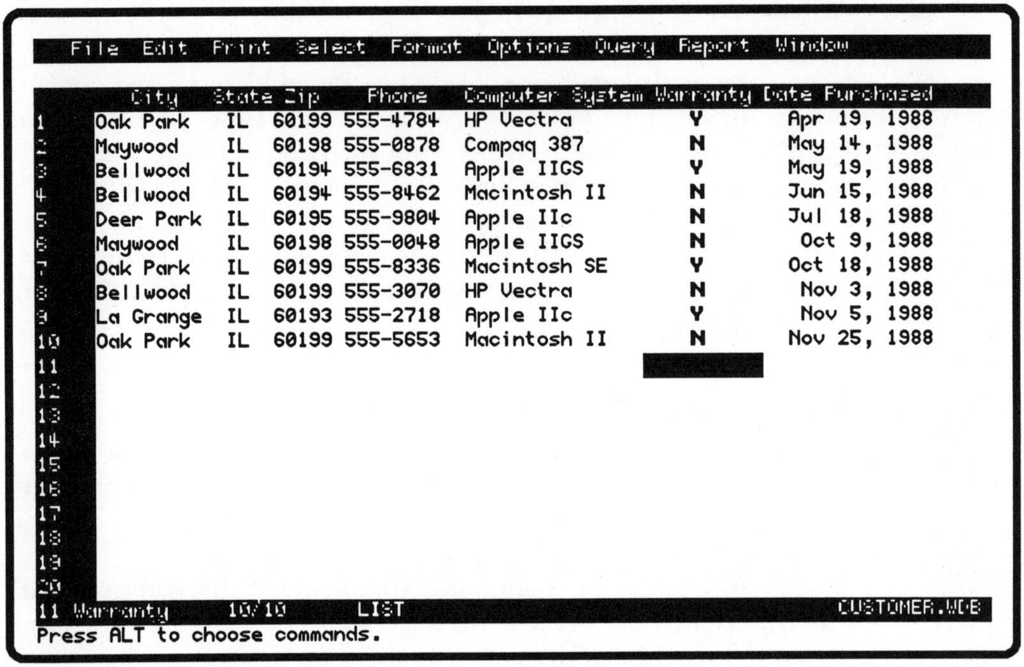

	City	State	Zip	Phone	Computer System	Warranty	Date Purchased
1	Oak Park	IL	60199	555-4784	HP Vectra	Y	Apr 19, 1988
2	Maywood	IL	60198	555-0878	Compaq 387	N	May 14, 1988
3	Bellwood	IL	60194	555-6831	Apple IIGS	Y	May 19, 1988
4	Bellwood	IL	60194	555-8462	Macintosh II	N	Jun 15, 1988
5	Deer Park	IL	60195	555-9804	Apple IIc	N	Jul 18, 1988
6	Maywood	IL	60198	555-0048	Apple IIGS	N	Oct 9, 1988
7	Oak Park	IL	60199	555-8336	Macintosh SE	Y	Oct 18, 1988
8	Bellwood	IL	60199	555-3070	HP Vectra	N	Nov 3, 1988
9	La Grange	IL	60193	555-2718	Apple IIc	Y	Nov 5, 1988
10	Oak Park	IL	60199	555-5653	Macintosh II	N	Nov 25, 1988
11							
12							
13							
14							
15							
16							
17							
18							
19							
20							

File Edit Print Select Format Options Query Report Window

11 Warranty   10/10   LIST   CUSTOMER.WDB
Press ALT to choose commands.

Figure 3-16 The NAME dialog box

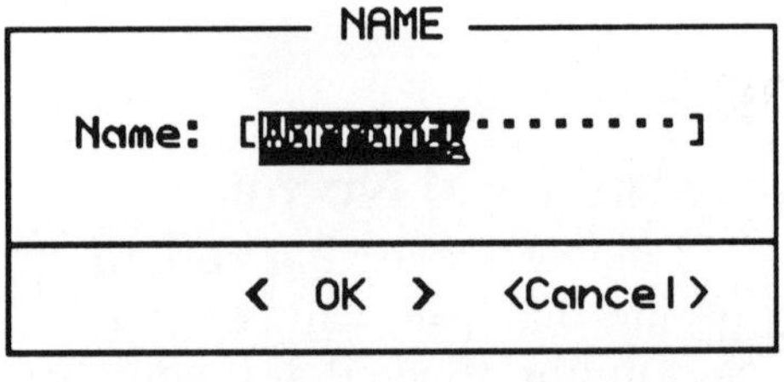

```
┌──────────── NAME ────────────┐
│                              │
│   Name: [Warranty········]   │
│                              │
├──────────────────────────────┤
│      < OK >   <Cancel>       │
└──────────────────────────────┘
```

Figure 3-17 Narrow the Wty column

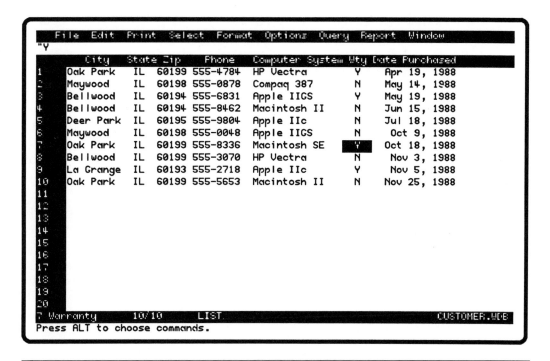

This would be a good time to save your database document again because you're going to mess it up while you learn about editing your data. After you've completed the next section, you'll revert to the version of the document you've just saved.

☰ Editing Data

Editing your data means being able to add new information, as well as changing and/or deleting existing information. This section will demonstrate the commands and techniques that *Works* provides for editing.

Adding a Record

Works allows you to add one or more records either at the bottom of the list or between existing records. Adding a record at the bottom is the easiest. Just move the cursor to the data cell under the last entry for First Name. This action selects the cell and allows you to type in data. Type the name **Patrick**. As you do, "Patrick" appears on the formula bar.

As in the Form display, pressing (Enter) accepts the entry; pressing (↓) accepts the entry and highlights the box below; pressing (Tab) accepts the entry and highlights the box to the right. So, press (Tab) after typing Patrick. The rest of the record is entered the same way, by typing the entry and pressing (Tab). (No, you don't have to enter the rest of the record.)

Suppose you wanted to insert a new record between the fourth and fifth records in your list. To do this, you have to first insert a blank record between records 4 and 5. Highlight the data box containing the First Name of the fifth record, the name "David." Pull down the Select menu and choose **Record**. This highlights the entire record. Now, pull down the Edit menu and choose **Insert**. Figure 3-18 shows the result. Notice that the blank record is inserted *above* the record that contained the cursor.

Pressing (Esc) deselects the record and leaves the First Name cell highlighted. This time let's finish typing the record. Here's the data (or you can make up your own): Patrick, LaMaster, 211 Baker St., Maywood, IL, 60198, 555-4701, Macintosh SE, Y, 6/23/88, Brown.

After you've finished typing the record, press (Home) to return the cursor to the first column. Notice that the window scrolls to follow the highlighted data cell. You might wonder how much data you can type into a single cell. The answer is 255 characters. If the box isn't wide enough to display all the characters in the entry, then the excess characters just aren't displayed. But they're still "there" in your computer's memory, and you can see them on the formula bar when you select the cell.

Deleting a Record

Let's delete the partial record you began entering at the bottom of the list. Move the cursor to any cell in the last record, then choose **Record** from the Select menu (Figure 3-19).

Figure 3-18 Insert a blank record

	First Name	Last Name	Address	City	State	Zip	Phone
1	Susan	Larson	324 Elm St.	Oak Park	IL	60199	555-4784
2	Chuck	Maddox	1344 W. Archer	Maywood	IL	60198	555-0878
3	LuAnn	Smith	749 First Ave.	Bellwood	IL	60194	555-6831
4	Merre Lynn	Hare	54 Third Ave.	Bellwood	IL	60194	555-8462
5							
6	David	Barr	1212 Wood Drive	Deer Park	IL	60195	555-9804
7	Valerie	Popeck	649 Pinetree Ct.	Maywood	IL	60198	555-0048
8	Ogden	Spruill	2214 Orchard	Oak Park	IL	60199	555-8336
9	Dave	Workman	1417 East End	Bellwood	IL	60199	555-3070
10	Sue	Eddins	314 Euclid Circle	La Grange	IL	60193	555-2718
11	Rosemary	Semenchuk	914 Cherry Lane	Oak Park	IL	60199	555-5653
12	Patrick						
13							
14							
15							
16							
17							
18							
19							
20							

File Edit Print Select Format Options Query Report Window

5 First Name   12/12   LIST   CUSTOMER.WDB

Press ALT to choose commands.

To delete this record, pull down the Edit menu and select **Delete**. Actually, there are two commands that delete record data, **Delete** and **Clear**. **Clear** removes the entries from the record, but leaves a blank record. **Delete** removes the entire record, data cells and all.

Copying Data

The **Copy** command is used to duplicate data in your database. (*Note*: In Chapter 7, you'll see how to copy data from one database to another, and from a database to other *Works* applications.) *Works* will copy any amount of data, individual cells, groups of cells, records, entire fields, or whole databases. You tell *Works* how much data you want to copy by highlighting it.

Copying an individual cell is easiest. Just move the cursor to the cell, and type ⟨Shift⟩ + ⟨F3⟩ (or select **Copy** from the Edit menu). The

Figure 3-19 Highlight the entire record prior to deleting it

```
 File  Edit  Print  Select  Format  Options  Query  Report  Window

       First Name  Last Name      Address       City     State Zip    Phone
 1    Susan       Larson      324 Elm St.       Oak Park   IL  60199 555-4784
 2    Chuck       Maddox      1344 W. Archer    Maywood    IL  60198 555-0878
 3    LuAnn       Smith       749 First Ave.    Bellwood   IL  60194 555-6831
 4    Merre Lynn  Hare        54 Third Ave.     Bellwood   IL  60194 555-8462
 5    Patrick     LaMaster    211 Baker Street  Maywood    IL  60198 555-4701
 6    David       Barr        1212 Wood Drive   Deer Park  IL  60195 555-9804
 7    Valerie     Popeck      649 Pinetree Ct.  Maywood    IL  60198 555-0048
 8    Ogden       Spruill     2214 Orchard      Oak Park   IL  60199 555-8336
 9    Dave        Workman     1417 East End     Bellwood   IL  60199 555-3070
10    Sue         Eddins      314 Euclid Circle La Grange  IL  60193 555-2718
11    Rosemary    Semenchuk   914 Cherry Lane   Oak Park   IL  60199 555-5653
12    Patrick
13
14
15
16
17
18
19
20
12 Last Name     12/12       LIST                              CUSTOMER.WDB
Press ALT to choose commands.
```

word COPY appears on the status line. Then, move the cursor to the cell you want to copy to, and press (Enter).

To copy larger amounts of data, you have to highlight them first. Suppose you wanted to copy three cells (City, State, and Zip) of the second record into record 12. Move the cursor to the City cell in the second record and hold down (Shift) while you press ⟶ twice. This highlights the three cells you want to copy. Press (Shift) + (F3) to enter the copy mode. Move the cursor to the City cell of record 12, and press (Enter) (Figure 3-20). (*Note*: If there is data in the cells you're copying to, that data is thrown away without warning!)

Copying whole records or entire fields is just as easy, but here are two shortcuts that will speed the highlighting process. Place the cursor in a cell of the record or field you want to highlight. Then, press (Control) + (F8) to highlight the record containing the cell, or (Shift) + (F8) to highlight the field containing the cell.

Figure 3-20 Copying three fields at once

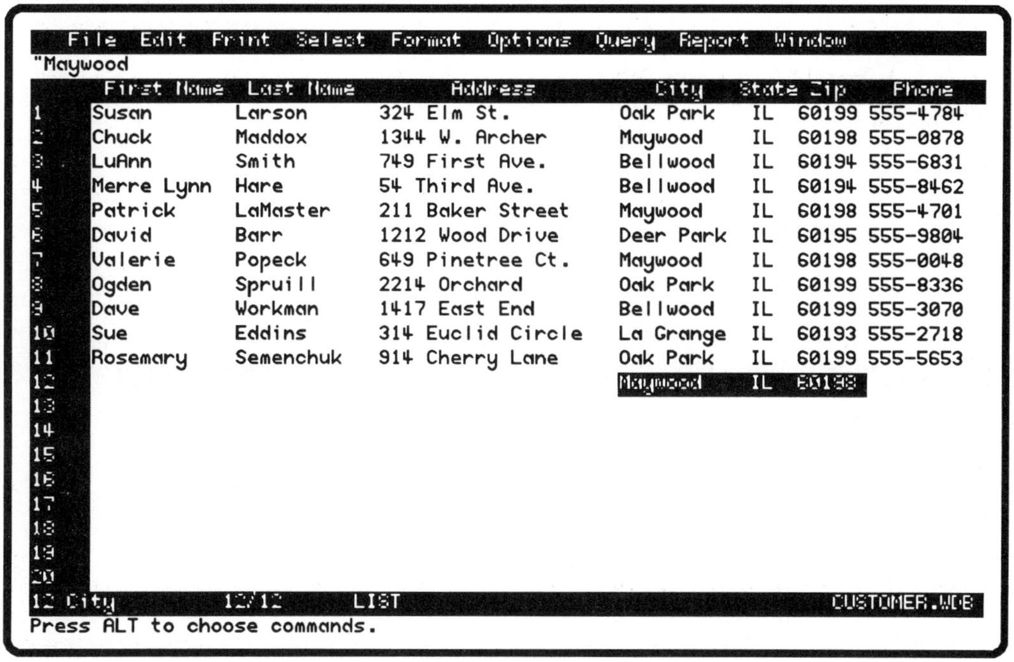

Moving Data

The **Move** command differs from the **Copy** command in three ways. First, the original data doesn't remain after the move. Second, only whole records or entire fields can be moved. And third, the destination cells for the moved record or field must be completely highlighted before the move can be completed. You saw this earlier when you moved the First Name field one column to the left.

Restoring the Database

I warned you that you were going to mess up your database document. Let's restore from the last saved version. Select **Close** from the File menu and press Ⓝ to indicate that you *don't* want to save the changes. *Works* throws away the file.

Then, select **Open** from the File menu and choose the CUSTOM-ER.WDB file. Refer to Chapter 2 if you need help restoring your file.

☰ Organizing Your Data

At this point, you may be wondering why there is a separate application called database. You could have set up tabs in a word processor document so that the various fields would line up in columns. Why bother using the database at all?

The answer is that a database allows you to manipulate data in ways that a word processor cannot. For example, *Works* allows you to sort or arrange the records in your database by any field.

Sorting Records

Suppose you wanted to display the records in your Customer database in alphabetical order, by last name. This would be virtually impossible to do in the word processor, but it's easy to do in the database.

Pull down the Query menu and choose **Sort**. Figure 3-21 shows the SORT dialog box.

Figure 3-21   The SORT dialog box

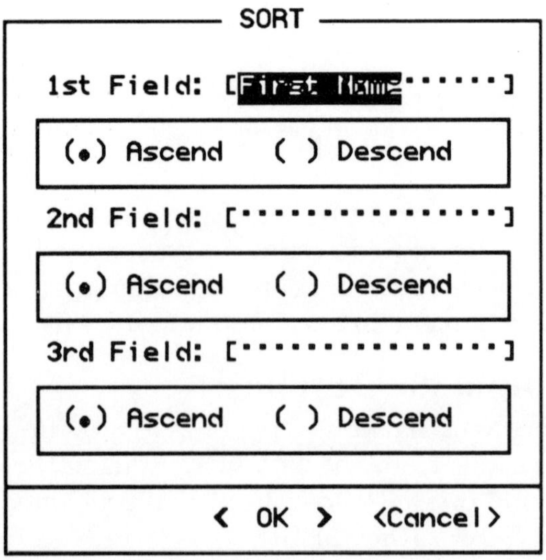

```
┌──────────── SORT ────────────┐
│                              │
│  ┌─────────────────────────┐ │
│  │ 1st Field: [First Name······] │
│  │                         │ │
│  │ (•) Ascend   ( ) Descend│ │
│  └─────────────────────────┘ │
│  ┌─────────────────────────┐ │
│  │ 2nd Field: [·············] │
│  │                         │ │
│  │ (•) Ascend   ( ) Descend│ │
│  └─────────────────────────┘ │
│  ┌─────────────────────────┐ │
│  │ 3rd Field: [·············] │
│  │                         │ │
│  │ (•) Ascend   ( ) Descend│ │
│  └─────────────────────────┘ │
│                              │
│  ┌─────────────────────────┐ │
│  │    ‹ OK ›   ‹Cancel›    │ │
│  └─────────────────────────┘ │
└──────────────────────────────┘
```

Works selects the First Name field by default because it was the first field you created. Type **Last Name** in the **1st Field**: text box. *Works* gives you the option of sorting in Ascend (A to Z) or Descend (Z to A) order. Accept the default choice of Ascend, and press (Enter) (Figure 3-22).

Figure 3-22   The records are sorted by Last Name

	First Name	Last Name	Address	City	State	Zip	Phone
1	David	Barr	1212 Wood Drive	Deer Park	IL	60195	555-9804
2	Sue	Eddins	314 Euclid Circle	La Grange	IL	60193	555-2718
3	Merre Lynn	Hare	54 Third Ave.	Bellwood	IL	60194	555-8462
4	Susan	Larson	324 Elm St.	Oak Park	IL	60199	555-4784
5	Chuck	Maddox	1344 W. Archer	Maywood	IL	60198	555-0878
6	Valerie	Popeck	649 Pinetree Ct.	Maywood	IL	60198	555-0048
7	Rosemary	Semenchuk	914 Cherry Lane	Oak Park	IL	60199	555-5653
8	LuAnn	Smith	749 First Ave.	Bellwood	IL	60194	555-6831
9	Ogden	Spruill	2214 Orchard	Oak Park	IL	60199	555-8336
10	Dave	Workman	1417 East End	Bellwood	IL	60199	555-3070

File Edit Print Select Format Options Query Report Window
"David

1 First Name   10/10   LIST   CUSTOMER.WDB
Press ALT to choose commands.

Notice that entire records were rearranged when the Last Names were alphabetized. In other words, all the entries that made up the Larson record, for example, before the sort are still with the Larson record.

Sorting on More Than One Field

The **Sort** command lets you specify up to three fields to sort on. Suppose you wanted to sort your list of customers by City, and within City by Last Name. In this example, City would be the *primary* sort field; Last Name would be the *secondary* sort field.

Display the SORT dialog box, and enter **City** for the 1st Field. Then, press (Alt) + (2) to move the cursor to the **2nd Field**: text box, type **Last Name**, and press (Enter). Figure 3-23 shows the effect of this dual sorting.

Figure 3-23 Sorting on two fields

```
 File  Edit  Print  Select  Format  Options  Query  Report  Window
"Dave
        First Name  Last Name    Address          City     State Zip   Phone
1    Dave        Workman    1417 East End     Bellwood   IL   60199 555-3070
2    LuAnn       Smith      749 First Ave.    Bellwood   IL   60194 555-6831
3    Merre Lynn  Hare       54 Third Ave.     Bellwood   IL   60194 555-8462
4    David       Barr       1212 Wood Drive   Deer Park  IL   60195 555-9804
5    Sue         Eddins     314 Euclid Circle La Grange  IL   60193 555-2718
6    Chuck       Maddox     1344 W. Archer    Maywood    IL   60198 555-0878
7    Valerie     Popeck     649 Pinetree Ct.  Maywood    IL   60198 555-0048
8    Ogden       Spruill    2214 Orchard      Oak Park   IL   60199 555-8336
9    Rosemary    Semenchuk  914 Cherry Lane   Oak Park   IL   60199 555-5653
10   Susan       Larson     324 Elm St.       Oak Park   IL   60199 555-4784
11
12
13
14
15
16
17
18
19
20
1 First Name      10/10      LIST                              CUSTOMER.WDB
Press ALT to choose commands.
```

Let's do one more sort. Display the SORT dialog box again. Type **Date Purchased** in the **1st Field**: text box, then press (Alt) + (2). Press (Del) to erase the entry for 2nd Field, and finally, press (Enter). This brings the records back to their original order. (*Note*: For fields that are formatted as date or time fields, Ascend means chronological, Descend means reverse chronological.)

Finding a Record

Works makes it easy to locate a particular record. I'll grant you that with only ten records in your database, locating any one of them is pretty simple; after all, you can see all ten in the window at the same time. But what if your customer database contained several hundred records, and you needed to find one of them? If you knew the customer's Last Name, you could sort the file by Last Name, and then scroll until you found the name. Suppose, though, you couldn't remember the customer's name. In fact, all you could remember is that the customer lives on a street that has the word "tree" in it—Peachtree, or Greentree, or something like that.

In this situation, *Works*' **Search** command can save you a great deal of time. Instead of searching through all your customers' addresses, looking for a street name containing "tree," pull down the Select menu and choose **Search**. The dialog box (Figure 3-24) prompts you to type in the string of characters you're searching for. (*Note*: The term "string" refers to any group of text characters.) Type in **tree**, and press (Enter).

Figure 3-24 The SEARCH dialog box

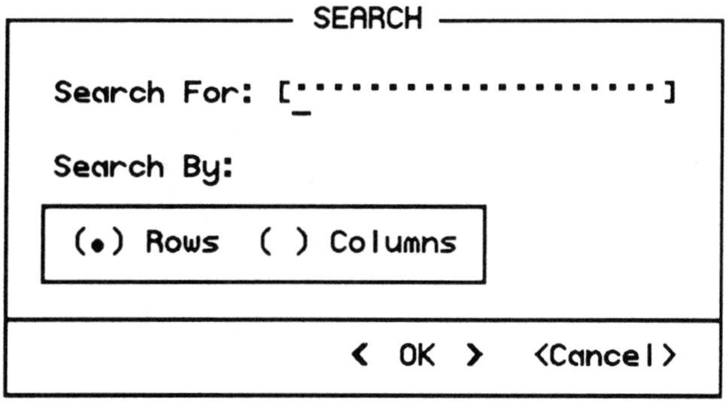

```
┌──────────────── SEARCH ────────────────┐
│                                         │
│   Search For:  [•················•]     │
│                _                        │
│                                         │
│   Search By:                            │
│                                         │
│   ┌─────────────────────────────────┐   │
│   │  (•) Rows   ( ) Columns         │   │
│   └─────────────────────────────────┘   │
│                                         │
├─────────────────────────────────────────┤
│              ‹ OK ›    ‹Cancel›         │
└─────────────────────────────────────────┘
```

Works begins its search from the current cursor position but searches through the entire database.

If the entry found by **Search** isn't the one you want, you can repeat the search by pressing (F7). If *Works* can't find the string, it will display an Alert box saying "No match."

Notice that you didn't tell *Works* to search only the Address field for your text string. As a matter of fact, *Works* looked at every field of every record in the database trying to find the four letters "tree." If those four letters existed in some other field (a City named Treemont, for example), that entry would have been found. As you can imagine, with hundreds of records to examine, instead of just ten, the search could take several seconds or even a minute or two. To speed the search, you could choose the appropriate Search By option (in the dialog box). For example, if you knew the search string was in the Address field, you could move the cursor to the top of the Address column, then display the SEARCH dialog box. After typing in the search string, you would press (Alt) + (C) to tell *Works* to search by *columns* instead of by its default choice of rows. *Works* would then start searching at the top of the Address column and proceed down the column.

Another way of finding a record is by its record number. The **Go To** command, also in the Select menu, displays a dialog box that lets you enter a record number. When you press (Enter), the cursor moves to that record, scrolling the window if necessary.

A second function of the GO TO dialog box is to move the cursor to a field chosen from the Fields list box. This feature is useful if you've hidden a field by reducing its column width to 0.

Record Selection

Suppose you wanted to see a list of customers who bought Macintosh computers before October 1, 1988, and who had not purchased an extended warranty. (Perhaps you want to send them a special letter to try to get them to buy your store's warranty, before the manufacturer's warranty expires.) *Works'* Query feature was created for just such a situation. It allows you to display only those records that meet your specifications.

Choose **Define** from the Query menu. Figure 3-25 shows the resulting window. This window looks like the Form window, but note the word QUERY on the status line. The Query window allows you to set up what are called *comparison criteria*. After you've set up these criteria, only those records whose entries conform to the criteria will be displayed. In the above example, you need to set up three comparison criteria:

1   Customers who have purchased Macintosh computers
2   Customers with an "N" for Warranty (Wty)
3   Customers with Date Purchased earlier than 10/1/88

Each of these comparisons is created separately within the Query window. For the first criterion, you want to select records whose Computer System field begins with "Macintosh."

Use the arrow keys to move the cursor to the Computer System data cell. Now type **Macintosh*** into the cell and press (Enter). (*Note:* It doesn't matter whether you type upper- or lowercase letters. The comparison is not case-dependent.) You have just set up the first

Figure 3-25 The Query window

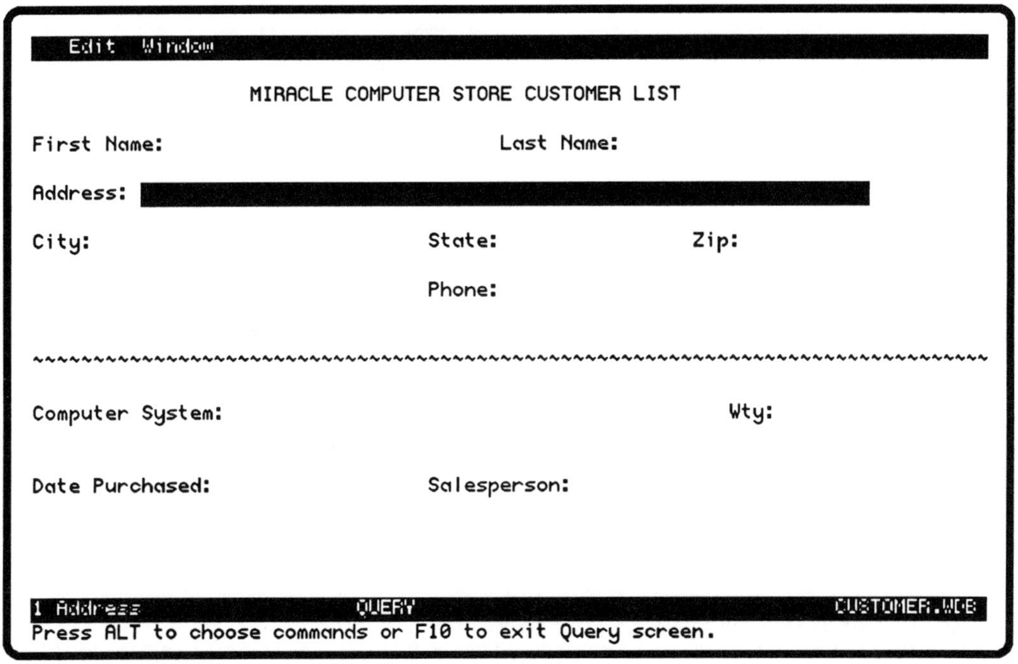

```
 Edit  Window
                    MIRACLE COMPUTER STORE CUSTOMER LIST

First Name:                      Last Name:

Address: ████████████████████████████████████████████████████

City:                   State:              Zip:

                        Phone:

~~~~~~~~~~~~~~~~~~~~~~~~~~~~~~~~~~~~~~~~~~~~~~~~~~~~~~~~~~~~~~~~~~~~~

Computer System:                              Wty:


Date Purchased:          Salesperson:



 1 Address              QUERY                    CUSTOMER.WDB
 Press ALT to choose commands or F10 to exit Query screen.
```

comparison. You've told *Works* to display only those records with entries in the Computer System field that begin with "Macintosh." The asterisk (*) after the word tells *Works* to accept as a match any entry that begins with the characters preceding the asterisk. Your screen should look like Figure 3-26.

Let's see how *Works* uses this single criterion to select records. Press (F10) (or choose **Exit Query** from the Edit menu). Figure 3-27 shows the three records that meet your first criterion. Scroll the window so that you can see the Computer System field.

Return to the Query window by selecting **Define** from the Query menu. The second condition you want to impose is to show records with an entry of "N" for Warranty. Move the cursor to the Wty data cell, and enter **N** into this cell. Press (F10) and confirm that *Works* displays only two records that meet both criteria.

Return once more to the Query window, and move the cursor to the Date Purchased data cell. The last criterion is Date Purchased

Figure 3-26 Enter the first query criterion

```
 Edit  Window
"Macintosh*
                    MIRACLE COMPUTER STORE CUSTOMER LIST

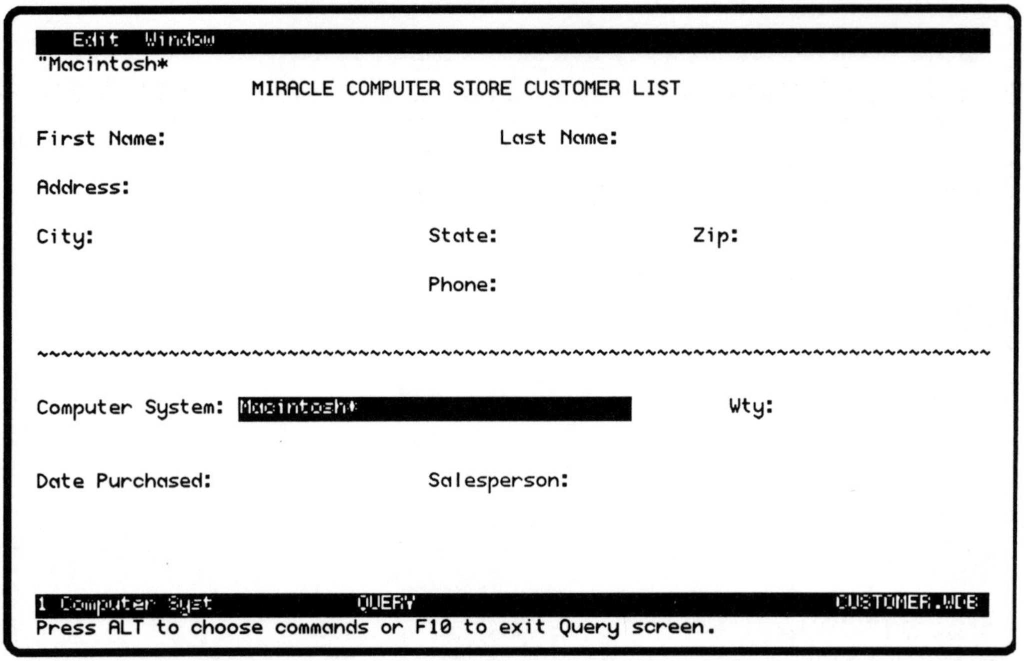

First Name:                        Last Name:

Address:

City:                     State:              Zip:

                          Phone:

~~~~~~~~~~~~~~~~~~~~~~~~~~~~~~~~~~~~~~~~~~~~~~~~~~~~~~~~~~~~~~~~~~~~~~~~~~~~~

Computer System: Macintosh*                    Wty:


Date Purchased:           Salesperson:



1 Computer Syst            QUERY                      CUSTOMER.WDB
Press ALT to choose commands or F10 to exit Query screen.
```

entries earlier than 10/1/88. Mathematically speaking, the term *earlier* translates as *less than,* and is represented by the symbol "<." The formula for the statement "earlier than 10/1/88" is:

< '10/1/88'

You must place single quotes around the date. Figure 3-28 shows the completed Query window. Press (F10), and see that only one record matches all three criteria.

Suppose you wanted to view records of customers who had purchased either Macintosh or Apple computers before 10/1/88 and without a warranty. You need to tell *Works* to accept Computer System entries that either begin with "Macintosh" or begin with "Apple." The Query window uses a special symbol (⌷) to indicate a logical *or,* but the syntax for the combined criterion is somewhat more complex than you've used so far.

You've actually been using an abbreviated format with the previously entered criteria. For example, while *Works* accepted the

Figure 3-27   Three records match the first criterion

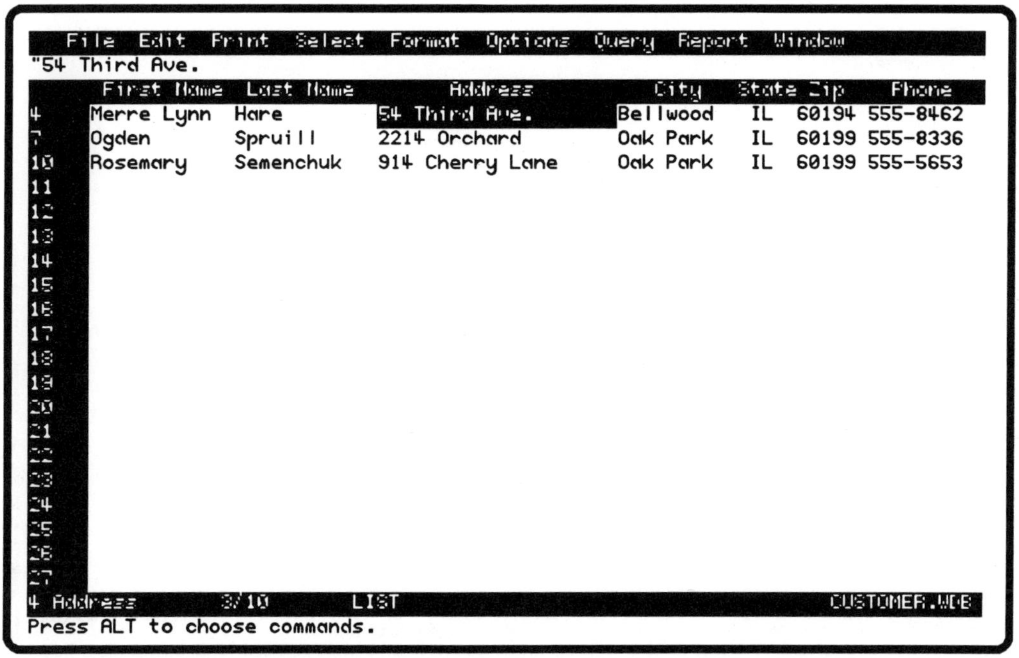

single character, N, for the Warranty criterion, the proper format is: ="N". Similarly, the proper format for the original Computer System condition is: ="Macintosh*".

To combine two (or more) conditions so that *Works* will treat them in an "either/or" sense, you separate the two criteria by a ┋ symbol. Thus, the correct format to indicate either a Computer System beginning with Macintosh or a Computer System beginning with Apple is:

=="Macintosh*" ┋ ="Apple*"

(*Note*: In my version of *Works*, 1.05, single quotes ['] are use to surround comparison numbers; double quotes ["] are used to surround comparison text.) Type this criterion into the Computer System cell, press (F10), and see that *Works* selects two records that meet the combined criteria.

Figure 3-28   Enclose the date in single quotes

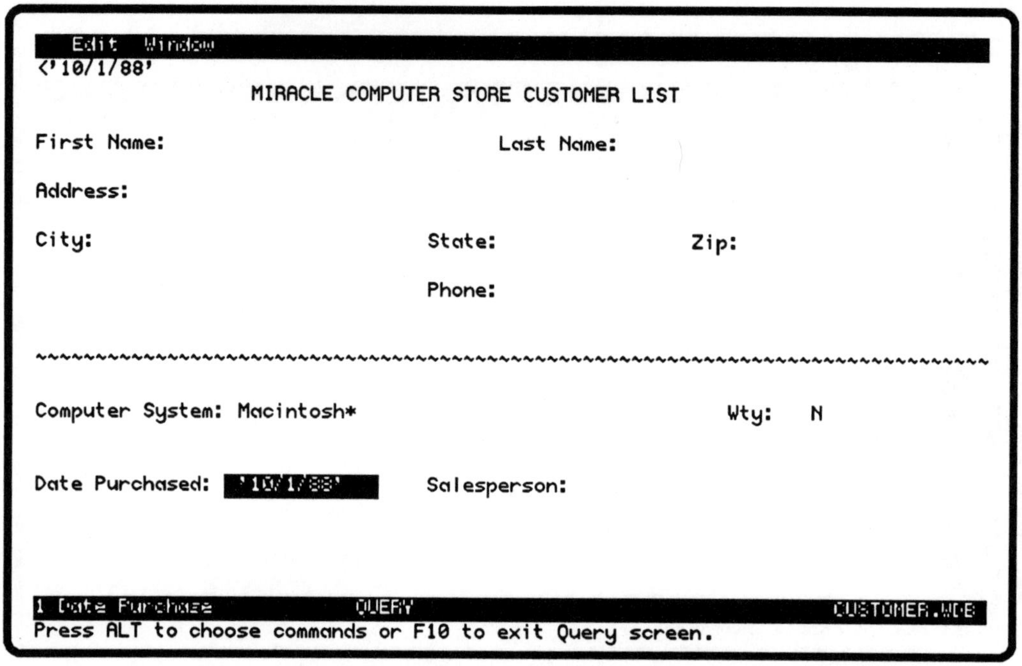

```
 Edit  Window
<'10/1/88'
                    MIRACLE COMPUTER STORE CUSTOMER LIST

 First Name:                        Last Name:

 Address:

 City:                     State:              Zip:

                           Phone:

 ~~~~~~~~~~~~~~~~~~~~~~~~~~~~~~~~~~~~~~~~~~~~~~~~~~~~~~~~~~~~~~~~~~~~

 Computer System: Macintosh*                   Wty:    N

 Date Purchased:  '10/1/88'      Salesperson:


 1 Date Purchase              QUERY                    CUSTOMER.WDB
 Press ALT to choose commands or F10 to exit Query screen.
```

To display all of the records again, choose **Show All Records** from the Query menu. You'll find further examples of record selection in Chapter 8.

The two Edit menu commands in the Query window, **Clear** and **Delete**, are used to erase criteria from cells. **Clear** erases the currently highlighted cell. It has the same effect as pressing (Del). **Delete** erases query criteria from *all* cells so that you can define an entirely new query.

☰ Printing Your Database

If you pull down the Print menu from either the List or Form windows, you'll see the normal printing commands, **Layout** and **Print**. Refer to Chapter 2 for a complete description of these commands and their respective dialog boxes. The only printing you can do from either the List display or the Form display is to print the records as they appear in the List window. Try it.

Figure 3-27   Three records match the first criterion

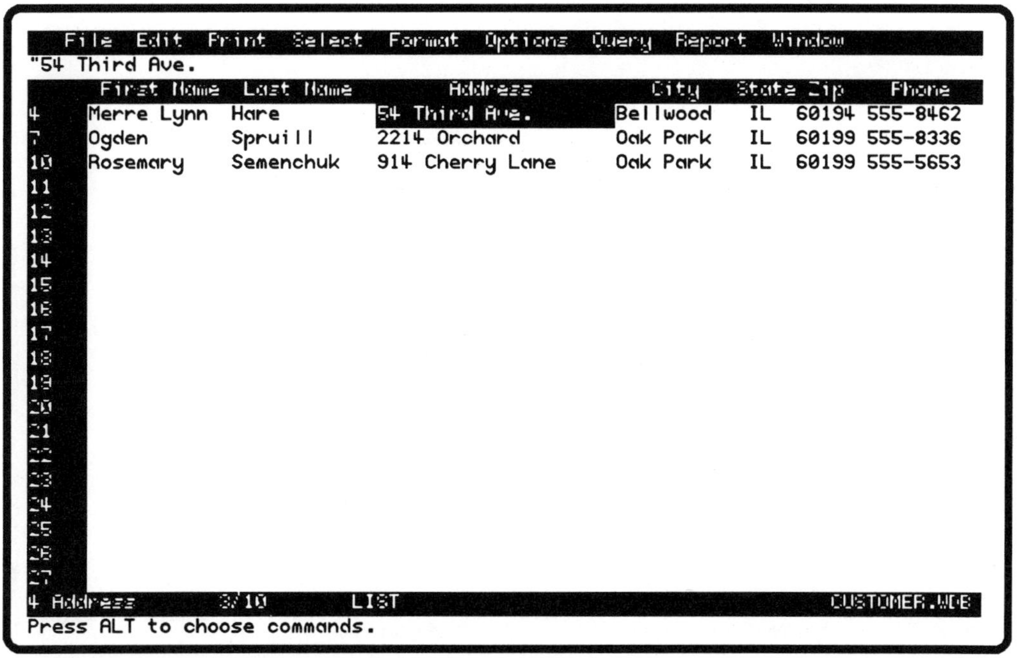

```
   File  Edit  Print  Select  Format  Options  Query  Report  Window
"54 Third Ave.
         First Name  Last Name      Address        City    State Zip    Phone
4   Merre Lynn   Hare          54 Third Ave.  Bellwood  IL   60194 555-8462
7   Ogden        Spruill       2214 Orchard   Oak Park  IL   60199 555-8336
10  Rosemary     Semenchuk     914 Cherry Lane Oak Park IL   60199 555-5653
11
12
13
14
15
16
17
18
19
20
21
22
23
24
25
26
27
4 Address          3/10         LIST                            CUSTOMER.WDB
Press ALT to choose commands.
```

single character, N, for the Warranty criterion, the proper format is: ="N". Similarly, the proper format for the original Computer System condition is: ="Macintosh*".

To combine two (or more) conditions so that *Works* will treat them in an "either/or" sense, you separate the two criteria by a ┋ symbol. Thus, the correct format to indicate either a Computer System beginning with Macintosh or a Computer System beginning with Apple is:

=="Macintosh*" ┋ ="Apple*"

(*Note*: In my version of *Works*, 1.05, single quotes ['] are use to surround comparison numbers; double quotes ["] are used to surround comparison text.) Type this criterion into the Computer System cell, press (F10), and see that *Works* selects two records that meet the combined criteria.

Figure 3-28   Enclose the date in single quotes

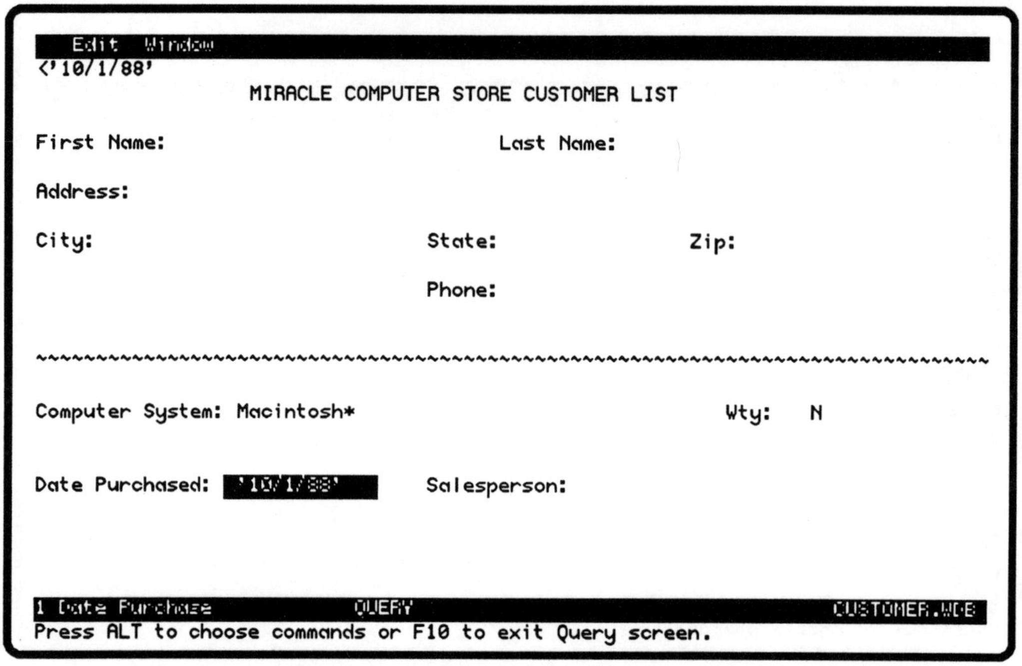

```
┌─────────────────────────────────────────────────────────────────┐
│ ▐ Edit   Window                                                   │
│ <'10/1/88'                                                        │
│              MIRACLE COMPUTER STORE CUSTOMER LIST                 │
│                                                                   │
│ First Name:                       Last Name:                      │
│                                                                   │
│ Address:                                                          │
│                                                                   │
│ City:                      State:              Zip:               │
│                                                                   │
│                            Phone:                                 │
│                                                                   │
│ ~~~~~~~~~~~~~~~~~~~~~~~~~~~~~~~~~~~~~~~~~~~~~~~~~~~~~~~~~~~~~~~~~~   │
│                                                                   │
│ Computer System: Macintosh*                    Wty:    N          │
│                                                                   │
│ Date Purchased:  '10/1/88'       Salesperson:                     │
│                                                                   │
│                                                                   │
│ 1 Date Purchase            QUERY                   CUSTOMER.WDB    │
│ Press ALT to choose commands or F10 to exit Query screen.         │
└─────────────────────────────────────────────────────────────────┘
```

To display all of the records again, choose **Show All Records** from the Query menu. You'll find further examples of record selection in Chapter 8.

The two Edit menu commands in the Query window, **Clear** and **Delete**, are used to erase criteria from cells. **Clear** erases the currently highlighted cell. It has the same effect as pressing (Del) . **Delete** erases query criteria from *all* cells so that you can define an entirely new query.

☰ Printing Your Database

If you pull down the Print menu from either the List or Form windows, you'll see the normal printing commands, **Layout** and **Print**. Refer to Chapter 2 for a complete description of these commands and their respective dialog boxes. The only printing you can do from either the List display or the Form display is to print the records as they appear in the List window. Try it.

Display the LAYOUT dialog box and change the left and right margins to 0 inches. Save your database file, then select **Print** from the Print menu, and notice that there is a special feature in the PRINT dialog box that wasn't present when you printed from the word processor: Print Record and Field Labels. Ignore this option for the moment, and print the database.

Notice that the fields are printed in the order that they appear in the List window. You'll see exactly the same printout whether you print from the List window or the Form window. Choose **Print** again, and this time press `Alt` + `L` to select the Print Record and Field Labels feature. Then press `Enter`. Now your printout contains record numbers and field names.

Works can produce much more sophisticated printouts of your data, but you have to create a Report first.

☰ Creating a Report

Pull down the Report menu and select **Define**. Figure 3-29 shows the Report window.

Suppose you wanted to print just the names (last and first), telephone number, street address, and city for each customer in your database. You would like your report to begin with a two-line title, perhaps

Miracle Computer Store
Customer List

You'd like the five field names (Last Name, First Name, etc.) to appear underlined as column headings followed by the records, double-spaced and listed alphabetically by last name.

Creating a report consists of inserting a series of rows in the Report window. The *type* of row you choose to insert, and the data you place in the cells of the row, determine the appearance of your report. *Works'* report generator has six types of rows that you can use to create your reports. Let's look at a list of them.

Row Definitions

Move the cursor to the top cell of column A, and press `Control` + `F8` (or choose **Row** from the Select menu) to highlight the entire first row. Then, select **Insert** from the Edit menu. The six row types are listed in the INSERT dialog box (Figure 3-30).

Figure 3-29 The Report window

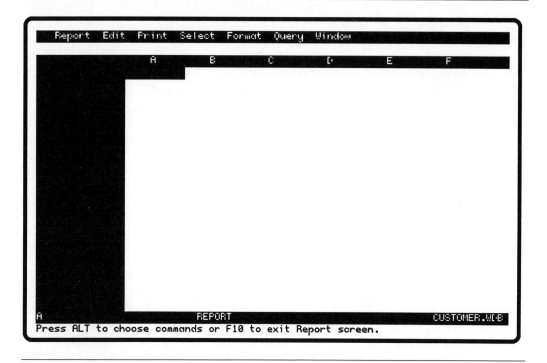

Figure 3-30 The INSERT dialog box for the Report generator

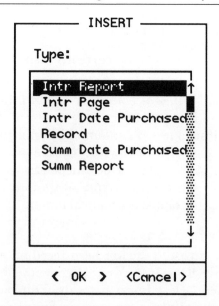

I'll identify and define all six row types here, even though you'll only use two of them in this report, so that if you need to refer to these row definitions, they'll all be in the same place.

Intr Report   *Report Introduction*   This row type contains text that appears once at the beginning of the report. It is typically used for the report title, but it may also be used for column headings in a single-page report. If the row contains no text, a blank line is left in the report.

Intr Page   *Page Introduction*   This row type contains text that appears once on every page of the report. It is typically used for column headings in multiple-page reports. It is generally *not* used for page numbers. That function is provided by the Header/Footer line in the LAYOUT dialog box.

Intr (field)   *Group Introduction*   There may be up to three of these lines in the INSERT dialog box, depending on the contents of the SORT dialog box. *Works'* reports are designed to use what are called break fields, and this line contains text that will appear when a change (or break) occurs in the specified field. See the next project for an example using break fields.

Record   *Record Detail*   The line contains the names of fields whose data you want to list in the report. When the report is generated, this line will print once for every record currently displayed in the database. If the row is blank, a blank line will be inserted into the report for each record processed. This technique will be used to doublespace the report.

Summ (field)   *Group Summary*   This is a summary line, and there may be up to three of these lines in the INSERT dialog box, depending on the contents of the SORT dialog box. Cells in this line may contain text or mathematical functions (such as sum, average, count, etc.). Summ lines appear each time a change (or break) in a field occurs. The functions summarize the data that has been listed since the last break in the field. See the next project for an example using break fields.

Summ Report   *Report Summary*   These lines appear once at the end of the report. Cells in this line may contain text or mathematical functions (such as sum, average, count, etc.). The functions summarize all the data that has been listed.

Creating a Report Title

Highlight the Intr Report type in the INSERT dialog box, and press (Enter). *Works* creates a row in your report of type, Intr Report (Figure 3-31). Move your cursor to the second row, and let's create three more rows of the same type.

Press (Control) + (F8) to highlight the second row, and then hold down (Shift) while you press (↓) twice so that rows 2, 3, and 4 are all highlighted. Display the INSERT dialog box, highlight Intr Report in the list box, and press (Enter). Now the first four rows are Intr Report rows.

Let's put some data in these rows. Move the cursor to row 1, column C, and type **Miracle Computer Store**. Notice that when you press (Enter),

Figure 3-31   Select Intr Report for the first row

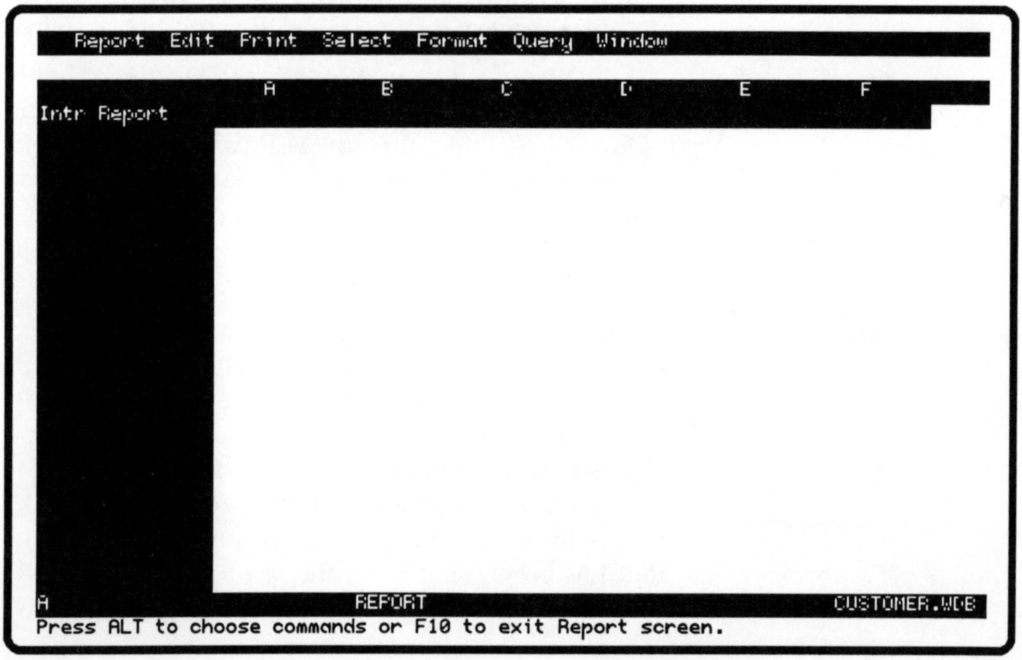

the text extends into adjacent cells to the right. Move the cursor to column C of the second row, and type **Customer List**. Again, the text extends into the next cell.

Let's tell *Works* to display both lines of text in bold. Place the cursor in either of the column C cells, and hold down either (Shift) while you move the cursor to the other column C cell. This highlights both column C cells. Now, select **Style** from the Format menu, press (Alt) + (B) to select bold, and press (Enter) to accept your style selection.

You might decide that the second line would look better if it were centered relative to the first line. You don't have to retype the line; you can edit it instead. Highlight the C cell in the second row, and press (F2). This places *Works* in the edit mode (see the word EDIT on the status line?), and moves the cursor up to the formula bar. Use the (←) to move the cursor under the "C" in "Customer," type four spaces, and press (Enter) Compare your report title with Figure 3-32.

Figure 3-32   Enter a report title in the first two rows

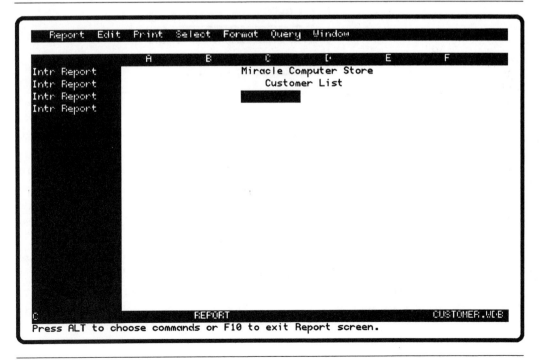

Column Headings

Let's leave row 3 blank, and place field names in the cells of row 4 for column headings. You could type the field names directly into the cells, but *Works* will do it for you.

Place the cursor in the first cell of row 4. You'd like this to be the First Name column. Pull down the Edit menu and select **Field Name** (Figure 3-33). Use the arrow keys to highlight the First Name field, and press (Enter). *Works* inserts the selected field name into the highlighted cell.

Figure 3-33   The FIELD NAME dialog box

Move the cursor to the next cell in row 4, and repeat the process. This time, choose Last Name. Continue inserting fields into the next three cells (Phone, Address, and City, respectively). Then compare your Report window with Figure 3-34.

You wanted to underline those column headings, so highlight the entire row ((Control) + (F8)), display the STYLE dialog box, press (Alt) + (U) to select underline, then press (Enter).

Since the data for some fields is longer than others, it makes sense to change the width of the five columns. Use the **Width** command in the Format menu (as you did earlier) to change the columns to the following widths:

Figure 3-34   Enter the five field names in row 4

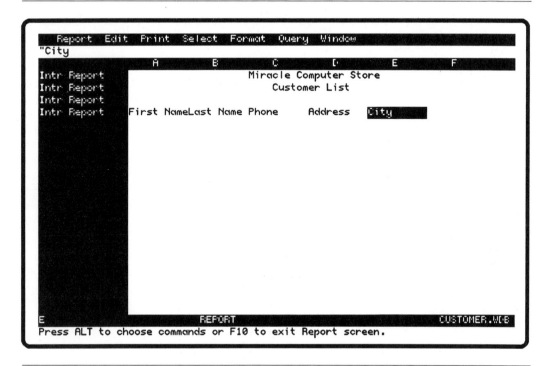

First Name	12
Last Name	12
Phone	10 (unchanged)
Address	20
City	10 (unchanged)

Your Report window should look like Figure 3-35.

Report Data

Now let's tell *Works* to print the data from your database under the column headings. Highlight row 5, and display the INSERT dialog box. This time, select the Record row type and press (Enter).

You have to tell *Works* which field to display in each cell of the Report row. And because this is data, rather than text, each cell entry must begin with an (=) symbol. Again, you could type the information directly into the cells, but once more *Works* will do it for you.

Figure 3-35 Vary the column widths to suit the fields

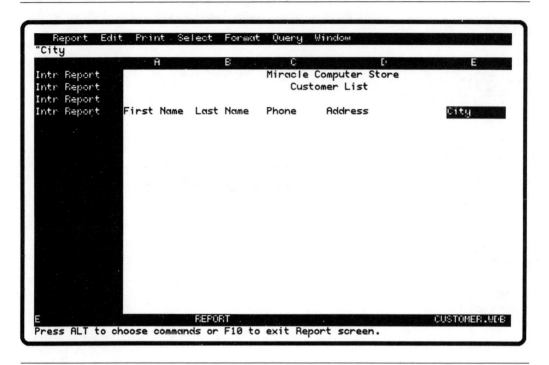

Highlight the first cell in row 5, and select **Field Value** from the Edit menu. The dialog box for FIELD VALUE is virtually identical to the one for FIELD NAME (Figure 3-36).

Select First Name from the list, press (Enter), and *Works* inserts =**First Name** into the highlighted cell. Repeat the process with the remaining four cells in the row, choosing the appropriate field from the FIELD VALUE dialog box (Figure 3-37).

In order to print the cells double-spaced, highlight row 6, and use the INSERT dialog box to define this row as Record type. You'll leave this row blank in your report.

Report Sorting

You want the data in your report to be sorted alphabetically by last name. Display the SORT dialog box by selecting **Sort** from the Query menu.

Figure 3-36   The FIELD VALUE dialog box

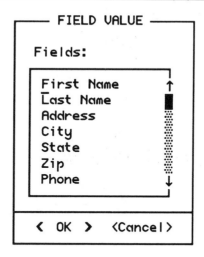

Figure 3-37   Enter the five field values in row 5

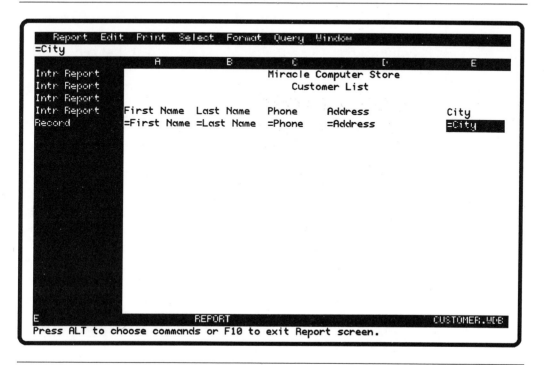

Type **Last Name** into the **1st Field**: text box. If there is a field name entered for **2nd Field**:, press (Alt) + (2) and then (Del) to erase it. Do the same for the **3rd Field**: text box, if necessary.

If there is an "X" next to the Break option for 1st Field, press (Alt) + (G) to disable the feature. Compare your completed dialog box with Figure 3-38. Then, press (Enter).

Figure 3-38   Deselect the Break option before closing the dialog box

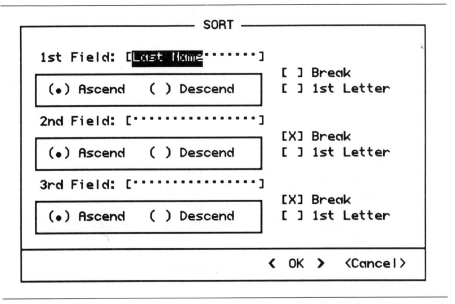

Printing the Report

Select **Layout** from the Print menu, and change the Left and Right Margins to 0. You can also delete the default Footer if you wish, since this will be a one-page report.

Close the LAYOUT dialog box, and press (F10) to return to the List window. Save your database file again, and note that your report format will be saved as part of the file.

You can view the report before you print it by selecting **View** from the Report menu. The report will pause every screenfull; press (Enter) to see the next section. Print the report by pulling down the Print menu, selecting **Print Report**, and pressing (Enter).

Other Report Features

If you pull down the Report menu, you'll see your report listed at the bottom of the menu. It's called Report1 and has a bullet (•) next to it indicating that it's the currently selected report. *Works* allows up to eight separate report definitions for each database file. So that you can better remember what the different report formats are, you can change the name of the report to something more informative than "Report1."

Select **Reports** from the Report menu (Figure 3-39). With Report1 highlighted in the list box, press Alt + N to move the cursor to the **Name:** text box. Name this report **Customer List**, and press Alt + R to Rename. Then, press Esc to close the dialog box.

Figure 3-39   Use the REPORTS dialog box to rename the report

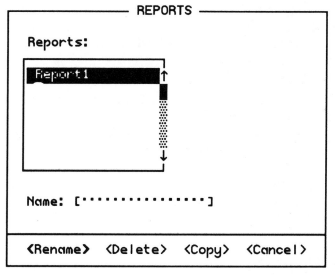

The REPORTS dialog box has other uses, too. You can delete reports from your database (remember, you can only have eight), or you can copy a report. Copying a report format is useful if you want to make a small change in a complex report and leave the original one unchanged.

Once you've changed the report name, you'll see the name you gave to the report when you pull down the Report menu. With more than one report created for a single database, you have to select which is the *active* report. The choice is made in the Report menu, and the active report is indicated by a bullet symbol.

It is the active report that's printed when you select the **Print Report** command. And it's the active report that's displayed when you choose **Define** from the Report menu.

You can create a new report by selecting **New** from the Report menu. *Works* supplies you with a series of default rows to get you started, but you can delete any or all of them by highlighting the rows and selecting **Delete** from the Edit menu.

PROJECT 4: REPAIR CENTER ACTIVITY

Our second database exercise involves the service technicians of the Miracle Computer Store. You want to track the time and materials costs for the repairs performed by each of your three techs.

From the repair tickets they submit, you know how much time they spent performing each repair and the price of parts they used. You also know that repair time is billed at $45 per hour and that all repair parts are marked up 50%. (This means that your profit on repair parts is 33%, or $1/3$ of the customer price.)

You want a report that lists revenues from the sale of parts and labor, totaled for each technician and grand totaled at the end.

Designing the Database

Consider the columns (fields) of information you'll want for each repair. You'll want to include:

- The tech's name
- The date of the repair
- The time to repair (in hours)
- Labor cost (calculated by the database at $45 per hour)
- Customer price of parts
- Store profit on parts (calculated at $1/3$ of parts price)
- Gross repair revenue (the sum of parts profit and labor)

Creating the Fields

Create a new database by pulling down the File menu and selecting **New**. Select **Database**, then press (Enter). Refer to Table 3-3 for a list of the seven fields that comprise your REPAIR database. Type each field name into the Form Design window, remembering to add a colon to each field name before you press (Enter). Use the techniques you learned in the previous project to position the fields as shown in Figure 3-40. Then, press (F10) to enter the Form window.

Table 3-3   Field names for Project 4

Field Names
Tech
Repair Date
Time
Labor
Parts Price
Parts Margin
Gross Revenue

Formatting the Fields

Before you begin entering data, you need to format 6 of the 7 fields. Start with the Repair Date field. Highlight its data cell, and then select **Time/Date** from the Format menu. Select the first format, Month, Day, Year, from the dialog box, and accept the Short date form.

Next, highlight the Time cell, and select **Fixed** with 2 decimal places from the Format menu.

Highlight the Parts Price cell, and select **Dollar** with 2 decimal places.

Computed Fields

The Labor, Parts Margin, and Gross Revenue fields are to be defined as *computed* fields. That is, their entries will be computed from data in other fields. Change the format of the Labor cell to Dollar with 2 decimal places. Then, with the Labor cell still highlighted, enter a formula that will compute labor cost based on $45 per hour of Time. The formula for Labor is Time multiplied by 45. The asterisk, *, is the symbol *Works* uses to signify multiplication. To enter this formula, type =**Time*45** and press (Enter). (*Note*: Before you can enter formulas

Figure 3-40 Form design for Project 4

```
┌─────────────────────────────────────────────────────────┐
│  ▐ Edit  Format  Window                                  │
│  Gross Revenue:                                           │
│                                                           │
│                                                           │
│   Tech: _____        Repair Date: _____   │
│                                                           │
│                                                           │
│   Time: _____              Labor: _____          │
│                                                           │
│                                                           │
│   Parts Price: _____       Parts Margin: _____   │
│                                                           │
│                                                           │
│                  ▐ Gross Revenue: _____                │
│                                                           │
│                                                           │
│                                                           │
│  Pg 1                    DESIGN                DATA1.WDB  │
│  Type field names. Press ALT to choose commands or F10 to exit Form Design. │
└─────────────────────────────────────────────────────────┘
```

that define computed fields, you must be in the Form window, not the Form Design window.)

If you mistype the formula or the name of a field and *Works* can't figure out what you mean, you'll see a special alert message saying: "Invalid message or wrong operand type." Retype the formula, press (Enter), and all will be well.

Format the Parts Margin cell as Dollar with 2 decimal places. Its value is determined by taking 33%, or ⅓, of the value in Parts Price. Therefore, its formula is: =**Parts Price/3**. (*Note*: The / symbol is used to indicate division.)

Format Total Revenue as you did the previous two fields. Its computed value is the sum of Labor and Parts Margin, so its formula is simply: =**Labor+Parts Margin.**

Finally, display the STYLE dialog box for Tech, Repair Date, Time, and Parts Price. For each field, press (Alt) + (K) to unlock the field, then press (Enter) to close the dialog box. Leave the remaining three fields locked (*Works'* default state). Then, select **Protect** from the Options menu.

Save this document as REPAIR.

Enter the Data

Table 3-4 contains ten sets of data for your database. Please type them all in so that the totals in your report will agree with mine. Notice that you only have to enter data for four fields; the other three are computed by *Works*. Because you enabled the **Protect** option, the cursor skips over those fields that are *locked*. That's why you had to unlock the four fields into which you intended to type data.

Table 3-4 Data for Project 4

Tech	Repair Date	Time	Parts Price
Scott	12/3/88	1.5	88.50
Cheryl	12/3/88	.5	27.00
Cheryl	12/3/88	1	0.00
Brad	12/3/88	1	48.00
Scott	12/3/88	2	165.00
Brad	12/3/88	1.5	57.00
Cheryl	12/3/88	1.5	99.00
Brad	12/3/88	1	72.00
Scott	12/3/88	.5	0.00
Cheryl	12/3/88	1.5	135.00

After you have entered data for all ten records, save the document again. Then, choose **View List** from the Options menu (Figure 3-41), and remove cell protection by selecting **Protect** again. I've changed the column widths so that all seven would fit on the screen. (*Note*: You could have entered the data in the List window instead of the Form window.)

☰ Creating a Summarizing Report

I had two objectives when I thought up this database exercise. One was to demonstrate the use of calculated fields. The other was to show the summarizing features of the report generator.

Laying out the Report

The report I have in mind is pictured in Figure 3-42. There is a three-line report title followed by a line containing the seven column headings.

Figure 3-41   Enter the ten records from Table 3-4

	Tech	Repair Date	Time	Labor	Parts Price	Parts Margin	Gross Revenue
File Edit	Print	Select Format	Options	Query	Report	Window	
1	Scott	12/3/88	1.50	$67.50	$88.50	$29.50	$97.00
2	Cheryl	12/3/88	0.50	$22.50	$27.00	$9.00	$31.50
3	Cheryl	12/3/88	1.00	$45.00	$0.00	$0.00	$45.00
4	Brad	12/3/88	1.00	$45.00	$48.00	$16.00	$61.00
5	Scott	12/3/88	2.00	$90.00	$165.00	$55.00	$145.00
6	Brad	12/3/88	1.50	$67.50	$57.00	$19.00	$86.50
7	Cheryl	12/3/88	1.50	$67.50	$99.00	$33.00	$100.50
8	Brad	12/3/88	1.00	$45.00	$72.00	$24.00	$69.00
9	Scott	12/3/88	0.50	$22.50	$0.00	$0.00	$22.50
10	Cheryl	12/3/88	1.50	$67.50	$135.00	$45.00	$112.50
11							
12							
13							
14							
15							
16							
17							
18							
19							
20							

`11 Tech            10/10        LIST                          REPAIR.WDB`

`Press ALT to choose commands.`

The data is sorted by Tech and a break occurs whenever the tech's name changes. At each break, totals are printed for that tech's Time, Labor, Parts Price, Parts Margin, and Gross Profit. At the end of the report, totals for all techs are printed as well as other results.

Begin by selecting **Define** from the Report menu. Since this is the first report for this database, the Report screen will be blank. To make it easier to refer to individual cells in the report, let's refer to the cells by the row and column that define them. For example, the cell in the upper left corner we'll call A1. The cell next to it will be B1. The cell under B1 is B2, and so on.

Highlight the first three rows and use the INSERT dialog box to define these rows as Intr Report rows (refer to the previous project if you need help). Define the next two rows as Intr Page rows. Define row 6 as a Record row.

Display the SORT dialog box, and verify that the 1st Field is Tech and that the Break option is checked. The 2nd Field and 3rd Field text boxes should be empty. This is the default setting for the dialog box.

Figure 3-42 The report for Project 4

```
                        Miracle Computer Store
                        Repair Activity Report

Tech      Repair Date  Time     Labor     Parts Price    Parts Margin Gross Revenue

Brad         12/3/88   1.00    $45.00       $48.00         $16.00        $61.00
Brad         12/3/88   1.50    $67.50       $57.00         $19.00        $86.50
Brad         12/3/88   1.00    $45.00       $72.00         $24.00        $69.00

   Brad totals:        3.50   $157.50      $177.00         $59.00       $216.50

Cheryl       12/3/88   0.50    $22.50       $27.00          $9.00        $31.50
Cheryl       12/3/88   1.00    $45.00        $0.00          $0.00        $45.00
Cheryl       12/3/88   1.50    $67.50       $99.00         $33.00       $100.50
Cheryl       12/3/88   1.50    $67.50      $135.00         $45.00       $112.50

 Cheryl totals:        4.50   $202.50      $261.00         $87.00       $289.50

Scott        12/3/88   1.50    $67.50       $88.50         $29.50        $97.00
Scott        12/3/88   2.00    $90.00      $165.00         $55.00       $145.00
Scott        12/3/88   0.50    $22.50        $0.00          $0.00        $22.50

  Scott totals:        4.00   $180.00      $253.50         $84.50       $264.50
-------------------------------------------------------------------------------
  Grand totals:       12.00   $540.00      $691.50        $230.50       $770.50

Average time per repair:           1.20 Hours

Average cost per repair:      $123.15
```

Highlight the next three rows in the report, and define them as Summ Tech rows. Last, define the next six rows as Summ Report rows. Compare your Report window with Figure 3-43.

Adjust the width of columns A through G according to the following chart.

Column	Width
A	8
B	12
C	6
D	10
E	14
F	15
G	14

Figure 3-43 The 15 rows that will define the report

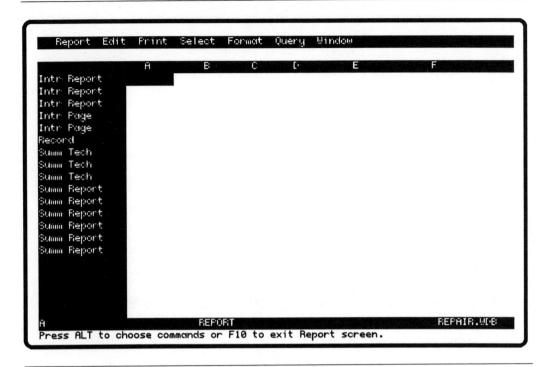

Type **Miracle Computer Store** into cell D1, and **Repair Activity Report** into cell D2. Then, highlight both cells, D1 and D2, and change their format style to bold.

Leave row 3 blank. Enter the field names into the first seven cells of row 4. Use the FIELD NAME dialog box, as you did in the previous database project, or type the field names yourself. Notice that this report uses an Intr Page row for the column headings instead of an Intr Report row. Should the report run longer than one page, column headings in an Intr Page row would be printed at the top of each page.

When you've finished entering field names into row 4, highlight the entire row and change its format style to underline. Skip row 5.

Use the FIELD VALUE dialog box to enter field names preceded by an = symbol into the first seven cells of row 6. Then, compare your Report window with Figure 3-44.

Group Summarizing

Leave row 7 blank. Row 8 will contain the formulas that compute the sum of the Time, Labor, Parts Price, Parts Margin, and Gross

Figure 3-44 Enter the field names and the field values in the appropriate rows

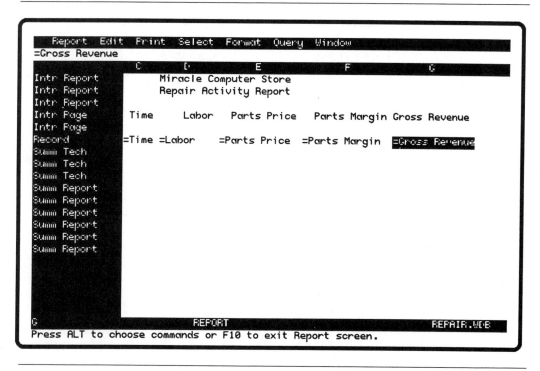

Profit fields for each tech. These totals are often referred to as *group* totals. The group, in this case, is the group of entries for each tech.

Works has seven summarizing functions: sum (SUM), average (AVG), number of entries (COUNT), maximum value (MAX), minimum value (MIN), standard deviation (STD), and variance (VAR).

The first group summary value you want is the sum of the Time entries. Highlight cell C8 (the Time cell for row 8), then select **Field Summary** from the Edit menu. The FIELD SUMMARY dialog box (Figure 3-45) aids you in creating the appropriate summarizing formula. It has two list boxes: one with field names, the other containing the seven summarizing functions.

Use the arrow keys to select the Time field, and since the Sum function is the default choice, press (**Enter**). *Works* inserts the formula **=SUM(Time)** into the highlighted cell.

All the summarizing formulas are entered with the same technique. One at a time, select cells D8 through G8. Display the FIELD

Figure 3-45 Use the FIELD SUMMARY dialog box to enter summarizing formulas

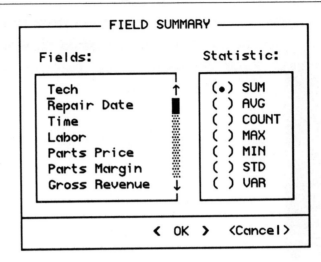

SUMMARY dialog box, and select the appropriate field to create the summarizing formula. Complete line 8 by typing **totals**: into cell B8 and =**Tech** into cell A8. Change the style of cell A8 to right alignment.

The contents of cells A8 and B8 will print "Brad totals" at the break following Brad's entries, "Cheryl totals" at the break following Cheryl's entries, etc.

Highlight all of row 8 and change its style to bold (Figure 3-46). Leave row 9 blank.

Grand Totals

Row 10 is the first Summ Report row. I drew a line in this row to mark the end of group totals and the beginning of grand totals. Drawing a line is easy, but there is one little trick you need to know. If you just type a row of dashes into cell A10, *Works* will treat the dashes as minus signs and display a "Formula too complex" message. If you begin your string of dashes with a quote (i.e., "------), *Works* will treat the dashes as text.

Grand totals are created in row 11. The formulas for grand totals are exactly the same as those for group totals. The only difference is that they're entered into a Summ Report row instead of a Summ Tech row.

Because the formulas are identical, you can *copy* the formulas instead of typing them again. Highlight cells C8 through G8 (you

Figure 3-46 The completed Summ Tech row

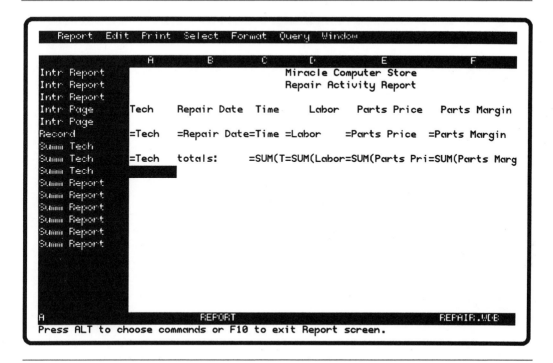

```
  Report   Edit   Print   Select   Format   Query   Window

                    A          B          C          D          E          F
Intr Report                              Miracle Computer Store
Intr Report                              Repair Activity Report
Intr Report
Intr Page    Tech    Repair Date  Time     Labor    Parts Price   Parts Margin
Intr Page
Record      =Tech   =Repair Date=Time =Labor      =Parts Price  =Parts Margin
Summ Tech
Summ Tech   =Tech    totals:           =SUM(T=SUM(Labor=SUM(Parts Pri=SUM(Parts Marg
Summ Tech
Summ Report
Summ Report
Summ Report
Summ Report
Summ Report
Summ Report


A                        REPORT                           REPAIR.WDB
Press ALT to choose commands or F10 to exit Report screen.
```

can hold down (**Shift**) as you move the cursor, to highlight the range of cells). Press (**Shift**) + (**F3**) (or select **Copy** from the Edit menu) to enter the copy mode. Then, move the cursor to cell C11, and press (**Enter**). That was quick, and saved you some typing time, too. Finish row 11 by typing **Grand totals**: into cell A11. Highlight the entire row, and change its style to bold.

The final two summary computations demonstrate the flexibility of *Works'* report generator. Type **Average time per repair**: into cell A13. Use the FIELD SUMMARY dialog box to insert the formula =**AVG(Time)** into cell D13. Change the format of this cell to **Fixed** with 2 decimal places. Type the word **Hours** into cell E13. Then, format the entire row as bold.

Type **Average cost per repair**: into cell A15. Because the formula for average repair cost is more complex than a single summarizing function (it's actually the sum of two functions), type the formula =**AVG(Labor)+AVG(Parts Price)** directly into cell E15. Format this cell as **Dollar** with 2 decimal places. Then change the style of the entire row to bold. Figure 3-47 shows the completed report form.

Figure 3-47 The completed report form

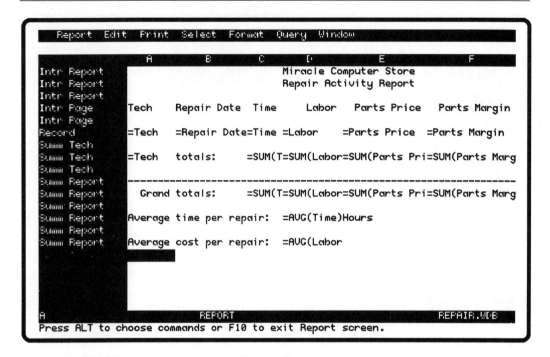

Printing the Report

Display the LAYOUT dialog box, and change the Left and Right Margins to 0 inches. View the report on screen using the **View** command in the Report menu. While you can't see effects such as bold or underline on the screen, you can see that all of the summarizing features work properly.

Return to the List window and save the database. Then, print the report with the **Print Report** command, and compare it with Figure 3-42.

Works can print a summary of your report, containing only the introduction and summarizing rows. Select **Print Report** again, and press (Alt) + (A) to accept the option Print All But Record Rows. Press (Enter), and compare the resulting summary report with the detail report you printed earlier.

Note: The Print All But Record Rows option remains in effect for this report until you cancel it by pressing (Alt) + (A) again while displaying the PRINT dialog box.

Inserting Page Breaks

You might want the data for each tech to be on a separate page. If
you do, just insert a page break below the group summary row.

Highlight row 9, then select **Insert Page Break** from the Print menu.
A >> symbol appears at the left edge of the row indicating a page break
has been inserted. Print the report again, and see that each tech's data
is on its own page.

If you want to remove the page break, highlight the row with the
>> symbol, and select **Delete Page Break** from the Print menu.

☰ Final Comments

If I had written this book as a textbook, you would see a list of student
exercises here. Since it's not a textbook, all I can do is strongly
recommend that you practice using the commands and techniques
discussed in this chapter. It doesn't matter what subjects you use for
your practice databases. You might want to list all the major possessions
in your home, for example, giving the location, description, cost, and
date purchased for each item. Or you could create a birthday list of
your friends and relatives, sorted by birth date, to remind you when
to send birthday cards. (I use a list like this all the time.)

The point is to use the knowledge you've acquired to create your
own applications. Then, as questions arise, you can refer back to this
chapter for help.

Chapter **4**
THE SPREADSHEET

In the last two chapters, I didn't have to define the functions of either a word processor or a data base. I took it for granted that you had been writing notes and letters long before you thought of using a word processor and that you had been making lists of things long before computer databases became available.

The spreadsheet application is different. The features and uses of electronic spreadsheets have no precomputer analog. In fact, most new computer users probably have never seen a spreadsheet before. So, before you begin the first spreadsheet project, let's talk about what a spreadsheet is and how it can be used.

In some ways, a spreadsheet resembles the List display of a *Works* database file. Each piece of data is typed into a box, or cell, and the cells are arranged in a grid of rows and columns. The rows and columns are labeled so that you can refer to an individual cell by its row and column labels. In a *Works* spreadsheet, rows are numbered from 1 to 4096, while columns are lettered from A to IV (that is, from A to Z, then AA to AZ, BA to BZ, and so on to IV) for a total of 256 columns. Each cell is referred to by the column and row that contain it. For example, the cell in the third column, fourth row would be referred to as cell C4. The cell to the right of C4 would be D4, and so on.

Cells can contain either text (sometimes called labels) or numerical values. A cell's value also can be defined from the contents of other cells. For example, you could define the contents of one cell as the sum of the contents of two other cells.

By now, you may very well be asking, "What's the point? Why bother with spreadsheets at all?" The point is that spreadsheets allow you to do computations in seconds that would take hours or days to perform by hand. Moreover, you don't need to be a mathematical wizard or a computer programmer to use this computational power. But, as with any other application, you have to have an idea of what you want the spreadsheet to do.

To introduce you to the world of spreadsheets, I have chosen three representative projects. First, we'll let *Works* compute commissions for the salespersons of your business, the Miracle Computer Store. Second, we'll create a table of monthly mortgage payments for a new home you're thinking of buying. And third, we'll set up a customer invoice form.

PROJECT 5: SALES COMMISSIONS

Your sales staff (Mary, Ron, Ed, Maggie, Charles, and Chris) is paid a monthly commission on the computer equipment they sell. Their commission is computed at 16% of the gross margin. You want to set up a spreadsheet that will list the names of your salespersons, their gross sales for the month, and the cost of items they sold. You want the spreadsheet to compute gross margins (the difference between gross sales and cost) and commissions.

Creating a New Spreadsheet

Begin by booting up *Works*. From the NEW dialog box, select Spreadsheet, and press (Enter). Figure 4-1 shows the blank spreadsheet.

This is a good place to remind you that you're seeing just a small part of the total spreadsheet. Your window shows you columns A through G and rows 1 through 20. Moving the cursor allows you to shift the window to display other areas of the spreadsheet.

The Split Bars

Just as with the List display in a database, the spreadsheet window has both horizontal and vertical split bars. These are used to divide the window display into two or four "panes," allowing you to view two or four different sections of the spreadsheet at the same time. Refer to the section *Dividing the Window*, in Chapter 3, for more information on using the split bars.

Column Widths

When you create a new spreadsheet, *Works* uses certain default, or standard, values in its display. You can change some of these display characteristics to suit your own preferences or the needs of a particular application. For example, *Works* makes all the columns the same width. You can widen (or narrow) any column, just as you did with the List display in the database.

Figure 4-1 A blank *Works* spreadsheet

Suppose you decide you want to widen column C. To do this, move your cursor to any cell in column C. Select **Width** from the Format menu, and enter the desired column width (Figure 4-2). You can use this technique to set a different width for any or all of the columns in your spreadsheet.

Selecting One or More Cells

The cursor itself is used to select the particular cell (or group of cells) you want to work with at the moment. Move the cursor to cell A1, and notice that the cell location, "A1," appears at the left of the status line.

If you want to select a group of cells, just hold down (Shift) while you move the cursor until you've highlighted all the cells you want. For example, if you want to select cells B3 through B10, place the cursor in cell B3, hold down (Shift), and press ⬇ seven times to reach cell B10. Then, release the (Shift). This is called highlighting a range of cells.

Figure 4-2   The WIDTH dialog box

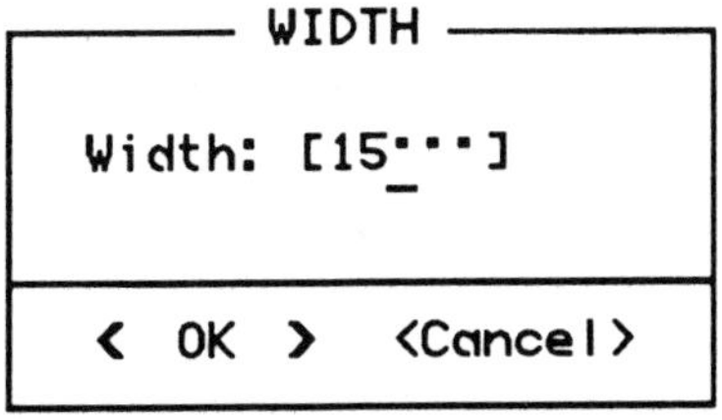

```
┌──────── WIDTH ────────┐
│                       │
│   Width: [15˙˙˙]       │
│          _            │
│                       │
├───────────────────────┤
│   < OK >   <Cancel>   │
└───────────────────────┘
```

Works indicates a range of cells by joining the first cell and last cell with a colon. If you look at the left end of the status line, you'll see the range of cells you've just highlighted, "B3:B10." You can deselect (or "unhighlight") the range by pressing (Esc) or typing any key.

Another method of highlighting a range of cells uses the Extend key, (F8). Place the cursor back in cell B3, if you've moved it. Press (F8) once to enter the Extend mode (note the word EXTEND on the status line). Then use (↓) to highlight the range B3:B10. The end result is the same as the (Shift) key method—cells B3 through B10 are highlighted. Press (F8) again to cancel Extend.

Note: Mouse users can use the "click and drag" method to highlight a range of cells.

Works makes it easy to select entire rows or columns. If you want to select row 6, for example, move the cursor to any cell in row 6. Then, choose **Row** from the Select menu or press (Control) + (F8). (Mouse users can just click on the row number along the left edge of the window.) If you want to highlight more than one row, hold down (Shift) while you move the cursor. (Mouse users just click and drag through the row numbers.) Similarly, entire columns may be selected by choosing **Column** from the Select menu, pressing (Shift) + (F8), or, if you have a mouse, clicking on the column letters at the top of the window.

If you want to highlight all the rows (or all the columns) in the spreadsheet, you first choose **Row** and then **Column** from the Select menu. (Mouse users can click in the area that's above row 1 and to the left of column A.) Again, to unhighlight cells, just press (Esc) or move the cursor.

Resetting the Column Widths

Let's ask *Works* to make all the columns the same width. First, highlight the entire spreadsheet using the above technique. Select **Width** from the Format menu. The standard default value is 10, but let's make our columns a little wider. Type **14**, and press (Enter). All the columns should now be the 14 spaces wide.

☰ Entering Text

Let's begin your Commissions spreadsheet by entering column headings. Highlight cell A3, and type the heading **Salesperson**. Notice that the characters you type appear on the formula bar (the line below the menu bar) and not in the cell (Figure 4-3). If you mistype, use (Backspace) to erase your mistake. To transfer the data from the formula bar to the cell, you can do one of three things. You can press (Enter), (Tab), or an arrow key. All three actions transfer the data from the formula bar to the highlighted cell, but pressing (Tab) or an arrow key moves the cursor as well. If you press (Tab), the cell immediately to the right (B3, in this example) becomes the selected cell. Pressing an arrow key moves the cursor in the direction of the arrow.

Figure 4-3   Cell contents are entered and edited on the formula bar

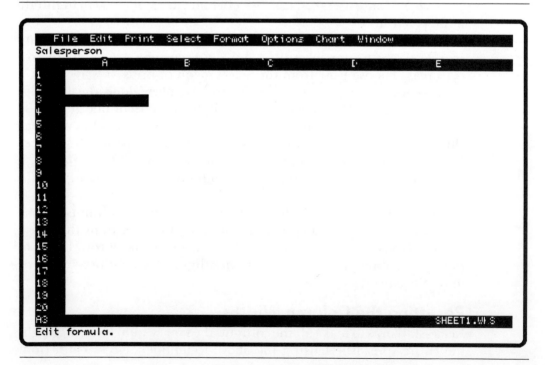

Press (Tab) both to enter **Salesperson** into cell A3 and to select cell B3. Type **Gross Sales** in cell B3, **Cost** in C3, **Gross Margin** in D3, and **Commission** in E3. Figure 4-4 shows these five column headings.

Figure 4-4   Enter the column headings on row 3

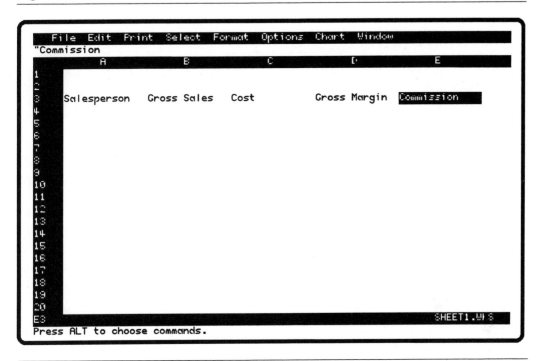

≡ Formatting Text

Works allows you to format text you've typed into spreadsheet cells. As with any text, you have to select it before you can change its format. First, let's underline all five cells in row 3, so highlight the entire row.

Pull down the Format menu and select **Style**. This is the same STYLE dialog box you saw in the database projects in the last chapter. Press (Alt) + (U) to underline the text (Figure 4-5). Then press (Enter) to close the dialog box.

Figure 4-5   The STYLE dialog box

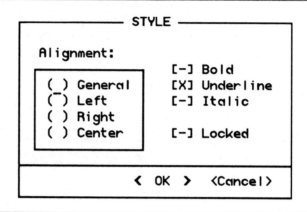

Deselect row 3 by moving the cursor. Then, select cells B3:E3. Display the STYLES dialog box again, and change the alignment of these cells to Right by pressing (Alt) + (R).

Close the dialog box, and compare your spreadsheet with Figure 4-6. As usual, *Works* doesn't show emphasis such as underline on the screen. Instead, the text in the affected cells appears brighter. When you print the spreadsheet, an underline will be drawn through the entire width of the cell, not just under the text. That way, the underline will extend unbroken through the five cells in row C that contain text. Empty cells in that row will not be underlined.

Now type in the names of the six salespersons (Mary, Ron, Ed, Maggie, Charles, and Chris) in cells A4:A9.

This is a good time to save the spreadsheet to your *Works* Data disk. You can name it SALESCOM.

≡ Entering and Formatting Numbers

Table 4-1 gives you the values for Gross Sales and Cost for each salesperson. Enter the Gross Sales values in cells B4:B9 and Cost values in Cells C4:C9. Notice that *Works* automatically right-aligns the numbers (that's why you right-aligned the column headings). Compare your spreadsheet with the one in Figure 4-7.

Looking at the values for Gross Sales and Cost, it's difficult to see that they represent dollars. Let's format these cells to improve their appearance by adding dollar signs and commas.

Figure 4-6   The column headings have been right-aligned

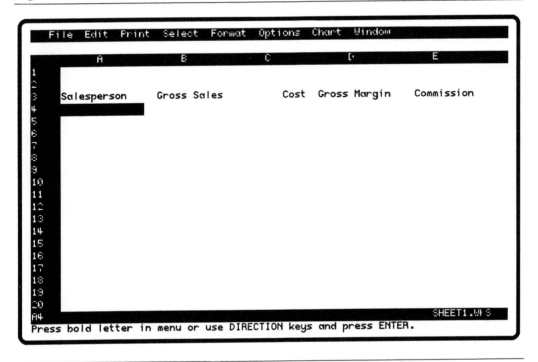

Table 4-1   Gross sales and cost values

Salesperson	Gross Sales	Cost
Mary	62525	51250
Ron	73418	59933
Ed	71631	57305
Maggie	87042	71698
Charles	56390	45475
Chris	111945	92136

First, select columns B and C using one of the techniques described above. Then, pull down the Format menu and choose **Dollar**. *Works* displays a DECIMALS dialog box (Figure 4-8) with a default value of 2 decimal places. Since none of the data contain decimal points, change the number of decimal places to 0, and press (Enter) .

Figure 4-7 Enter values for Gross Sales and Cost

```
  File   Edit   Print   Select   Format   Options   Chart   Window

            A            B            C          D           E
 1
 2
 3  Salesperson   Gross Sales        Cost  Gross Margin   Commission
 4  Mary               62525       51250
 5  Ron                73418       59933
 6  Ed                 71631       57305
 7  Maggie             87042       71698
 8  Charles            56390       45475
 9  Chris             111945       92136
10
11
12
13
14
15
16
17
18
19
20
C10                                               SALESCOM.WKS
Press ALT to choose commands.
```

Figure 4-8 The DECIMALS dialog box

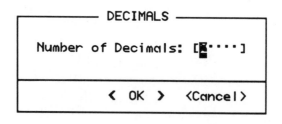

```
┌─────────── DECIMALS ───────────┐
│                                │
│   Number of Decimals: [2····]  │
│                                │
├────────────────────────────────┤
│       < OK >    <Cancel>       │
└────────────────────────────────┘
```

Unhighlight the columns. *Works* has added a dollar sign in front of each numerical entry, and commas where appropriate. Notice that the two text entries in cells B3 and C3 are unaffected by the numerical format change (Figure 4-9).

Figure 4-9 Apply Dollar format to columns B and C

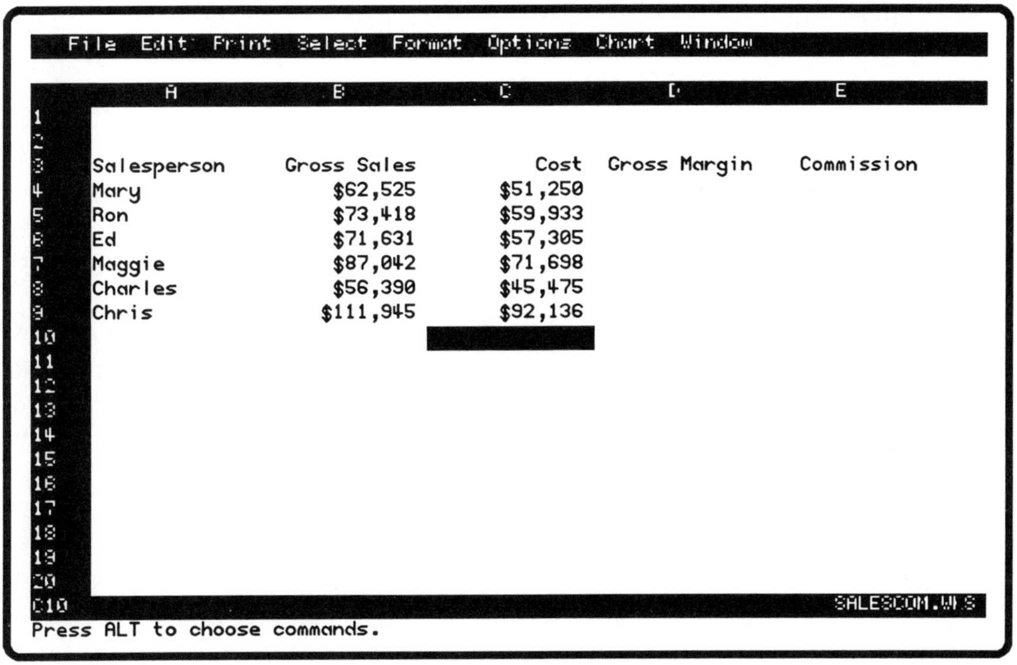

```
 File  Edit  Print  Select  Format  Options  Chart  Window
           A              B            C        D           E
 1
 2
 3   Salesperson    Gross Sales       Cost  Gross Margin   Commission
 4   Mary               $62,525    $51,250
 5   Ron                $73,418    $59,933
 6   Ed                 $71,631    $57,305
 7   Maggie             $87,042    $71,698
 8   Charles            $56,390    $45,475
 9   Chris             $111,945    $92,136
10
11
12
13
14
15
16
17
18
19
20
C10                                                    SALESCOM.WKS
Press ALT to choose commands.
```

☰ Spreadsheet Computations

The values for Gross Margin and Commission are to be calculated by the spreadsheet. Gross Margin is the difference between Gross Sales and Cost. Commission is 16% of Gross Margin.

Entering a Formula

Let's start by computing the Gross Margin for Mary. Highlight cell D4. *All* formulas begin with an equals symbol, =. Mary's Gross Margin is the difference between her Gross Sales and her Cost. Another way of saying this is that her Gross Margin is the difference between the value in cell B4 and the value in cell C4, or B4 – C4.

With cell D4 highlighted, type the formula **=B4-C4** and press ⟨Enter⟩. The result, 11275, should appear in cell D4. Notice that the value isn't formatted for dollars; you'll change that in a moment.

Arithmetic Operators and the Order of Operations

The minus sign, "-," is one of five arithmetic operators used by *Works* to calculate numerical results. Here is a list of all five:

Symbol	Operation
+	addition
–	subtraction or negation
*	multiplication
/	division
^	exponentiation (raising to a power)

As long as your formulas contain only one operator (3*B3, C12/C9, etc.), the order or sequence of operations is a moot point. But suppose, for example, you wanted to calculate the result of doubling the sum of two cells. Suppose the cells were C1 and C2. You might think that the appropriate formula would be 2*C1+C2 or perhaps C1+C2*2, but you'd be wrong in both cases.

When two or more operations occur in the same formula, *Works* performs them in a particular order. Negation is performed first. Exponentiation is performed next, followed by multiplication and division. Addition and subtraction are performed last. This means that in the example C1+C2*2, *Works* would multiply C2 by 2, and then add C1 to the result because multiplication is performed before addition.

You can force *Works* to add C1 and C2 first, before multiplying by 2, by enclosing the sum in parentheses: (C1+C2)*2. *Works* always performs operations in parentheses first.

Copying a Formula

You could continue calculating the next salesperson's Gross Margin by typing the formula =**B5–C5** into cell D5, but there is a spreadsheet command that greatly simplifies your work. The formulas for cells D5 through D9 are very similar to D4's. Only the cell references to Gross Sales and Cost change. *Works* has two special commands that both replicate a formula and automatically change the cell references. One of them is called **Fill Down** and is found in the Edit menu. (*Note:* The other special copying command is **Fill Right**, and you'll use it a little later.)

To use **Fill Down**, you must first select the cell with the original formula *and* the cells into which you want to copy the formula. To do this, start with cell D4 (the cell with the original formula) and highlight the range of cells, D4:D9. Now, select **Fill Down** from the Edit menu. All six Gross Margin values will be calculated.

With these cells still highlighted, use the **Dollar** command in the Format menu to change the numerical format to that of columns B and C (Figure 4-10).

Figure 4-10 Use **Fill Down** to copy the formula into the other 5 cells

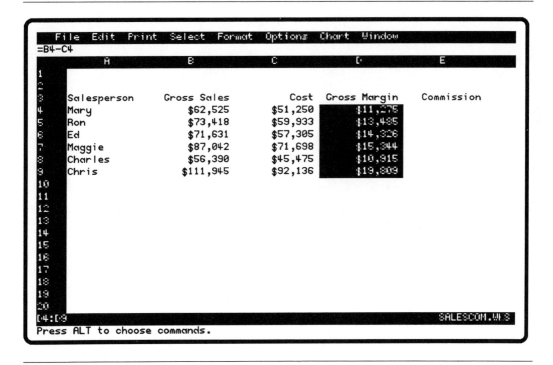

Calculating Commissions

Highlight cell E4, type the commission formula =**.16*D4** (16% of Gross Margin), and press (Enter). The result, 1804, should appear in cell E4. Copy this formula into the remaining Commission cells using the same technique you used with Gross Margins. Highlight cells E4:E9, and choose **Fill Down**.

Highlight column E and change the format to dollars, but leave the number of decimal places set at 2. Compare your spreadsheet with Figure 4-11.

Figure 4-11 Calculate the Commissions and format as Dollar

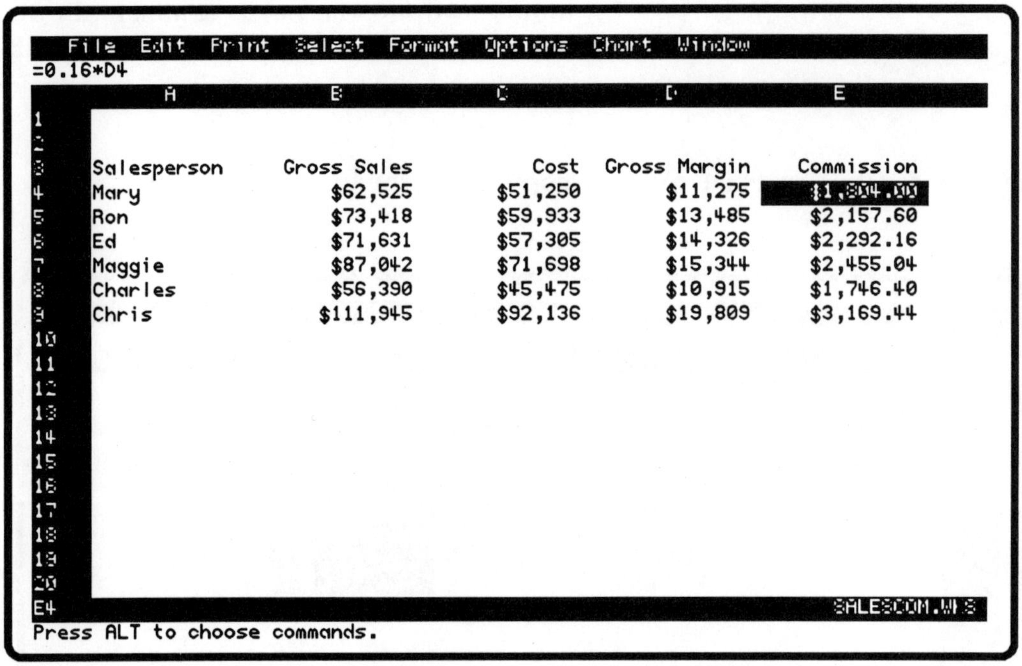

```
  File  Edit  Print  Select  Format  Options  Chart  Window
=0.16*D4
           A            B            C       D            E
1
2
3       Salesperson  Gross Sales     Cost  Gross Margin   Commission
4       Mary            $62,525    $51,250     $11,275    $1,804.00
5       Ron             $73,418    $59,933     $13,485    $2,157.60
6       Ed              $71,631    $57,305     $14,326    $2,292.16
7       Maggie          $87,042    $71,698     $15,344    $2,455.04
8       Charles         $56,390    $45,475     $10,915    $1,746.40
9       Chris          $111,945    $92,136     $19,809    $3,169.44
10
11
12
13
14
15
16
17
18
19
20
E4                                                      SALESCOM.WKS
Press ALT to choose commands.
```

≡ Using Functions in Formulas

You probably want to know the total Gross Sales for all six salespersons. One way of calculating this value is to add the values in cells B4:B9 (i.e., =B4+B5+B6+B7+B8+B9), but there's a much easier way. Type the word **Total** in cell A11, and then highlight cell B11.

Functions

Works provides over 50 predefined functions to assist you with your spreadsheet calculations. A function is a mathematical operation involving one or more values. (*Note*: All *Works* functions are numerical. That is, they only operate on numerical quantities, and they only produce numerical results.)

Works' functions are divided into six categories: Date and Time functions such as HOUR( ), MONTH( ), and NOW( ); Mathematical functions such as SUM( ), SIN( ), and ROUND( ); Logical functions such as TRUE( ), ISNA( ), and IF( ); Financial functions such as RATE( ), PMT( ), and NPV( ); Statistical functions such as SUM( ), COUNT( ), and STD( ); and special functions such as CHOOSE( ), VLOOKUP( ), and ERR( ). You can see a list of all *Works'* functions in the Help Index, under Functions.

The parentheses following the function name contain the values (or *arguments*) used by the function. For example, the square root function, SQRT( ), uses as its argument the number for which you want the square root, so that SQRT(2) evaluates as 1.414. Most arguments are numerical values (24, –3.5, etc.), cells (A1, B11, etc.), or ranges of cells (B4:B9, H6:Q6, D2:F5, etc.).

(*Note*: Ranges in which either the row or column remains constant for the first and last cells, such as A4:G4 or B2:B7, are referred to as one-dimensional ranges. Ranges that have different row and column values for the first and last cells, for example D2:F5, are considered two-dimensional.)

The SUM( ) function discussed below can take one or more individual cells and/or one or more ranges of cells for its argument. The expression SUM(G3,G5,K5:K8) tells *Works* to compute the result of adding the values in cells G3, G5, K5, K6, K7, and K8.

The SUM( ) Function

With cell B11 selected, enter the formula for the sum of the values in cells B4:B9 by typing =**SUM(B4:B9)**, and press (Enter). *Works* responds by displaying a value of $462,951 in cell B11. Figure 4-12 shows how your screen should appear. (*Note*: If you make a mistake, just retype the formula.)

Using Fill Right

You could use the same technique to sum up the columns for Cost, Gross Margin, and Commission. But the **Fill Right** command will create these three totals with one single operation. Highlight the range of cells B11:E11. Then, pull down the Edit menu, and select **Fill Right**.

Notice that the "no decimal place" format is copied along with the formula. If you want the total in E11 to be displayed to 2 decimal places, you'll have to highlight the cell and use the **Dollar** format again. Compare your spreadsheet with the one in Figure 4-13.

Displaying Formulas

Works will display either the values of the formulas you type into cells (the standard display), or the formulas themselves. Pull down

Figure 4-12   Use the SUM( ) function to calculate the total Gross
Sales

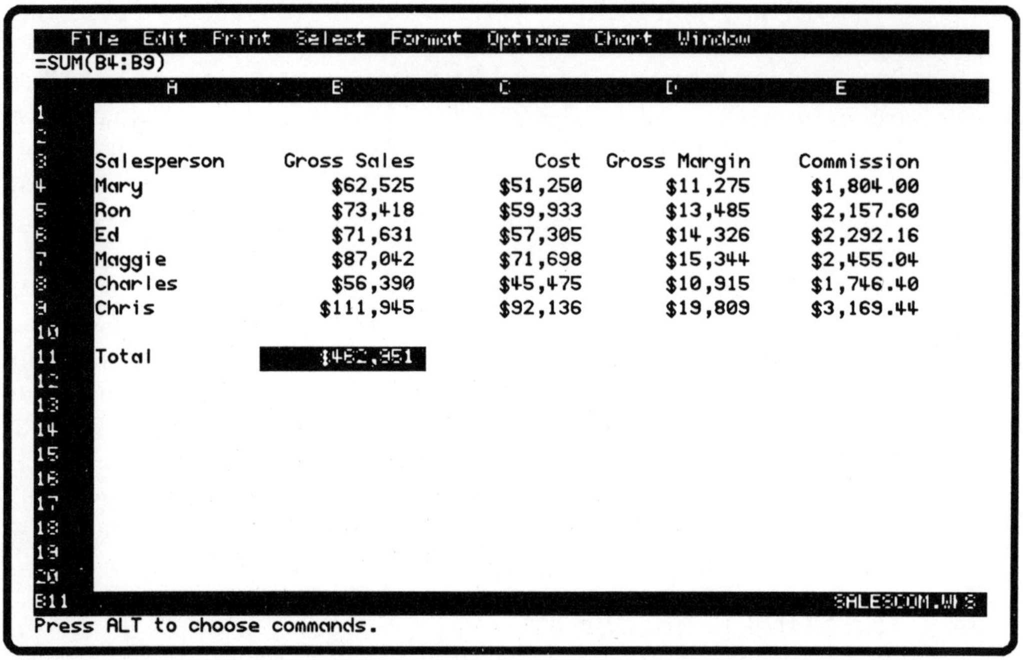

```
 File  Edit  Print  Select  Format  Options  Chart  Window
=SUM(B4:B9)
            A           B           C        D            E
1
2
3    Salesperson   Gross Sales      Cost  Gross Margin   Commission
4    Mary             $62,525    $51,250     $11,275     $1,804.00
5    Ron              $73,418    $59,933     $13,485     $2,157.60
6    Ed               $71,631    $57,305     $14,326     $2,292.16
7    Maggie           $87,042    $71,698     $15,344     $2,455.04
8    Charles          $56,390    $45,475     $10,915     $1,746.40
9    Chris           $111,945    $92,136     $19,809     $3,169.44
10
11   Total           $462,951
12
13
14
15
16
17
18
19
20
B11                                               SALESCOM.WKS
Press ALT to choose commands.
```

the Options menu, and select **Show Formulas** (Figure 4-14). Notice
that when you used the **Fill Right** command on the formula in B11,
Works automatically changed the argument (B4:B9) as it copied the
formula into cells C11, D11, and E11.

To change the display back to values, select **Show Formulas** again.

The Average Function

Let's use one more function with this first spreadsheet example. The
Average function, AVG( ), allows you to compute the average Gross
Sales, Cost, etc., for your six salespersons.

Highlight cell A12 and type the word **Average**. Move to cell B12,
and begin the average formula by typing the characters =**AVG(** into

Figure 4-13   Use **Fill Right** to copy the SUM( ) function into the three remaining Total cells

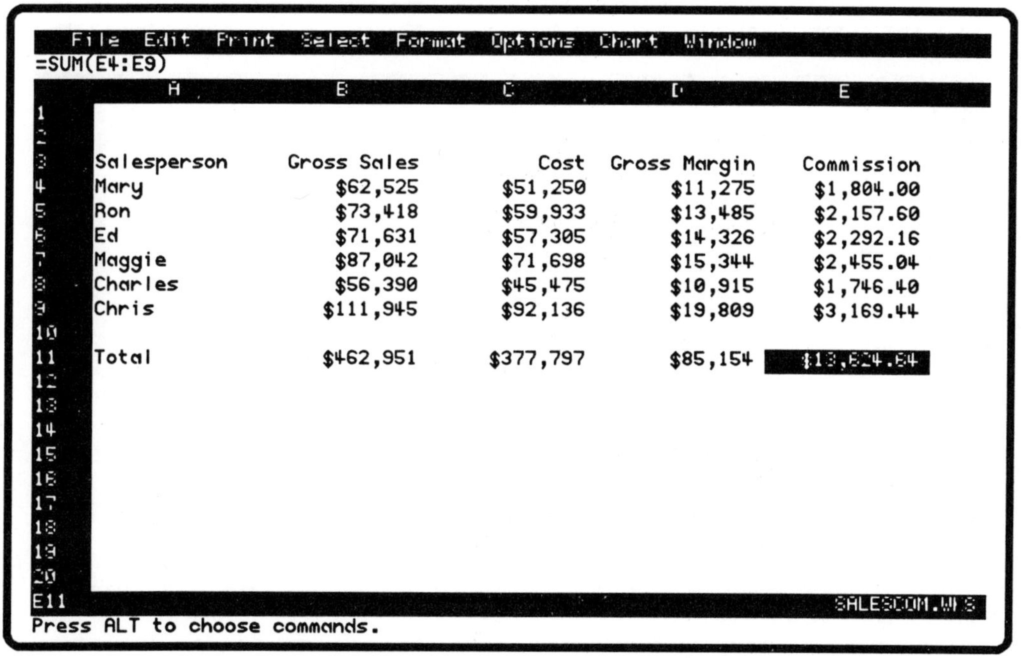

```
  File  Edit  Print  Select  Format  Options  Chart  Window
=SUM(E4:E9)
            A            B          C       D            E
 1
 2
 3   Salesperson   Gross Sales      Cost  Gross Margin   Commission
 4   Mary             $62,525    $51,250      $11,275     $1,804.00
 5   Ron              $73,418    $59,933      $13,485     $2,157.60
 6   Ed               $71,631    $57,305      $14,326     $2,292.16
 7   Maggie           $87,042    $71,698      $15,344     $2,455.04
 8   Charles          $56,390    $45,475      $10,915     $1,746.40
 9   Chris           $111,945    $92,136      $19,809     $3,169.44
10
11   Total           $462,951   $377,797      $85,154    $13,624.64
12
13
14
15
16
17
18
19
20
E11                                                   SALESCOM.WKS
Press ALT to choose commands.
```

the formula bar, but *don't* complete the formula yet. I want to show you another way of entering the cell range.

After you type the left parenthesis, use the arrow keys to highlight cell B4. Notice "B4" appears after the parenthesis on the formula bar. Press `F8` to extend the highlight, and press ⬇ until you've highlighted cells B4:B9. See that the range "B4:B9" is now on the formula bar (Figure 4-15). *Works* calls this method of selecting cells the *point* method. (*Note:* Mouse users can click and drag to highlight the range.) Complete the formula by typing the right parenthesis, and press `Enter`.

Use the **Fill Right** command (in the Edit menu) to copy this formula into cells C12, D12, and E12, so that you can see the average values for Cost, Gross Margin, and Commission. Again, use the **Dollar** format

Figure 4-14 Formulas used to compute Gross Margins and Commissions

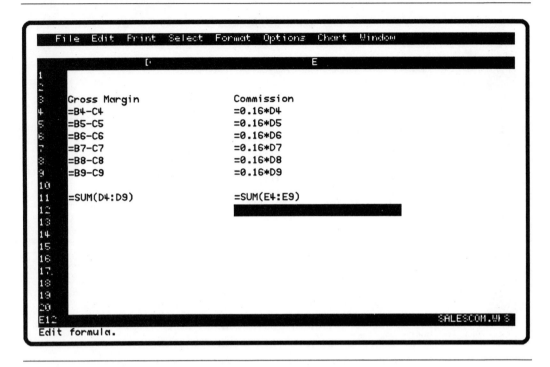

to change the display of cell E12 to 2 decimal places. Figure 4-16 shows the four averages.

≡ The Power of the Spreadsheet

Up until now, you've been using the spreadsheet as sort of a giant calculator. The real power of a spreadsheet lies in its ability to answer "what if" types of questions. For example, what if the commission rate were changed from 16% to 15% or 17%?

Highlight cell C15, begin with ten spaces, then type **Commission Rate =**, and press (Enter). Notice that *Works* automatically extended the text into cell D15.

Highlight cell E15, and type the current Commission Rate, **16%**, into it (Figure 4-17). *Works* will interpret 16% as 0.16. In fact, it displays a value of 0.16 on the formula bar.

Figure 4-15 Use the *point* method to define the range for the AVG( ) function

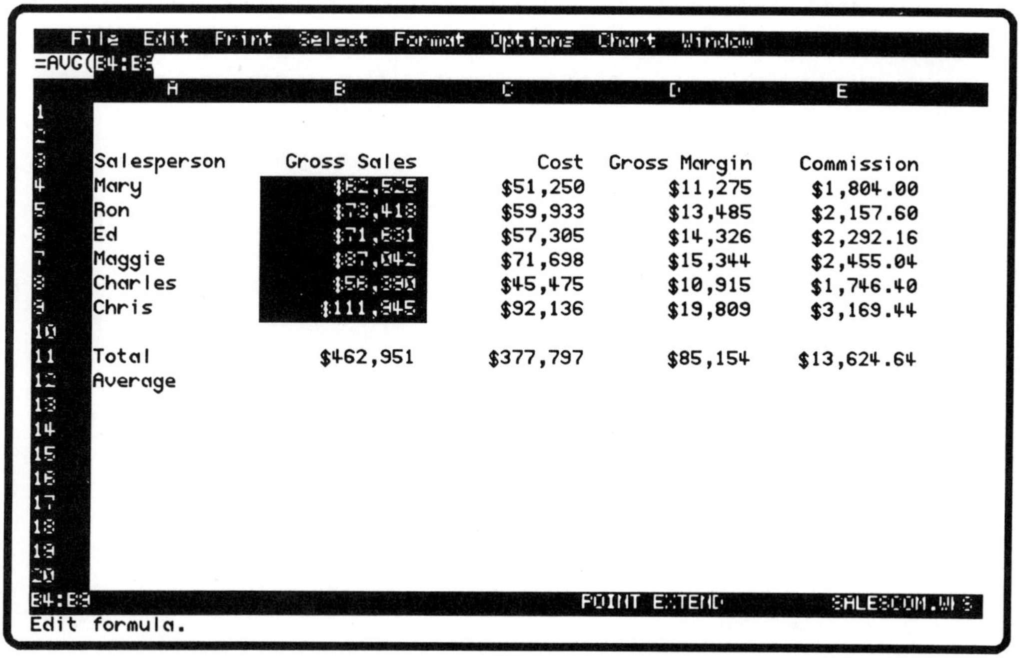

Select cell E4, and look at the formula displayed on the formula bar. You calculated Mary's Commission by multiplying 0.16 times the contents of cell D4, Mary's Gross Margin. Instead of using the constant value, 0.16, use the value in cell E15. Retype the formula as =**E15*D4**, and press (Enter). Notice that the result, $1,804.00, in cell E4 didn't change. You're still computing it by multiplying 0.16 times the Gross Margin. You're just getting the 0.16 value from cell E15.

Highlight cell E15 and change the Commission Rate to **17%**. As you press (Enter) to accept the new value, watch cell C4. Its value changed (to $1,916.75) as soon as you changed the Commission Rate. But the remaining five Commissions *didn't* change. Why not? They didn't change because their formulas still use 0.16 instead of the value in cell E15.

Figure 4-16 Copy and format the Average values as you did the
Totals

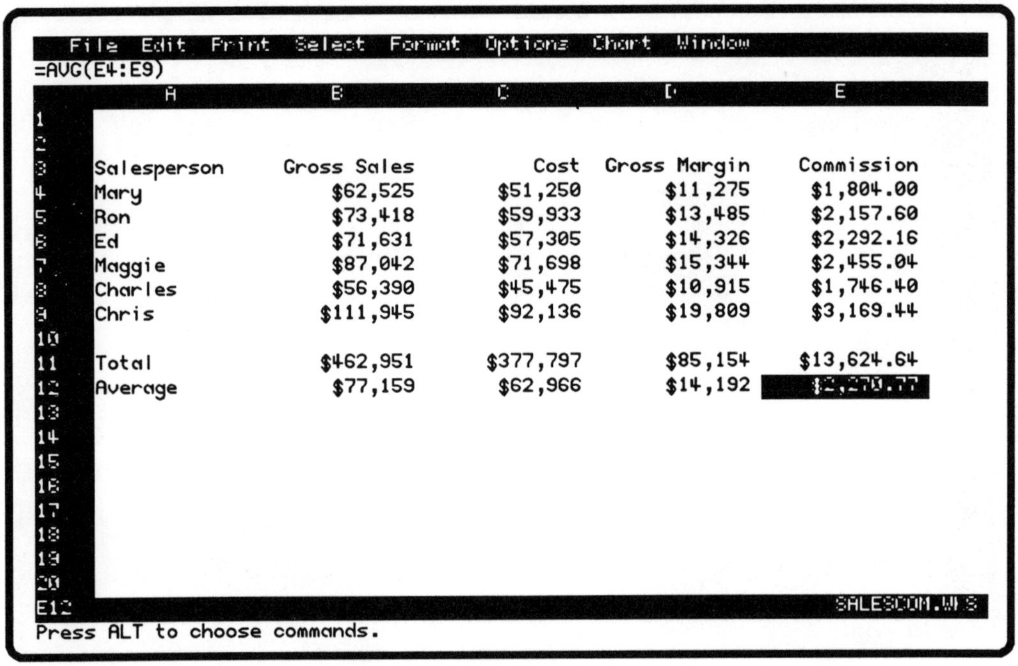

Let's use the **Fill Down** command to copy the formula in E4 into
cells E5 through E9. Highlight the range of cells, E4:E9, then choose
Fill Down from the Edit menu (Figure 4-18).

Absolute Cell Reference

What happened? Instead of the expected values, the other five
commissions were calculated to be $0.00. Select cell E5, look on the
formula bar, and you'll see why this happened. When you used the
Fill Down command, *Works* automatically incremented *both* cell
references from the formula in E4. In other words, when it copied
the formula E15*D4 from E4 to E5, it changed D4 to D5 *and E15
to E16*. The first change, from D4 to D5, is necessary so that Ron's
commission is calculated using his value for Gross Margin. But, when
Works changed the cell reference E15 to E16, there was nothing in
cell E16. *Works* interpreted this empty cell as having a value of zero.

Figure 4-17 16% is interpreted as 0.16

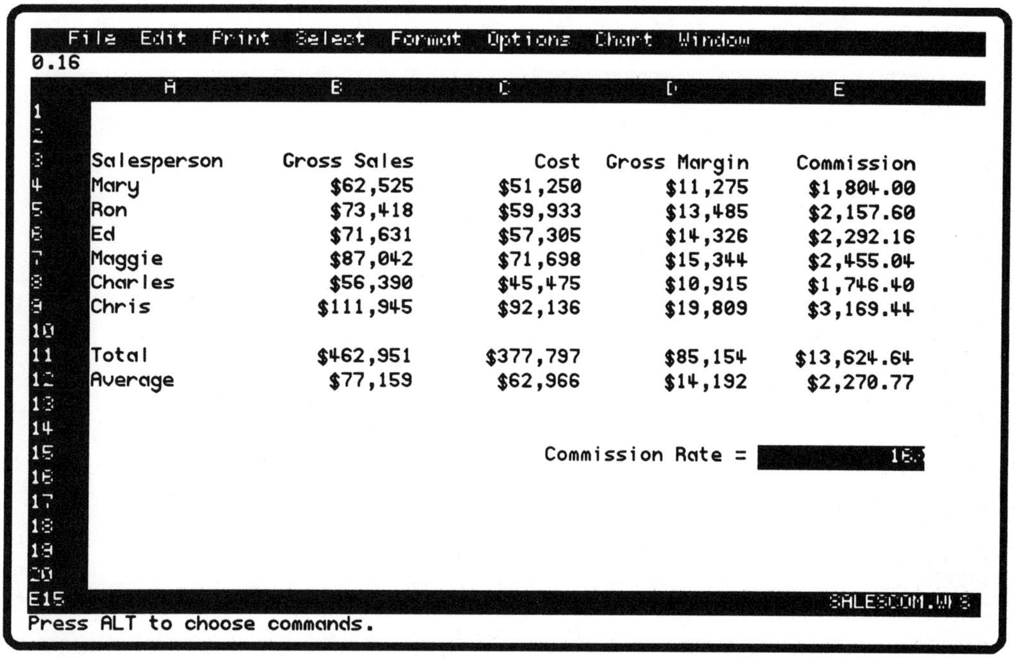

```
 File  Edit  Print  Select  Format  Options  Chart  Window
0.16
            A           B            C           D            E
 1
 2
 3  Salesperson  Gross Sales      Cost  Gross Margin   Commission
 4  Mary            $62,525    $51,250     $11,275     $1,804.00
 5  Ron             $73,418    $59,933     $13,485     $2,157.60
 6  Ed              $71,631    $57,305     $14,326     $2,292.16
 7  Maggie          $87,042    $71,698     $15,344     $2,455.04
 8  Charles         $56,390    $45,475     $10,915     $1,746.40
 9  Chris          $111,945    $92,136     $19,809     $3,169.44
10
11  Total          $462,951   $377,797     $85,154    $13,624.64
12  Average         $77,159    $62,966     $14,192     $2,270.77
13
14
15                           Commission Rate =            16%
16
17
18
19
20
E15                                                  SALESCOM.WKS
Press ALT to choose commands.
```

And that's why the Commission value for E5 (and the other cells) was computed to be zero.

One way around this problem is to put Commission Rate values in cells E16, E17, etc. This is a poor solution. A better solution is to tell *Works* to leave the reference E15 alone and not to increment it when the **Fill Down** command is used. That's the purpose of *Works'* Absolute Cell Reference feature. Here's how to use it.

Highlight cell E4, the cell with the original formula. The formula =**E15*D4** will appear on the formula bar. Change this formula to =**E15*D4**. The $ symbols in front of the column and row values of the cell reference tell *Works* to treat the reference as *absolute*. When you copy this formula to other cells with **Fill Down**, the reference to E15 will remain E15, while the reference to D4 will change with the row.

Press (Enter) to accept the change in cell E4's formula. Again, highlight cells E4 through E9, and use the **Fill Down** command (Figure 4-19). That's more like it!

Figure 4-18   Something went wrong when the formula was copied

```
  File  Edit  Print  Select  Format  Options  Chart  Window
=E16*D5
              A            B            C         D              E
 1
 2
 3  Salesperson    Gross Sales        Cost  Gross Margin    Commission
 4  Mary              $62,525      $51,250      $11,275      $1,916.75
 5  Ron               $73,418      $59,933      $13,485          $0.00
 6  Ed                $71,631      $57,305      $14,326          $0.00
 7  Maggie            $87,042      $71,698      $15,344          $0.00
 8  Charles           $56,390      $45,475      $10,915          $0.00
 9  Chris            $111,945      $92,136      $19,809          $0.00
10
11  Total            $462,951     $377,797      $85,154      $1,916.75
12  Average           $77,159      $62,966      $14,192        $319.46
13
14
15                                  Commission Rate =              17%
16
17
18
19
20
E5                                                      SALESCOM.WKS
Press ALT to choose commands.
```

What If

Now your spreadsheet can answer your "What if" question. Currently, your spreadsheet shows a Commission Rate of 17% (at least mine does). Change the value of E15 to 15%. Notice that not only are the individual Commission values recalculated, but also the Total Commission and Average Commission. Try different values for Commission Rate, and you'll begin to see what I meant about answering "What if" questions.

Naming Cells

Instead of referring to the commission rate in your formulas as cell E15, you can *name* the cell and then use the cell name in your formulas.

Try this. Highlight cell E15, then select **Name** from the Edit menu. Figure 4-20 shows the resulting dialog box. Type the name **Rate** into the **Name:** text box, and press (Enter).

Works closes the NAME dialog box, and it looks as if nothing has changed. But highlight one of the cells in the range E4:E9, and see that *Works* has changed the formula. For example, instead of =E15*D4, you'll see =Rate*D4. *Works* has substituted the cell name

Figure 4-19 Using an absolute reference for E15 solves the problem

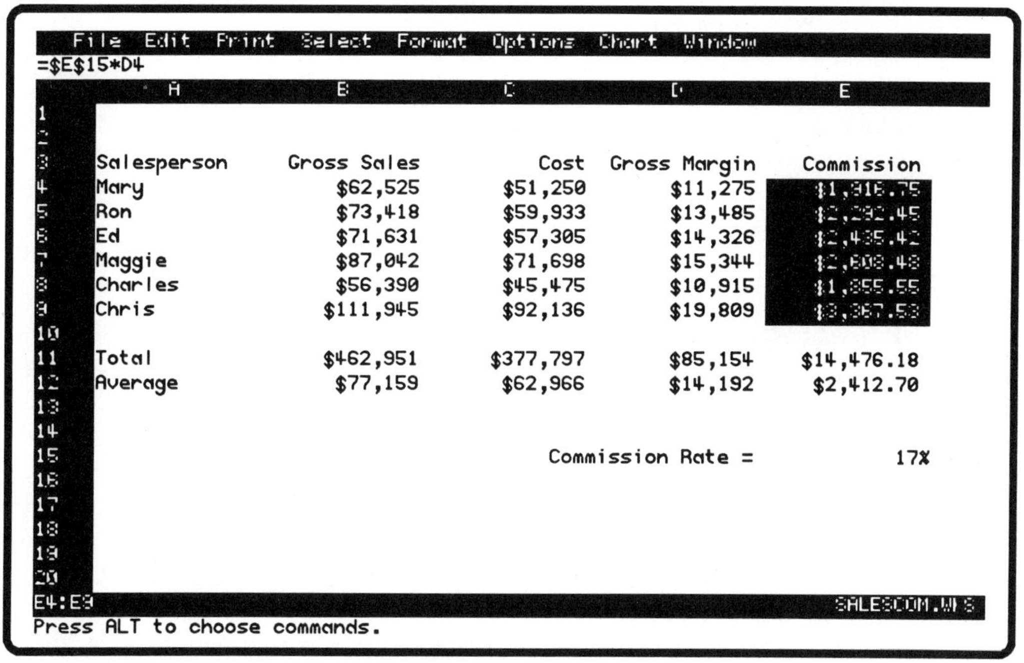

```
 File  Edit  Print  Select  Format  Options  Chart  Window
=$E$15*D4
              A              B              C            D              E
1
2
3   Salesperson    Gross Sales          Cost  Gross Margin    Commission
4   Mary             $62,525       $51,250       $11,275       $1,916.75
5   Ron              $73,418       $59,933       $13,485       $2,292.45
6   Ed               $71,631       $57,305       $14,326       $2,435.42
7   Maggie           $87,042       $71,698       $15,344       $2,608.48
8   Charles          $56,390       $45,475       $10,915       $1,855.55
9   Chris           $111,945       $92,136       $19,809       $3,367.53
10
11  Total           $462,951      $377,797       $85,154      $14,476.18
12  Average          $77,159       $62,966       $14,192       $2,412.70
13
14
15                                        Commission Rate =          17%
16
17
18
19
20
E4:E9                                                      SALESCOM.WKS
Press ALT to choose commands.
```

Figure 4-20 The NAME dialog box

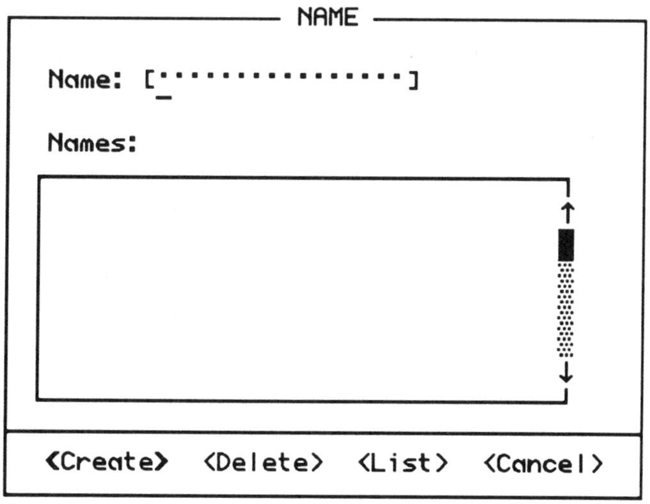

```
┌──────────────────── NAME ────────────────────┐
│                                               │
│    Name: [················]                   │
│          _                                    │
│                                               │
│    Names:                                     │
│          ┌──────────────────────────┐ ↑      │
│          │                          │ ▓      │
│          │                          │ ▒      │
│          │                          │ ▒      │
│          │                          │ ▒      │
│          │                          │ ▒      │
│          │                          │ ↓      │
│          └──────────────────────────┘        │
│                                               │
│   <Create>   <Delete>   <List>   <Cancel>     │
└───────────────────────────────────────────────┘
```

"Rate" in place of the cell reference "E15" in every formula that used the cell. From now on, you can type "Rate" instead of "E15," and *Works* will know to which cell you're referring.

You can also name ranges of cells. Highlight the range B4:B9, and display the NAME dialog box. Notice that *Works* has automatically entered the name, "Gross Sales," from the cell directly above the highlighted range. This is exactly the name you want, so press (Enter) to accept it. Look at cells B11 and B12, and see that *Works* has substituted "Gross Sales" for the range reference in the SUM( ) and AVG( ) functions.

Freezing Titles

Suppose you had so many salespersons (more than 20) that they couldn't all be displayed on the screen at the same time. You could always scroll the window to see a particular salesperson, but if you scrolled too far, the column titles in row 3 would scroll off the screen.

You could divide the window with the horizontal split bar (see above), but there's a better way of keeping the column titles in view. Move the cursor to highlight cell A4. Then, pull down the Options menu and select **Freeze Titles**.

It looks as if nothing happened, but scroll down to row 25 or so, and watch the column headings on row 3. They're "frozen" in place. You can cancel the effect by selecting **Unfreeze Titles**.

The cell that's highlighted determines which rows and/or columns will be frozen. Specifically, rows *above*, and columns to the *left* of, the highlighted cell will not scroll when you select **Freeze Titles**.

Manual vs. Automatic Calculation

Changing a single cell's value causes the entire spreadsheet to recalculate. This means that *Works* has to check every numerical cell to see if it was affected by the change. The larger your spreadsheet becomes, the more time this calculation process takes.

Works allows you to suspend automatic calculation with the **Manual Calculation** command. Pull down the Options menu, and choose **Manual Calculation**. Now change the Commission Rate in cell E15 and notice that none of the other cells whose values depend on E15 change.

To force *Works* to recalculate at any time, choose **Calculate Now** from the Options menu. To restore the automatic calculation feature, choose **Manual Calculation** again.

☰ Printing the Spreadsheet

Save your spreadsheet again, and check to see that your printer is turned on, selected, and has paper. Choose **Layout** from the File menu. The LAYOUT dialog box for the spreadsheet is identical to the ones for the word processor and the database. You have the same choices for paper size, margins, headers, and footers. (*Note*: Refer to Chapter 2 for complete descriptions of these features.) Change the left and right margins to 0 inches, delete the default footer, and close the dialog box.

Choose **Print** from the Print menu, and press (Enter). Your entire spreadsheet fits on a single page. If it hadn't, *Works* would have divided the spreadsheet so that columns would not have been split between pages.

You can force your own page breaks, horizontally and vertically, by highlighting a row or a column and selecting **Insert Page Break** from the Print menu. Page breaks you set can be removed with the **Delete Page Break** command.

When you're through experimenting with different values for commission rate, close the spreadsheet by selecting **Close** from the File menu.

☰ PROJECT 6: MORTGAGE PAYMENTS

Your company, the Miracle Computer Store, is doing well. So well, in fact, that you have decided to buy a new home. You anticipate paying about $125,000 for the home, financing 80 percent of it through your local bank. Before you actually go out house hunting, you would like to have some idea of what your monthly payments will be.

☰ Designing the Spreadsheet

One way of representing the information would be to list several interest rates across the top of the spreadsheet and several loan amounts down the left side. You could then use one of the spreadsheet's functions to compute the monthly payment for each combination. For the sake of simplicity, assume that the loan would be for 25 years (300 months).

Open a new spreadsheet, and begin by typing the title, **Monthly Mortgage Payments**, into C1. Use the STYLE dialog box to change the text emphasis of C1 to bold. Type the first interest rate, **9.5%**, into B3. (*Note*: *Works* allows you to enter a percentage value either as a percent or as its decimal equivalent.)

Widen column A to 15 spaces. Then, widen columns B through F to 12 spaces. In cell A5, type the loan amount, **100000** (80% of the $125,000 home you're hoping to buy). Highlight column A, and change its format to **Dollar** with no decimal places. Type **Annual Percent** in A3; then highlight row 3 and select **Underline** from the STYLE dialog box. Save this spreadsheet as PAYMENTS, and compare it with Figure 4-21.

The actual monthly payment will be computed in cell B5, but before you attempt the calculation, let's talk about some of the spreadsheet's financial functions.

Figure 4-21 Choose an initial loan rate and mortgage amount

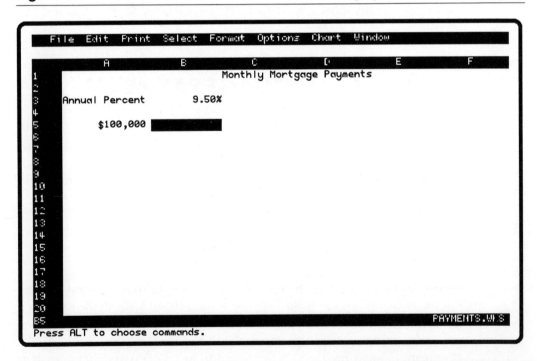

☰ Financial Functions

Of the 54 spreadsheet functions, 11 of them supply results useful in financial calculations. The function you want for your chart is PMT( ), which will calculate the payment for your loan. But before you try to use this function, you need to understand how to specify the three arguments it uses. To calculate the payment, you must specify the loan principal, the interest rate, and the number of payments, *in that order.*

Let's talk about the number of payments, first. You've decided on a 25-year mortgage. Since you'll be paying in monthly installments, that's a total of 300 payments.

Here comes the tricky part. The interest rate specified in the PMT( ) function must be based on the same time period as the payments. In other words, if the payments occur monthly, the interest rate used must be the *monthly* interest rate. That's no problem; you'll just divide the annual interest rate by 12.

The loan principal is the amount of money you receive from the bank, $100,000, or the value in A5.

The format of the PMT( ) function is PMT(Principal,Rate,Term). In the example we've been discussing, the following values would be used: PMT(100000,9.5%/12,300). Notice that the three arguments are separated by commas.

The first argument, 100000, is the loan amount in cell A5. The second argument, 9.5%/12, is the monthly interest rate—the annual rate divided by 12. Notice that you could have computed it by using the cell reference, B3, as B3/12. Therefore, you could (and should) express the Payment function as: PMT(A5,B3/12,300).

Now let's actually enter the formula. Select cell B5, type **=PMT(A5,B3/12,300)** and press Enter. The value 873.6966609 should appear in cell B5.

Change B5's format to **Dollar** with 2 decimal places (Figure 4-22). Notice that *Works* automatically rounds the value to the nearest penny.

☰ Completing the Table

Now that you have calculated the monthly payment for one loan amount and one interest rate, you can have *Works* compute the monthly payments for any loan amount and/or interest rate. You could, for

Figure 4-22 Enter the Payment function as shown

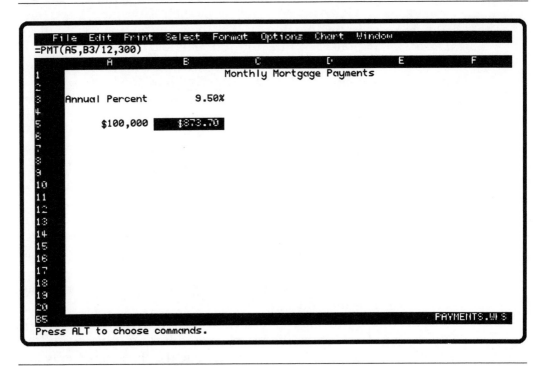

example, change the interest rate in B3 from 9.5% to 9.0% to see what effect this would have on the monthly payment.

Try it. Select cell B3, type **9%**, and press Enter. Notice that the resulting payment changed to $839.20.

Instead of typing different interest rates into B3, you could display several interest rate values across the top of your spreadsheet, in row 3. You might decide to show interest rates incremented by .25%—e.g., 9.00%, 9.25%, 9.50%, etc. A quick method of doing this is to use a formula, =B3+.25%, in cell C3, and then copy the formula across using **Fill Right**.

Begin by highlighting cell C3. Type the formula =**B3+.25%** and press ⌐Enter⌐. The value 0.0925 is correct; it's just not expressed as a percent. But you know what to do about that. Right! Highlight the entire row and change its format to **Percent**.

Now let's fill in the rest of the row of percent values. Highlight the range of cells, C3:F3. Pull down the Edit menu and choose **Fill Right**. Figure 4-23 shows the result.

Figure 4-23 Copy the percentage formula with **Fill Right**

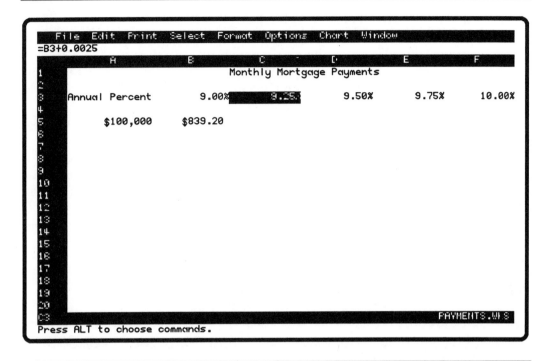

You can use **Fill Right** to copy the formula in B5 into cells C5:F5. Highlight the range B5:F5. Choose **Fill Right**.

Whoops! Small problem. Those new loan amounts don't look right, and they're *not* right. The problem is the relative reference to cell A5 in the Payment function. Highlight cell B5, and press F2 to enter the edit mode.

In the last project, you saw that placing $ symbols in front of both the row and column values in the cell reference (e.g., A5) made that cell reference absolute. That is, its value didn't change as the formula was copied to other rows or other columns. There are two other forms of cell referencing, neither completely relative nor completely absolute.

The expression $A5 will allow the cell reference to vary when it's copied to other rows, but *not* when it's copied to other columns. Similarly, the expression A$5 will allow the cell reference to vary when it's copied to other columns, but not when it's copied to other rows.

You want the reference to the loan amount in A5 to be "locked" in column A, so move the cursor on the formula bar under the "A" and type a $ to change the cell reference to "$A5."

Before you enter this modification, let's make one more change to the formula. Move the cursor under the "3" in cell reference "B3" and type another $, so that this cell reference now reads "B$3." This change locks the interest rate reference to row 3. Your formula should now read: =**PMT($A5,B$3/12,300)**

Press (Enter) to accept the new formula. Again, highlight the range B5:F5, and select **Fill Right**. That's better!

Let's add other loan amounts to column A of your table. Highlight cell A6, and type the formula =**A5+5000**. Press (Enter), and the value $105,000 will appear in A6. Highlight the range A6:A20, and choose **Fill Down** from the Edit menu (Figure 4-24).

Now for the payoff. Highlight all the cells B5:F20. Select **Fill Down**. It's almost magic.

Figure 4-24 Add absolute cell referencing to the payment formula

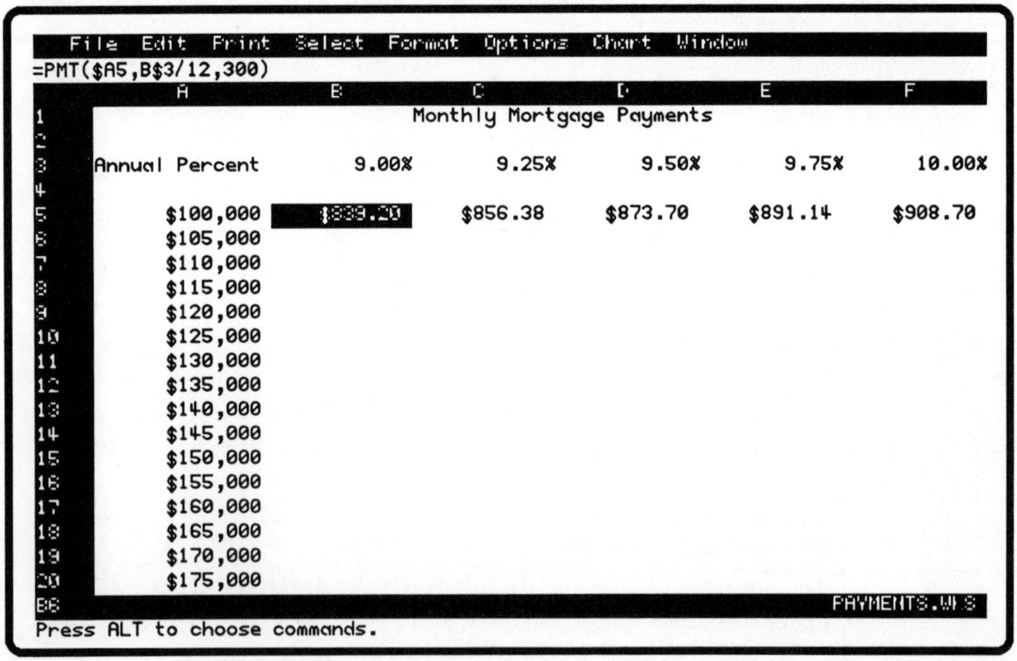

As a final touch, you can change the style of cells A5:A20 to bold. Compare your spreadsheet table with Figure 4-25.

Notice that if you change the loan rate value in cell B3, the other four loan rates will change, as will the entire body of the table. The same is true if you change the value of the initial loan amount in A5. That's why spreadsheets are so powerful. Print your spreadsheet and congratulate yourself.

PROJECT 7: THE CUSTOMER INVOICE

The last spreadsheet project is a simple customer invoice form. The basic layout is straightforward, but the project gives me the opportunity to demonstrate three special spreadsheet functions, as well as some of the standard commands you haven't used yet.

Figure 4-25 Fill in the rest of the table

	A	B	C	D	E	F
	File Edit Print Select Format Options Chart Window					
	=PMT($A20,F$3/12,300)					
1			Monthly Mortgage Payments			
2						
3	Annual Percent	9.00%	9.25%	9.50%	9.75%	10.00%
4						
5	$100,000	$839.20	$856.38	$873.70	$891.14	$908.70
6	$105,000	$881.16	$899.20	$917.38	$935.69	$954.14
7	$110,000	$923.12	$942.02	$961.07	$980.25	$999.57
8	$115,000	$965.08	$984.84	$1,004.75	$1,024.81	$1,045.01
9	$120,000	$1,007.04	$1,027.66	$1,048.44	$1,069.36	$1,090.44
10	$125,000	$1,049.00	$1,070.48	$1,092.12	$1,113.92	$1,135.88
11	$130,000	$1,090.96	$1,113.30	$1,135.81	$1,158.48	$1,181.31
12	$135,000	$1,132.92	$1,156.12	$1,179.49	$1,203.04	$1,226.75
13	$140,000	$1,174.87	$1,198.93	$1,223.18	$1,247.59	$1,272.18
14	$145,000	$1,216.83	$1,241.75	$1,266.86	$1,292.15	$1,317.62
15	$150,000	$1,258.79	$1,284.57	$1,310.54	$1,336.71	$1,363.05
16	$155,000	$1,300.75	$1,327.39	$1,354.23	$1,381.26	$1,408.49
17	$160,000	$1,342.71	$1,370.21	$1,397.91	$1,425.82	$1,453.92
18	$165,000	$1,384.67	$1,413.03	$1,441.60	$1,470.38	$1,499.36
19	$170,000	$1,426.63	$1,455.85	$1,485.28	$1,514.93	$1,544.79
20	$175,000	$1,468.59	$1,498.67	$1,528.97	$1,559.49	$1,590.23

F20   PAYMENTS.WKS
Press ALT to choose commands.

☰ Creating the Form

Figure 4-26 shows most of the text labels for a customer invoice form. Begin by creating a new, blank spreadsheet. Change the width of columns A and E to 12, and column C to 30 characters.

Figure 4-26 Begin this project by adjusting the column widths and entering the cell labels

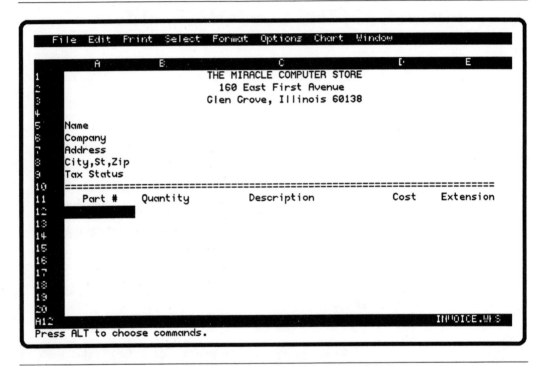

The labels (text) in cells C1:C3 have had their style changed to Center alignment, and Bold emphasis was chosen for C1. The labels in cells A5:A9 are displayed with the standard default format for text. (I'll explain the significance of Tax Status in a moment.)

What you can't see in Figure 4-26 is that cells B5:B8 have had their format changed, even though they're blank. Highlight this range of cells and choose Underline from the STYLE dialog box. That way, when you actually type in the customer's name and address, the text will appear underlined.

The labels in row 11 are centered and underlined.

Drawing a Line across the Screen

The line of equals signs in row 10 was made by typing a bunch of these symbols in cell A10 only, rather than by typing the symbol in all 5 cells (A10:E10).

Select A10, and hold down the equals sign key on your keyboard until you have generated a row of "=" symbols (about 74 of them). Press (Enter), and a row of equals signs should appear. Whoops!

What happened? The alert box (Figure 4-27) says "Missing operand." What does this mean? You'll remember that when you wanted to type a formula into a cell, you had to begin the formula with an equals sign. The equals sign alerted *Works* to interpret the rest of the cell's contents as a formula. Well, *Works* saw the first equals sign and is trying to interpret the rest of them as a formula. Anytime *Works* can't interpret a formula, it displays this dialog box to allow you to correct the formula.

Figure 4-27   Something's wrong with the formula

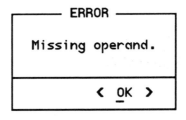

To correct the problem, you need to tell *Works* to treat the line of = symbols as text, and not as a formula. You do this by inserting a quote (") in front of the string of characters.

Press (Enter) to acknowledge the alert message. Then press (Backspace) once to position the cursor at the beginning of the text on the formula bar. Type a quote, and press (Enter) to accept.

Now the row of equals signs appears.

Classifying a Cell's Contents

At the beginning of this chapter, I said that spreadsheet cells could contain either text or numerical values. How does *Works* know whether a cell contains text or a numerical value? *Works* looks at the first character typed into the cell. If that character is an equals sign, the rest of the contents are interpreted as a formula. If the first character is a number, minus sign, plus sign, decimal point, or $ symbol, the contents are interpreted as a number. (*Note*: If a nonnumerical character appears later, for example: "160 East First Avenue," *Works* changes its mind and treats the entry as text.) Entries beginning with any other character are treated as text.

But suppose you want to type a number, or a row of equals signs, and force *Works* to treat the entry as text. You can do this by typing a quote symbol (") as the first character in the cell. *Works* won't display the quote in the cell, but will treat everything that follows as text. (*Note*: The database uses the same scheme to identify string or numeric data.)

Save this spreadsheet to your *Works* Data disk as INVOICE.

Inserting Rows and Columns

Often when you are setting up a spreadsheet, you need to insert one or more blank rows or columns. Suppose, for example, you wanted to insert a blank row between rows 9 and 10 of this spreadsheet to improve the "look."

Highlight any cell in row 10, and select **Insert** from the Edit menu. *Works* asks if you want to insert a row or a column (Figure 4-28). The default choice is Row, so press (**Enter**) to close the dialog box. The original row 10, and everything below it, is shifted down one row. And a new, blank row appears in row 10.

Figure 4-28   You can insert either a row or a column at the cursor position

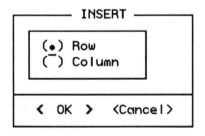

At this point in the development of your Invoice spreadsheet, all the data you've typed has been text, but I know what you're thinking. Suppose some of the cells contained formulas. What about their cell references? Don't worry. When you insert (or delete) rows or columns,

Works automatically changes all cell references in all the formulas to adjust for the added or deleted row or column.

When you insert a column, the column you first selected and all the columns to the right of that column are shifted to the right. The new column appears in the "vacated" space with the standard 10-character column width.

Save your spreadsheet again because you're going to mess it up a little.

☰ Editing Your Spreadsheet

You've used **Copy, Clear,** and **Move** in previous chapters. These commands work more or less the same way in the spreadsheet as they did in the word processor and the data base, but I thought some practice using them might be a good idea.

Copying Cells

The **Copy** command duplicates the contents of selected cells to a different group of cells in the spreadsheet.

Suppose you want to copy the cells A5:A9 into cells D1:D5. Highlight the range A5:A9, then select **Copy** from the Edit menu (or press ⧉Shift + ⧉F3). Notice the word COPY on the status line. *Works* is waiting for you to tell it where to copy the cell data. Highlight cell D1, and press ⧉Enter. *Works* copies the five cells A5:A9 into D1:D5 (Figure 4-29). *Caution:* Any existing data in cells D1:D5 is thrown away without warning.

Blanking Cells with Clear

A quick way to erase the contents of one or more cells is to highlight them, and choose **Clear**. Try it by highlighting cells A5:A9 and selecting **Clear** from the Edit menu. Poof, gone. No warning, and no **Undo** command to recover. Moral: Be careful when you use **Clear**.

When a cell is cleared, its formatting, if any, remains. You can blank entire rows or columns, or even the entire spreadsheet with **Clear**. All you do is highlight the desired cells before you select the command. As with the database, ⧉Shift + ⧉F8 highlights the column containing the cursor, while ⧉Control + ⧉F8 highlights the row containing the cursor.

Figure 4-29 Using the **Copy** command

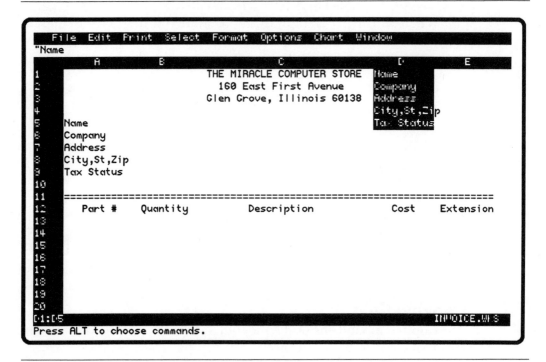

Moving Cells

To move the contents of cells A5:A9 to D1:D5, you used two commands: **Copy**, to duplicate the data into the "target" cells, and **Clear**, to erase the original data. **Move** accomplishes the same action with a single command. Let's move those five cells back to their original location.

Highlight cells D1:D5, and select **Move** from the Edit menu (or press (F3)). Highlight cell A5, and press (Enter).

You can move one or more cells, entire columns, or entire rows. If you try to move data into cells that already have their own data (in other words, nonempty cells), *Works* will throw away the existing data with no warning. So be careful where you move things.

If you begin a move (or a copy) and decide not to complete it, you can press (Esc) to abort the procedure.

Delete vs. Clear

You might wonder what the difference is between the commands **Delete** and **Clear**. **Delete** is used to remove entire rows or columns, and it removes them, cells and all. When you **Delete** a row, for example, that row completely disappears. By comparison, if you **Clear** an entire row, a row of blank cells remains.

Protecting Cells

Works allows you to protect cells so that they cannot be accidentally changed or erased. Select **Protect** from the Options menu. Now try to erase the contents of any cell with **Clear**. Try to type anything into any cell. When you press ⌐Enter⌐ , *Works* displays an alert box saying that "Locked cells cannot be changed."

Locked cells? Each cell in the spreadsheet can be either locked or unlocked. *Works* initially locks all cells in a new spreadsheet.

When you turn the **Protect** option on, two things happen. First, as you saw a moment ago, you are prevented from typing anything into locked cells. Second, most of the commands in the Edit menu and all of the commands in the Format menu become inoperative.

Let's see what happens when you unlock cells. Disable cell protection by selecting **Protect** again. (*Note*: You can tell whether cell protection is "on" by looking at the Options menu. If a bullet symbol [•] appears next to the **Protect** command, cell protection has been activated.) With cell protection off, highlight cells B5:B9. Display the STYLE dialog box, and notice that a dash appears in the Locked check box. Press ⌐Alt⌐ + ⌐K⌐ once, and an "X" appears in the check box. Press ⌐Alt⌐ + ⌐K⌐ again, and the check box becomes blank. This unlocks the highlighted cells. Close the dialog box.

Now, select **Protect**, highlight one of the cells in the range B5:B9, and type something into it. No problem. But, highlight any other cell outside that range, and the **Protect** feature will prevent you from altering that cell's contents. This is the procedure for selectively protecting cells in a spreadsheet.

Before continuing with the project, turn off cell protection.

Restoring the Spreadsheet

Throw away this version of your spreadsheet by selecting **Close** from the File menu. (You did save this spreadsheet earlier, didn't you?) Type **N** when *Works* asks you if you want to save any changes. Then, select **Open** from the File menu, and read in the INVOICE.WKS spreadsheet from your data disk. (*Note*: Refer to Chapter 2 if you need help with the OPEN dialog box.)

☰ Adding the Formulas

Let's fill in some data on your Customer Invoice. Figure 4-30 shows data for a typical customer. Tax Status refers to whether the customer pays state sales tax or is tax exempt. For this sample spreadsheet, I've set up a numerical code for Tax Status. A "1" means normal sales tax (in this example, 7%), "2" means tax exempt. Enter a **1** in cell B9 for the Tax Status code, and change the alignment to Left with the STYLE dialog box. While you're changing formats, change columns D and E to Dollar with 2 decimal places. And change cells B13:B16 to Center alignment. Enter all the customer data from Figure 4-30 into your spreadsheet.

Figure 4-30 Enter the invoice data

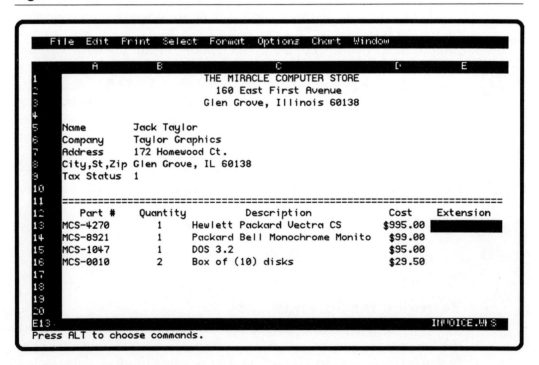

The Extension value, in column E, is the product of Quantity times Cost. Select cell E13, and enter the formula **=B13*D13**. Press (Enter) to accept the formula. Copy this formula into cells E14:E16 using the **Fill Down** command. (*Note*: Refer to Project 6 if you need help with this command.)

Type 12 underscore characters (_) into cell C17. Type the label **Merchandise Total** into C18 and change the alignment to Right. Compute the total for merchandise in cell E18 using the formula **=SUM(E13:E16)**. (*Note*: you'll find a complete discussion of the Sum function in Project 5.)

Scroll the spreadsheet down, and add the labels you see in Figure 4-31 to cells C19 through C22. Change their format to Align Right, and make C22 bold.

Figure 4-31 Compute the Extensions and use the SUM( ) function to calculate the total

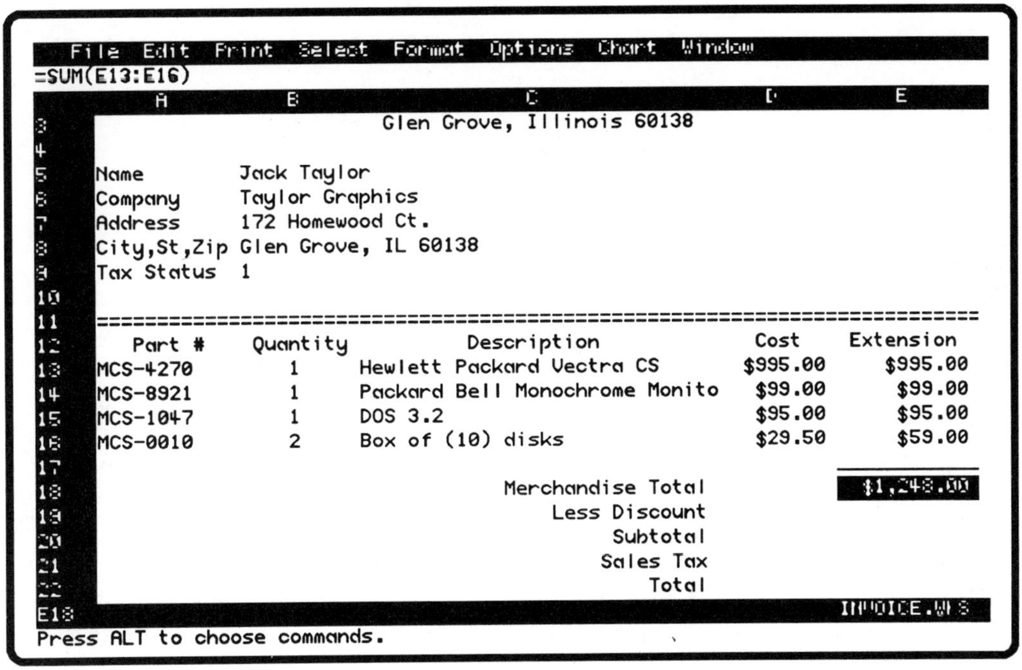

Using a Lookup Table

As part of the holiday promotion for your store, you have advertised a special discount, based on the amount of merchandise a customer buys. If a customer's purchases total less than $500, no discount is given. Between $500 and $1,000, you're offering a 5% discount. From $1,000 to $2,000, the discount increases to 8%. From $2,000 to $4,000, it's 10%; and above $4,000, you'll discount 12%. Table 4-2 summarizes this discount schedule.

Table 4-2   Discount rate schedule for lookup table

Merchandise Total	Discount
0	0%
500	5%
1000	8%
2000	10%
4000	12%

You need a way of looking up the correct discount, based on the merchandise total. In the example you've been using, the $1,248 total should result in a discount of 8%. How do we get *Works* to do this?

First, let's copy the discount schedule from Table 4-2 into the spreadsheet. Scroll the spreadsheet down to row 50. Type the discount schedule into columns A and B, beginning at row 50 (Figure 4-32). Change the format of cells A50:A54 to Dollar with 0 decimal places.

What we need now is a function that will compare the merchandise total with the values in A50:A54, find the largest value that is either less than or equal to the merchandise total, and return the appropriate value from column B.

Let me explain that again, using the merchandise total of $1,248. Compare this value with the first value in column A of your lookup table (that's what a table like this is called). Is $0 either less than or equal to $1,248? Yes, so look at the next value in the table. Is $500 either less than or equal to $1,248? Yes, so look at the next value in the table. Is $1,000 either less than or equal to $1,248? Yes, so look at the next value in the table. Is $2,000 either less than or equal to

Figure 4-32   Enter the lookup table

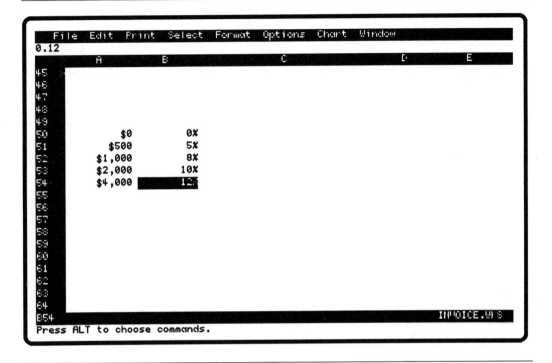

$1,194? No, so $1,000 is the *largest* value in the table that is either less than or equal to $1,248.

Now look at the cell in column B that is adjacent to $1,000 in column A (B52). It contains a value of 8%. This is the value you want the VLOOKUP( ) function to return.

Actually, *Works* supplies two lookup functions that will do the job: HLOOKUP( ) and VLOOKUP( ). HLOOKUP( ) (or Horizontal Lookup) assumes that the two sets of data (merchandise total and discount percent, in this example) are arranged in two *rows*. VLOOKUP( ) (or Vertical Lookup) assumes that the two sets of data are arranged in two columns, as is the case here. So, we'll use the VLOOKUP( ) function.

Scroll up and highlight D19, the cell that will contain the Lookup function. Change its format to Percent with no decimal places.

With D19 still highlighted, begin the lookup formula by typing **=VLookup(.**

The VLOOKUP( ) function requires three arguments. The first is the value to be compared—in this example, the Merchandise Total value in E18. Type **E18** and a comma. The second argument is the cell range of the entire lookup table. For your lookup table, that range is from A50 to B54, so type **A50:B54** and another comma. The third argument is the number of the column that contains the results of the lookup.

Your lookup table consists of two columns. Think of the cursor sitting in the first column of your lookup table. How far would it have to move in order to be in column B? One column, right? Type **1**, as the third argument in the VLOOKUP( ) function, close the parentheses, and press (Enter) (Figure 4-33). A discount rate of 8% should appear in D19.

Let's test the VLOOKUP( ) function. Change the quantity value in B13 from 1 to 2. This will change the Extension price in E13 to $1,990.00, change the Merchandise Total to $2,243.00, and should change the discount rate to 10%. Change the quantity in B13 back to 1.

Figure 4-33 VLOOKUP( ) returns the correct percent from the lookup table

```
   File  Edit  Print  Select  Format  Options  Chart  Window
=VLOOKUP(E18,A50:B54,1)
        A          B              C              D        E
 5   Name        Jack Taylor
 6   Company     Taylor Graphics
 7   Address     172 Homewood Ct.
 8   City,St,Zip Glen Grove, IL 60138
 9   Tax Status  1
10
11   ===========================================================
12      Part #   Quantity       Description        Cost    Extension
13   MCS-4270        1     Hewlett Packard Vectra CS  $995.00   $995.00
14   MCS-8921        1     Packard Bell Monochrome Monito $99.00    $99.00
15   MCS-1047        1     DOS 3.2                  $95.00    $95.00
16   MCS-0010        2     Box of (10) disks        $29.50    $59.00
17                                                           _____
18                              Merchandise Total             $1,248.00
19                               Less Discount        8.
20                                    Subtotal
21                                   Sales Tax
22                                       Total
23
24
D19                                                       INVOICE.WKS
Press ALT to choose commands.
```

You want cell E19 to compute the actual discount, in dollars. The discount is the product of the discount rate times the merchandise total. Select E19, type the formula =**D19*E18**, and press Enter. With an 8% discount rate, the actual discount in E19 should be $99.84.

Compute the Subtotal (merchandise total minus discount) in cell E20 with the formula =**E18-E19**. The value $1,148.16 should appear in E20.

The N/A Function

Before you compute the Sales Tax in your Invoice, I'd like to modify the Lookup table a bit. Use the **Go To** command to highlight cell B50. Choose **Go To** from the Select menu, type **B50** in the **Reference**: text box (Figure 4-34), and press (Enter).

Figure 4-34   The GO TO dialog box

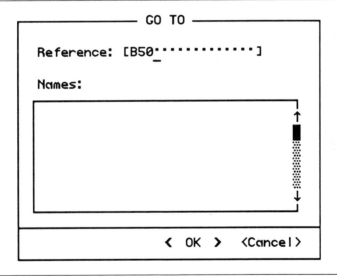

If a customer purchases less than $500, the discount rate is 0%. Instead of the 0% value, I'd like the Lookup function to return a value of N/A (Not Available). *Works* has a special function, called NA( ) (surprisingly enough), that you can substitute for the 0 value in B50. With B50 selected, type =**NA( )**, and press (Enter).

Scroll back to the main body of the invoice, using either **Go To** or the arrow keys.

To see that the Lookup function returns N/A as a value when the total is less than $500, change the Quantity value in B13 to 0 (Figure 4-35). What happened? Lookup returned a value of N/A, as expected, in D19. But N/A also appeared in cells E19 and E20. The reason is that the value, N/A, is not the same as a value of 0. And any calculation that uses a value of N/A will automatically evaluate to N/A itself. Since the discount in E19 depends on the value in D19, an N/A in D19 causes an N/A in E19. Similarly, the Subtotal result in E20 depends on the contents in E19. So E20 shows an N/A value, too. What can you do about this?

Figure 4-35   Testing the NA( ) function

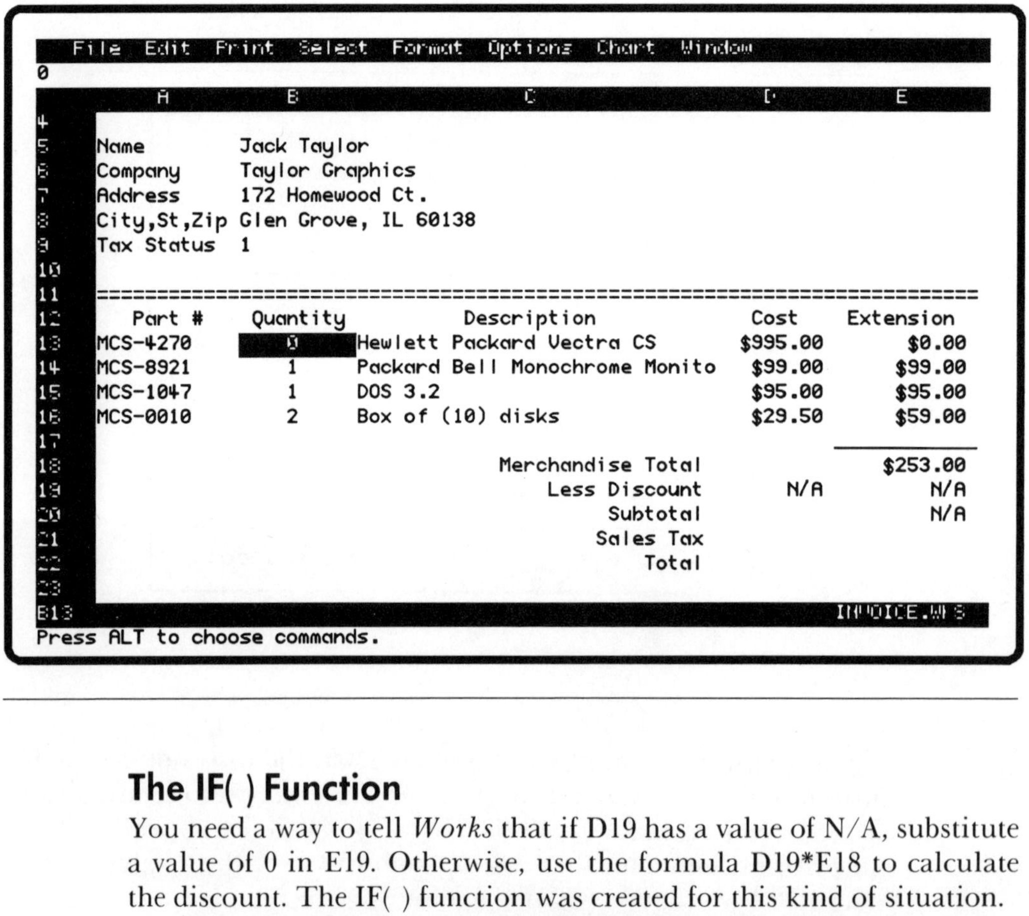

The IF( ) Function

The IF( ) Function

You need a way to tell *Works* that if D19 has a value of N/A, substitute a value of 0 in E19. Otherwise, use the formula D19*E18 to calculate the discount. The IF( ) function was created for this kind of situation.

The IF( ) function tests a condition to see if it is true or false. If the condition is true, one result is returned; if the condition is false, another result is returned. Here's an example of the function: IF(A1>0,25,100). The first argument is the condition, in the example, A1>0. The second argument, 25, is the value the function will return if the condition is true—in other words, if the contents of A1 are greater than 0. The third argument is the value the function will return if the condition is *not* true, that is, if A1 is not greater than 0.

The > symbol is one of six comparisons that may be performed. Here is a list of all six.

Symbol	Comparison
=	equals
<	is less than
<=	is less than or equal to
>	is greater than
>=	is greater than or equal to
<>	is not equal to

Here is how you can use the IF( ) function to avoid a value of N/A appearing in E19. One way uses the function ISNA( ) as the IF function's comparison. The formula =IF(ISNA(D19),0,D19*E18) says that if the value in cell D19 is N/A, return a value of 0. If, however, D19 contains anything except N/A, compute the result that is the product of D19 times E18.

Select cell E19, and type in the above formula. Press (Enter), and compare the result with Figure 4-36. Then, change the Quantity value in B13 back to 1.

The CHOOSE( ) Function

The Tax Status value in B9 was created to control the charging of Sales Tax. Some of your customers may belong to organizations that are exempt from sales tax. When the tax code value in B9 is 1, *Works* should calculate standard sales tax at 7% of the Subtotal. When the tax code is 2, no tax should be charged. The CHOOSE( ) function is perfect for this situation.

CHOOSE( ) takes a minimum of two arguments. The first argument is an index value. The second, third, fourth, etc., arguments are possible results returned by the Choose function. Here is an example. The formula =Choose(G5,14,85,52) will return a value of 14 if G5, the index value, has a value of 0. It will return a value of 85 if G5 has a value of 1, a value of 52 if G5 has a value of 2, and so on.

You don't have to stop at three choices. You can have as many choices in a Choose function as you want, as long as you don't exceed

Figure 4-36 Use IF( ) to solve the N/A problem

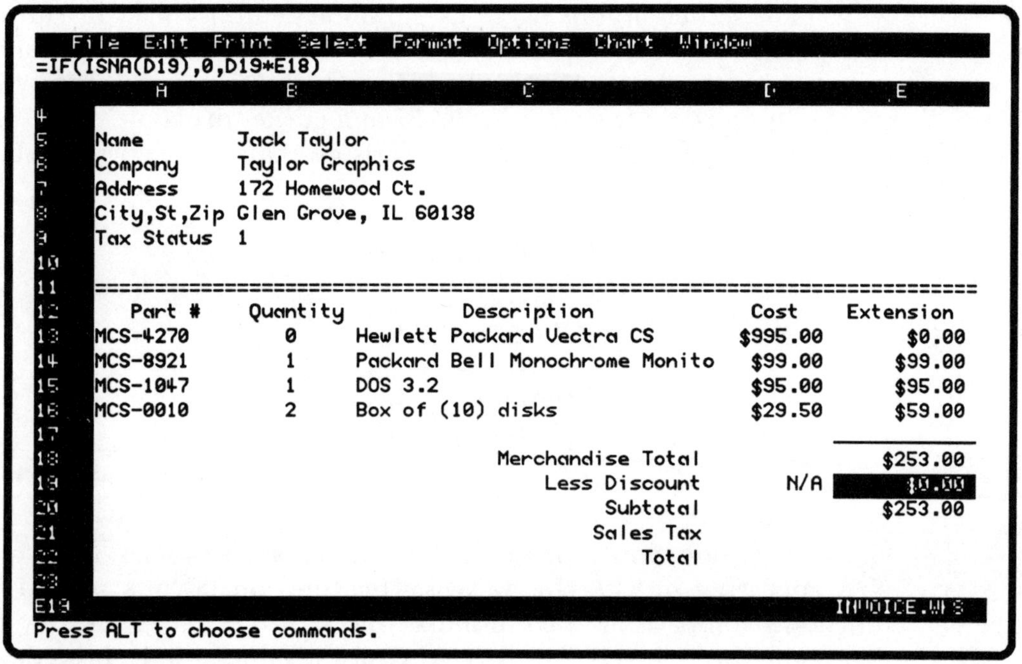

```
   File  Edit  Print  Select  Format  Options  Chart  Window
=IF(ISNA(D19),0,D19*E18)
            A              B                   C                 D          E
 4
 5    Name          Jack Taylor
 6    Company       Taylor Graphics
 7    Address       172 Homewood Ct.
 8    City,St,Zip   Glen Grove, IL 60138
 9    Tax Status    1
10
11    ===================================================================
12       Part #     Quantity          Description           Cost    Extension
13    MCS-4270         0       Hewlett Packard Vectra CS   $995.00      $0.00
14    MCS-8921         1       Packard Bell Monochrome Monito  $99.00    $99.00
15    MCS-1047         1       DOS 3.2                      $95.00     $95.00
16    MCS-0010         2       Box of (10) disks            $29.50     $59.00
17
18                               Merchandise Total                    $253.00
19                                  Less Discount          N/A          $0.00
20                                       Subtotal                     $253.00
21                                      Sales Tax
22                                          Total
23
E19                                                              INVOICE.WKS
Press ALT to choose commands.
```

the maximum number of characters allowed in any formula, 256. There is one caution you must observe when using CHOOSE( ). The index value must not be less than 0, nor greater than the number of possible results.

Select cell D21 for the location of the tax percentage, and change its format to **Percent** with no decimal places. Type in the formula **=CHOOSE(B9,ERR( ),7%,0%)** (Figure 4-37). With a value of 1 in B9, the tax in D21 should be 7%. (I'll explain the ERR( ) function in a moment.)

Now, what about that expression, ERR( ), in the CHOOSE( ) function? Suppose you were to forget to enter a value into cell B9. *Works* interprets a blank cell as having a value of 0. Select B9, and choose **Clear**. The cleared cell evaluates as 0, and the CHOOSE( ) function selects the first of its options, ERR( ). Instead of returning a value of 7% or 0%, the CHOOSE( ) function displays "ERR" in D21. That's what *Works* returns when it encounters an ERR( ) function. (*Note: Works* will also display "ERR" if it cannot evaluate a formula.)

Figure 4-37 Use CHOOSE( ) to compute the tax percentage

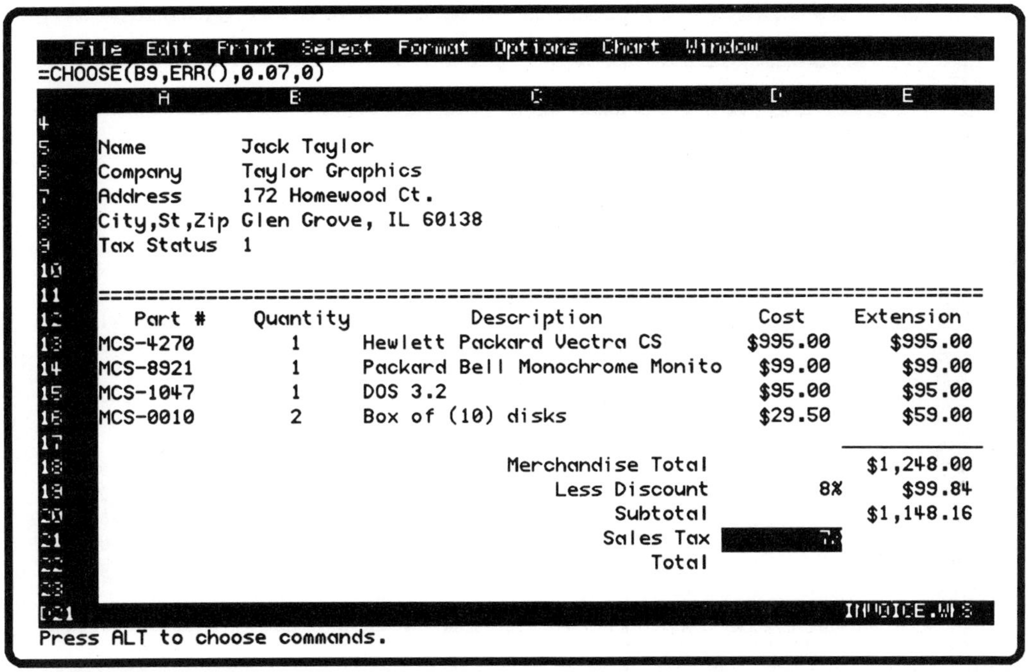

Enter a value of 1 in B9 again, and CHOOSE will return the 7% value in D19.

Complete the spreadsheet by computing the actual tax in cell E21, using the formula =D21*E20. Then calculate the Total in E22 as the sum of E20 and E21 (=E20+E21). Compare your spreadsheet with Figure 4-38.

☰ Printing Part of the Spreadsheet

You want to print out the invoice portion of the spreadsheet, but not the Lookup table. This is easy if you insert a page break between the invoice and the table. Scroll the spreadsheet down to row 45, highlight this row, and select **Insert Page Break** from the Print menu. *Works* will place a page break indicator, », just after the row number. This will place the invoice on page 1 and the lookup table on page 2.

Figure 4-38 Calculate the Sales Tax and Total

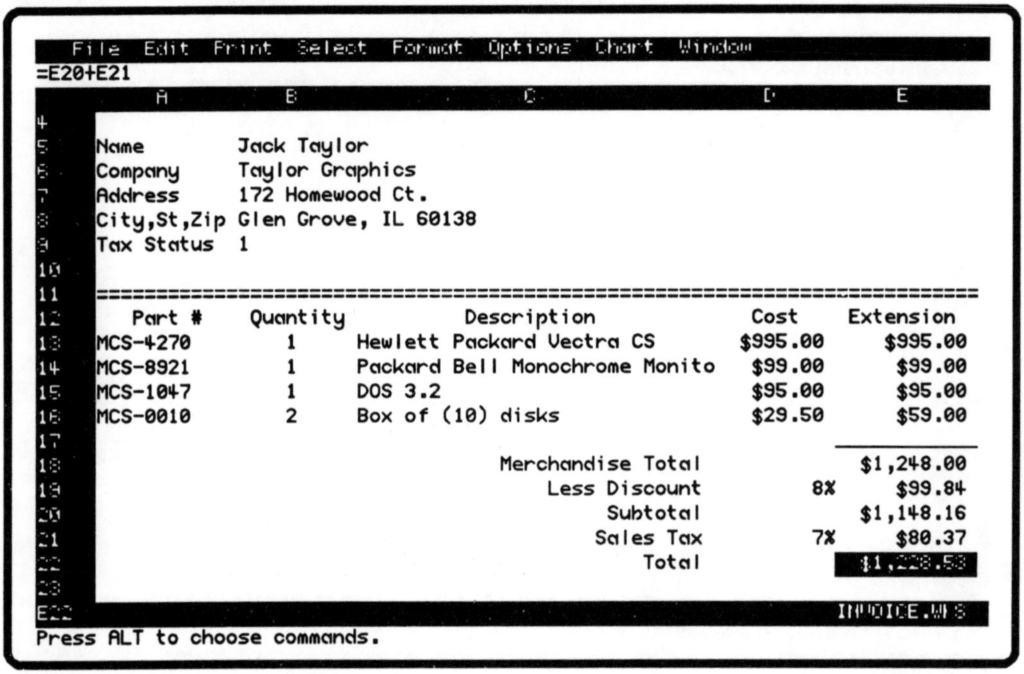

```
 File  Edit  Print  Select  Format  Options  Chart  Window
=E20+E21
           A          B              C                D         E
 4
 5     Name       Jack Taylor
 6     Company    Taylor Graphics
 7     Address    172 Homewood Ct.
 8     City,St,Zip Glen Grove, IL 60138
 9     Tax Status 1
10
11     ================================================================
12       Part #    Quantity        Description        Cost     Extension
13     MCS-4270       1      Hewlett Packard Vectra CS  $995.00   $995.00
14     MCS-8921       1      Packard Bell Monochrome Monito $99.00  $99.00
15     MCS-1047       1      DOS 3.2                    $95.00    $95.00
16     MCS-0010       2      Box of (10) disks          $29.50    $59.00
17
18                                  Merchandise Total            $1,248.00
19                                     Less Discount    8%          $99.84
20                                          Subtotal             $1,148.16
21                                         Sales Tax    7%          $80.37
22                                             Total             $1,228.53
23
E22                                                        INVOICE.WKS
Press ALT to choose commands.
```

Save your spreadsheet. Make sure your printer is turned on and selected, then choose **Print** from the Print menu, and look at its dialog box (Figure 4-39). Normally, you print all the pages of your documents. This time, you'll select the option Print Specific Pages.

Press (Alt) + (S) to place an "X" in the Print Specific Pages option. Then, press (Alt) + (G) to move the cursor to the **Pages:** text box, type 1, and press (Enter).

Only page 1, containing the invoice portion of your spreadsheet, will be printed. Figure 4-40 shows the printed invoice.

Another way to print part of a spreadsheet is to highlight the section you want to print, then choose **Set Print Area** from the Print menu. When you print the spreadsheet, only those cells that were highlighted when you selected **Set Print Area** will be printed. To print all of the spreadsheet again, highlight the entire spreadsheet (press (Control) + (F8) followed by (Shift) + (F8)). Then select **Set Print Area**.

otot necessary here.

Figure 4-39 Use the PRINT dialog box to print page 1 only

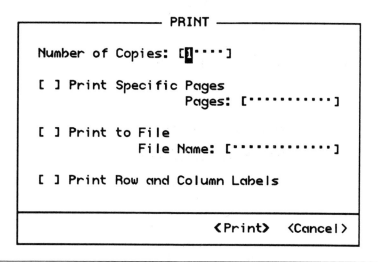

Figure 4-40 Page 1 of the INVOICE spreadsheet

```
                    THE MIRACLE COMPUTER STORE
                      160 East First Avenue
                     Glen Grove, Illinois 60138
Name         Jack Taylor
Company      Taylor Graphics
Address      172 Homewood Ct.
City,St,Zip  Glen Grove, IL 60138
Tax Status   1

================================================================
  Part #    Quantity      Description          Cost    Extension
MCS-4270       1      Hewlett Packard Vectra CS  $995.00   $995.00
MCS-8921       1      Packard Bell Monochrome Monito $99.00  $99.00
MCS-1047       1      DOS 3.2                    $95.00    $95.00
MCS-0010       2      Box of (10) disks          $29.50    $59.00

                      Merchandise Total                 $1,248.00
                         Less Discount         8%          $99.84
                              Subtotal                  $1,148.16
                             Sales Tax         7%          $80.37
                                 Total                  $1,228.53
```

☰ Final Comments

If you've gotten this far, you've just finished the hardest chapter in the book. You've used all the Edit commands except the **Copy Special** command, and you'll use this command in Chapter 8. You've used all the Print commands (except **Font** and **Print Chart**, which I'm saving for the next chapter). You've used all of the Select commands, most of the Format commands, and all the Options.

Only the Chart commands have been ignored—and for good reason. They're the subject of Chapter 5. Before you go on, though, I recommend that you review any of the commands or procedures that may seem a little hazy to you. Repeat the projects, or parts of them; better yet, create your own projects. The spreadsheet, more than any other application, requires a great deal of practice before it becomes truly useful.

Yes, I know you didn't use all the functions in the chapter projects. For space reasons, I had to choose what I hope was a representative sampling. Many of the functions behave similarly, so that your experience here should help you to understand how to use functions that were not discussed.

If you run into trouble, you can always send a question to me via the *Works* Bulletin Board. (*Note*: The bulletin board is discussed in Chapter 6.)

We still have lots to do, so move on to Chapter 5 as soon as you're ready.

Chapter **5**
SPREADSHEET GRAPHICS

This chapter is really an extension of Chapter 4. It covers the one major spreadsheet topic not mentioned there: drawing graphs or charts from spreadsheet data. *Works* can draw two principal types of charts: Series (line, bar, multiple bar, etc.) and Pie.

I've designed three projects that should illustrate most of the charting features. The first two use data from the first spreadsheet project in Chapter 4, the project on sales commissions. If you haven't done this project, I suggest you take a few minutes and create the spreadsheet— at least the first three columns of it.

The last charting project will use data from a spreadsheet you'll create as part of the project.

PROJECT 8: A PIE CHART OF GROSS SALES

Your first charting project will be a pie chart, using data from the Commissions spreadsheet you constructed in the last chapter. Boot up *Works* or, if you're already in the program, choose **Open** from the File menu. From the OPEN dialog box, highlight and open SALESCOM.WKS from the list of documents on your *Works* Data disk.

You would like to draw a pie chart illustrating the Gross Sales of your sales staff. Before you draw the chart, though, notice that the values for the pie wedges, the Gross Sales values, are in column B from row 4 to row 9. The salespersons' names are in column A.

Drawing the Chart

Pull down the Chart menu, and select **New**. Notice the changes in the menu bar (the lack of File and Edit menus, and the presence of the Data menu) and the word CHART on the status line (Figure 5-1). This is the chart window.

To draw your pie chart, *Works* needs to know the values to use for the pie wedges. The values for the wedges are in cells B4:B9. You know this, but you need to let *Works* know it before it can plot your pie chart.

Highlight the range B4:B9. Then, pull down the Data menu and select **1st Y-Series**. This action assigns the range of highlighted cells to the 1st Y-Series, and *Works* creates a pie chart from the values specified in the 1st Y-Series.

Figure 5-1   The Chart window

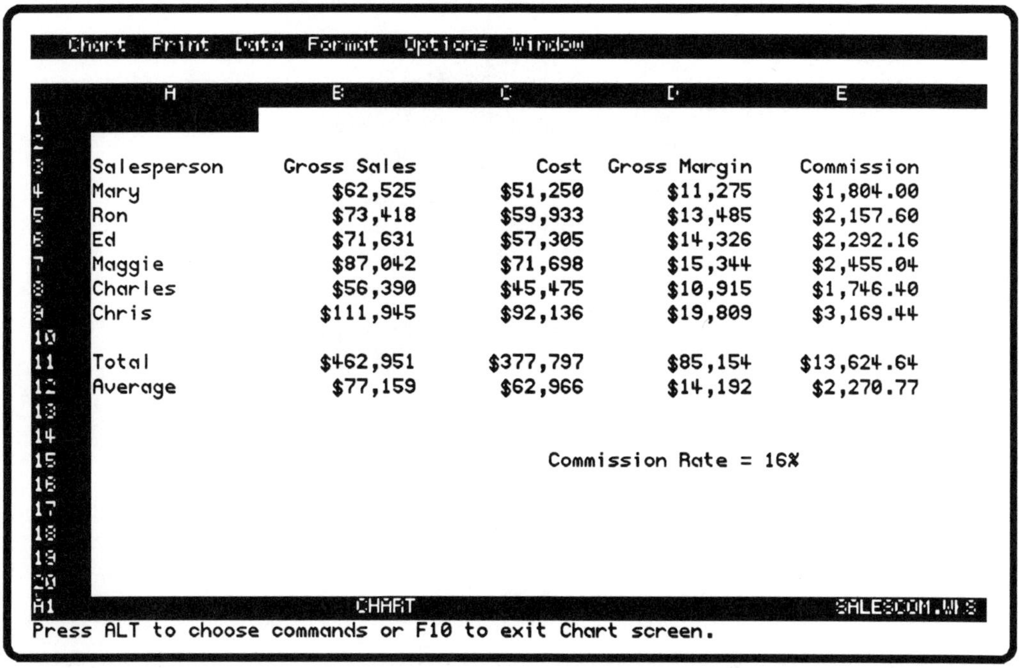

```
┌─────────────────────────────────────────────────────────────────┐
│  Chart  Print  Data  Format  Options  Window                     │
│ � ═══════════════════════════════════════════════════════════════ │
│          A            B            C          D            E      │
│ 1                                                                 │
│ 2                                                                 │
│ 3    Salesperson  Gross Sales     Cost   Gross Margin  Commission │
│ 4    Mary            $62,525    $51,250    $11,275     $1,804.00  │
│ 5    Ron             $73,418    $59,933    $13,485     $2,157.60  │
│ 6    Ed              $71,631    $57,305    $14,326     $2,292.16  │
│ 7    Maggie          $87,042    $71,698    $15,344     $2,455.04  │
│ 8    Charles         $56,390    $45,475    $10,915     $1,746.40  │
│ 9    Chris          $111,945    $92,136    $19,809     $3,169.44  │
│ 10                                                                │
│ 11   Total         $462,951   $377,797    $85,154    $13,624.64   │
│ 12   Average        $77,159    $62,966    $14,192     $2,270.77   │
│ 13                                                                │
│ 14                                                                │
│ 15                       Commission Rate = 16%                    │
│ 16                                                                │
│ 17                                                                │
│ 18                                                                │
│ 19                                                                │
│ 20                                                                │
│ A1 ────────────────── CHART ──────────────────── SALESCOM.WKS ─  │
│ Press ALT to choose commands or F10 to exit Chart screen.        │
└─────────────────────────────────────────────────────────────────┘
```

Let's view this pie chart. First, pull down the Format menu and select **Pie**, so that *Works* knows what type of chart to draw. Then, select **View** from the Chart menu (Figure 5-2).

Works creates a pie chart with six wedges, one for each value in the range B4:B9. Each wedge is drawn with a different pattern. (*Note*: If you have a color monitor, each wedge will appear in a different color instead of a different monochrome pattern. If you wish to see the wedges in patterns instead of colors, select **Format for B&W** from the Options menu.) The size of each wedge is determined by the ratio of each value divided by the sum of all six values. This ratio, expressed as a percent, is used to label each wedge.

But you'd like to know *which* salesperson corresponds to each wedge. You want *Works* to label the wedges with the names in column A of your spreadsheet. Press any key to display the Chart window. Then, highlight the range A4:A9, and select **X-Series** from the Data menu. For pie charts, X-Series holds the range of cells used to label the pie wedges.

Figure 5-2 A pie chart from the SALESCOM spreadsheet

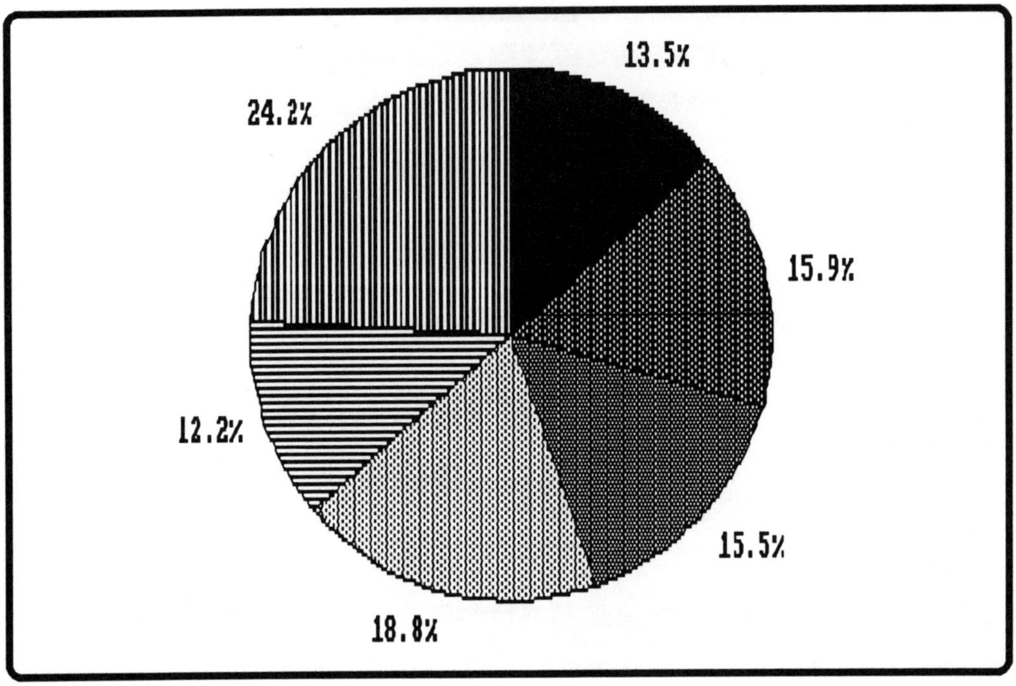

Display the pie chart again (choose **View** from the Chart menu), and see that *Works* has, indeed, labeled the wedges with the names of your salespeople (Figure 5-3).

≡ Customizing the Chart

Let's add a title to your pie chart. Return to the Chart window (by pressing any key). Choose **Titles** from the Data menu. Figure 5-4 shows the TITLES dialog box. Type **"GROSS SALES** in the **Chart Title:** text box, press (Tab), and type **"Week of December 1** in the **Subtitle:** text box.

(*Note*: Begin the Chart Title and Subtitle with quotes ["] so that *Works* will treat your entries as text. Otherwise, *Works* will check to

Figure 5-3   Add labels to the chart

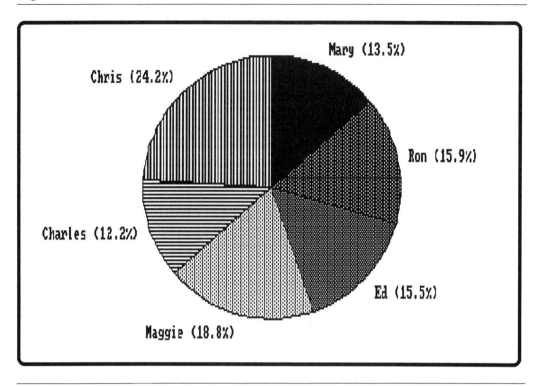

Figure 5-4   The TITLES dialog box

```
┌──────────────────── TITLES ────────────────────┐
│                                                 │
│  Chart Title:  [·····················]          │
│  Subtitle:     [·····················]          │
│  X-Axis:       [·····················]          │
│  Y-Axis:       [·····················]          │
│  Right Y-Axis: [·····················]          │
│                                                 │
├─────────────────────────────────────────────────┤
│              <  OK  >   <Cancel>                │
└─────────────────────────────────────────────────┘
```

see if your title has been used as a cell reference name. If it has, and "Gross Sales" was used this way in the last chapter, *Works* will substitute the cell value for the cell reference name. Beginning your title with ["] prevents this from happening.)

Close the dialog box, and view the chart again. Notice that the chart title is centered at the top of the chart, with the subtitle directly below it.

Suppose you wanted to emphasize Chris' contribution to the gross sales. One way of doing this is to *explode* Chris' pie wedge. Here's how. Pull down the Format menu, and select **Data Format**. The dialog box lists the pie wedges by number (in the **Slices:** list box), the available colors (in the **Colors:** list box), and the available patterns (in the **Patterns:** list box). Use the ↓ and ↑ keys to scroll through the slices, and you'll see that each slice, by default, uses "Auto" for both color and pattern. This choice cycles the colors of the pie wedges if you have a color monitor, or cycles the patterns if you have a monochrome monitor.

Ignore the colors and patterns for now (they're discussed in the next project). Chris' wedge is number 6 because Chris is the sixth salesperson listed in the spreadsheet. Highlight number 6 in the **Slices:** list box. Press Alt + E to select the Exploded option for this slice (Figure 5-5). Then press Alt + F to format this slice. Close the dialog box by pressing Esc.

Figure 5-5 The DATA FORMAT dialog box

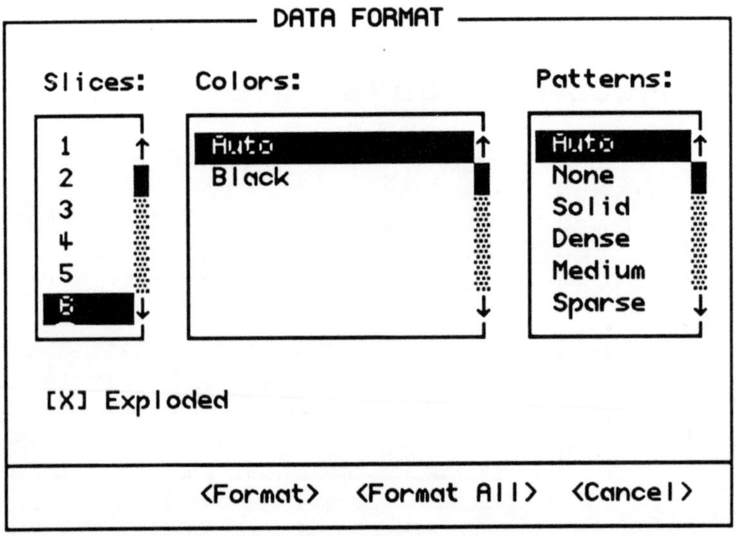

View the pie chart and see the effect of exploding one of the slices. You can draw a box around the chart by selecting **Show Border** from the Options menu. Figure 5-6 shows the finished chart.

If you display the Chart menu, you'll see your pie chart listed at the bottom as "Chart1." You can rename the chart to something more descriptive with the CHARTS dialog box. Select **Charts** from the Chart menu. Press (Alt) + (N) to move the cursor to the **Name:** text box. Type the name **Gross Sales**. Then, press (Alt) + (R) to rename the chart. Notice that the chart name changes in the **Charts** list box. Close the dialog box by pressing (Esc).

Now, pull down the Charts menu, and see that the chart's new name appears at the bottom of the menu. Roll up the menu by pressing (Esc).

When you save your spreadsheet, and now would be a good time to do it, *Works* saves your charts (up to eight of them) along with

Figure 5-6   Explode a pie slice to emphasize it

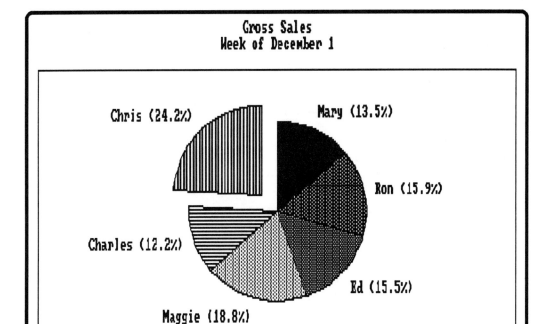

the spreadsheet. (*Note*: You can't save from the Chart window. Select **Exit Chart** from the chart menu, then save the spreadsheet. To return to the Chart window, choose **Define** from the Chart menu.)

☰ Printing the Chart

To complete this project, let's print the pie chart. First, however, you need to tell *Works* which printer to use. When you ran the *Works* Setup program, you selected at least one text printer and at least one chart printer. You may be using the same printer for both purposes, but you need to identify your choice for chart printer to *Works*. Choose **Select Chart Printer** from the Print menu, highlight your choice for chart printer (Figure 5-7), and press (Enter). (*Note*: You must be in the Chart window to see this command in the Print menu.)

Figure 5-7   You must select a chart printer before you can print the chart

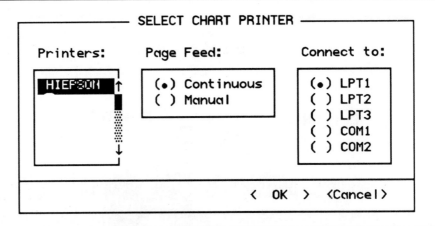

```
┌─────────────── SELECT CHART PRINTER ───────────────┐
│                                                      │
│   Printers:       Page Feed:        Connect to:      │
│  ┌──────────┐↑   ┌───────────────┐  ┌──────────────┐ │
│  │ HIEFSON  │    │(•) Continuous │  │(•) LPT1      │ │
│  │          │    │( ) Manual     │  │( ) LPT2      │ │
│  │          │    └───────────────┘  │( ) LPT3      │ │
│  │          │                       │( ) COM1      │ │
│  │          │↓                      │( ) COM2      │ │
│  └──────────┘                       └──────────────┘ │
│                                                      │
│                          <  OK  >   <Cancel>         │
└──────────────────────────────────────────────────────┘
```

If the Printers list box is empty, you didn't specify a chart printer during the *Works* setup procedure. If you want to print your chart, you'll have to exit the Chart window, save your spreadsheet, quit *Works*, and rerun the Setup program to add a chart printer. Then, run *Works*, open the SALESCOM spreadsheet, and resume the project.

Once you've selected a chart printer, printing is easy—just select **Print** from the Print menu. But before you print, let's change the *font* for the chart's title, subtitle, and labels.

Pull down the Print menu, and select **Title Font**. *Works* provides a variety of fonts for the chart title. Each font comes in one or more sizes. The fonts you'll see in the **Fonts:** list box depend on your choice for chart printer.

Highlight the Bold Italic Roman B font (you may have to scroll the **Fonts:** list box). Then, press (Alt) + (S) to move the cursor to the **Sizes:** list box, and highlight the 36 point size (Figure 5-8). Press (Enter) to accept.

Figure 5-8 Change the font and size of the chart's title

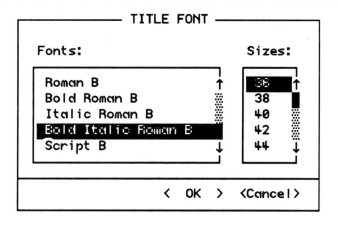

Pull down the Print menu again, and select **Other Font**. This dialog box looks and behaves exactly the same as the TITLE FONT dialog box, but the choices you make in the OTHER FONT dialog box affect all of the text in your pie chart *except* the title. Choose Bold Roman B font in a size of 18 points. Press (Enter), and let's look at the pie chart.

Select **View** from the Chart menu, and you won't see any difference in the appearance of the pie chart's text. That's because it takes extra time to draw those special fonts you chose for chart text. By default, *Works* ignores your font choices and displays its own *screen* font, which it can draw quickly. You can tell *Works* to display the fonts you've chosen by selecting **Show Printer Fonts** from the Options menu.

Try it. Return to the Chart window, select **Show Printer Fonts**, and view the pie chart again. This time, you'll see the fonts you've chosen (Figure 5-9).

Figure 5-9 Show fonts as they will be printed

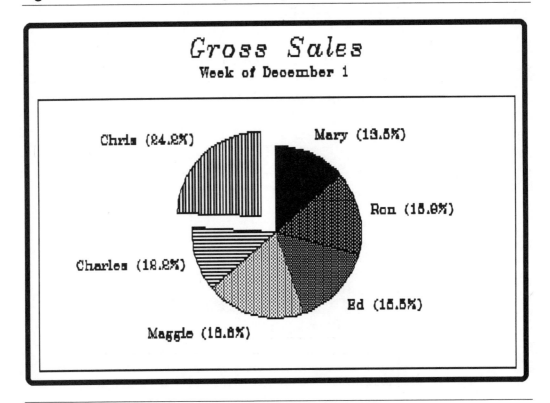

Print the chart. Then, leave the Chart window by selecting **Exit Chart** from the Chart menu. Save the spreadsheet, and go on to the next project.

PROJECT 9: A SERIES CHART OF GROSS SALES AND COST

If you are continuing from the previous project, your screen shows the SALESCOM spreadsheet. If you are not continuing from the previous project, boot *Works* and open the SALESCOM.WKS spreadsheet.

You would like to draw a bar chart showing the Gross Sales and the Cost values for all of your salespersons.

≡ Drawing the Series Chart

Choose **New** from the Chart menu, then pull down the Format menu and select **Bar**. Highlight the Gross Sales values, B4:B9, and assign this range to the **1st Y-Series** (in the Data menu). Highlight the Cost values, C4:C9, and assign this range to the **2nd Y-Series**. Then, highlight the names of your salespersons, A4:A9, and assign the range to **X-Series**.

After you've assigned all three ranges, check your selections by choosing **Series** from the Data menu (Figure 5-10). The SERIES dialog box displays your choices for the X-Series, and up to six Y-Series. Each Y-Series defines the values for a set of (in this case) bars. The X-Series defines the range of labels (or values) for the X-axis.

Figure 5-10   The SERIES dialog box shows assigned data ranges

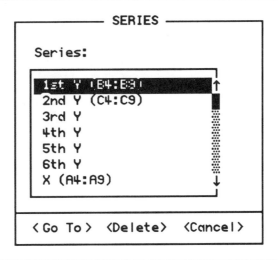

The SERIES dialog box, in addition to showing the current ranges for the X- and Y-Series, provides a convenient method of highlighting any of the ranges. For example, select 2nd Y (C4:C9), press $\boxed{\text{Enter}}$, and the range of Cost cells is highlighted.

Display the bar graph by selecting the **View** command (Figure 5-11). Notice that *Works* has chosen different patterns for the Gross Sales and Cost bars, and that it has automatically scaled the Y-axis. Notice also that the Y-axis values are formatted in dollars because both sets of Y-Series data were formatted that way.

Figure 5-11 Different data series are represented by different bar patterns

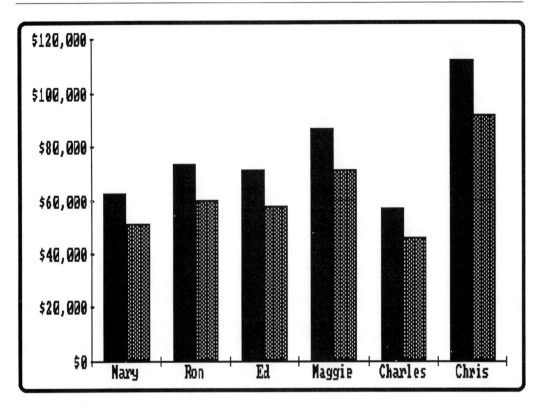

Scaling the Graph

Press any key to return to the Chart window, and select **Y-Axis** from the Options menu. The Y-AXIS dialog box contains, among other things, three text boxes for Minimum, Maximum, and Interval. By default, all three are set to "Auto." Auto tells *Works* to use 0 for the minimum value if none of the plotted values are negative, to choose an appropriate interval ($20,000), and to set the maximum value to be the minimum (0) plus six intervals.

You can change any or all of these scaling values. For example, enter **20000** for the Minimum, **120000** for the Maximum, and **10000** for the interval (Figure 5-12). You can move the cursor from one text box to the next by pressing ⌨Tab⌨.

Close the dialog box, view the graph, and see that *Works* has divided the Y-axis into ten intervals instead of six (Figure 5-13).

Figure 5-12   Use the Y-AXIS dialog box to change the axis scale

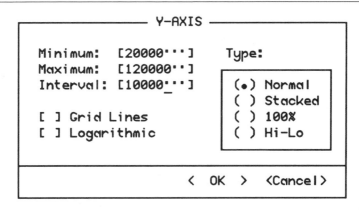

Figure 5-13   The vertical axis has been rescaled

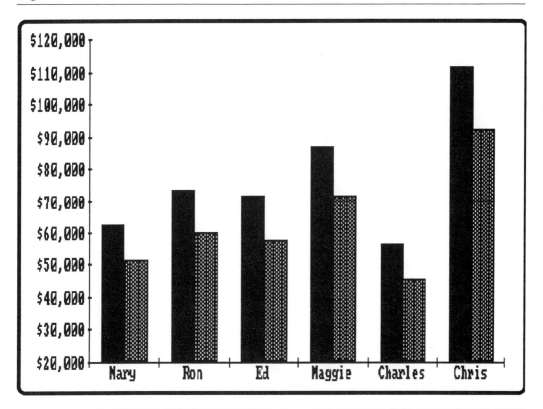

Display the Y-AXIS dialog box and reset the three scaling values to "Auto."

Labeling the Chart

Let's label your bar graph, using some of the techniques you learned in the last project as well as some new ones. First, display the TITLES dialog box (select **Titles** from the Data menu). Enter labels for the Chart Title, Subtitle, X-Axis, and Y-Axis as shown in Figure 5-14.

Figure 5-14   Enter these titles for your bar chart

```
┌──────────────────── TITLES ────────────────────┐
│                                                 │
│  Chart Title:  ["SALES AND COSTS·····]          │
│  Subtitle:     ["Week of December 1··]          │
│  X-Axis:       ["SALES STAFF·········]          │
│  Y-Axis:       ["AMOUNT··············]          │
│  Right Y-Axis: [·····················]          │
│                _                                │
│                                                 │
├─────────────────────────────────────────────────┤
│                        <  OK  >   <Cancel>      │
└─────────────────────────────────────────────────┘
```

You used Chart Title and Subtitle labels in the last project. The X-Axis label is horizontally centered at the bottom of the chart. The Y-Axis label is rotated 90° and vertically centered at the left edge of the chart. Close the dialog box, view the chart, and you'll see what I mean.

Anytime you plot more than one set of Y values, creating more than one set of bars (or lines), you need to identify the bars. *Works* plots each set of bars in its own pattern, but you need a key to indicate which pattern corresponds to each data set. The second labeling technique provides this identification.

Pull down the Data menu, and select **Legends**. The LEGENDS dialog box (Figure 5-15) creates the legends for the various sets of bars in your bar graph. As the dialog box opens, the 1st Y data set is selected. Press Alt + L to move the cursor to the **Legends:** text box, and type **Sales**. Then press Alt + C to create the legend.

Figure 5-15   Create legends to identify data sets

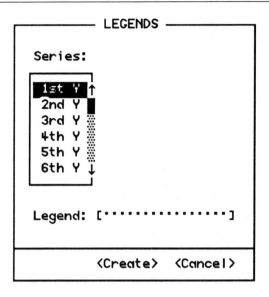

Your cursor should be back in the **Series**: list box. (*Note*: If your version of *Works* is older than version 1.05, you'll need to redisplay the LEGENDS dialog box each time you create a new legend.) Highlight 2nd Y in the list box, press Alt + L , and type **Costs** into the **Legends**: text box. Press Alt + C to create this legend, then press Esc to close the dialog box.

View your bar graph, and compare it with Figure 5-16.

Evaluating Your Graph

Looking at the bars that comprise your graph, it's difficult to estimate the value of the individual bars. *Works* can aid you in evaluating the bars in two ways.

First, *Works* can draw grid lines horizontally and/or vertically across your graph. Let's add horizontal grid lines. Select **Y-Axis** from the Options menu. Press Alt + G to place an "X" in the Grid Lines option, then press Enter to close the dialog box.

View the graph, and see that horizontal grid lines have been drawn at each Y-Axis value (Figure 5-17).

Figure 5-16   Titles and legends have been added to the chart

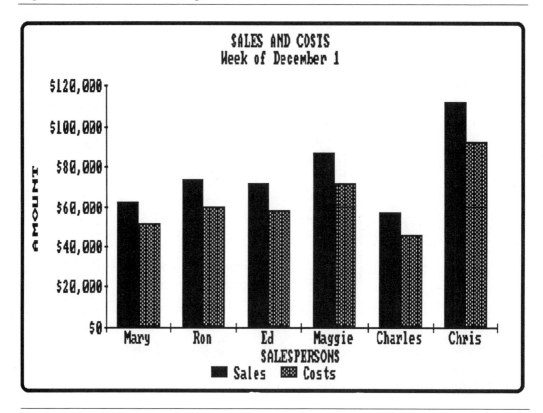

Sometimes, you need to be able to evaluate the bars with greater precision than just estimating to the nearest grid line. In such cases, you can tell *Works* to place numerical values at the top of each bar.

Return to the Chart window, and highlight the range of Gross Sales values, B4:B9. Then, pull down the Data menu and select **Data Labels**. 1st Y is automatically chosen when you enter the dialog box, so press (Enter) to assign the range of values you had highlighted, B4:B9, as labels for the 1st Y-Series. Pressing (Enter) also closes the dialog box.

Next, highlight the range of Costs, C4:C9, and display the DATA LABELS dialog box again. Highlight 2nd Y in the **Series:** list box, and press (Enter) to assign the values in C4:C9 as labels for the 2nd Y-Series. Display the dialog box once more, and compare it with Figure 5-18. This time, because you're not assigning a cell range to a Y-Series, press (Esc) to close the dialog box.

Figure 5-17   Grid lines help you estimate the bar values

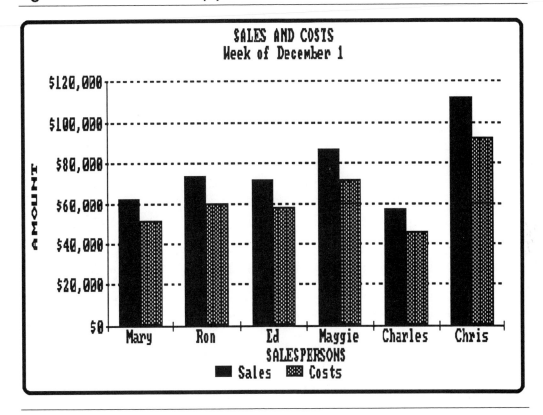

Figure 5-18   Assign the two sets of data as Data Labels

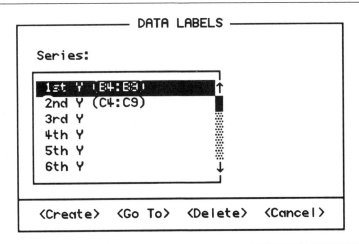

If your dialog box didn't match Figure 5-18, go back and repeat the above procedure. New highlighted ranges will replace existing ones. You can delete label ranges from one or more Y-Series by selecting the Y-Series (1st Y, 2nd Y, etc.) in the **Series:** list box, and pressing ⟨Alt⟩ + ⟨D⟩. Just be sure you close this dialog box by pressing ⟨Esc⟩.

Before you view the results of adding data labels, remove the grid lines you drew earlier. Display the Y-AXIS dialog box, press ⟨Alt⟩ + ⟨G⟩ to remove the "X" from the Grid Lines option, and close the dialog box. Now, view the graph and compare it with Figure 5-19.

Changing the Bar Pattern

If you look closely at your screen (or at Figure 5-19), you'll see that part of each 2nd Y (Costs) data label is obscured by the Gross Sales bar to its left. For example, the data label for the first Cost bar should

Figure 5-19 Some of the Data Labels are obscured by the Sales bars

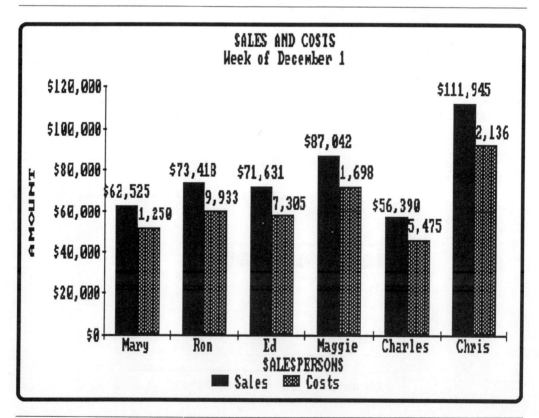

be "$51,250" but only "1,250" appears on the screen. The first two characters of the data label are "lost" in the Gross Sales bar.

One way to solve this problem is to change the pattern of the 1st Y (Gross Sales) bars to something less intense than solid black, so that the data label characters will show through. Bar patterns are set in the DATA FORMAT dialog box, so select **Data Format** from the Format menu.

With 1st Y highlighted in the **Series:** list box, press Alt + P to move the cursor to the **Patterns:** list box. Use the ↓ key to highlight the Sparse pattern, then press Alt + F to format the 1st Y bars with this pattern. Close the dialog by pressing Esc.

View the graph once more, and see that the Cost data labels can now be seen in their entirety (Figure 5-20).

Figure 5-20   Changing the bar pattern solves the problem

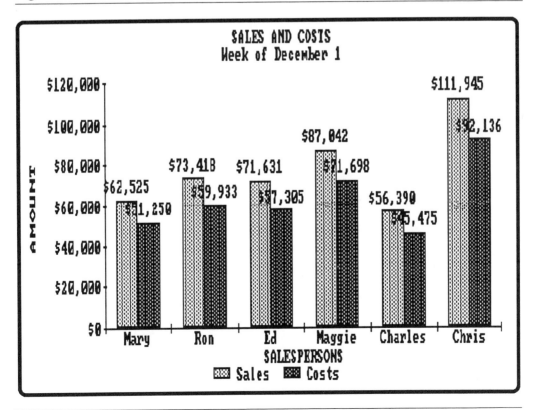

Return to the spreadsheet window by selecting **Exit Chart** from the Chart menu. Save your spreadsheet. Then, print the chart with the **Print Chart** command. Notice that you can print your chart either directly from the spreadsheet or from the Chart window. From the *spreadsheet*, you use the **Print Chart** command (**Print** is used to print the spreadsheet itself); from the *Chart window*, you use the **Print** command.

Change the name of your graph from "Chart1" to "Sales and Costs" by using the CHARTS dialog box. Refer to the previous project if you need help with this procedure.

≡ Mixed Line and Bar Graphs

When you plot two or more Y-Series on the same graph, you don't have to plot all the series as bars (or all of them as lines, for that matter). *Works* lets you mix bars and lines on the same graph. For example, you might decide to plot Gross Sales as bars and Costs as a line. Here's how to do this.

If you've been following along, you should be in the spreadsheet window, and your SALESCOM spreadsheet should have two charts, "Gross Sales" and "Sales and Costs." If you pull down the Chart menu, you'll see these two chart names at the bottom of the menu. Make sure "Sales and Costs" is the selected chart; it should have a bullet (•) beside it. If it doesn't, select it by pressing the number of the chart, probably 2. Then, enter the Chart window for this chart by selecting **Define** from the Chart menu.

Now that you're in the Chart window for "Sales and Costs," select **Mixed Line & Bar** from the Options menu. The resulting dialog box, Figure 5-21, allows you to assign line or bar representations to each of the Y-Series in your graph. Both 1st Y-Series and 2nd Y-Series are currently defined as bar because you selected **Bar** from the Format menu when you began the graph.

To represent Costs as a line, rather than as bars, press (Alt) + (C). Then, close the dialog box by pressing (Enter). That's all there is to it. View the graph, and see that Gross Sales is still represented by bars, while Costs are drawn in with a line (Figure 5-22).

Return to the spreadsheet (select **Exit Chart**), save your work, then close the spreadsheet by selecting **Close** from the File menu.

Figure 5-21   Assign one of the data sets to be plotted as a line graph

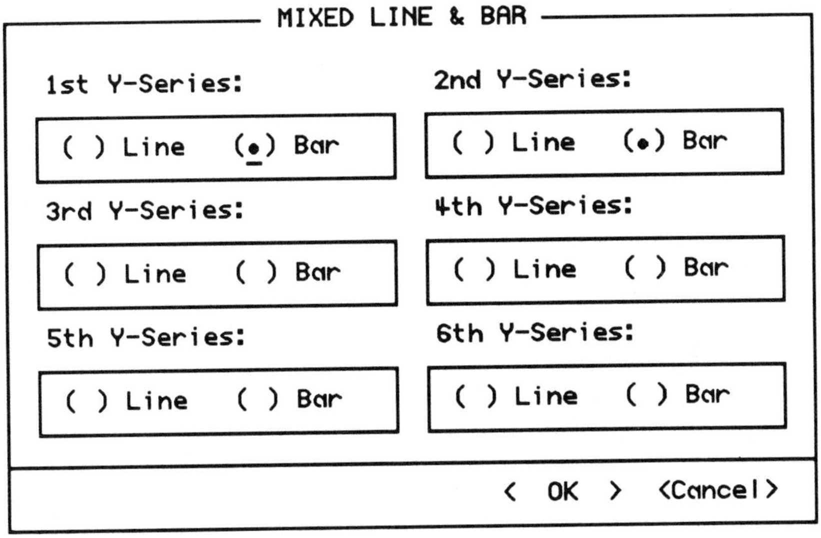

```
┌──────────────── MIXED LINE & BAR ────────────────┐
│                                                   │
│   1st Y-Series:            2nd Y-Series:          │
│  ┌─────────────────────┐  ┌─────────────────────┐ │
│  │ ( ) Line   (•) Bar  │  │ ( ) Line   (•) Bar  │ │
│  └─────────────────────┘  └─────────────────────┘ │
│   3rd Y-Series:            4th Y-Series:          │
│  ┌─────────────────────┐  ┌─────────────────────┐ │
│  │ ( ) Line   ( ) Bar  │  │ ( ) Line   ( ) Bar  │ │
│  └─────────────────────┘  └─────────────────────┘ │
│   5th Y-Series:            6th Y-Series:          │
│  ┌─────────────────────┐  ┌─────────────────────┐ │
│  │ ( ) Line   ( ) Bar  │  │ ( ) Line   ( ) Bar  │ │
│  └─────────────────────┘  └─────────────────────┘ │
│                                                   │
├───────────────────────────────────────────────────┤
│                      <  OK  >   <Cancel>          │
└───────────────────────────────────────────────────┘
```

PROJECT 10: A MATHEMATICAL GRAPH

This last chart project will create a graph of the three trigonometric functions: Sine, Cosine, and Tangent. You'll first create a table of angles ranging from 0° to 360°, in 10° increments. Then you'll compute the functions and plot them. You can use this technique to plot any function for any range of values. Just make sure that the function is defined for each value in the range (e.g., don't try to plot the Log of 0 or the Tangent of 90°, both of which yield undefined values).

Generating the Data

Create a new spreadsheet document. Begin by typing the label, **Angle**, into cell A1, **Sine** into B1, **Cosine** into C1, and **Tangent** into D1. Then, change the alignment of these four cells to Right.

Figure 5-22 You can mix bar and line graphs on the same chart

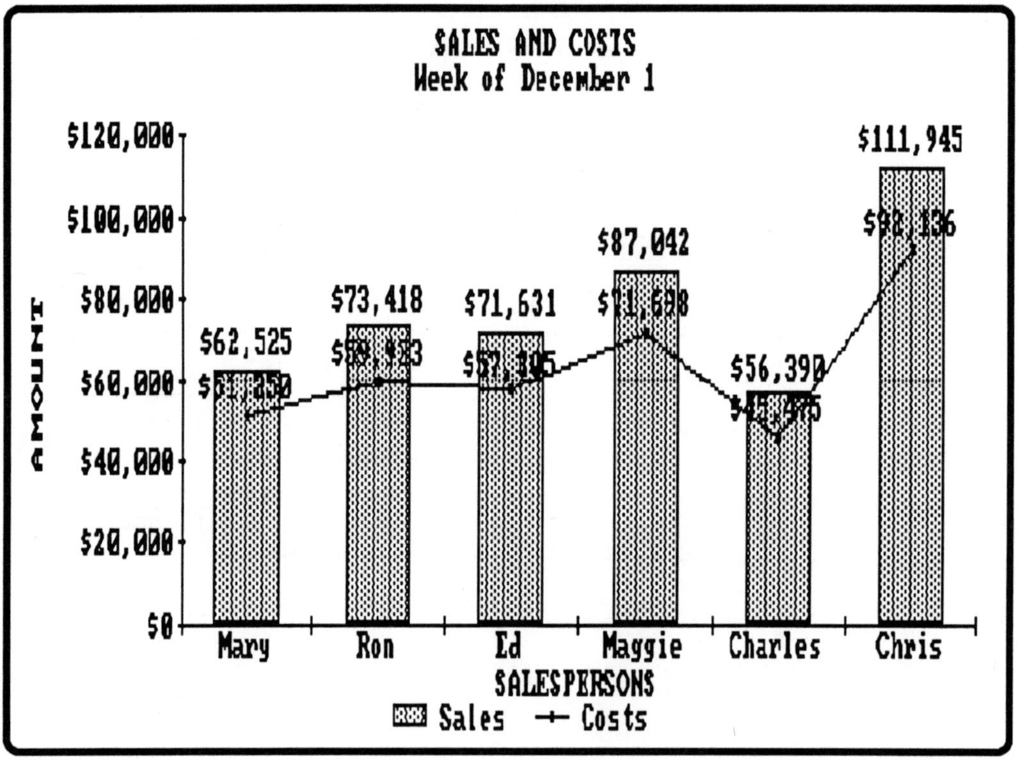

You want to calculate values for the three functions using angles from 0° to 360° in increments of 10°, so let's list these 37 values in A2:A38. Select cell A2, type the first value, **0**, and press (Enter).

You want to increment the angle value by 10° (0, 10, 20, 30, etc.), but instead of entering the value 10 into A3, enter the formula =**A2+10.** (Don't forget to press (Enter) after you've typed the formula into A3.)

Now you can copy A3's formula into the next 35 cells and *generate* the rest of the angle values. Highlight all the cells from A3 to A38. With A3:A38 highlighted, choose **Fill Down**, and move the cursor to unhighlight the cells (Figure 5-23). That sure beats typing all those values, doesn't it?

Select cell B2. This cell will contain the formula for computing the Sine of the angle in A2. You might think that this formula is simply =SIN(A2), but it isn't. All trigonometric functions that use angles for their arguments expect the angles to be expressed in *radians*, not

Figure 5-23 Use **Fill Down** to generate the Angle values

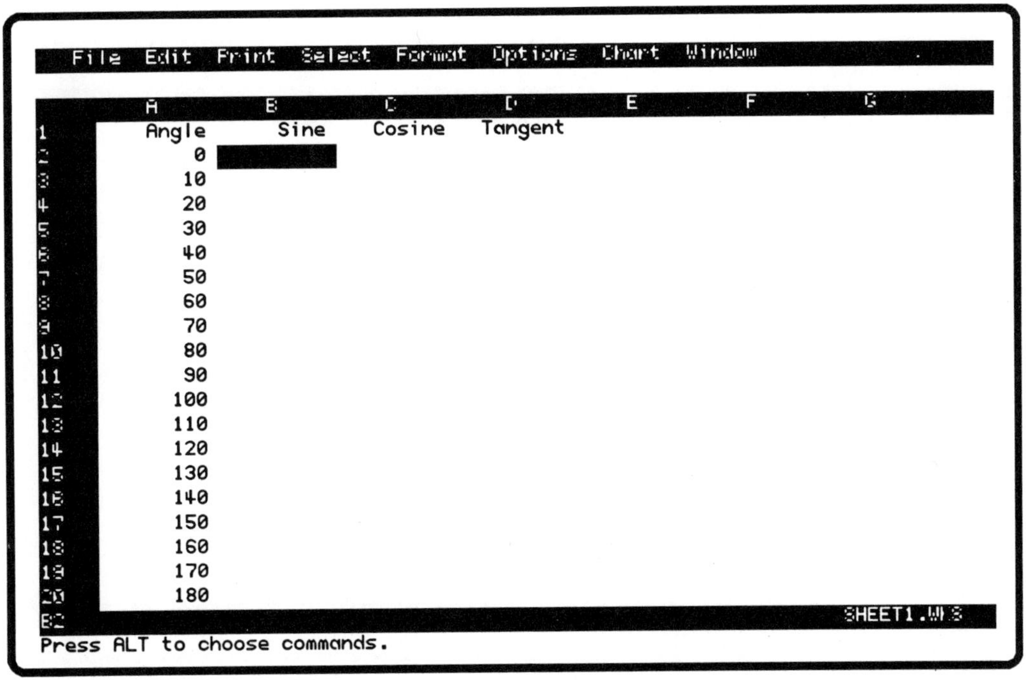

```
 File   Edit   Print   Select   Format   Options   Chart   Window        .

          A           B          C          D        E        F        G
  1     Angle        Sine      Cosine     Tangent
  2        0    ▮▮▮▮▮▮▮▮▮▮
  3       10
  4       20
  5       30
  6       40
  7       50
  8       60
  9       70
 10       80
 11       90
 12      100
 13      110
 14      120
 15      130
 16      140
 17      150
 18      160
 19      170
 20      180
                                                              SHEET1.WKS
 Press ALT to choose commands.
```

degrees. (*Note*: As there are 360° in a circle, so there are 2π radians in a circle. A radian is about 57.5°.) You can easily convert degrees to radians by multiplying by $\pi/180$. *Works* has a function for π, called PI( ), so the correct formula for the sine of the angle in A2 is =SIN(A2*PI( )/180). Enter this formula in cell B2, then copy the formula into cells B3:B38 with **Fill Down** (Figure 5-24). I know the values don't line up. That's because the default numerical format is General, which displays as many decimal places as will fit in each cell. You might be tempted to format the cells in columns B, C, and D to Fixed with 4 decimal places, for example, but don't do it. Leave the cells in General format. After all, it's the *graph* of this data in which you're interested, not the data itself.

Compute the values for Cosine and Tangent using the same procedure as you used for Sine values. Enter the formula =**COS(A2*PI( )/180** into cell C2, and copy it into C3:C38. Similarly, type the formula =**TAN(A2*PI( )/180)** into D2, and copy it into D3:D38 (Figure 5-25). Notice the value for the Tangent of 90° (cell D11). *Works* is telling

Figure 5-24 Don't change the format of the Sine values

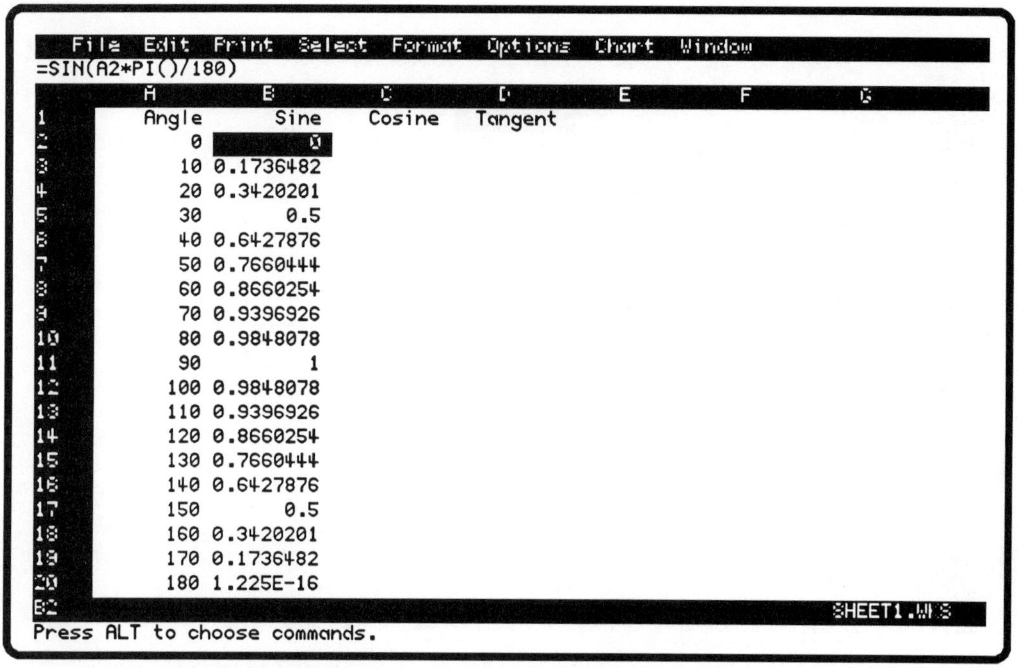

```
   File  Edit  Print  Select  Format  Options  Chart  Window
=SIN(A2*PI()/180)
         A          B          C          D          E          F          G
1     Angle       Sine     Cosine    Tangent
2        0          0
3       10  0.1736482
4       20  0.3420201
5       30        0.5
6       40  0.6427876
7       50  0.7660444
8       60  0.8660254
9       70  0.9396926
10      80  0.9848078
11      90          1
12     100  0.9848078
13     110  0.9396926
14     120  0.8660254
15     130  0.7660444
16     140  0.6427876
17     150        0.5
18     160  0.3420201
19     170  0.1736482
20     180  1.225E-16
B2                                                          SHEET1.WIS
Press ALT to choose commands.
```

you that this value is very large. That's not surprising considering that the Tangent of 90° is undefined.

This is a good time to save your spreadsheet.

≡ Plotting the Functions

In the last project, you defined each Y-Series (Gross Sales and Costs) separately. *Works* has a special *speed charting* mode that lets you define several Y-Series in one step.

Speed Charting

Highlight all the cells in the range B1:D38 (everything except the Angle column). Then, pull down the Chart menu and select **New**. This not only assigns various portions of the highlighted cells to appropriate graph parameters, but also displays the Chart window.

Figure 5-25   Notice the exceptionally large value for cell D11

	A	B	C	D	E	F	G
	Angle	Sine	Cosine	Tangent			
1	0	0	1	0			
2	10	0.1736482	0.9848078	0.176327			
3	20	0.3420201	0.9396926	0.3639702			
4	30	0.5	0.8660254	0.5773503			
5	40	0.6427876	0.7660444	0.8390996			
6	50	0.7660444	0.6427876	1.1917536			
7	60	0.8660254	0.5	1.7320508			
8	70	0.9396926	0.3420201	2.7474774			
9	80	0.9848078	0.1736482	5.6712818			
10	90	1	6.123E-17	1.633E+16			
11	100	0.9848078	-0.173648	-5.671282			
12	110	0.9396926	-0.34202	-2.747477			
13	120	0.8660254	-0.5	-1.732051			
14	130	0.7660444	-0.642788	-1.191754			
15	140	0.6427876	-0.766044	-0.8391			
16	150	0.5	-0.866025	-0.57735			
17	160	0.3420201	-0.939693	-0.36397			
18	170	0.1736482	-0.984808	-0.176327			
19	180	1.225E-16	-1	-1.22E-16			

Press ALT to choose commands.

Tell *Works* you want to plot a line graph by pulling down the Format menu and selecting **Line**.

To show you the effect of speed charting, display the SERIES dialog box (select **Series** from the Data menu), and see that the first three Y-Series have been defined (Figure 5-26). Close this dialog box, and display the LEGENDS dialog box. Notice that the legend for the 1st Y-Series will be the contents of cell B1, the legend for the 2nd Y-series will be the contents of cell C1, and so forth. Speed charting is responsible for this, as well. Close the dialog box.

Let's assign the angles in column A as X-axis labels. Highlight the range A2:A38, and select **X-Series** from the Data menu.

Manual Scaling

Now, let's view the graph. Select **View** from the Chart menu (Figure 5-27). Not quite what you expected, is it? Both axes are messed up, and the graph itself makes no sense at all.

Figure 5-26 Speed charting enters several sets of data at one stroke

Figure 5-27 This is not the graph we expected to see

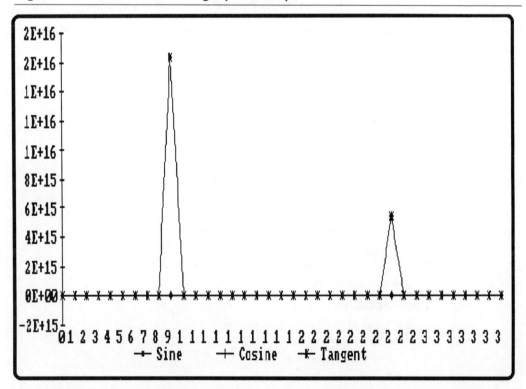

Part of the problem is the undefined values for the Tangents of 90° and 270°. These values are so large that the rest of the values are lost in the background. Rather than allow *Works* to automatically scale the Y-axis so that all the points are visible, let's set up a more useful scale.

Select **Y-Axis** from the Options menu. Change the Minimum value to -1, and the Maximum value to 1. Leave the Interval set to Auto. Close the dialog box, and view the graph again (Figure 5-28). That's better, but the X-axis is still unreadable.

This is due to *Works* trying to display an X-axis label for each and every data point. There just isn't room for 37 labels along the X-axis.

Select **X-Axis** from the Options menu. The Label Frequency option determines how often X-axis labels are displayed. The default value is 1, which means that *Works* tries to insert a label for every data

Figure 5-28   Rescaling the Y-Axis results in a proper display of the three functions

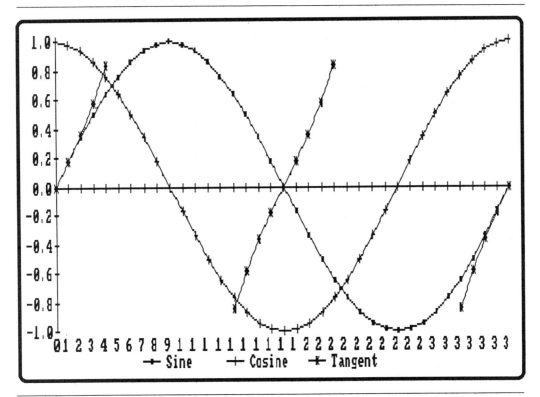

point. Press (Alt) + (L) to move the cursor to the Label Frequency text box, and change the frequency value to 4 (Figure 5-29).

Press (Enter) to close the dialog box, and view the graph again. That's better.

Figure 5-29   Set the Label Frequency to 4 to correct the X-Axis labels

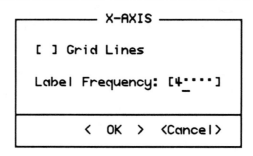

≡ Customizing the Graph

Your graph of trigonometric functions is presentable now, but you can make several additional modifications that will greatly improve its "look."

Changing Line Markers and Patterns

In the last project, you used the DATA FORMAT dialog box to alter the pattern of one of the sets of bars. When you plot line graphs, this dialog box controls both the line patterns and the markers that are placed at each data point.

Display this dialog box by selecting **Data Format** from the Format menu. By default, *Works* chooses Auto for line Colors, Patterns, and Markers. If you own a color monitor, choose Red for the 1st Y Series, Dark Green for the 2nd Y Series, and Dark Blue for the 3rd Y Series. For each color change, press (Alt) + (C) to move the cursor to the **Colors:** list box, highlight your color choice, and press (Alt) + (F) to format the data series. (*Note*: If you own a monochrome monitor, your color choices are only Auto and Black. Either choice results in the same black line, so you might as well accept the choice of Auto for all three data series.)

Ignore the **Patterns**: list box for now, and concentrate on the markers. Choose an o marker for the 1st Y Series, a Filled box (■) marker for the 2nd Y Series, and an x marker for the 3rd Y Series. For each change, press (Alt) + (M) to move the cursor to the **Markers**: list box, select the marker, then press (Alt) + (F) to confirm.

Close the dialog box by pressing (Esc). View the graph again, and compare it with Figure 5-30. Notice that the new choices for markers (and colors, if you changed them) are indicated by the legends at the bottom of the graph.

Figure 5-30   Choose markers that clearly identify your graphs

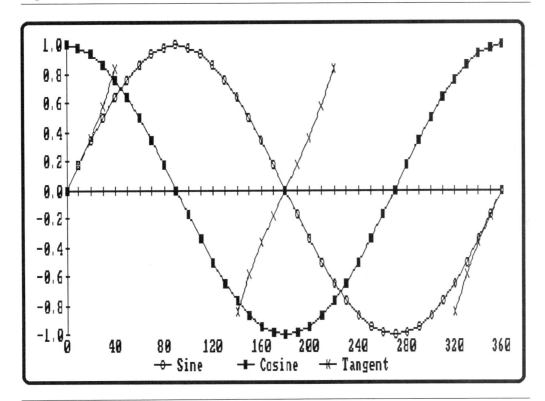

Another way of labeling line graphs is by changing the line patterns and not using markers.

Display the DATA FORMAT dialog box. Change the marker for each of the three data series to None while choosing Solid pattern for 1st Y, Dashed pattern for 2nd Y, and Dotted pattern for 3rd Y. Don't forget to press (Alt) + (F) to lock in each change.

Close the dialog box, and view the graph (Figure 5-31). The legends again indicate the different line patterns.

Figure 5-31   Another way of identifying graphs is by using different line patterns

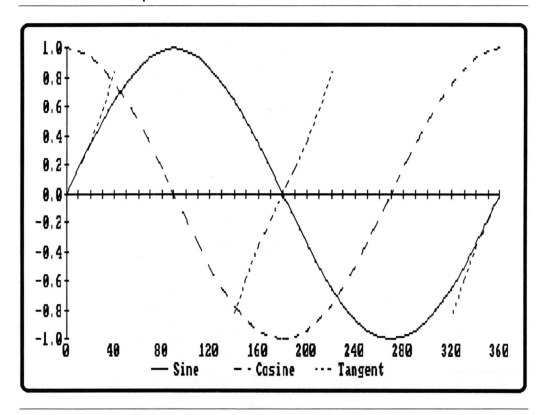

Two Y-Axes

Look at the graphs of the three trig functions, especially the Tangent. If you're familiar with this function, you'll see that the true shape of the graph isn't being displayed. Too many of the Tangent's data points lie outside the range –1 to +1. You could extend the Y-Axis, for example, from –10 to +10. This would display almost all of the Tangent's data points, but would also compress the Sine and Cosine graphs to one-tenth of their original height.

The ideal solution would be to plot the Sine and Cosine functions using a Y-axis scale of –1 to +1 while plotting the Tangent function using a Y-axis scale of –10 to +10, on one single graph. *Works'* **Two Y-Axes** feature lets you do this. It sets up one Y-axis on the left, and another Y-axis on the right. You can define different scales for each Y-axis, and assign individual data series to either Y-axis. Here's how it works.

Pull down the Options menu, and select **Two Y-Axes**. The dialog box (Figure 5-32) assigns each Y-series to either the left or right Y-axis. The 3rd Y-Series represents Tangent data, so press (Alt) + (F) to assign this series to the Right Y-axis. Press (Enter) to close the dialog box.

Figure 5-32 Assign the Tangent graph to the Right Y-Axis

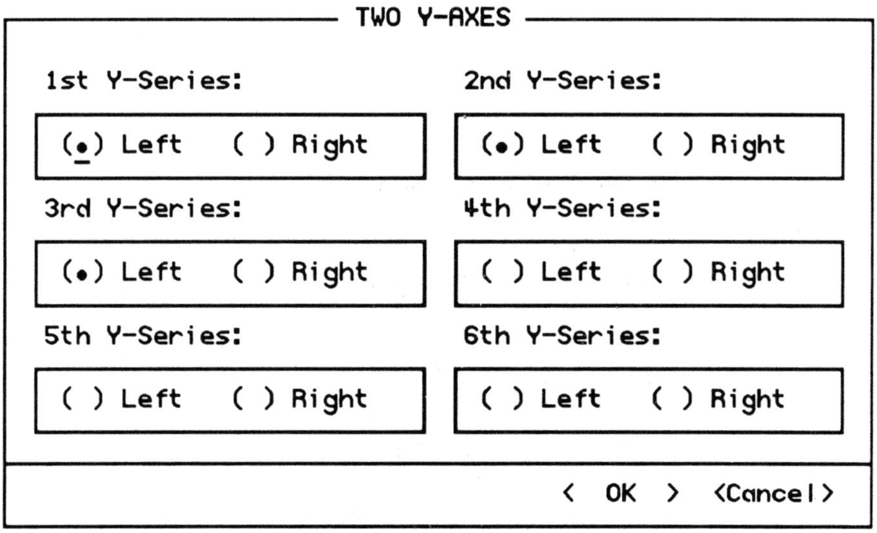

```
  ──────────────────── TWO Y-AXES ────────────────────

   1st Y-Series:              2nd Y-Series:
   ┌─────────────────────┐    ┌─────────────────────┐
   │ (•) Left   ( ) Right│    │ (•) Left   ( ) Right│
   └─────────────────────┘    └─────────────────────┘
   3rd Y-Series:              4th Y-Series:
   ┌─────────────────────┐    ┌─────────────────────┐
   │ (•) Left   ( ) Right│    │ ( ) Left   ( ) Right│
   └─────────────────────┘    └─────────────────────┘
   5th Y-Series:              6th Y-Series:
   ┌─────────────────────┐    ┌─────────────────────┐
   │ ( ) Left   ( ) Right│    │ ( ) Left   ( ) Right│
   └─────────────────────┘    └─────────────────────┘

                              <  OK  >   <Cancel>
```

Select **Right Y-Axis** from the Options menu. This dialog box is identical to the Y-AXIS dialog box that you've used before. Change the Minimum value to –10 and the Maximum value to 10. Then press (Enter) to close the dialog box.

View the graph once more, and see the effect. Now the shape of the Tangent function is clearly displayed (Figure 5-33).

Figure 5-33   The Tangent graph uses the Right Y-Axis

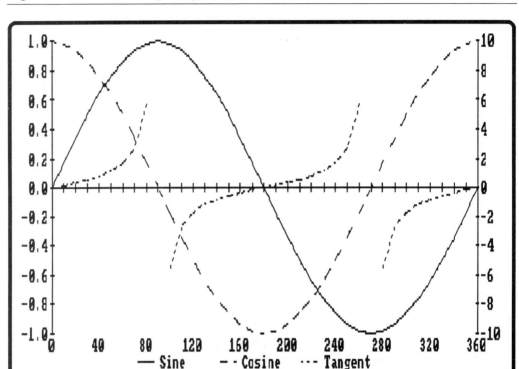

Finally, use the TITLES dialog box to add a Chart Title: **TRIGONOMETRIC FUNCTIONS**; Subtitle: **Sine, Cosine, & Tangent**; X-Axis: **ANGLE (Degrees)**; Y-Axis: **Sine & Cosine**; and Right Y-Axis: **Tangent** to your graph. Compare this graph with Figure 5-34.

Return to the spreadsheet window with the **Exit Chart** command, and save your work. Then, print the chart. If you like, you can return to the Chart window (with **Define**) and use **Title Font** and **Other Font** commands to change the font and size of the text in your chart.

☰ Final Comments

Feel free to experiment with plotting different types of charts. It's the only way you'll become familiar with the various chart features. The ability to plot functions, as you did in Project 10, can be used in a

Figure 5-34 Finish the Trig Functions graph by adding titles

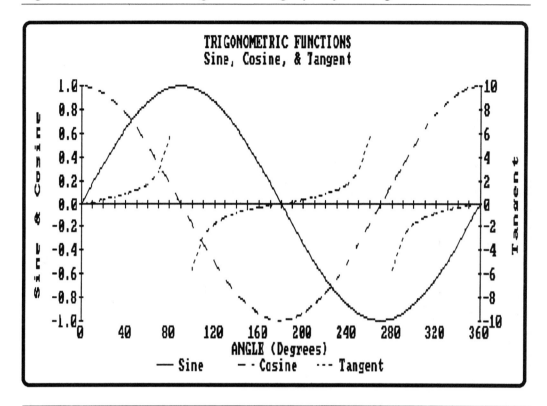

variety of ways, including displaying the solution to simultaneous equations (for those of you who are mathematically inclined).

In general, it is easier to see relationships when values are charted graphically than when they are displayed in a table. Make use of this fact when you are creating your own reports. In Chapter 7, you'll see how to paste spreadsheet charts directly into your word processor documents.

Chapter **6**
DATA COMMUNICATIONS

One of the many advantages that owning a microcomputer grants you is the ability to communicate with other computers and computer owners, anywhere in the world, via telephone. Yes, I know, you have always been able to call up and talk to other people, but now your computer can talk directly with other computers. This allows you to share data and other information as well as chit-chat.

Data communications is the name of the process whereby two computers talk to each other. In order to data communicate, you need four things: a computer, access to a telephone, a modem (described below), and a computer program that teaches your computer how to "talk" over telephone lines. (The "computer program" is, of course, the communications section of *Works*.)

When *you* talk over the phone, an element in the telephone mouthpiece converts the sound of your voice into electrical impulses that can be transmitted over the phone lines. At the other end, those impulses are converted back into sound for the other party to hear. Similarly, when your computer wants to talk on the telephone, a device is needed to convert computer "sounds" into a form that can be carried over the same phone lines. This device is called a *modem*. The word modem is actually a contraction of the words *mo*dulate and *dem*odulate. The modem modulates (converts) the signal coming from the sending computer so that it can be carried by the phone line and demodulates the signal as it passes from the phone line into the receiving computer.

There are many brands of modems currently available. I've worked successfully with modems manufactured by Hayes Computer Products, Inc., Prometheus Products, Inc., and USRobotics. All three of these manufacturers build modems that are referred to as *Hayes-compatible*.

Modems, like any other piece of computer equipment, have to be told how to operate. Several years ago, the folks at Hayes Computer Products developed a collection of modem commands and command codes that became an industry standard. The term *Hayes-compatible* means that the modem understands all (or most) of the standard Hayes commands. And the communications section of *Works* was specifically designed to talk to Hayes-compatible modems.

Note: *Works* will work with non-Hayes-compatible modems, but not as easily. If you haven't purchased your modem as yet, I strongly recommend that you buy one that's Hayes-compatible. By the way, there are two general types of modems. One type connects directly with the phone line by plugging into the phone jack on the wall; the other, called an acoustic modem, provides a cradle for the telephone handset to rest in. I recommend you buy the direct connect, rather than the acoustic, type of modem. Direct connect modems are more expensive, but worth it. They are less susceptible to room noise and other sounds and come with additional features unavailable with acoustic modems. These extra features include the ability to dial a telephone number automatically, answer the phone when it rings, and hang up the phone when your computer is through talking.

There is only one project for this chapter. In it, you'll learn all of the features of *Works* communications. A communications project must, by its very nature, involve two computers—yours and somebody else's. Rather than assume that you would be communicating with one of the major computer networks (The Source, CompuServe, Delphi, GEnie, etc.), I've set up a special "computer bulletin board" service, exclusively for the readers of this book. In the following project, all exercises are designed to be performed in conjunction with the *Working with Works* Bulletin Board System (or WWWBBS, for short).

The WWWBBS serves two purposes. First, it allows me to create a communications project in which I can control the responses you'll see when you dial up. Second, I've designed the bulletin board so that if you encounter problems using *Works* on your computer, you can call up the WWWBBS and leave a message for me, describing the problem. You can even send me a copy of a troublesome *Works* file. I will do my best to resolve the problem, and you can read the answer the next time you call.

But, before we get into these special bulletin board features, let's do the project.

PROJECT 11: COMMUNICATING WITH A BULLETIN BOARD SYSTEM

Begin by creating a new communications document. Boot *Works*, and select Communications in the NEW dialog box. Then press ⌐Enter⌐. Figure 6-1 shows the communications window.

Protocol Settings

Before your computer can communicate with another computer, there has to be agreement between them on what are called communication *protocols*. These protocols describe the entire communication process— how fast data is sent, how the computers will verify that data has been

Figure 6-1   The communications window

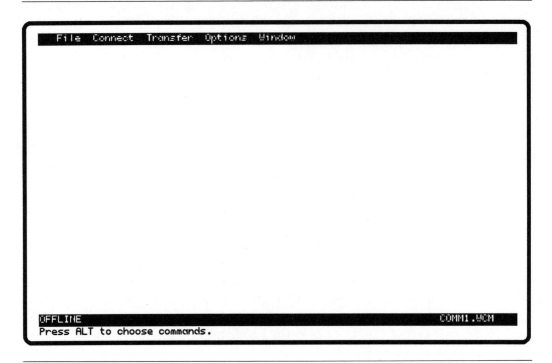

received correctly, and a variety of other things. You might wonder why *Works* doesn't set these protocol values for you. Well, *Works* does choose default protocol values, but different computers require different values. Most of the protocol values are set in two dialog boxes: TERMINAL and COMMUNICATIONS.

Terminal Options

Pull down the Options menu, and select **Terminal** (Figure 6-2). You don't have to change anything in this dialog box to communicate with my bulletin board system (BBS), so the explanation that follows is optional. If you'd like to learn about options in the TERMINAL dialog box, read on. If not, you can close the dialog box and skip ahead to the next section.

Terminal Type   Data communication between computers existed long before Microsoft *Works*. In fact, it existed long before there were such things as microcomputers. In those dim, dark days, devices called *terminals*

Figure 6-2 Accept the default settings of the TERMINAL
dialog box

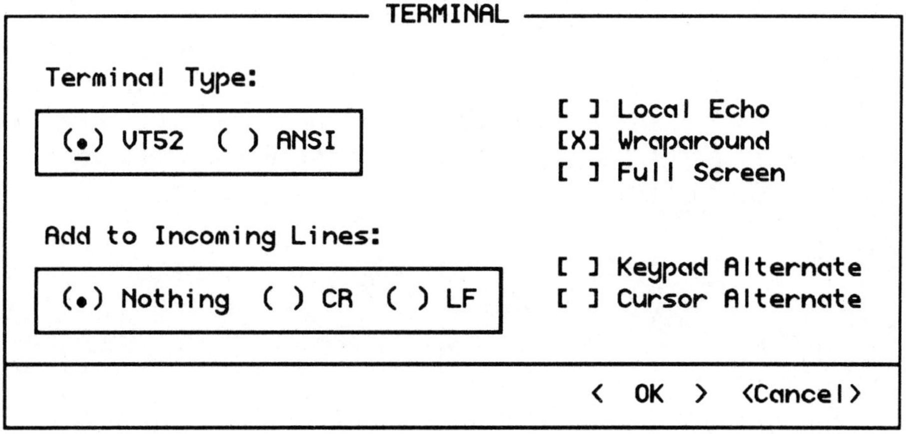

```
┌──────────────────── TERMINAL ────────────────────┐
│                                                   │
│  Terminal Type:                  [ ] Local Echo   │
│  ┌─────────────────────────┐     [X] Wraparound   │
│  │ (•) VT52  ( ) ANSI      │     [ ] Full Screen  │
│  │     ‾                    │                      │
│  └─────────────────────────┘                      │
│                                                   │
│  Add to Incoming Lines:          [ ] Keypad Alternate │
│  ┌─────────────────────────┐     [ ] Cursor Alternate │
│  │ (•) Nothing ( ) CR ( ) LF │                    │
│  └─────────────────────────┘                      │
│                                                   │
├───────────────────────────────────────────────────┤
│                              <  OK  >  <Cancel>   │
└───────────────────────────────────────────────────┘
```

were used to data communicate. Special commands were devised to tell these terminals to perform tasks such as moving the cursor and clearing the screen.

Two popular terminal types (then and now) are VT52 and ANSI. *Works* is written to *emulate* (that is, behave like) either of these terminal types. My BBS doesn't care which terminal type, if any, you emulate, so you can accept the default choice of VT52.

Add to
Incoming
Lines

When a computer sends text to your PC, the text is sent a line at a time. Most computers send a carriage return character (CR) and a line feed character (LF) at the end of each line. If they don't, you can use the Add to Incoming Lines options and have *Works* add one or both of these characters to each incoming line. My BBS supplies both characters, so accept the default choice of Nothing.

Local Echo

When your PC sends text to another computer, each character is usually *echoed* back. (*Note*: This feature is often referred to as *full duplex*.) *Works* knows and expects this echo. Actually, it's the echo from the remote computer, rather than the actual character you type, that's displayed on your screen. Some remote computers don't echo. (This is referred to as *half duplex*.) If you want to see the characters that you type appear on your screen, *Works* must echo them locally. That's the purpose of the Local Echo option. My BBS *does* echo characters, so you won't need this option. In fact, if you use Local Echo when communicating with my BBS, or with any full duplex computer, each character you type will appear doubled on your screen.

Wraparound

Your PC's screen is 80 characters wide. Most computers you communicate with know this and keep the length of the text lines they send to fewer than 80 characters. But what happens if the line is longer than 80 characters? With the Wraparound option selected, its default setting, lines longer than 80 characters are automatically *wrapped around* to the next line. If you deselect this option, portions of lines longer than 80 characters are ignored and are not displayed. My BBS is careful not to send lines longer than 80 characters, but you may as well leave the Wraparound option selected.

Full Screen

The communications window, like all of *Works* application windows, uses the top line for the menu bar and the bottom two lines for status and instructions. The Full Screen option hides these lines while you're communicating, so that you can use all 24 lines on your screen. If you select this feature (and I recommend that you *don't* until you are more familiar with data communications), pressing (Alt) will display the three hidden lines.

Keyboard & Cursor Alternate

The Keyboard Alternate and Cursor Alternate options are used in conjunction with the two terminal types, VT52 and ANSI. The original VT52 and ANSI terminals have keys that transmit special sequences of characters. Your PC's keyboard doesn't have those terminal keys, so *Works* modifies the action of the keypad keys to emulate the special-purpose terminal keys. Since my BBS doesn't look for any terminal emulation, you can ignore both of these options.

The end result of this discussion of the TERMINAL dialog box is that you can accept all of *Works'* default settings, and this is true for most (but not all) of the computers with which you'll communicate. Close the dialog box, and let's look at the Communication options.

Communication Options

Display the COMMUNICATION dialog box by selecting **Communication** from the Options menu (Figure 6-3). This dialog box can be somewhat intimidating, but the choices it offers have to be decided upon before your computer can talk to another computer.

Figure 6-3   Select a baud rate that matches your modem

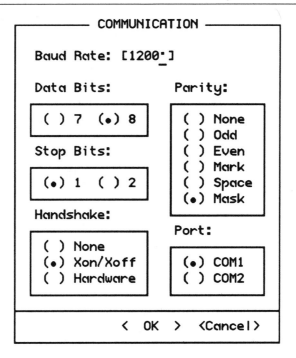

There are six items in the COMMUNICATION dialog box. The choices for most of them depend on the computer you're calling up. Many of the items are rather technical in nature, and all you really need to know about them is which choice to make. However, if you're interested in understanding the concepts of baud rate, parity, and such, I have included brief explanations of each item. Feel free to skip over the explanations and just read the settings. You'll find the settings choices for the WWWBBS in the last paragraph of each explanation.

Baud Rate

Your computer can send out data at a variety of different rates. When it sends data to a serial printer (a serial printer accepts data in the same format as a modem), characters are sent at a rate of almost 1000 per second. Your computer sends each character as a stream of 1's and 0's, and it takes eight of these 1's and 0's (called bits) to define a single character. For example, when your PC sends the letter "A" to a printer or modem, it really sends 01000001.

In addition to the eight bits that define each character, there are one or two extra bits that indicate where one character ends and the next character begins in the stream of bits. That's a total of either 9 or 10 bits per character. The number of *bits* per second that a computer sends out is called the baud rate. When your computer sends data to a serial printer, the data is sent at 9600 baud—that equates to about 1000 characters per second. But a telephone line cannot carry data as quickly as your printer cable can.

There are a number of reasons for this. The facts that phone lines are shared, that the lines go through switching systems, and that they are much longer than your printer cable all play a part in limiting the maximum baud rate that they can handle. The modems themselves have similar limitations, so that the maximum baud rate used over standard telephone lines is 2400 baud. (*Note*: Data communications technology is constantly being improved. By the time you read this, the maximum baud rate may be higher.) Practically speaking, most modems are built to send and receive data at rates of 300, 1200, and/or 2400 baud.

Before you can select a baud rate in the COMMUNICATION dialog box, you have to make sure of two things. First, your modem has to support the rate you choose, and second, the computer you're attempting to communicate with has to be expecting the baud rate. If your computer sends at 2400 baud and my computer is expecting you to send at 1200 baud, my computer is never going to understand your computer.

The WWWBBS is designed to communicate at 300, 1200, or 2400 baud. (It automatically senses which rate you're using.) If your modem can operate at 2400 baud, change the default choice in the dialog box to 2400. If your modem can only communicate at 1200 baud, accept the default value of 1200. If your modem operates only at 300 baud, enter 300.

Data Bits

When your **PC** sends data to your printer, each character is defined by eight bits (1's and 0's). When data is sent through a modem over the phone, each character can be defined by either 8 bits or 7 bits. It doesn't matter which value is used, but both computers must agree.

The WWWBBS uses a data size of 8 bits, so accept the default choice of 8 data bits.

Stop Bits

After your computer sends 7 or 8 data bits defining a particular character, it sends 1 or 2 special bits, called stop bits. These bits mark the division between individual characters. My computer, the one you'll be calling in a moment, expects a single stop bit so, again, accept the the *Works* default value of 1 stop bit.

Parity

Telephone lines are susceptible to noise or static. This noise can cause bits of data to become lost or, even worse, can make a 1 bit appear to be a 0, and vice versa. There are several schemes to assure data integrity; in other words, to verify that the character sent was the character received.

One method is to add an extra bit (called the parity bit) to each string of 7 or 8 character bits. This bit is used as a check that the previous 7 or 8 bits were received correctly. There are several techniques used to generate the parity bit, but the two most popular are *odd parity* and *even parity*.

With odd parity, for example, the purpose of the parity bit is to make sure that the sum of the

1 bits for each character (including the parity bit) adds up to an odd number. To do this, the computer adds up all the 1 bits in the data for each character. If the sum of the 1 bits is an *odd* number (1, 3, 5, or 7 1 bits) the parity bit would be a 0, so that the sum of the 1 bits in data plus parity would remain odd. If, on the other hand, the sum of the 1 bits in the data is an *even* number (0, 2, 4, 6, or 8 1 bits), the computer would generate a 1 for the parity bit, so that the sum of the 1 bits (data plus parity) would again be odd. As an example, suppose the computer sent the letter "A". The data bits for A are 01000001. If the computer used *odd* parity to verify data, it would create a 1 parity bit, so that the sum of the 1 bits (data plus parity) would be an odd number, 3.

Now that you know all about parity, I'll tell you that most computer data services, including the WWWBBS, don't use the parity bit at all! They (and I) use a different method of data verification altogether. That's why Mask is *Works'* default choice and the parity value you should use. (*Note*: The Mask option is equivalent to None but has the additional effect of telling *Works* to ignore the eighth data bit.)

Handshake

Have you ever been talking to someone and trying to write down what is being said? Occasionally, you fall behind and have to ask the other person to pause for a moment to let you catch up. Well, your computer and the computer you're calling need to be able to do the same thing. Occasionally, data comes in too rapidly for the computer to process properly. The method whereby one computer can tell another computer to pause for a while and then continue is called *handshaking*. And, as you can imagine, there are several handshaking schemes.

One scheme uses a separate signal, carried along its own wire, to indicate whether to pause or continue sending. This handshake method is called *hardware handshake*. It is most often used when two computers are communicating over short distances and the computers are directly connected to each other through a cable, rather than through telephone lines.

When computers communicate by phone, the most common form of handshaking is *Xon/Xoff*. The terms *Xon* and *Xoff* represent special characters (specifically, Control + Q and Control + S) that can be sent at any time by the receiving computer (or by you). The Xoff character tells the sending computer to pause until it receives an Xon character, after which it can resume sending.

The WWWBBS uses Xon/Xoff handshaking, and by coincidence (ha!), Xon/Xoff is the default choice.

Port

The last option in the COMMUNICATION dialog box allows you to specify how your modem is connected to your computer. Your PC has two serial connections (called ports), at least one of which will be present at the rear of the case. The ports are identified as COM1 and COM2.

When you (or your computer dealer) attached the modem to your PC, you selected one of the two ports. The Port selection you make in the dialog box must match the port to which your modem is connected. In most cases, this will be COM1; that's why COM1 is the default choice. Occasionally, COM1 is used for a serial printer or a mouse, in which case the modem is connected to COM2.

For your convenience, I've listed all the TERMINAL and COMMUNICATION settings for the WWWBBS in Table 6-1. Close the COMMUNICATION dialog box by pressing Enter.

☰ Calling the Bulletin Board

All you have to do to connect to the bulletin board is to dial the number. First, though, make sure that your modem is properly connected. Unless your modem is on a card that's plugged into your PC, there will be a cable connecting the modem to the COM1 or COM2 port on your computer, and a power cord that plugs into a standard wall outlet.

Table 6-1   Settings for the bulletin board

Item	Setting
Terminal Type	VT52 or ANSI
Add to Incoming Lines	Nothing
Local Echo	No
Wraparound	Yes
Full Screen	No (Yes, as you get more experience)
Keypad Alternate	No
Cursor Alternate	No
Baud Rate	300, 1200, or 2400 (the highest rate your modem supports)
Data Bits	8
Stop Bits	1
Parity	Mask (or None)
Handshake	Xon/Xoff
Port	COM1 or COM2 (probably Com1)

Another cable connects the modem to the telephone wall jack (unless yours is an acoustic modem).

If your modem has switches on it, leave them at their factory settings. If you've altered their settings, refer to the modem's manual for the correct switch positions. Some common modem options that are often controlled by switches are:

DTR	Stands for Data Terminal Ready, and should be held or forced On.
DCD	Stands for Data Carrier Detect, and also should be forced On.
Single or Multi-line Phone	Depends on your telephone but will probably be Single.

Here's how you can check out your Hayes-compatible modem to see that it and your computer are talking to each other, before you actually dial the bulletin board. With your modem connected and turned on, pull down the Connect menu, and choose **Connect**. If you had entered a telephone number in the PHONE dialog box (see below), *Works* would automatically dial that number. Since you haven't given *Works* a phone number, choosing **Connect** just tells *Works* to "pay attention" to what you type. Until you Connect, *Works* ignores the keyboard. Notice that when you Connect, the word OFFLINE is replaced by an elapsed time counter at the left end of the status line.

Type **at**, and press (Enter). You may not see the characters at on your screen. It depends on whether your modem echoes the characters back to the computer. But your modem should respond, "OK," and you should see these characters on your screen (Figure 6-4). (*Note*: If your modem isn't Hayes-compatible or is an acoustic modem, don't bother trying this test.)

Figure 6-4   Your modem should respond "OK" when you type "at"

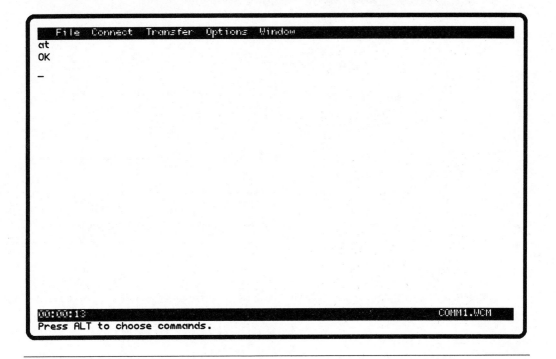

If your modem has responded with "OK," it and your PC are communicating with each other. Select **Connect** from the Connect menu to go *offline*. *Works* will display an alert box asking you if it's OK to disconnect. Press (Enter), and the status line will indicate the OFFLINE state.

If your modem is Hayes-compatible and it didn't respond with "OK," try typing "at" again. If you still get no response, check the cable connecting the modem to the PC (for external modems). Make sure that the modem is turned on and that *Works* is in Connect mode. There should be a bullet

(•) next to the **Connect** command in the Connect menu. Try the other COM port in the COMMUNICATION dialog box. If you still can't get a response, ask your computer dealer for help.

Entering a Phone Number

If your modem has an auto-dial feature, you must "teach" *Works* the number to call. Pull down the Options menu, and select **Phone**. Figure 6-5 shows the resulting dialog box.

Figure 6-5   Enter the BBS' phone number

```
┌─────────────────────── PHONE ───────────────────────┐
│                                                      │
│   Phone Number:  [·······························]    │
│                   _                                  │
│                                                      │
│   Modem Setup:   [·······························]    │
│                                                      │
│   Dial Type:                                         │
│   ┌──────────────────────────┐                       │
│   │  (•) Tone  ( ) Pulse     │   [ ] Automatic Answer │
│   └──────────────────────────┘                       │
│                                                      │
├──────────────────────────────────────────────────────┤
│                        <  OK  >   <Cancel>           │
└──────────────────────────────────────────────────────┘
```

Phone Number   Each communications document allows you to store one telephone number, along with all the settings in the TERMINAL and COMMUNICATION dialog boxes.

Currently, my BBS' phone number is 312-260-9660. I say "currently" because my phone company has just announced that as of November 1, 1989, my area code will change from 312 to 708. I'll assume that you're reading this prior to the changeover date and use "312," but if November 1, 1989, has come and gone, please substitute the new area code.

With the cursor in the **Phone Number**: text box, type the *Works* bulletin board number: **1-312-260-**

9660. The dashes are optional; *Works* and your Hayes-compatible modem will ignore them. (*Note*: If you live within the 312 calling area, type **260-9660** as the Phone Number.)

Modem Setup

I mentioned earlier that all Hayes-compatible modems understand a common set of commands. The **Modem Setup**: text box allows you to issue a string of commands to your modem *before* it dials the phone number. These commands control parameters such as the modem's speaker volume, the types of messages the modem returns, the modem's echo feature, etc. For now, you can ignore this option. Later on, you might want to read the modem manual to determine what commands, if any, you'd like to issue to your modem. (*Note*: If your modem isn't Hayes-compatible but *is* capable of automatic dialing, you should place the command for dialing the BBS phone number into this text box.)

Dial Type

Assuming that your modem can dial a telephone number automatically and that it is Hayes-compatible, the only other piece of information *Works* needs to know is whether your phone service supports Tone or Pulse dialing. *Works* assumes Tone, but if Touch-Tone® isn't available in your area or if you haven't paid for the option (there is an extra charge for Touch-Tone® service), choose Pulse for the Dial Type. (*Note*: If your modem either doesn't support auto-dialing or isn't Hayes-compatible, it doesn't matter which Dial Type you choose.)

Automatic Answer

This feature allows your modem to answer the phone automatically when it rings. With this feature enabled, a remote computer could call your PC and connect to it without your presence. My BBS has this feature enabled so that it will answer automatically when you call. But since you're initiating the call, leave this feature disabled.

Close the **PHONE** dialog box, and save this communication document to your data disk. Use the name WWWBBS.WCM.

Dialing the Bulletin Board

Here comes the big moment. Choose **Connect** from the Connect menu.
If your modem supports automatic dialing, you should hear the number
being dialed through the modem's built-in speaker.

If your modem can't dial a phone number automatically, use your
telephone to dial the number and, if your modem is an acoustic modem,
place the telephone handset in the modem's holder.

Most modems have a small speaker inside that allows you to hear
the call being placed. After the number is dialed, you will hear the
phone ring once, my modem will pick up the phone, and the two
modems will beep at each other for a few seconds. Then your modem's
speaker will stop monitoring the call, and you'll see the word "Connect"
on your screen. (*Note*: Depending on the baud rate your modem uses
and the messages it sends, you may see "Connect," "Connect 1200,"
or "Connect 2400.") The "Connect" message indicates that a connection
has been made between your PC and another computer.

Press (Enter) (the program I'm using for the bulletin board expects
you to do this). The WWWBBS will respond with a welcoming message,
and your screen should look like Figure 6-6. (*Note*: If you're operating
your modem at 300 or 2400 baud, the first line of the welcoming message
will indicate that baud rate.) Congratulations, you've just connected
with your first BBS (bulletin board system)! If all is well, skip the
next section and read *It Worked*!

It Didn't Work

OK. Suppose you didn't get the welcoming message. What do you do
now? First, wait a few seconds, and try pressing (Enter) again. If you
still don't see the message, type three plus symbols, +++, and wait a
few seconds. This action tells your Hayes-compatible modem to
disconnect from the phone line. (If your modem isn't Hayes-compatible,
you'll have to hang up the phone manually.)

If you were listening to the modem's speaker, you could hear
whether your call was answered. If it wasn't answered, either it rang
without being picked up, or you heard a busy signal. If the phone
rang several times without being answered, check that you, or *Works*,
dialed the correct number. If you're sure that you called the right
number, then the BBS has been temporarily turned off. I'm probably
doing maintenance (reading and sending messages, etc.). If the line
was busy, another reader is communicating with the BBS. All callers
are limited to 15 minutes per session, so the board will be available
shortly. In any case, call back in a few minutes. The WWWBBS operates
24 hours a day, every day.

Figure 6-6   Welcome to the WWWBBS

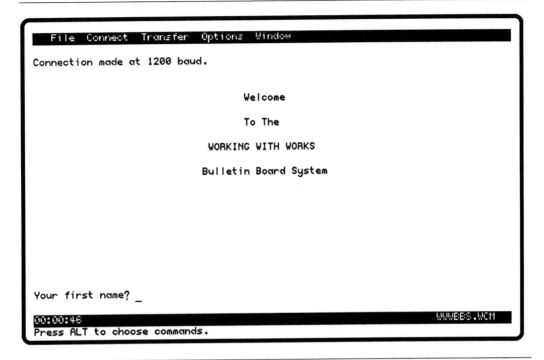

If your modem didn't dial when you selected **Connect**, and you have a Hayes-compatible modem, try typing **at** and press ⏎Enter. If the modem responds "OK," select **Dial Again** from the Connect menu.

If you got the "Connect" message on your screen, your computer successfully connected to my BBS. If you didn't get the "welcome" message after you pressed Return, then either my BBS has a problem (unlikely, but possible) or, more probably, one (or more) of the options in the COMMUNICATION dialog box differs from the values specified in Table 6-1. If you're sure the settings are correct, wait a day and try again. I check on the BBS at least once a day.

Finally, if your modem absolutely refuses to respond, no matter what you (or *Works*) try to do, take your system (modem *and* PC) to your local computer dealer and have someone there check the modem's operation.

It Worked!

At the bottom of the screen, the BBS is asking for your first name. Type it in, and press ⏎Enter. (*Note:* The bulletin board expects you to press (Enter) after every response.) Next, type in your last name, and wait for the BBS to check the caller directory (or userlog). Because this is the first time you've called the WWWBBS, your name won't be in the userlog (at least it shouldn't be), and you'll see a verification message listing your whole name and asking if you typed your name correctly (Figure 6-7). Type **Y** or **N** (you can type your responses in either upper- or lowercase).

Figure 6-7 Enter your first and last names

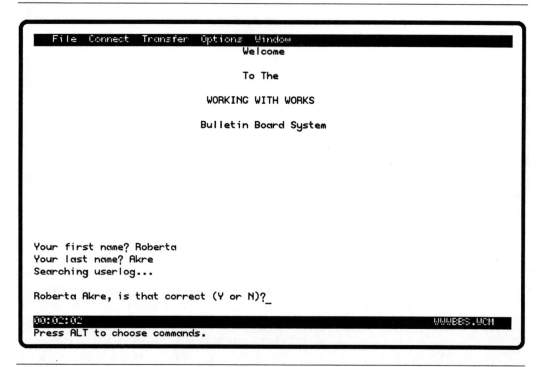

(*Note*: If, instead of the verification message, the BBS asks you immediately for your "password," someone else whose name is the same as yours has registered with the WWWBBS at some earlier time. Press (Enter) several times until the BBS stops asking you for a password that you don't know. The BBS will "log off" or disconnect. Dial the WWWBBS again by selecting the **Dial Again** command, and type your name slightly differently. Use a nickname or your middle name, anything to differentiate your name from the one already registered with the BBS.)

Next, the bulletin board wants to know the city and state you're calling from. Enter this information.

Now you get to enter your own password. Think up a password that is at least 3 but not more that 8 characters long. Type it in, then, when the BBS asks you to verify it, type it again. Notice that when you type the password the second time, asterisks are transmitted to your screen instead of the actual characters you type. This is for security. From now on, when you type your password to gain access to the WWWBBS, you'll see only asterisks repeated on your screen.

This is a good time to write down the name and the password you used to register with the WWWBBS so that you won't forget them. (No, I don't think you're going to forget your own name, but you might forget your password.)

WWWBBS Log On Data

First name: _____

Last name: _____

Password: _____

Terminal Characteristics

After you've verified your password, the bulletin board is going to ask you some questions about the operation of your computer and communications software. The first question concerns how your system treats carriage returns and linefeeds. The BBS will send two rows of periods and will then ask you if you see one row or two. You'll see one row, so type 1.

The second test will tell the BBS how to clear your screen, which it does every time it prints a menu (more about menus in a moment). The bulletin board sends a line of text, "Hello World," and then sends a special command that tells some computer systems to clear the screen. Unfortunately, *Works* doesn't recognize this "clear screen" command, so you'll still see the line "Hello World" on your screen. Therefore, answer **Y** to the question. Now the BBS knows that in order to clear your screen, it has to send a bunch of linefeed symbols that will scroll any text up and off the top of the window.

The last question gives you the option of using a feature called *Hot Menus*. Normally, you must press (Enter) after each response, including menu responses. If you choose the Hot Menus option, you can select menu choices by pressing a single key—you won't have to press (Enter). For the time being, though, answer **N** to this option (Figure 6-8). You can change your mind later, and this way you'll know that you must always press (Enter) after *every* type of response.

Registration

My bulletin board currently supports readers of three of my computer books—*Working with Works* and *Word Power*, both written for the Macintosh computer, and this book, *Working with PC Works*. Each group of readers communicates within its own section of the BBS. So the bulletin board needs to know whether you're a PC owner or a Macintosh owner.

Figure 6-8 Configure the BBS for your computer

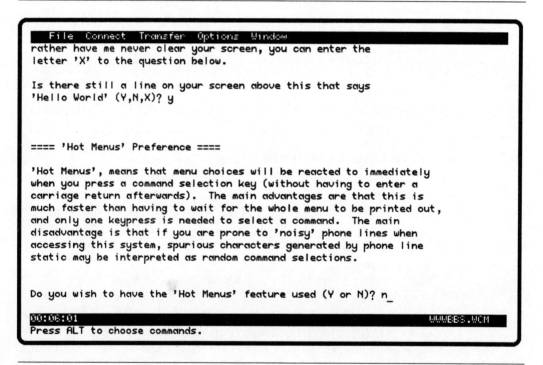

After you complete the last question about your terminal, you'll see the Main Menu screen for first-time callers. There are only two options, New caller registration and Log off.

Enter a 1 to select New caller registration. The BBS asks "Are you a Macintosh user (Y/N)?" Respond by typing **N**. You are now registered as a *Working with PC Works* reader (Figure 6-9). Press (Enter).

Figure 6-9   Register as a *Working with PC Works* reader

```
 File  Connect  Transfer  Options  Window




                    *** IDENTIFICATION AND REGISTRATION ***

Because this BBS is used to support both Macintosh and MS-DOS
users, I need to know which type of computer you're using.

Please answer Yes or No ('Y' or 'N') to the following question.

Are you a Macintosh user (Y/N)? n

Thank you. You're now registered as a "Working With PC Works" reader
and can access electronic mail and file transfer sections.

Please press <RETURN> or <ENTER> to continue._

 00:05:10                                                  WWWBBS.WCM
 Press ALT to choose commands.
```

The Main Menu

After you've registered as a *PC Works* reader, your screen will clear, and you'll see the standard Main Menu. All of the features in the WWWBBS are presented as menu choices. This is the same technique used by most BBSs and all information services. Currently, the Main Menu shows five choices (Figure 6-10).

The first choice, Caller Information, displays a menu with options allowing you to change your password, change your terminal characteristics (Hot Menus), see a list of other callers to the BBS, etc. The second choice, Exercises for Project 11, shows you another menu that you will use in the next section of this project.

I'll discuss the third and fourth options in the second part of this chapter, after you complete Project 11. The last option in the Main Menu allows you to log off, or disconnect, from the BBS. Below the choices, you'll see a line telling you how much time you have remaining in this communications session. Each session is limited to 15 minutes so that everyone will have an opportunity to connect with the

Figure 6-10 The bulletin board's Main Menu

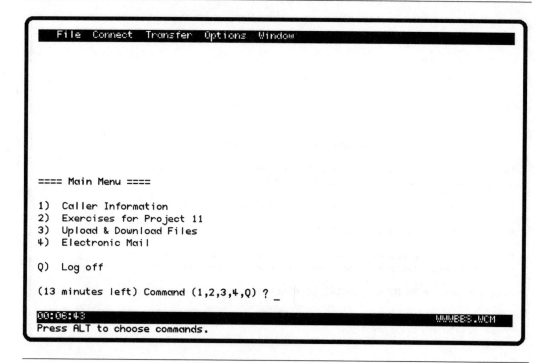

```
  File  Connect  Transfer  Options  Window




==== Main Menu ====

1)  Caller Information
2)  Exercises for Project 11
3)  Upload & Download Files
4)  Electronic Mail

Q)  Log off

(13 minutes left) Command (1,2,3,4,Q) ? _
00:08:43                                          WWWBBS.WCM
Press ALT to choose commands.
```

WWWBBS. You'll also see a list of allowed responses to the menu choices—in this case 1,2,3,4,Q.

In order to select a menu choice, you must type the single character that precedes the item in the menu.

Logging Off

I know you want to start sending and receiving data to and from the BBS. But right now, I'd like you to log off from the system. This way you'll get a chance to read about the various operations you're going to perform, and when you call up the BBS to actually do the exercises, you'll have the full 15-minute session to work with.

Type **Q** (for Quit) as your selection from the Main Menu. Type **Y**, indicating that you really want to disconnect now.

In a few seconds, the BBS tells you it has disconnected and advises you to hang up your modem (Figure 6-11). If you have a Hayes-compatible modem, *Works* will automatically hang up your modem. If your modem is not Hayes-compatible, type whatever command it

Figure 6-11   Logging off the BBS

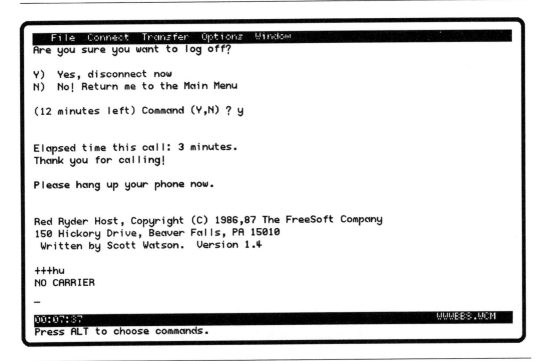

```
 File  Connect  Transfer  Options  Window
Are you sure you want to log off?

Y)  Yes, disconnect now
N)  No! Return me to the Main Menu

(12 minutes left) Command (Y,N) ? y


Elapsed time this call: 3 minutes.
Thank you for calling!

Please hang up your phone now.


Red Ryder Host, Copyright (C) 1986,87 The FreeSoft Company
150 Hickory Drive, Beaver Falls, PA 15010
 Written by Scott Watson.  Version 1.4

+++hu
NO CARRIER

-

00:07:37                                          WWWBBS.WCM
Press ALT to choose commands.
```

needs to hang up the phone. If yours is an acoustic modem, place the handset back on the telephone.

You have just been initiated into the world of data communications.

≡ Sending and Receiving Data

There are many reasons to use your computer to talk to other computers. Bulletin boards of various types abound. Most are dedicated to special interests of one sort or another. Some bulletin boards are for users of particular programs (such as *Works*); others are for people who share a common vocation (medicine or law, for example). Then there are the major public access computer networks, such as CompuServe, The Source, Dow Jones, GEnie, and Delphi. These services provide an incredible variety of features, from special interest groups (called

SIGs) and home shopping by computer to stock market quotes and entire encyclopedias of information.

However you decide to use *Works'* data communications tool, even if you're just calling up a friend who has a computer, you need to know how to send and receive information. In the telecommunications world, this is called "uploading" and "downloading."

Text vs. Files

There are two general types of computer information that are uploaded and downloaded: text and files. When you send *text* to another computer, all you're sending are the characters that comprise the message. No special attributes (e.g., boldface, underlining, or formatting of any kind) are sent along with the characters. You can send the text characters one at a time, as you type them, or you can prepare the message in advance and send it after you connect with the other computer. But the key concept regarding transmitted text is that only characters are sent and received, nothing else.

Sending (and receiving) *files*, on the other hand, is a different matter altogether. When you transmit a file, you send an entire document. It doesn't matter what's inside the document. If it's a word processor document, all the special formatting characteristics are included. If you send a spreadsheet, the entire spreadsheet, including formulas and charts, is transmitted. You can send and receive pictures, even entire computer programs, as long as they are transmitted as files.

In this part of the project, you'll be sending and receiving both text and files. As you might expect, there are four exercises: sending text, receiving text, sending a file, and receiving a file. The files you'll be receiving from the BBS have already been created and are waiting for you to download them.

You'll need to create the text you'll be sending to the BBS, but you can use one of the existing *Works* documents you created in an earlier chapter as the file to be uploaded.

Sending Text

One of the major features of a computer bulletin board or information service is its ability to play mail carrier. This feature is called *electronic mail* or *Email*, and it allows you to send and receive messages from anyone else who calls the same computer.

Usually, the steps for sending a message are as follows: You log on to the *host* computer (my bulletin board, for example). You select the electronic mail feature from a menu. You choose to send a message (as opposed to reading messages sent to you). You type the name of the person to whom you're sending the message and, perhaps, a brief description of the message (welcome, help, etc.). Then you input the message itself and send it.

Because most commercial computer networks charge you for the time you are connected to them, the less time you spend sending a message, the less you are charged. While the WWWBBS is free to owners of *Working with PC Works*, telephone long distance charges mount up quickly. For that reason, any technique that shortens the *connect time* is one you should master. One such technique is preparing electronic mail messages *off line* (not connected to the host computer).

Works allows you to prepare communications text messages in the word processor, and I'd like you to do that now. As soon as you've created the message in the word processor, you'll dial up the WWWBBS and send the message to me, the System Operator.

Create a new word processor document by choosing **New** from the File menu and then pressing (Enter) (the word processor tool is selected by default). Figure 6-12 shows a typical message to the System Operator (or Sysop).

Figure 6-12   Create a sample text message in the word processor

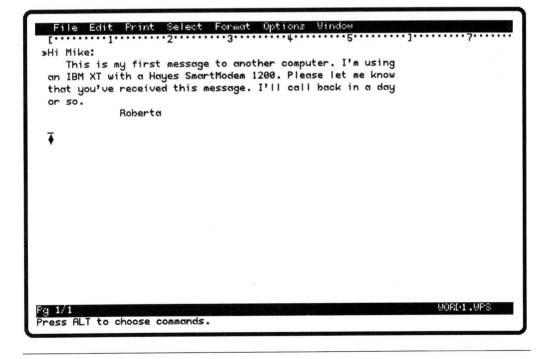

Don't feel that you have to copy the message word for word. Feel free to type any message you like. Here are a couple of guidelines you should use when you create electronic mail messages off line. Don't leave any blank lines in your message (above, within, or below). My bulletin board and many others interpret a blank line as signifying the *end* of the message. And keep your messages fairly short—less than 40 lines. If you need to send a lengthier message, break it into two or more parts and send them as separate messages.

After you've typed the last line of your message, press (Enter), but don't leave any extra blank lines at the bottom of the document. Then, display the LAYOUT dialog box and change the values of the following options:

Option	New Value
Top Margin	0″
Bottom Margin	0″
Left Margin	0″
Right Margin	1.5″
Footer	Delete default Footer
Header Margin	0″
Footer Margin	0″

Close the LAYOUT dialog box and display the SAVE AS dialog box by selecting **Save**. (If necessary, use the Other Drives and Directories list box, (Alt) + (O), to select the disk drive containing your data disk.) Name this document MESSAGE., and be sure to include the period at the end of the name. Then, because you intend to use this document for data communications, press (Alt) + (P) to choose the Plain option (Figure 6-13). Press (Enter) to save the file to your data disk, and when *Works* asks if it's OK to lose the document's formatting (a result of choosing the Plain option), press (Enter) again.

You can leave this document on your *Works* desktop and display the Communications window. Pull down the Window menu, and select **1 WWWBBS.WCM**.

Now let's send the message. Dial the WWWBBS by selecting **Dial Again** from the Connect menu. (*Note: Works* must be *online* for the **Dial Again** command to be active. If the status line displays the OFFLINE message, select the **Connect** command instead of **Dial Again**.) Press (Enter) after you see the word "Connect" on your screen. Type

Figure 6-13 Save the document as a Plain text file

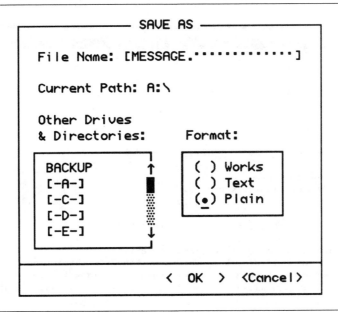

your name, first name then last, as you're prompted. And then type in your password, exactly as you typed it the first time you called the BBS. (*Note*: This process, from dialing the BBS to typing your password, is called "logging on" to the bulletin board system.)

At the Main Menu, choose item 2, Exercises for Project 11, by typing **2** and pressing (Enter). (Always press (Enter) after each response.)

The Project 11 Exercises menu has five options (plus Return to the Main Menu). You want to send a text message to me, so type **1** for Send text.

Before you can send a message, the bulletin board needs to know *who* you're sending it to. I am the "System Operator" or "Sysop." Type one name or the other. The BBS then verifies that there is such a person called System Operator or Sysop registered.

Next, you're asked for a brief (40 characters or fewer) description of your message. Call it a "First Text Message." At this point, your screen should look like Figure 6-14.

The BBS is now waiting for you to input the actual message. You could type it in, but you prepared the message off line so that you wouldn't have to take the time typing it in while you were connected. Pull down the Transfer menu, and select **Send Text**. *Works* displays a dialog box (Figure 6-15) that shows the names of all of the documents

Figure 6-14 You're ready to send the text file

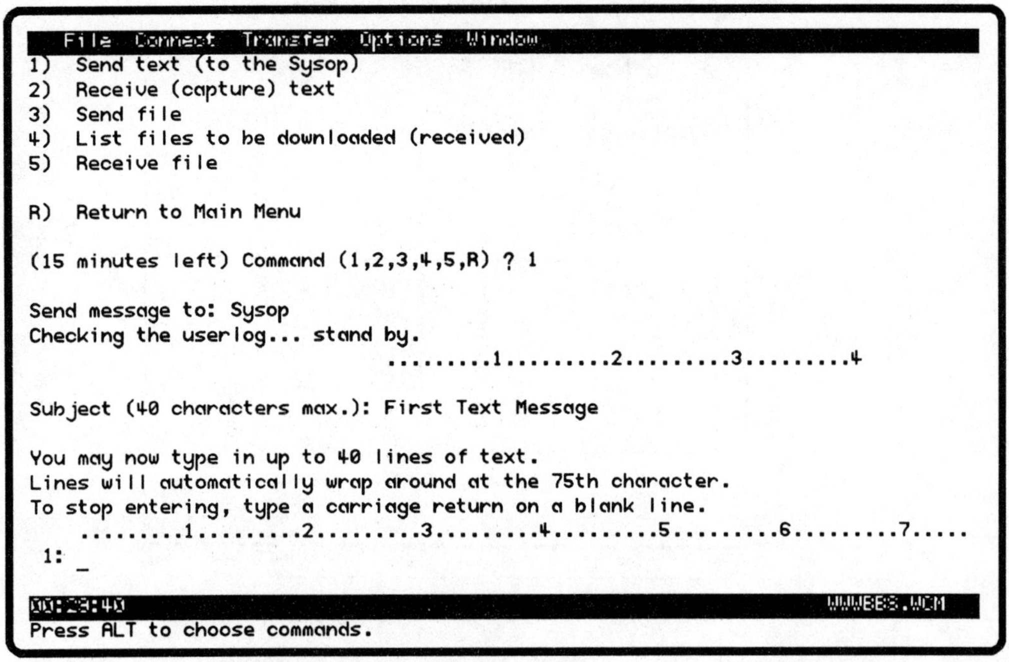

```
 File  Connect  Transfer  Options  Window
1)  Send text (to the Sysop)
2)  Receive (capture) text
3)  Send file
4)  List files to be downloaded (received)
5)  Receive file

R)  Return to Main Menu

(15 minutes left) Command (1,2,3,4,5,R) ? 1

Send message to: Sysop
Checking the userlog... stand by.
                        .........1.........2.........3.........4

Subject (40 characters max.): First Text Message

You may now type in up to 40 lines of text.
Lines will automatically wrap around at the 75th character.
To stop entering, type a carriage return on a blank line.
        .........1.........2.........3.........4.........5.........6.........7.....
  1:  _


00:29:40                                              WWWBBS.WCM
Press ALT to choose commands.
```

on your *Works* Data disk that have file names ending with a period. That's why you gave the name "MESSAGE." to your word processor document. "MESSAGE" should be the only document in the Files list box. Press Alt + F to move the cursor to this list box, then highlight the MESSAGE file name and press Enter.

Works transmits the text in the document, and to the BBS it appears the same as if you were typing it in.

After the message has been sent, press Enter. The BBS gives you a variety of options (Figure 6-16) for handling the message. These options allow you to actually send the message to me, throw it away without sending it, look at the message to verify that the BBS received it correctly, edit the message, and so forth.

Type **L** (List), for example, and your text message will be retyped. Type **S**, for Save, and your message is placed in my "mail box." During the next day, I'll read the message and send you an acknowledgment.

Figure 6-15 Select the MESSAGE file

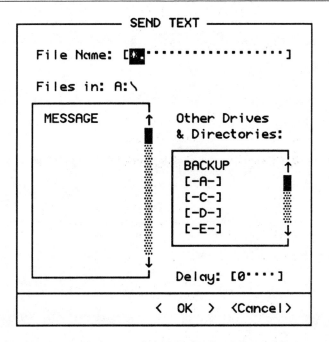

The next time you log on to the BBS, you can choose the Electronic Mail option, and you'll be able to read my message to you. (*Note*: The last section of this chapter explains the use of the BBS electronic mail feature.)

Press (Enter), and the BBS will display the Project 11 Exercises menu again.

Receiving Text

I have left a text message on the bulletin board for you to receive. The second option in the Project 11 menu displays this message, so type **2**.

If you were to log off the BBS and quit *Works,* the text you received would disappear. In fact, if you just press the Return key (which you're being prompted to do), the message will be scrolled off the top of the screen. Once text has been scrolled off the window, there's no way to look at it again.

Most of the text you receive, BBS menus, for example, you don't need to see again. But if you want to review the message I sent to

Figure 6-16   Send the text file

```
  File  Connect  Transfer  Options  Window
(15 minutes left) Command (1,2,3,4,5,R) ? 1

Send message to: Sysop
Checking the userlog... stand by.
                     .........1.........2.........3.........4

Subject (40 characters max.): First Text Message

You may now type in up to 40 lines of text.
Lines will automatically wrap around at the 75th character.
To stop entering, type a carriage return on a blank line.
     .........1.........2.........3.........4.........5.........6.........7.....
 1: Hi Mike:
 2:    This is my first message to another computer. I'm using an IBM XT
 3: with a Hayes SmartModem 1200. Please let me know that you've received
 4: this message. I'll call back in a day or so.
 5:          Roberta
 6:


C)ancel, S)ave, L)ist, I)nsert, D)elete, A)dd, E)dit: (C,S,L,I,D,A,E)? _

00:31:45                                              WWWEES.WCM
Press ALT to choose commands.
```

you, you need a way to save the text to your data disk. The **Capture Text** command lets you do this.

You should be looking at the Project menu again (press Enter if it isn't displayed). Choose **Capture Text** from the Transfer menu. The dialog box (Figure 6-17) is prompting you for a file name and a disk location. Make sure your data disk is specified as the Current Path (use the **Other Drives & Directories**: list box, if necessary). Name the file CAPTEXT, and press Enter.

From now on, until you turn off the **Capture Text** feature, everything that appears in the Communications window will be saved to your data disk in a file called CAPTEXT.

Choose option 2 from the Project 11 menu, so that my text message is sent again to your computer. This time, though, the message is also being saved to disk. Now, instead of pressing Enter at the prompt, pull down the Transfer menu and choose **End Capture Text**. Now the text coming to your screen is no longer being saved to disk.

Figure 6-17   Change the file name to CAPTEXT

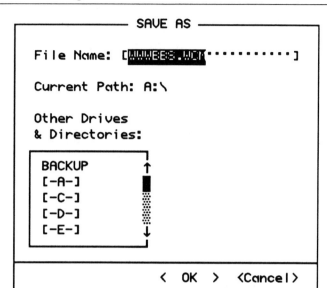

Sending a File

In a few moments, you'll be sending one of your *Works* files to me. It doesn't matter which one you choose, but I'm going to assume it will be PROPOSAL.WPS, a word processor document you created in Chapter 2. If you don't have this file on your data disk, or if you'd rather send a different file—even a non-*Works* file—that's fine.

By the way, don't worry about running out of time on the WWWBBS. You are limited to 15 minutes per call, but you can always call back and have another 15-minute session. Another thing you should know is that the BBS monitors your activity (or rather your inactivity). If you don't type anything for five minutes, the BBS figures you've gone to sleep and logs you off automatically.

Choose option 3, Send File, from the Project 11 Exercises menu on the BBS. The bulletin board wants to know what method (protocol) it should use to check for transmission errors. Choose the *second* protocol, XMODEM-Checksum.

The BBS asks if the file you're uploading was created on a Macintosh computer. Since your file was created on a PC, respond by typing **N**. Next, the BBS will advise you how much disk space it has available for storing your file. And then it will ask you for a file name for your file. Normally, you would choose a descriptive name, such as Sample File. But because so many readers will be sending their files to the WWWBBS, and since each file must have a unique file name, type your name (or the first 12 characters of it) as the file name. Finally, the BBS will prompt you to send the file (Figure 6-18).

Figure 6-18   Get ready to send your file

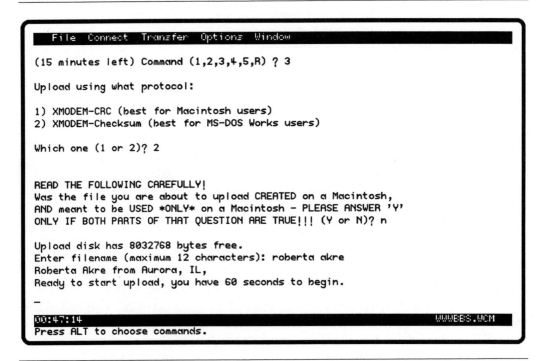

```
  File  Connect  Transfer  Options  Window

(15 minutes left) Command (1,2,3,4,5,R) ? 3

Upload using what protocol:

1) XMODEM-CRC (best for Macintosh users)
2) XMODEM-Checksum (best for MS-DOS Works users)

Which one (1 or 2)? 2


READ THE FOLLOWING CAREFULLY!
Was the file you are about to upload CREATED on a Macintosh,
AND meant to be USED *ONLY* on a Macintosh - PLEASE ANSWER 'Y'
ONLY IF BOTH PARTS OF THAT QUESTION ARE TRUE!!! (Y or N)? n

Upload disk has 8032768 bytes free.
Enter filename (maximum 12 characters): roberta akre
Roberta Akre from Aurora, IL,
Ready to start upload, you have 60 seconds to begin.

_

00:47:14                                            WWWBBS.WCM
Press ALT to choose commands.
```

Don't worry about the 60-second time limit; you have plenty of time. Pull down the Transfer menu, and choose **Send Protocol**. Figure 6-19 shows the SEND PROTOCOL dialog box. Notice that at the right of the dialog box there are two Send Formats, Binary and Text. Accept the default choice, Binary. If necessary, use the Other Drives & Directories to select the disk drive containing your data disk. Then, choose "PROPOSAL.WPS" from the **Files:** list box, and press (Enter).

Works will immediately display a box that shows your file's progress as it is being transmitted (Figure 6-20). The two protocols you've chosen—Binary for *Works,* and XMODEM-Checksum for the BBS—work together to transmit your file in sections or "blocks." As each block is sent from your computer to my BBS, a check is made

Figure 6-19   Choose a file to upload

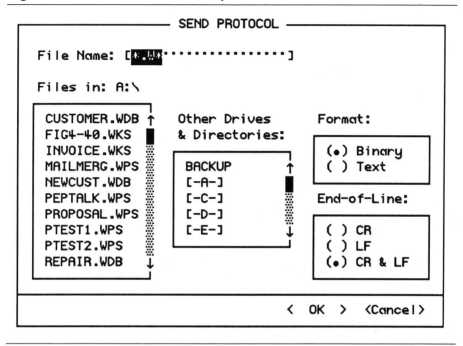

Figure 6-20   You can watch your file being sent

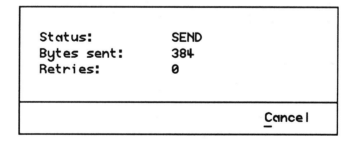

to see if it was received correctly. If there is a transmission error, the block is retransmitted.

After all the blocks have been successfully transmitted and received, press (Enter). The BBS tells you: "The file transfer concluded successfully."

When the BBS asks you if the file you uploaded was meant to be used on a Macintosh, answer **N**. You'll then be asked for the version number or release date of the transmitted file. Ignore this, and just press (Enter). For the file description, enter the type of file (word processor, database, etc.) and your name (Figure 6-21).

Figure 6-21   Describe the uploaded file

```
 File  Connect  Transfer  Options  Window


The file transfer concluded successfully.


Is this file meant to be used on a Macintosh (Y or N)? n

If you know it, please enter the version number or release date
of this file so that others won't download a version they already
have.  If you don't know it, just enter a carriage return.

Version number or release date (maximum 8 characters):


Enter a description of the file, up to 60 characters long,
that will help others decide if the file would be useful to them.
If you would like this file to be accessible by the system operator
only, put a '*' character as the first character of the description.
             ..........1.........2.........3.........4.........5.........6
Description: Word Processor file from Roberta Akre_

01:14:31                                                    WWWBBS.WCM
Press ALT to choose commands.
```

That's all there is to sending a file to another computer. Actually, the version number and file description requests have nothing to do with the file transfer process. The WWWBBS uses this information as part of its filing system.

Receiving a File

The last of the four exercises will show you how to receive, or download, a file from another computer. Before you can tell the BBS to download the file to you, you have to know the name of the file. That's the purpose of the fourth option in the Project 11 Exercises menu.

Type 4, and the WWWBBS will list the files available for you to download. Actually, for this exercise, there is only one file, called PROJECT 11 (Figure 6-22).

Figure 6-22   View the list of files for downloading

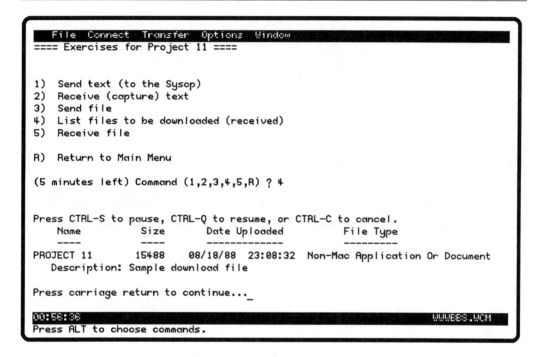

Press (Enter) to display the Project menu again. Now that you know the name of the file, choose option 5. The file name is, of course, PROJECT 11, and you will choose protocol 2, XMODEM-Checksum, as you did when you were sending a file (Figure 6-23).

Again, don't let the 60-second time factor make you feel rushed. Select **Receive Protocol** from the Transfer menu of *Works*. The RECEIVE PROTOCOL dialog box (Figure 6-24) looks much like the one for SEND PROTOCOL, but without the Files list box. Make sure

Figure 6-23 Select XMODEM-Checksum protocol

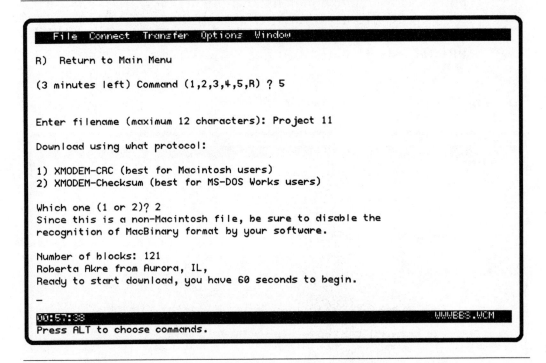

```
   File  Connect  Transfer  Options  Window

R)  Return to Main Menu

(3 minutes left) Command (1,2,3,4,5,R) ? 5


Enter filename (maximum 12 characters): Project 11

Download using what protocol:

1) XMODEM-CRC (best for Macintosh users)
2) XMODEM-Checksum (best for MS-DOS Works users)

Which one (1 or 2)? 2
Since this is a non-Macintosh file, be sure to disable the
recognition of MacBinary format by your software.

Number of blocks: 121
Roberta Akre from Aurora, IL,
Ready to start download, you have 60 seconds to begin.

-

00:57:38                                         WWWBBS.WCM
Press ALT to choose commands.
```

that the drive containing your data disk is named as the Current Path. (If necessary, use the Other Drives & Directories list box.) Enter the name SPIRAL.WKS for the File Name, and accept the default Receive Format, Binary (Figure 6-24).

Press (Enter), and the WWWBBS will begin sending the file to your computer. Again, you'll see a box on your screen marking the progress of the file as it's being received (Figure 6-25).

When the file has been completely received, press (Enter) and you'll see the Project menu once more. Return to the Main Menu (type **R**), and log off from the BBS.

Did It Work?

You sent and received a total of four documents, either as text or as files. Were they *really* transmitted? The two you sent to the BBS will be read and acknowledged (more about that in a minute). The two you received—one captured text, the other a file—should be on your *Works* Data disk.

Figure 6-24 Name the file you're about to download

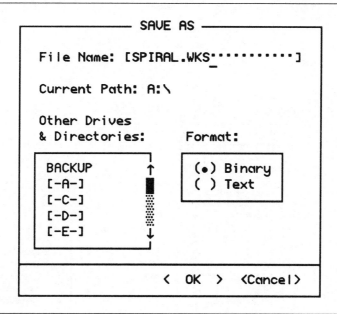

Figure 6-25 The Receive File status box

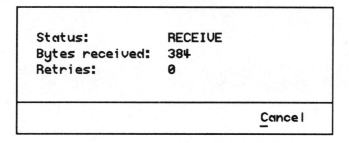

Choose **Open** from the File menu, and let's look at the captured text document. Don't worry if the document's name, CAPTEXT, doesn't appear in the **Files:** list box. By default, *Works* only displays files with an *extension* beginning with the letter "W." (*Note:* See Chapter 2 for the discussion of *Works'* file extensions.) CAPTEXT is really on your Data disk; it's just not displayed in the list box.

Replace the default file name "*.W*" in the File Name text box with the three characters, *.*, and press (Enter). This tells *Works* to display *all* the files on your data disk. Now you should see the CAPTEXT document in the **Files**: list box (Figure 6-26). Select this file, and press (Enter).

Figure 6-26 Choose CAPTEXT from the OPEN dialog box

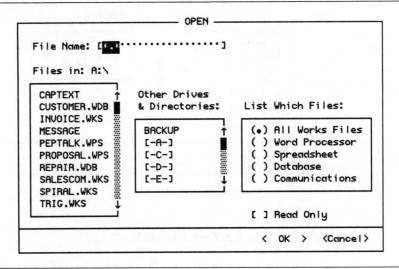

Because this file is a pure text file, rather than a *Works* file (word processor, spreadsheet, etc.), you need to tell *Works* how to interpret the file—as a word processor file, spreadsheet file, or database file (Figure 6-27). Press (Enter) to accept the default choice of Word Processor.

Figure 6-27 Open the CAPTEXT file as a word processor document

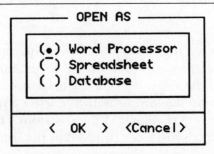

It may look as if this document is blank, but remember that the BBS began the message with several blank lines. Scroll down, and you'll see the message. You can edit the document by deleting the blank lines at the top, and the "Press any key to continue" line at the bottom. Then you can resave the document.

Open the SPIRAL.WKS file you downloaded from the BBS. I won't tell you what's in this file. Let it be a surprise. But you'll know the file was correctly received when you open it.

Now, how about the files you sent to me? As I mentioned earlier, I will acknowledge them through the BBS. As soon as I read them (by the end of the next day, for sure), I'll write an electronic mail message to you and "post" it on the WWWBBS. The next time you log on, you can read your message in Electronic Mail.

In the next section, you will learn how to read and send electronic mail and how to use the other features of the WWWBBS as well.

SPECIAL FEATURES OF THE *WORKING WITH WORKS* BULLETIN BOARD SYSTEM

To my knowledge, this is the first time an author has offered assistance to his readers through a computer bulletin board service. In addition to being used with the exercises in Project 11, the WWWBBS was set up to provide you with a source of technical support for Microsoft *Works*.

When a problem arises with *Works*, help is a phone call away. This help comes from three separate areas. First, fellow callers to the WWWBBS will see your question in the public message section. People who share a common interest (the use of a computer program like *Works*, for example) are remarkably willing to offer assistance. And, because the BBS is free (except for long distance phone charges), I encourage you to call frequently and check the public message section.

Second, I will read each request for assistance and answer all the questions I can. If I need to see your *Works* file, so that I can better understand your problem, you can transmit the file to me using the BBS' File Transfer section.

Third, if I can't solve the problem, I will refer it to the folks at Microsoft, who have expressed great interest in this bulletin board support concept. One of the benefits Microsoft hopes to gain is user reports of actual program faults (bugs). Every program has them; that's why new versions of programs are released periodically. The more information we provide Microsoft about their program, the better the program will become.

☰ The Caller Information Menu

In addition to the exercises for Project 11, in the WWWBBS, there are three other sections. Each of these is accessed through the Main Menu.

The first choice in the Main Menu is Caller Information. This section offers four utilities (Figure 6-28). The first allows you to change your password. Remember to write down the new password so that you won't forget it.

Figure 6-28 The BBS' Caller Information Menu

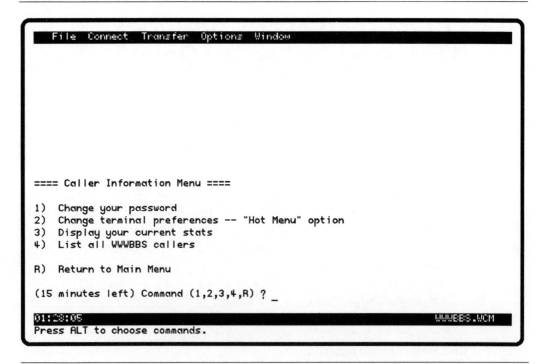

```
 File  Connect  Transfer  Options  Window




==== Caller Information Menu ====

1)  Change your password
2)  Change terminal preferences -- "Hot Menu" option
3)  Display your current stats
4)  List all WWWBBS callers

R)  Return to Main Menu

(15 minutes left) Command (1,2,3,4,R) ? _

01:28:05                                    WWWBBS.WCM
Press ALT to choose commands.
```

The second option in this section lets you change what are called "terminal preferences." You saw these preferences when you first signed on to the BBS. Two of the preferences you might decide to change are "clear screen" and Hot Menus. Currently, the BBS clears your screen (by issuing a number of blank lines) before it prints each menu. You can choose not to have the BBS clear your screen ("X" response).

You can also select the Hot Menus option to speed up the BBS' response to your menu choices. Normally, the BBS prints the entire menu, then prints a line listing all the acceptable choices, and then waits for you to type one of these choices and press ⎡Enter⎤. If you select the Hot Menus option, you don't have to wait for a menu to be printed on your screen; you can type your selection immediately. You don't even have to press ⎡Enter⎤.

The third Caller Information option, Display your current stats, lists your current status on the WWWBBS. It tells you how many times you've called the BBS, when you last called, the number of files you have uploaded and downloaded, how many messages you have sent, etc.

The List all WWWBBS callers option prints a chronological list of all the callers to the BBS. When you want to send a message to another caller, you must know his or her name. This option is also available in the Electronic Mail section of the BBS.

≡ The File Transfer Menu

Selecting option 3 from the BBS' Main Menu displays the File Transfer Menu (Figure 6-29). The menu has four options: three of them for downloading a file from the BBS to your PC, the fourth for uploading a file from your computer to the BBS. The files for downloading are those contributed by you and other *Working with PC Works* readers. They may be *Works* spreadsheet templates, public domain programs, or other interesting files. You are welcome to download and use any or all of them.

To see a list of the available files, choose option 1 from the File Transfer menu. Make a note of the names of the files you wish to download.

The second option displays specific information about a particular file, so you'll need the file's name. The BBS will display the file type,

Figure 6-29 The File Transfer Menu

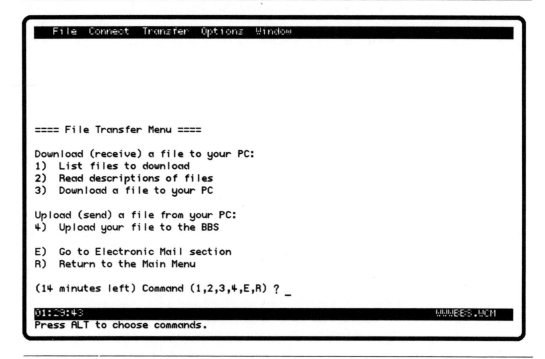

the date the file was uploaded to the BBS, the size of the file, the version number, and a description. Of all this information, the file size is probably the most useful. With it, you can estimate the time it will take to download the file. If you are communicating at 1200 baud (see the discussion of baud rate earlier in this chapter), it takes about 10 seconds to transmit 1000 bytes of data. A 30,000-byte file, therefore, would take about five minutes to download. At 300 baud, that same file would take about 20 minutes. Don't worry about the 15-minute time limit. The BBS won't cut you off in the middle of a file transfer.

Option 3 in the File Transfer menu does the actual downloading. Again, you'll need the name of the file. You'll also be asked to choose the error-checking protocol, so be sure you select the second one: XMODEM-Checksum. After the BBS tells you that you have 60 seconds to begin downloading, pull down the Transfer menu in *Works*, and choose **Receive Protocol**. If necessary, select your *Works* Data disk with the Other Drives & Directories option. Type in a file name (you can use the same name as the one given by the BBS), and accept the default

Format, Binary. Press (Enter), and the file will be downloaded to your data disk. You can watch its progress on your screen.

If you decide not to download a file, just wait about a minute, and the BBS will abort the option. If you've already started downloading the file and you want to stop receiving it, press (Esc) or (Enter). When *Works* asks if you want to cancel the file transfer, press (Enter).

The last File Transfer option allows you to upload a file from your PC to the WWWBBS. You might use this option if you wanted to send a troublesome *Works* file to me. Or you might want to share a *Works* application document (a spreadsheet, for example) with other callers to the BBS.

To upload a file to the BBS, choose option 4 from the File Transfer menu. Select XMODEM-Checksum protocol, and use the file's actual name as the filename. Tell the BBS that your file is *not* a Macintosh file. When you're prompted to start uploading, pull down the Transfer menu and choose **Send Protocol**. Select the file from the list in the dialog box, leave the Format set to Binary, and press (Enter).

If you decide not to upload a file, just wait about a minute, and the BBS will abort the option. If you've already started uploading the file and you want to stop sending it, press (Esc) or (Enter). When *Works* asks if you want to cancel the file transfer, press (Enter).

☰ The Electronic Mail Menu

Electronic mail (Email) is the fourth option on the Main Menu. Virtually every electronic bulletin board and information service provides some sort of Email facility. Figure 6-30 shows the Electronic Mail Menu.

Usually, you're allowed to send two types of Email: private and public. That's why the six Email options are grouped into two categories.

The first Private Message option is specifically designed to allow you to send Email to me, the System Operator. You can prepare the message offline, as you did in the first Project 11 exercise, or you can type the message at the prompt.

Whenever you input a message, typing a blank line signifies that you've reached the end of the message. This means that you can't use blank lines to separate paragraphs in your message. (You can, however, press (Tab), and then press (Enter) to leave what looks like a blank line.) After you've typed the message's last line, press (Enter) one extra time, and the BBS will ask you what you want to do with the message.

Figure 6-30　The Electronic Mail Menu

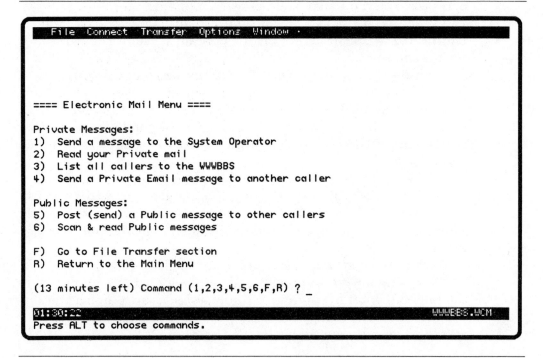

```
  File  Connect  Transfer  Options  Window .




==== Electronic Mail Menu ====

Private Messages:
1)  Send a message to the System Operator
2)  Read your Private mail
3)  List all callers to the WWWBBS
4)  Send a Private Email message to another caller

Public Messages:
5)  Post (send) a Public message to other callers
6)  Scan & read Public messages

F)  Go to File Transfer section
R)  Return to the Main Menu

(13 minutes left) Command (1,2,3,4,5,6,F,R) ? _

01:30:22                                         WWWBBS.WCM
Press ALT to choose commands.
```

Your choices are (C) Cancel, (S) Save, (L) List, (I) Insert, (D) Delete, (A) Add, and (E) Edit.

Cancel lets you throw away the message without actually sending it. Save sends, or "posts," the message to the person you've specified. List retypes the message.

The remaining four choices are used to edit the message. Corrections are made to individual lines. That's why each line in your message is numbered. If you need to add a line at the top or between existing lines, use Insert. You'll be prompted for the number of the line *below* the line to be inserted. Delete removes a line from the message. Add is used to add a line at the bottom of the message, while Edit allows you to change a message line.

Most of the time, you'll prepare your messages offline, and do your editing in the *Works* word processor, so you won't need to use these editing commands. In fact, the only command you'll probably use is Save.

The second Electronic Mail feature, Read your Private mail, lets you see all the Private messages that were addressed to you and/or sent by you to someone else. After each message is printed, the BBS gives you three options. You can tell it to delete the message, you can reply to the message, or you can see the next Private message addressed to you, if there is one. When you reply, the BBS automatically addresses the reply to the caller who sent the original message.

For long messages, you need a way to tell the BBS to pause the output from the BBS, so that you have time to read the message before it scrolls off the top of the screen. You could use the Capture Text command to record the message to your data disk, but there's an easy way to temporarily halt the flow of data from a remote computer. Type (Control) + (S). The BBS will stop its listing. (It may print another line or so before it recognizes the pause command.) To resume the listing, type (Control) + (Q). (*Note*: Typing (Control) + (S) sends a special character to the BBS. This character is recognized as an Xoff command. (Control) + (Q) generates a character that is recognized as an Xon command. See the discussion of handshaking at the beginning of this chapter.)

You are urged to delete messages after you read them. The BBS has a limited amount of storage space for messages. Periodically, I will delete any messages more than 30 days old. (*Note*: You can only delete messages that were sent either to you or by you.)

When you want to send a private message (or a public message, for that matter), you need to know the exact name of the intended person. The third Email option, List all callers to the WWWBBS, prints a list of every caller to the bulletin board. This is the same utility you'll find in the Caller Information Menu, discussed earlier.

When you want to send a Private message to someone other than the System Operator, you'll use option 4, Send a Private Email message to another caller. The only difference between this option and option 1 is that option 4 lets you specify a caller's name and a brief description of the message.

The remaining two options deal with public access messages. Option 5 lets you send a message either to an individual caller or to "All" callers, to be posted in the Public message section. These messages, whether they're addressed to an individual caller or to "All," can be read by everyone. The procedure for sending a Public message is the same as for sending a Private one.

When you want to read Public messages, use option 6, Scan & read Public messages. When you scan messages you see only the description of the message. You then can decide whether you want to read the entire message. To avoid having to look at messages you have read before, the BBS offers several scanning options.

When you first select option 6, you can choose to scan (N) New messages since last call, (F) Forward chronologically, (R) Reverse chronologically, or (I) Individually. New will display only those messages that have been posted since the last time you called the BBS.

Forward will display all Public messages in the order they were posted. You'll see a range of message numbers (e.g., 1 - 45), and the Forward scan will begin with the message number you specify.

Reverse will also display all Public messages, but will start with the newest message and work backwards. You'll probably want to start with the highest message number.

Scanning Individually requires that you know the number of the message. This option is useful if you want to reread a message.

As you scan through the messages, you can decide which of them you want to read. If you read the message, you can then delete it (if it's either to you or from you), reply to it, or go on to the next message. You can stop scanning whenever you want by pressing (Enter) instead of one of the lettered responses.

☰ Final Comments

I won't promise that the above section describes *all* the features of the WWWBBS. At the moment it does, but the software I'm using to run the bulletin board allows me to add features at any time. The bulletin board program, by the way, is called *Red Ryder Host*, and is available from The Freesoft Company—in case you'd like to run your own bulletin board system. Their address is displayed every time you log off the BBS.

In previous chapters, I've exhorted you to practice using the tools and techniques you've learned in the projects. This time I don't think I'll have to urge you to data communicate. There are so many bulletin boards, each unique in its own way, not to mention the nationwide information services (CompuServe, *et al.*), that your main problem will be getting enough sleep (and paying your telephone bill).

Chapter **7**
INTEGRATING THE APPLICATIONS

Up until now, you've been treating each of the *Works* applications—word processor, database, spreadsheet, and communications—as a separate tool, complete unto itself. But, as you knew when you bought the software, *Works* is an *integrated* package. This means that documents created with one *Works* application can be used in and by other applications.

Actually, you've already used data from a word processor document in the communications project (sending text) in Chapter 6. That exercise gave you just a foretaste of *Works*' integration capabilities.

The three integration projects in this chapter demonstrate most of the ways data from one application can be used in another. Three separate mail merge exercises comprise the first project. Each exercise merges data from a database into a word processor document.

The second project illustrates how to add spreadsheet and database tables to a word processor document, while the third project lets you combine spreadsheet charts with the same document.

PROJECT 12: MAIL MERGE LETTERS, LABELS, AND ENVELOPES

As the owner of the Miracle Computer Store, you are responsible for promoting your store to the rest of the community. One of your ideas is to advertise a special holiday sale to your regular customers. You want to send each customer a personalized letter, but you don't want to have to type each letter separately. This is where *Works*' ability to merge data from a database into the word processor becomes really useful.

Creating a Form Letter

The terms *form letter* or *merge letter* describe a document that uses data from a database to provide information such as the inside address and salutation. Look at the sample letter in Figure 7-1. The words printed in italics show the areas where you'll want to substitute individualized customer data.

(*Note*: You're going to use customer data from a database project in Chapter 3. The document is called CUSTOMER.WDB, and if you don't have it on your data disk, I recommend that you stop here, go back to Chapter 3, and create the database.)

Figure 7-1   Text for the form letter

December 1

Title   First Name   Last Name
Address
City,   State   Zip

Dear *Title   Last Name*:

We at the Miracle Computer Store want to thank you for your
past patronage. We want you to know that we value you as a
customer and as a friend. And we want to say this with more
than just words, so:

Starting today, and for the rest of this month, we are
offering special holiday discount pricing -- not to everyone,
but just to long-term MCS customers, like you. These special
discounts extend to our entire inventory of computers,
computer peripherals, and computer supplies.

Because we have recently added to our staff, we ask that you
bring this letter when you come to our store. This will
assure that you receive the special pricing we feel you
deserve.

Our new holiday season hours are from 9 AM to 8 PM, Monday
through Friday, and from 9 AM to 6 PM on Saturday. Hope to
see you soon.

Sincerely,

J.P. Smithson, President

Writing the Letter

Begin the project by starting a new word processor document. Type the letter as you see it in Figure 7-1, but leave the areas printed in italics blank. Figure 7-2 shows the first few paragraphs of the letter as you should type it. Leave five blank lines between the date and the salutation ("Dear"), and type a space after the word "Dear" before you press (Enter). Save the document with the name, MAILMERG.

Figure 7-2 Leave space for the inside address

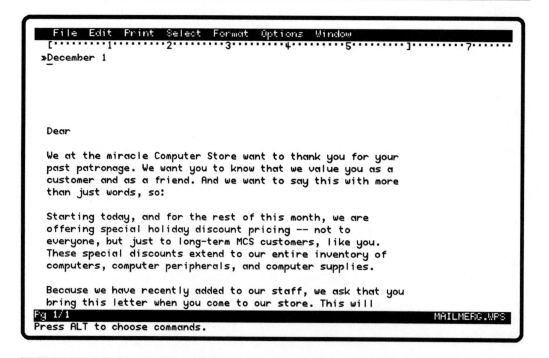

Open the Database

The data you wish to merge into this letter is in a database document called CUSTOMER.WDB, and in order for *Works* to merge data from this file into your letter, the database document must be on the desktop. Use the **Open** command to load CUSTOMER.WDB.

Look at the file (Figure 7-3). Notice that there are fields (columns) for First Name, Last Name, Address, City, State, and Zip. This is exactly the data you want in your form letter. Only one field is missing. You need to know the "Title" (Mr., Mrs., Ms., Dr., etc.) for each of your

Figure 7-3 The Customer database

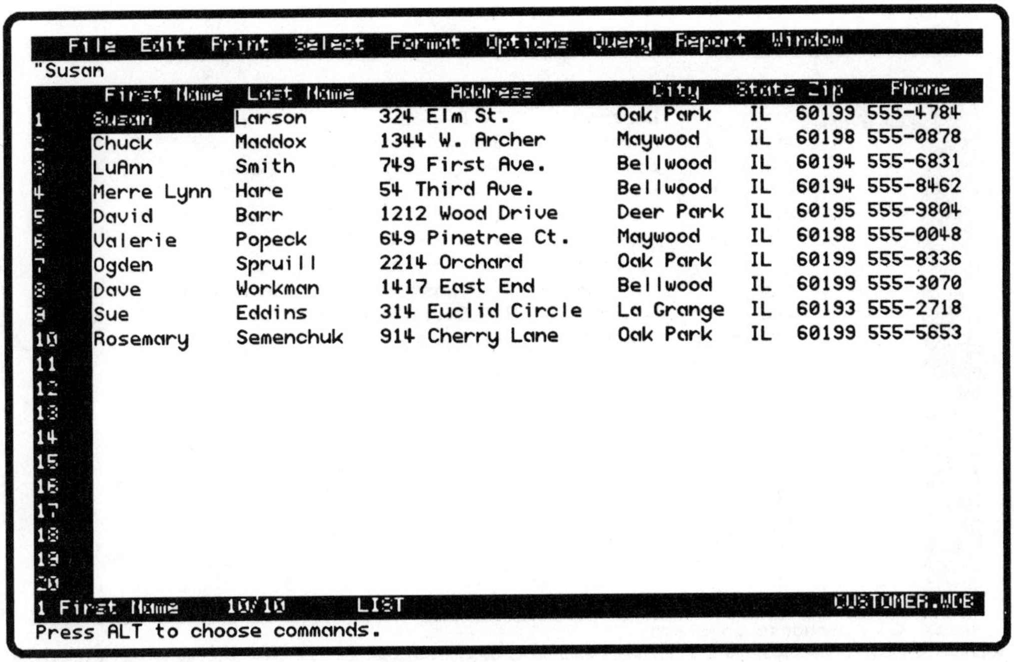

customers, so that you can refer to them as: Ms. Susan Larson, Mr. Chuck Maddox, and so forth.

Adding a New Field to the Database

With the cursor in the First Name column, select **Insert** from the Edit menu, choose Column from the INSERT dialog box, and press Enter. *Works* inserts a blank column to the left of the column containing the cursor (Figure 7-4).

With the cursor in this new column, use the **Name** command in the Edit menu to name the new field "Title." Figure 7-5 shows the Title field. (*Note*: I've also narrowed the field width and entered field data for each customer.)

Merging the Data

Both *Works* documents, CUSTOMER.WDB and MAILMERG.WPS, should now be on your desktop. Pull down the Window menu and choose **1 MAILMERG.WPS** to display the letter.

Figure 7-4   Insert a blank column to the left of the First Name column

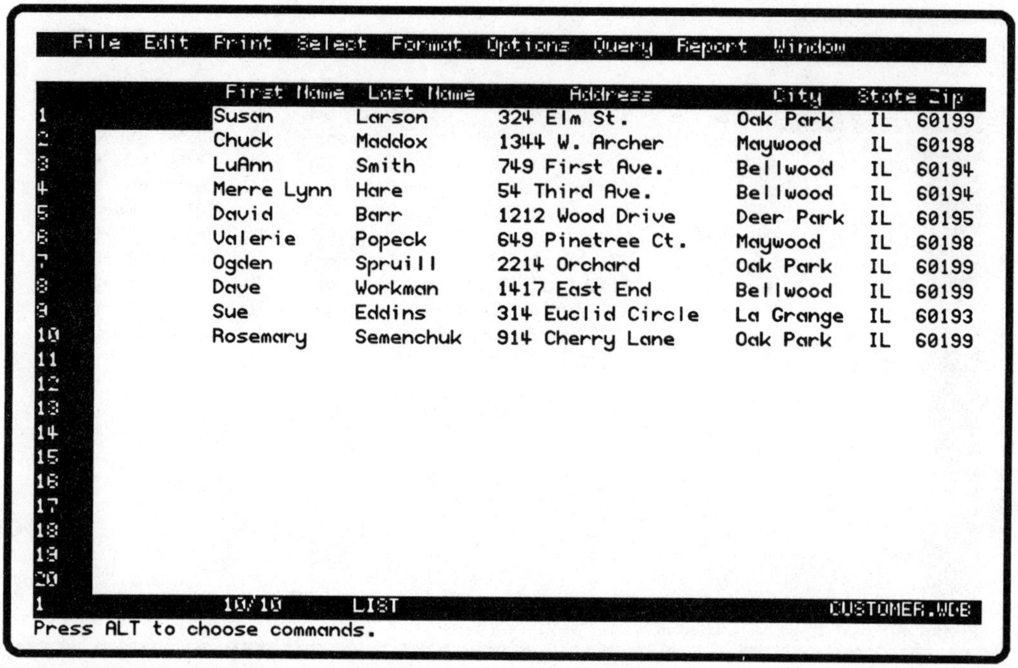

```
┌─────────────────────────────────────────────────────────────────────┐
│  File  Edit  Print  Select  Format  Options  Query  Report  Window    │
│ ╔═════════════════════════════════════════════════════════════════╗  │
│ ║         First Name   Last Name     Address        City   State Zip║  │
│ 1 ║        Susan        Larson       324 Elm St.     Oak Park  IL 60199│
│ 2 ║        Chuck        Maddox       1344 W. Archer  Maywood   IL 60198│
│ 3 ║        LuAnn        Smith        749 First Ave.  Bellwood  IL 60194│
│ 4 ║        Merre Lynn   Hare         54 Third Ave.   Bellwood  IL 60194│
│ 5 ║        David        Barr         1212 Wood Drive Deer Park IL 60195│
│ 6 ║        Valerie      Popeck       649 Pinetree Ct. Maywood  IL 60198│
│ 7 ║        Ogden        Spruill      2214 Orchard    Oak Park  IL 60199│
│ 8 ║        Dave         Workman      1417 East End   Bellwood  IL 60199│
│ 9 ║        Sue          Eddins       314 Euclid Circle La Grange IL 60193│
│10 ║        Rosemary     Semenchuk    914 Cherry Lane Oak Park  IL 60199│
│11 ║                                                                  ║  │
│12 ║                                                                  ║  │
│13 ║                                                                  ║  │
│14 ║                                                                  ║  │
│15 ║                                                                  ║  │
│16 ║                                                                  ║  │
│17 ║                                                                  ║  │
│18 ║                                                                  ║  │
│19 ║                                                                  ║  │
│20 ║                                                                  ║  │
│ 1      10/10        LIST                              CUSTOMER.WDB     │
│ Press ALT to choose commands.                                         │
└─────────────────────────────────────────────────────────────────────┘
```

The inside address will consist of three lines. The first line contains the customer's Title, First Name, and Last Name (Mr. Chuck Maddox, for example). You want to tell *Works* to insert these three pieces of data from the CUSTOMER database into your form letter. Here's how to do this.

Place the cursor on the second blank line below the date. Now, pull down the Edit menu, and select **Insert Field**. Figure 7-6 shows the INSERT FIELD dialog box.

The **Databases**: list box shows the names of the database documents that are currently open on your *Works* desktop. The only one that's open is CUSTOMER.WDB. Highlight this name by pressing ⬇. Now, the **Fields**: list box, which had been empty, shows the names of all the fields in the selected database. (*Note*: The fields are displayed in the order that they appear in the database's List window.)

Move the cursor to the **Fields**: list box by pressing (Alt) + (F). The first field you want to insert into your form letter is Title, so highlight this field, and then press (Enter).

Figure 7-5   Name the new column and enter data

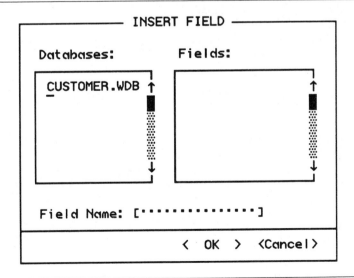

	Title	First Name	Last Name	Address	City	State	Zip
1	Ms.	Susan	Larson	324 Elm St.	Oak Park	IL	60199
2	Mr.	Chuck	Maddox	1344 W. Archer	Maywood	IL	60198
3	Dr.	LuAnn	Smith	749 First Ave.	Bellwood	IL	60194
4	Ms.	Merre Lynn	Hare	54 Third Ave.	Bellwood	IL	60194
5	Dr.	David	Barr	1212 Wood Drive	Deer Park	IL	60195
6	Prof.	Valerie	Popeck	649 Pinetree Ct.	Maywood	IL	60198
7	Mr.	Ogden	Spruill	2214 Orchard	Oak Park	IL	60199
8	Dr.	Dave	Workman	1417 East End	Bellwood	IL	60199
9	Prof.	Sue	Eddins	314 Euclid Circle	La Grange	IL	60193
10	Ms.	Rosemary	Semenchuk	914 Cherry Lane	Oak Park	IL	60199

File Edit Print Select Format Options Query Report Window

11 Title   10/10   LIST   CUSTOMER.WDB
Press ALT to choose commands.

Figure 7-6   Select the Customer database

INSERT FIELD

Databases: Fields:

CUSTOMER.WDB

Field Name: [··············]

< OK >   <Cancel>

Works inserts what's called a *Placeholder* (Figure 7-7). The Placeholder indicates the name of the database field and is inserted into the document at the location of the cursor.

You can delete a Placeholder the same way you delete anything in a document—highlight it, and press Del.

Figure 7-7 Insert the Title Placeholder

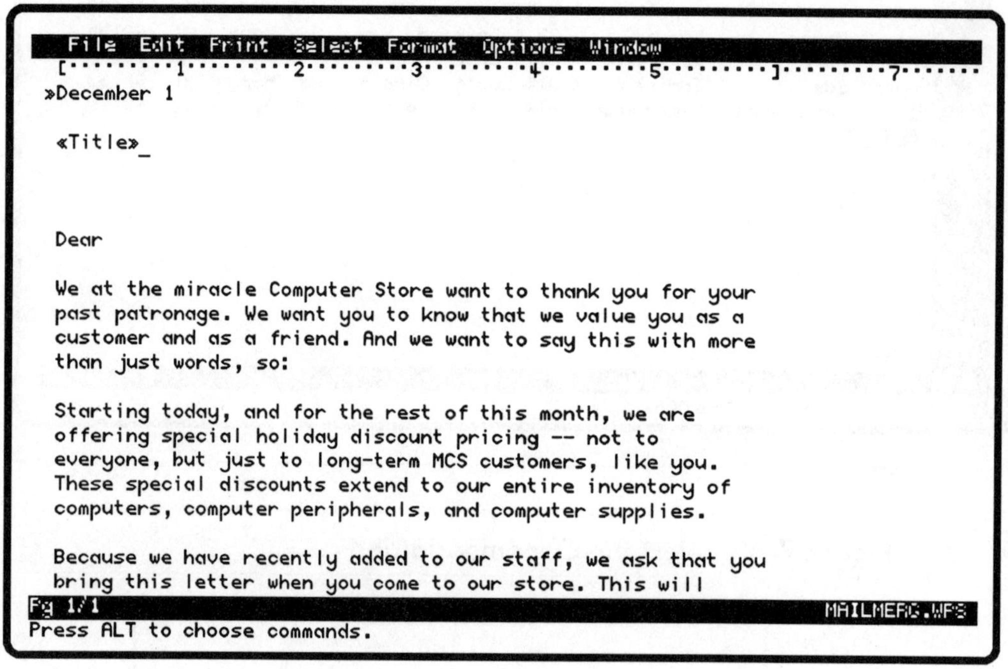

```
 File  Edit  Print  Select  Format  Options  Window
[········1·········2·········3·········4·········5·········]·········7·······
»December 1

 «Title»_


 Dear

 We at the miracle Computer Store want to thank you for your
 past patronage. We want you to know that we value you as a
 customer and as a friend. And we want to say this with more
 than just words, so:

 Starting today, and for the rest of this month, we are
 offering special holiday discount pricing -- not to
 everyone, but just to long-term MCS customers, like you.
 These special discounts extend to our entire inventory of
 computers, computer peripherals, and computer supplies.

 Because we have recently added to our staff, we ask that you
 bring this letter when you come to our store. This will
 Pg 1/1                                          MAILMERG.WPS
 Press ALT to choose commands.
```

You want the next field, First Name, to be inserted to the right of the Title, so type a space (to separate the Title from the First Name), and choose **Insert Field** again. This time highlight the First Name field, and press Enter. Now add the Last Name Placeholder by typing another space, choosing **Insert Field**, highlighting Last Name, and pressing Enter (Figure 7-8).

Use the arrow keys to move the cursor to the beginning of the next line (*don't* press Enter), and let's add the second line of the inside address. Choose **Insert Field**, highlight Address, and press Enter. Then move the cursor to the next line.

Figure 7-8   Insert the next two Placeholders on the same line

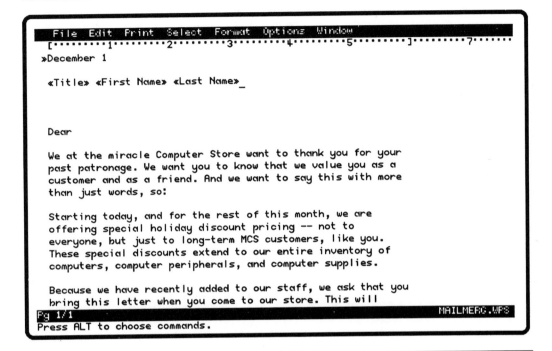

```
  File  Edit  Print  Select  Format  Options  Window
[••••••••1•••••••••2••••••••3••••••••••4•••••••••5••••••••]•••••••••7•••••••
»December 1

«Title» «First Name» «Last Name»_



Dear

We at the miracle Computer Store want to thank you for your
past patronage. We want you to know that we value you as a
customer and as a friend. And we want to say this with more
than just words, so:

Starting today, and for the rest of this month, we are
offering special holiday discount pricing -- not to
everyone, but just to long-term MCS customers, like you.
These special discounts extend to our entire inventory of
computers, computer peripherals, and computer supplies.

Because we have recently added to our staff, we ask that you
bring this letter when you come to our store. This will
Pg 1/1                                          MAILMERG.WPS
Press ALT to choose commands.
```

The third inside address line consists of three fields: City (followed by a comma and a space), State (followed by a space), and Zip. Insert these three fields on the same line using **Insert Field**.

Finally, move the cursor to the end of the salutation line, and insert Placeholders for Title and Last Name (separated by a space, and followed by a colon). Compare your letter with Figure 7-9.

Save the document again so that the file on your data disk includes the Placeholders.

Printing the Form Letters

Let's print out the letters. First, display the LAYOUT dialog box, and delete the default Footer. There's no need to print a page number for a one-page letter.

Next, if you're printing the form letters on letterhead stationery rather than continuous form paper, select the Manual Page Feed option in the SELECT TEXT PRINTER dialog box.

Figure 7-9   All of the Placeholders have been inserted

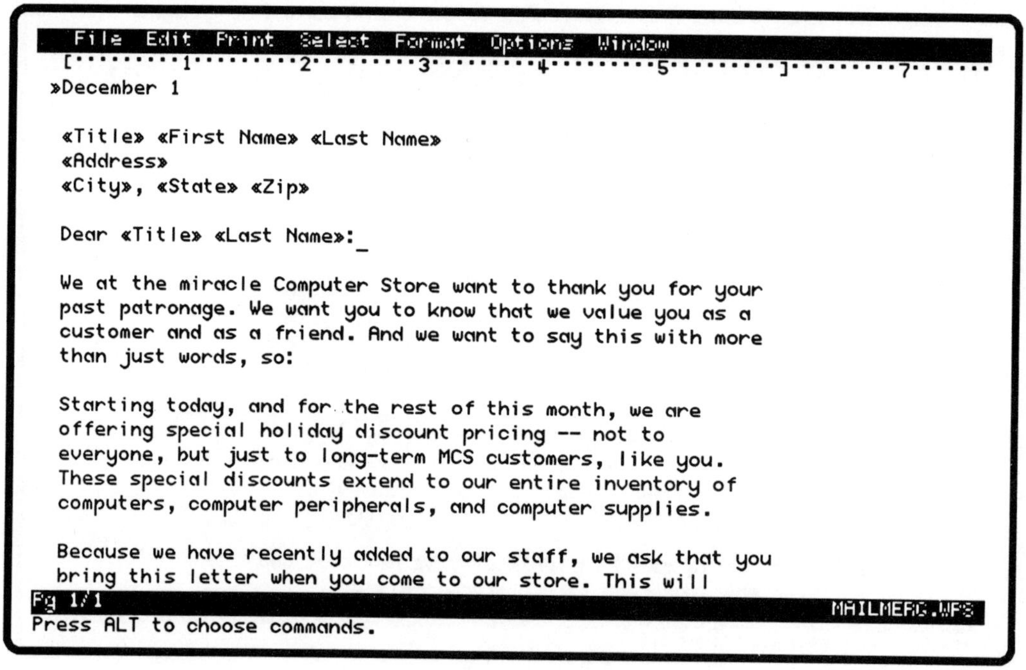

```
 File  Edit  Print  Select  Format  Options  Window
[·········1········2·········3·········4·········5·········]·········7·······
»December 1

«Title» «First Name» «Last Name»
«Address»
«City», «State» «Zip»

Dear «Title» «Last Name»:_

We at the miracle Computer Store want to thank you for your
past patronage. We want you to know that we value you as a
customer and as a friend. And we want to say this with more
than just words, so:

Starting today, and for the rest of this month, we are
offering special holiday discount pricing -- not to
everyone, but just to long-term MCS customers, like you.
These special discounts extend to our entire inventory of
computers, computer peripherals, and computer supplies.

Because we have recently added to our staff, we ask that you
bring this letter when you come to our store. This will
Pg 1/1                                                   MAILMERG.WPS
Press ALT to choose commands.
```

Then, pull down the Print menu, and choose **Print Merge**. The PRINT MERGE dialog box (Figure 7-10) shows the open databases on the desktop. Your CUSTOMER database is already highlighted, so press (Enter).

Works then displays the usual PRINT dialog box. Leave the number of Copies set at 1. This tells *Works* to print one copy of the form letter for every record displayed in the database's List window.

Press (Enter), and *Works* will print ten copies of your form letter, one for each customer record in your CUSTOMER.WDB database. If you chose the Manual Page Feed option, *Works* will prompt you to insert each sheet of paper.

You can stop printing at any time by pressing (Esc). But even though your computer immediately stops sending characters to your printer, the printer may continue printing for a while. Most printers have their own memory, and may have stored several hundred, or even a couple of thousand, characters sent by your computer but not yet printed. The printer will keep going until all the characters in its memory have been printed. The only way to stop the printer is to turn it off.

Figure 7-10   The PRINT MERGE dialog box

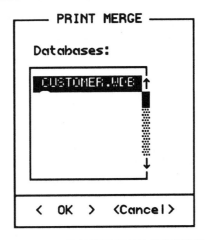

Using Selected Records from the Database

When *Works* merges data from a database in a letter, it takes the data in the order that the records appear in the database. In other words, Susan Larson's letter was printed first because hers was the first record listed in the database (at least her name was first in my CUSTOMER database).

This means that *Works* will print the form letters in whatever order you arrange the records in the database. You can use this feature to print your letters in Zip code order, for example. Just sort the database by Zip before you print the form letters.

You can also use the database's Query features to display only a portion of the records (e.g., only customers who have purchased Apple equipment, or only customers who haven't purchased warranties, etc.). *Works* will print form letters only for those records that are currently displayed in the database.

Labels

You can merge a database with a word processor document to print mailing labels or envelopes. In both cases, you need to create a word processor document consisting of Placeholders only. In fact, the Placeholders you need are the very ones you used for the inside address of your Merge Letter.

Creating the Label Document

You can use the same procedure you used above to insert the seven Placeholders (Title, First Name, Last Name, Address, City, State, and Zip) in a new word processor document, or you can use *Works'* **Copy** command to copy the Placeholders from your form letter into the new document.

Let's use the **Copy** method. (*Note*: If you haven't created the form letter document, use the techniques described above to insert Placeholders in your Labels document. Also, be sure that the CUSTOMER database is open on your *Works* desktop.)

To copy the Placeholders, highlight all three lines of the inside address. Then select **Copy** from the Edit menu.

Now, create a new word processor document by selecting **New** from the File menu. Choose Word Processor from the NEW dialog box, and when the new, empty document appears on the screen, press (Enter). This completes the **Copy** command and inserts the three highlighted lines into the new word processor document (Figure 7-11). (*Note*: You can use this same Copy technique to combine text from several different word processor documents.)

Save this document with the file name LABELS.WPS

What's in a Label?

Before you begin printing labels, let's talk about the labels themselves. Mailing labels are available in several formats: single-column format (called one-up), or multiple-column format (two-up, three-up, etc.). *Works* can handle both single-column and multiple-column labels. This example uses single-column labels, but there's an example of two-column labels in Chapter 8.

Labels also come in a variety of sizes. It is important that you know the exact size of the labels you're using, so take a ruler and measure them. You need to know both the width and the height. For the height, measure from the *top* of one label to the *top* of the next label. The labels I'm using are 3.5 inches wide and 1 inch high. They appear continuously, without header or footer space, on 12-inch long sheets (i.e., there are 12 labels from the top of one sheet to the top of the next sheet). (*Note*: Some labels, especially those that are more than 1 inch high, come in sheets with header and footer space at the top and bottom of each sheet. There's an example of printing onto this type of label form in Chapter 8.)

Figure 7-11   Insert Placeholders for mailing labels

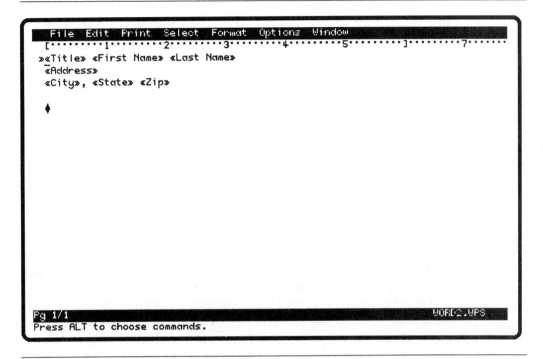

Changing the Layout

You want *Works* to print each customer's address at the same position on successive labels, so you have to tell *Works* what size labels you're using, and how the labels are arranged on the sheet.

Much of this information is entered in the LAYOUT dialog box, so choose **Layout** from the Print menu. Table 7-1 lists the Layout values for the labels I'm using.

Assuming you're using similar labels (they're very common), change your LAYOUT dialog box to match Table 7-1. If your continuous form labels are different from mine, let the values you enter into this dialog box reflect the measurements of your label sheets. For

Table 7-1   Layout values for labels

Parameter	Value
Top Margin	0
Bottom Margin	0
Left Margin	0
Right Margin	0
Page Length	12"
Page Width	3.5"
Footer	Delete default Footer
Header Margin	0
Footer Margin	0

example, the vertical distance from one perforation in the sheet to the next determines the Page Length, while the horizontal distance from the left edge of the first label to the right edge of the last label (for multicolumn labels) determines the Page Width.

If there is header and/or footer space on your label sheets, measure these distances and enter them, respectively, in the Top Margin and Bottom Margin text boxes. The Left Margin, Right Margin, Header Margin, and Footer Margin will be 0 for all labels. Be sure to delete the default Footer from the Footer text box. Figure 7-12 shows the LAYOUT dialog box for my labels. Close the dialog box by pressing (Enter).

Printing the Labels

Let's print some labels. Labels must be threaded through the tractor pins on your printer. You have to use the tractor because the printer's friction roller would allow the labels to slip out of alignment. Be sure that the printer's paper release lever is set to the *pin feed* position. Adjust the tractors to conform to the width of your labels. After you've threaded the labels through the pins, turn the platen knob to roll the labels around the platen and out through the front of the printer.

WARNING: Never try to roll labels backwards through the printer. The labels tend to peel off from their backing and can become stuck to the platen or the platen guide (a real mess). When you're finished printing labels and you want to remove them, tear the labels at the rear of the printer and roll *forward* the remaining labels.

Verify that the Continuous Page Feed option is set in the SELECT TEXT PRINTER dialog box.

Figure 7-12   LAYOUT settings for mailing labels

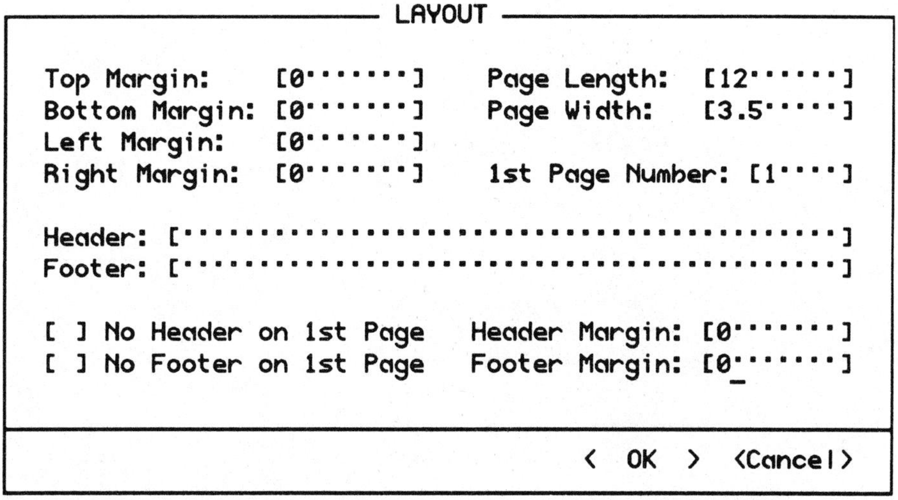

```
┌────────────────────── LAYOUT ──────────────────────┐
│                                                     │
│  Top Margin:      [0·······]   Page Length:   [12······]  │
│  Bottom Margin:   [0·······]   Page Width:    [3.5·····]  │
│  Left Margin:     [0·······]                             │
│  Right Margin:    [0·······]   1st Page Number: [1·····]  │
│                                                     │
│  Header: [·········································]  │
│  Footer: [·········································]  │
│                                                     │
│  [ ] No Header on 1st Page   Header Margin: [0·······]  │
│  [ ] No Footer on 1st Page   Footer Margin: [0·······]  │
│                                                     │
├─────────────────────────────────────────────────────┤
│                            <  OK  >   <Cancel>      │
└─────────────────────────────────────────────────────┘
```

Aligning the labels in the printer is a trial-and-error process. You can adjust the horizontal position of the labels by releasing the tractor release levers on your printer and sliding both tractors to the left or right. (*Note*: If you can't move the labels far enough to the left so that printing starts at an appropriate place on the label, you can increase the Left Margin value in the LAYOUT dialog box.)

The vertical alignment of the labels in your printer determines where the first line of text is printed. In a moment, you'll enter values into the PRINT LABELS dialog box that will ensure that first lines of successive labels are spaced one label height apart (one inch, for my labels). Aligning the labels vertically ensures that the first line is printed at an appropriate place on the label.

Select **Print Labels** from the Print menu (Figure 7-13). Press ↓ to highlight the CUSTOMER.WDB file in the database's list box. *Works'* default values of 1″ and 3.5″ for, respectively, Vertical and Horizontal Label Spacing exactly match the labels I'm using. If your labels are different, press Tab to move the cursor to the appropriate text box, and enter the values for your labels. Vertical Label Spacing should be measured from the top of one label to the top of the next label. Horizontal Label Spacing should be measured from the left edge to the right edge of a single label.

Figure 7-13   Select the merging database

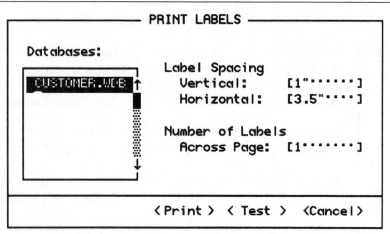

You can check the label alignment by printing a single label. Choose Test by pressing (Alt) + (T) in the PRINT LABELS dialog box. *Works* will display its standard PRINT dialog box. Press (Enter), and one label will be printed.

After the test label has been printed, *Works* will ask if you want to "Print all labels or reprint the test labels?" If you're dissatisfied with the placement of text on the label, you can realign the labels in your printer and repeat the testing procedure by pressing (Alt) + (T). If the alignment is correct, press (Enter) to print all labels.

As with the previous form letter example, *Works* will print one label for each record in the database. If you want to print labels for certain records only or want to print the labels in a particular order, use the commands in the database's Query menu to select and/or sort the records before you choose **Print Labels**. Remember, you can move between *Works* documents with the Window menu.

You can stop printing labels by pressing (Esc).

Save the LABELS document once more, so that the special Layout settings are saved, too.

≡ Envelopes

Envelopes are printed manually, one at a time. They're easier than labels are to set up, but they're more difficult to print because you have to stand at the printer and hand feed each envelope. However, many people (your MCS customers, for example) prefer receiving mail in individually addressed envelopes rather than in envelopes with labels stuck to them.

Creating a Document for Envelopes

Again, you need to create a separate word processor document for the Placeholders that are used in the address. You can either insert Placeholders (for Title, First Name, etc.) into the new document with the **Insert Field** command as you did in the Form Letter exercise above, or you can **Copy** the Placeholders from the Labels or the Form Letter document and into a new document. Either way, once you have the Placeholders in a new word processor document, save this document with the name ENVELOPE.WPS. (I know this document looks just like the Labels document in Figure 7-11, but printing envelopes requires different Layout settings than you use to print labels. That's why you're creating a separate document for envelopes.) Remember that the database document, CUSTOMER.WDB, must be open on your desktop.

Layout for Envelopes

In a moment, you're going to configure the LAYOUT dialog box to print envelopes. I'm going to assume that you have standard size (4.125″ × 9.5″) business envelopes. Don't worry if you're using some other size; just substitute your envelope's dimensions for mine in the following section.

  Display the LAYOUT dialog box, and change the Top Margin to 2 (inches), the Bottom Margin to 0, the Left Margin to 4.5, and the Right Margin to 0. (*Note*: As a general rule, set the Left Margin to a little less than half of the envelope's length, and the Top Margin to about half its height.) Leave the Page Length set to 11 inches (you're printing manually, so the Page Length, as long as it's greater than the envelope's length, doesn't matter). Change the Page Width to 9.5 inches (or the width of your envelopes). Delete the default Footer, and change both Header and Footer Margins to 0. Then close the dialog box.

Printing Envelopes

Display the SELECT TEXT PRINTER dialog box, and press (Alt) + (A) to choose Manual Page Feed. (*Note*: The options you set in the LAYOUT dialog box are only used with the document in which they were set; i.e., each document has its own LAYOUT settings. The options you set in the SELECT TEXT PRINTER dialog box, however, are "permanent"—that is, they remain the same for any succeeding document you print, until you change them.)

Select **Print Merge**, highlight the CUSTOMER.WDB file in the list box, and press `Enter`. When *Works* displays the PRINT dialog box, press `Enter` again. In a few moments, you'll see a special alert box advising you to insert the next sheet of paper (Figure 7-14). This is your cue to insert an envelope. Be sure that the paper release lever on your printer is set to the *friction feed* position.

Figure 7-14 *Works* prompts you to insert the next envelope

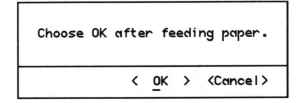

Most printers will position the envelope for you. Deselect the printer by pressing the Select or On-Line switch. The printer's On-Line light will turn off. Insert an envelope, hold it gently against the printer roller, and press the Form Feed switch on the printer. The printer will roll the envelope to the proper position. Now press the On-Line switch so that the On-Line light is on.

Press `Enter`, and *Works* will print the first envelope.

A few moments after the envelope has finished printing, *Works* will tell you to insert the next envelope. Do so, then press `Enter`, and *Works* will print the next envelope. If you decide not to print all the envelopes, you can press `Esc`.

Note: If you see an alert box saying "Print Error: Continue printing?" you probably forgot to press the On-Line switch on your printer. The On-Line light must be on before your printer will print. Press the On-Line switch, then press `Enter`. If you didn't see the special alert box prompting you to "Choose OK after feeding paper," you didn't select the Manual option in the SELECT TEXT PRINTER dialog box.

The three applications in this project—form letter, labels, and envelopes—demonstrate the most common uses of the *Works'* mail merge utility, but this utility is only one of the ways you can combine information from two or more *Works'* documents.

PROJECT 13: MERGING DATABASE AND SPREADSHEET TABLES INTO THE WORD PROCESSOR

Works was designed to allow you to move data easily from a spreadsheet or a database into a word processor document. (*Note:* You can also move data from a spreadsheet to a database, or vice versa.) The method is simple and can be summarized in a single sentence: **Copy** from one document into the other. Oh, you'll see some special techniques that will improve the "look" of your combined documents, but basically, this project will let you practice copying data between *Works* documents until you're comfortable doing it.

You'll be using three documents created in earlier projects: PEPTALK.WPS, a word processor document from Chapter 2, REPAIR.WDB, a database from Chapter 3, and SALESCOM.WKS, a spreadsheet from Chapters 4 and 5. If you haven't done these exercises, you can go and create them now, or you can use your own files.

I'm going to assume that you have the above documents, that you've booted *Works,* and that you've opened all three documents so that they're sitting on *Works'* desktop.

Display PEPTALK, if it isn't already displayed, by choosing it from the Window menu. Scroll down to the paragraph beginning "One final thought" and insert the following paragraph above it:

> **I thought you might be interested in the sales figures for last month. November was a good month for us, and you're all to be congratulated.**

Notice that the new paragraph is automatically justified because the text above and below it has this format (Figure 7-15).

Copying Cells from a Spreadsheet

Display the spreadsheet by choosing **SALESCOM.WKS** from the Window menu (Figure 7-16). Suppose you wanted to copy the first, second, and fourth columns from this spreadsheet into your memo. Copying the first two columns is easy; in fact, let's do it for practice.

Select cells A3:B12 (refer to Chapter 4 if you're not sure how to do this). Choose **Copy** from the Edit menu. Now go back to your memo by choosing **PEPTALK.WPS** from the Window menu. Place the cursor

Figure 7-15 Insert a paragraph about sales figures

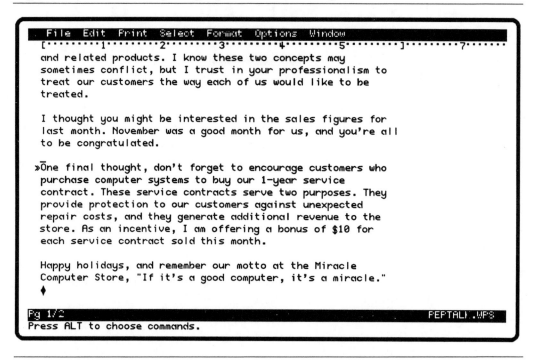

```
   File  Edit  Print  Select  Format  Options  Window
[·········1·········2·········3·········4·········5·········]·········7······
and related products. I know these two concepts may
sometimes conflict, but I trust in your professionalism to
treat our customers the way each of us would like to be
treated.

I thought you might be interested in the sales figures for
last month. November was a good month for us, and you're all
to be congratulated.

»One final thought, don't forget to encourage customers who
purchase computer systems to buy our 1-year service
contract. These service contracts serve two purposes. They
provide protection to our customers against unexpected
repair costs, and they generate additional revenue to the
store. As an incentive, I am offering a bonus of $10 for
each service contract sold this month.

Happy holidays, and remember our motto at the Miracle
Computer Store, "If it's a good computer, it's a miracle."
♦

Pg 1/2                                            FEPTALI.WPS
Press ALT to choose commands.
```

on the blank line below the paragraph you added a moment ago, and press ⏎ Enter . You can add an extra blank line above the inserted table by pressing ⏎ Enter again.

When you paste a section from a spreadsheet or database into a word processor document, each entry is "tabbed" into position. *Works* inserts appropriate tab markers in the ruler—left-aligned, right-aligned, decimal, etc.—according to the formatting of the spreadsheet cells. If you place the cursor within the copied table, you'll see the tabs *Works* inserted into the ruler (Figure 7-17). This feature lets you move individual columns left or right by highlighting the entire table and using the TABS dialog box to move the tab markers. By the way, the tabs for the column headings are different from those for the entries because their cells were formatted differently.

As I mentioned above, copying the first two columns of the spreadsheet was just a practice exercise because you wanted to copy columns 1, 2, *and* 4. Delete the spreadsheet section from your memo by highlighting it and pressing the ⌨ Del key. Display the SALESCOM

Figure 7-16   The SALESCOM spreadsheet

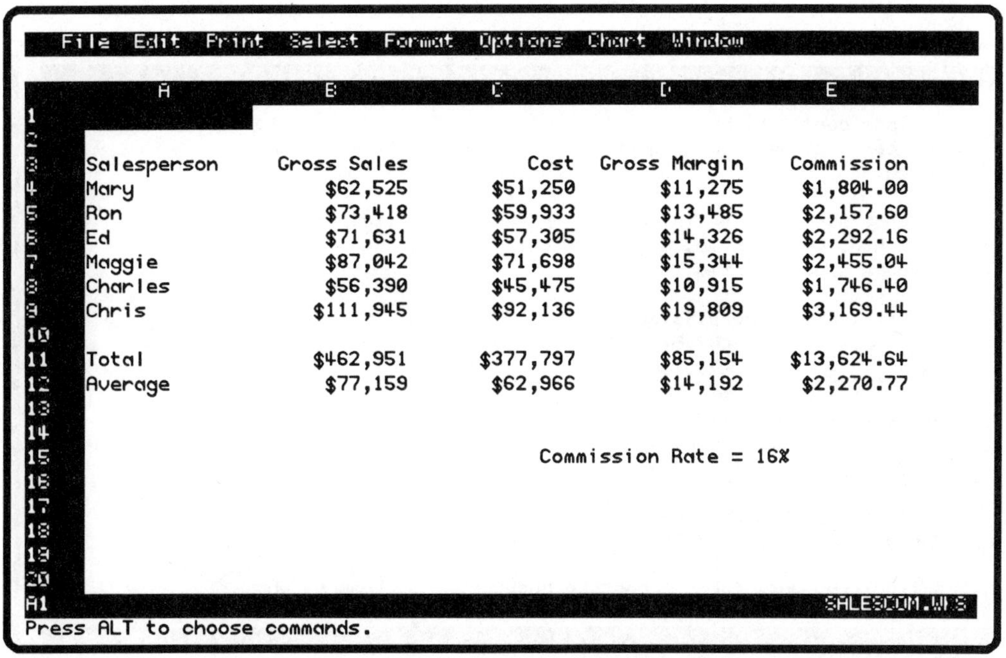

```
┌─────────────────────────────────────────────────────────────────────┐
│   File  Edit  Print  Select  Format  Options  Chart  Window           │
│─────────────────────────────────────────────────────────────────────│
│          A              B            C          D            E        │
│ 1                                                                     │
│ 2                                                                     │
│ 3  Salesperson    Gross Sales      Cost   Gross Margin   Commission   │
│ 4  Mary               $62,525   $51,250     $11,275     $1,804.00     │
│ 5  Ron                $73,418   $59,933     $13,485     $2,157.60     │
│ 6  Ed                 $71,631   $57,305     $14,326     $2,292.16     │
│ 7  Maggie             $87,042   $71,698     $15,344     $2,455.04     │
│ 8  Charles            $56,390   $45,475     $10,915     $1,746.40     │
│ 9  Chris             $111,945   $92,136     $19,809     $3,169.44     │
│ 10                                                                    │
│ 11 Total             $462,951  $377,797     $85,154    $13,624.64     │
│ 12 Average            $77,159   $62,966     $14,192     $2,270.77     │
│ 13                                                                    │
│ 14                                                                    │
│ 15                            Commission Rate = 16%                   │
│ 16                                                                    │
│ 17                                                                    │
│ 18                                                                    │
│ 19                                                                    │
│ 20                                                                    │
│ A1                                                    SALESCOM.WKS     │
│ Press ALT to choose commands.                                         │
└─────────────────────────────────────────────────────────────────────┘
```

spreadsheet again, and let's see how to copy those three columns to your memo.

Editing the Spreadsheet

One way of copying columns 1, 2, and 4 is to copy columns 1 through 4 and delete the third-column entries. The problem with this approach is that you have to edit each line of the copied section. A better approach is to do your editing in the spreadsheet. Here's one method.

Highlight columns G, H, and I, and widen them to 14 characters. Then, highlight cells A3:B12, and select **Copy**. Scroll horizontally, highlight cell G3, and press (Enter). *Works* copies cells A3:B12 into G3:H12.

Now, highlight cells D3:D12 and choose **Copy Special**. Scroll across, select cell I3, and press (Enter). *Works* displays its COPY SPECIAL dialog box (Figure 7-18). The dialog box allows you to add or subtract entire columns (or rows) of values, but it's the first option, Values Only, that you'll use here. Press (Enter) to accept this option. *Works* copies the values (and ignores the formulas) from D3:D12 into I3:I12.

Figure 7-17 Copy columns A and B from the spreadsheet to the word processor

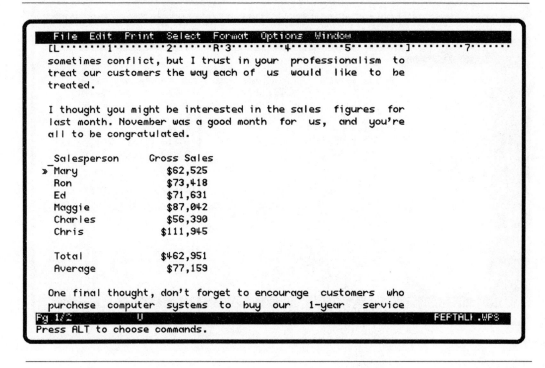

```
 File  Edit  Print  Select  Format  Options  Window
[L·······1·········2······R·3········4········5··········]········7······
sometimes conflict, but I trust in your  professionalism  to
treat our customers the way each of us  would  like  to  be
treated.

I thought you might be interested in the sales  figures  for
last month. November was a good month  for  us,  and  you're
all to be congratulated.

 Salesperson      Gross Sales
» Mary              $62,525
  Ron               $73,418
  Ed                $71,631
  Maggie            $87,042
  Charles           $56,390
  Chris            $111,945

  Total            $462,951
  Average           $77,159

One final thought, don't forget to encourage  customers  who
purchase  computer  systems  to  buy  our   1-year   service
Pg 1/2              U                                FEFTALI.WPS
Press ALT to choose commands.
```

Figure 7-18 Copy only values from column D

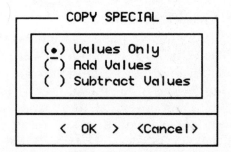

```
┌─── COPY SPECIAL ───┐
│                    │
│ (•) Values Only    │
│ ( ) Add Values     │
│ ( ) Subtract Values│
│                    │
├────────────────────┤
│  <  OK  >  <Cancel>│
└────────────────────┘
```

The reason you want to avoid copying the formulas is that only values are copied from the spreadsheet to the word processor, so that copying formulas serves no purpose and makes your spreadsheet needlessly more complex. Figure 7-19 shows the resulting three-column table.

Figure 7-19   Here are the 3 spreadsheet columns to be copied to the word processor

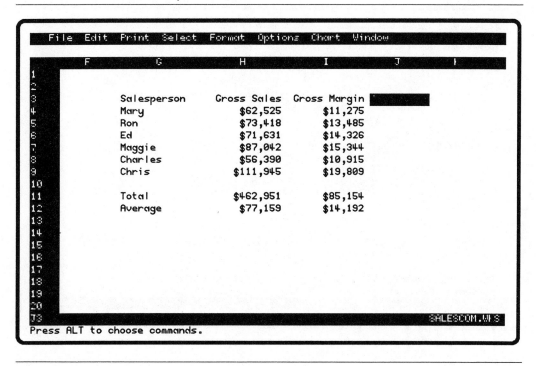

Editing the Table in the Word Processor

Now you can copy the three columns to your PEPTALK memo. Highlight cells G3:I12, and choose **Copy**. Display the memo (use the Window menu), position the cursor on the blank line below the newly typed paragraph, and press (Enter) (Figure 7-20).

Let's do some cosmetic formatting. Move the cursor to the first line of the table (the column headings) and display the TABS dialog box. Notice that in addition to the default tab marker, three tabs appear in the **Tabs**: list box. Change the .1″ tab marker to 1″, the 2.8″ tab marker to 3.5″, and the 4.2″ tab marker to 5″. Then close the dialog box by pressing (Esc). (*Note*: See the discussion on moving tab markers in Chapter 2, if you need help.)

Highlight the rest of the table (everything except the column headings), and use the TABS dialog box to move the three tab markers in the ruler to 1″, 3.5″, and 5″. Even though the tab markers for the body of the table are set to the same locations as those for the column

Figure 7-20 The spreadsheet table is inserted into the memo

```
 File  Edit  Print  Select  Format  Options  Window
[L·······1·······2······R·3·······4·R·····5·······]·······7·····
sometimes conflict, but I trust in your  professionalism  to
treat our customers the way each of  us  would  like  to  be
treated.

I thought you might be interested in the sales  figures  for
last month. November was a good month  for  us,  and  you're
all to be congratulated.

 Salesperson        Gross Sales  Gross Margin
» Mary               $62,525      $11,275
  Ron                $73,418      $13,485
  Ed                 $71,631      $14,326
  Maggie             $87,042      $15,344
  Charles            $56,390      $10,915
  Chris             $111,945      $19,809

  Total             $462,951      $85,154
  Average            $77,159      $14,192

One final thought, don't forget to encourage  customers  who
purchase  computer  systems  to  buy  our  1-year  service
Pg 1/2                                            PEPTALI.WPS
Press ALT to choose commands.
```

headings, you must set them separately because different alignment markers are used in the two sections (decimal vs. right-aligned). Close the TABS dialog box, and compare your screen with Figure 7-21.

≡ Copying Data from a Database

Your memo compliments MCS' sales force, but you feel that it also should praise the repair staff. Add the following paragraph below the table:

I don't want to forget our repair technicians. They're doing a super job, both satisfying customers and generating revenue.

Display the REPAIR.WDB database (Figure 7-22), and let's see what data you can copy and paste into your memo. (*Note*: If the records are not sorted alphabetically by technician name, use the **Sort** command

Figure 7-21   Use the TABS dialog box to realign the table

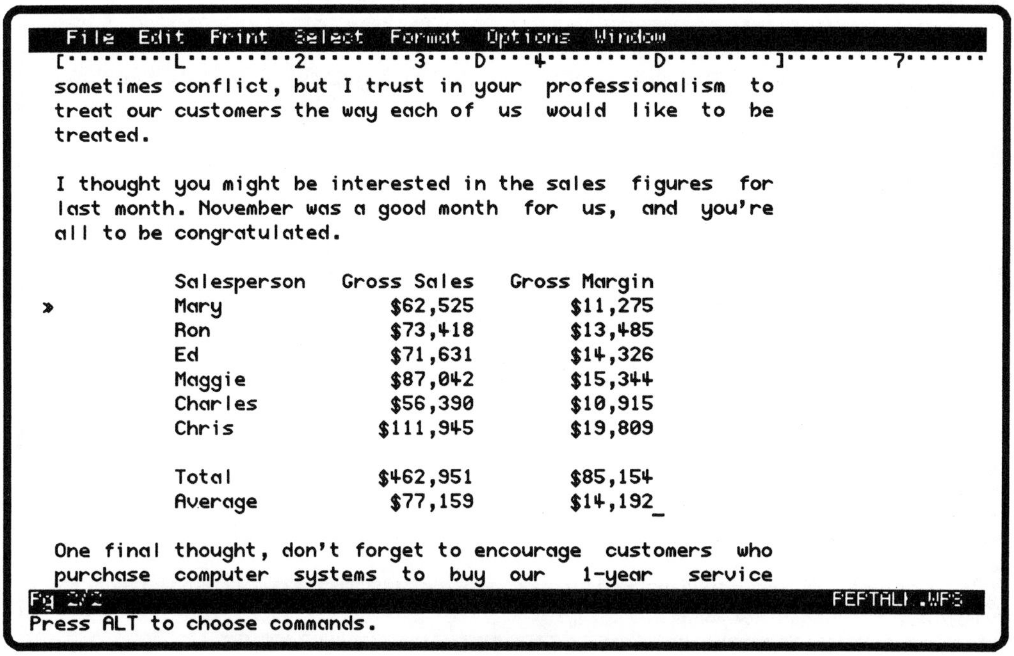

```
 File  Edit  Print  Select  Format  Options  Window
[·········L·········2·········3····D····4·········D·········]·········7······
sometimes conflict, but I trust in your  professionalism  to
treat our customers the way each of  us  would  like  to  be
treated.

I thought you might be interested in the sales  figures  for
last month. November was a good month  for  us,  and  you're
all to be congratulated.

             Salesperson    Gross Sales    Gross Margin
»            Mary             $62,525       $11,275
             Ron              $73,418       $13,485
             Ed               $71,631       $14,326
             Maggie           $87,042       $15,344
             Charles          $56,390       $10,915
             Chris           $111,945       $19,809

             Total           $462,951       $85,154
             Average          $77,159       $14,192_

One final thought, don't forget to encourage  customers  who
purchase  computer  systems  to  buy  our  1-year  service
 Pg 2/2                                           PEPTALI .WPS
Press ALT to choose commands.
```

in the Query menu to sort them.) You can select any number of entries, copy them to the Clipboard, and then paste them into your memo, just as you did with cells from the spreadsheet. The problem is that the data records themselves aren't what you really want. You want a summary of the Gross Revenue for your three repair technicians, and summaries are created in the report generator.

Creating a Summarizing Report

Pull down the Report menu, and choose **New**. Use the **Reports** command to change the report's name to "Summary."

Before you go any further with this report, let me give you some bad news. You can't copy the output of the report into your memo. That's right! The only thing you can do with a report is print it. You can't save the report (you can save its format, but not the report itself), and you can't copy it. But you *can* save a summary of your report (the subtotals and grand totals) to a text file on your data disk, and from there you can transfer this information from the text file into your memo.

Figure 7-22 The REPAIR database from Chapter 3

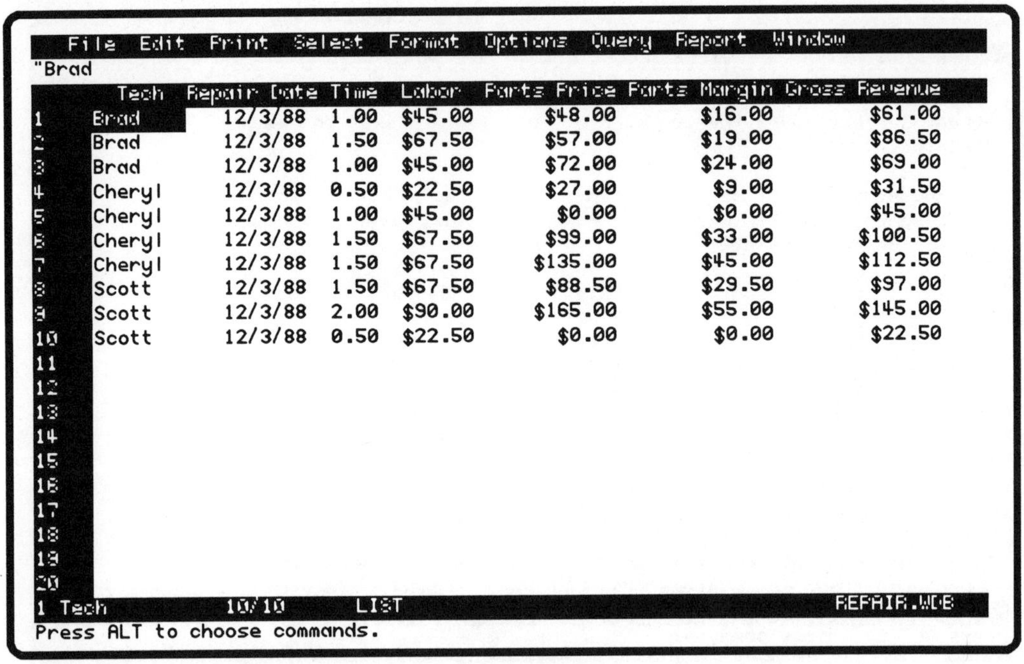

File Edit Print Select Format Options Query Report Window

"Brad

	Tech	Repair Date	Time	Labor	Parts Price	Parts Margin	Gross Revenue
1	Brad	12/3/88	1.00	$45.00	$48.00	$16.00	$61.00
2	Brad	12/3/88	1.50	$67.50	$57.00	$19.00	$86.50
3	Brad	12/3/88	1.00	$45.00	$72.00	$24.00	$69.00
4	Cheryl	12/3/88	0.50	$22.50	$27.00	$9.00	$31.50
5	Cheryl	12/3/88	1.00	$45.00	$0.00	$0.00	$45.00
6	Cheryl	12/3/88	1.50	$67.50	$99.00	$33.00	$100.50
7	Cheryl	12/3/88	1.50	$67.50	$135.00	$45.00	$112.50
8	Scott	12/3/88	1.50	$67.50	$88.50	$29.50	$97.00
9	Scott	12/3/88	2.00	$90.00	$165.00	$55.00	$145.00
10	Scott	12/3/88	0.50	$22.50	$0.00	$0.00	$22.50
11							
12							
13							
14							
15							
16							
17							
18							
19							
20							

1 Tech 10/10 LIST REPAIR.WDB

Press ALT to choose commands.

Let's continue formatting the report. When you created a new report form, *Works* set up seven columns, one for each field in your database. You want this report to contain data from just two fields: Tech and Gross Revenue. This means you have to delete all the other columns. Use the **Delete** command in the Edit menu to delete, one at a time, the columns separating Tech and Gross Revenue. Highlight and delete (with Del) the formulas in cells A4 and A5. Then, type =**Tech** into cell A4. Delete the second Intr Page row, and insert a blank Summ Report row above the existing one. Figure 7-23 shows the final report form.

Save the summary report to your data disk as a text file by selecting **Save As** from the Report menu. Type the file name, **REPAIR.RPT**, and press Enter.

Merging the Summary Report

Display your PEPTALK memo. (Select **PEPTALK.WPS** from the Window menu.) Then, choose **Open** from the File menu. Type **REPAIR.RPT** directly into the **File Name**: text box and press Enter.

Figure 7-23 The completed report form

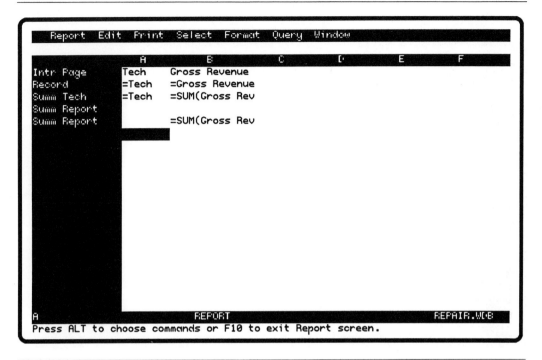

When *Works* asks how it should open this file, select the Spreadsheet option and press ⌷Enter⌷ (Figure 7-24). (I know it seems as if you should open the report summary as a word processor document, but trust me and open it as a spreadsheet.)

Highlight the cells A1:B6 and select the **Copy** command. Use the Window menu to return to the PEPTALK document, and place the cursor on the blank line below the "I don't want to forget" paragraph. Press ⌷Enter⌷ (Figure 7-25), and the cells from the spreadsheet are copied into your memo.

Feel free to underline the column headings and move the tab markers as you did with the previous table.

Save this version of your memo as a separate document with the **Save As** command. Name it PEPTALK1.WPS.

Figure 7-24 Open the saved report summary as a spreadsheet document

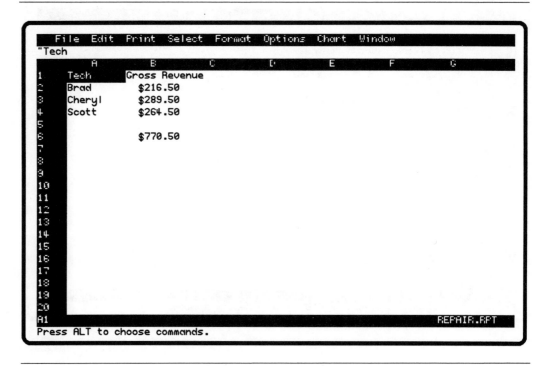

	A	B	C	D	E	F	G
	File Edit Print Select Format Options Chart Window						
	"Tech						
1	Tech	Gross Revenue					
2	Brad	$216.50					
3	Cheryl	$289.50					
4	Scott	$264.50					
5							
6		$770.50					
7							

A1

REPAIR.RPT

Press ALT to choose commands.

PROJECT 14: MERGING SPREADSHEET CHARTS

If you've been doing the exercises in this project (of course, you have), there are at least two versions of your office memo on your *Works* Data disk: PEPTALK.WPS and PEPTALK1.WPS. In this project, you'll replace the tables with spreadsheet charts.

If the PEPTALK1.WPS memo isn't on your *Works'* desktop, place it there now (use the **Open** command). Remove the sales table from the memo by highlighting the entire table and pressing Del. Then, place the cursor on the blank line below the "I thought you might" paragraph.

Save this version of your memo to your *Works* Data disk with the **Save As** command. Call it PEPTALK2.WPS.

Figure 7-25 Copy the report summary from the spreadsheet into your memo

```
 File  Edit  Print  Select  Format  Options  Window
[L········L·········2·········3·········4·········5·········]·········7······
              Ed            $71,631       $14,326
              Maggie        $87,042       $15,344
              Charles       $56,390       $10,915
              Chris        $111,945       $19,809

              Total        $462,951       $85,154
              Average       $77,159       $14,192

I don't want to forget our repair technicians. They're doing
a super job, both satisfying customers and generating
revenue.

 Tech     Gross Revenue
 Brad        $216.50
 Cheryl      $289.50
 Scott       $264.50

             $770.50

One final thought, don't forget to encourage customers who
purchase computer systems to buy our 1-year service
Pg 2/2                                              REPTALI.WPS
Press ALT to choose commands.
```

☰ Adding a Pie Chart

Let's insert a pie chart to present the sales figures graphically to your staff. Display the SALESCOM.WKS spreadsheet. If it's on your *Works* desktop, choose it from the Window menu; if it's not, **Open** it from your *Works* Data disk.

Preparing the Chart

You created this spreadsheet in Chapter 4 and created two charts from its data in Chapter 5. Let's create another chart, a pie chart, that will show the Gross Margin for all six salespersons.

To create the pie chart, choose **New** from the Chart menu. You want to plot values in column D, from row 4 through row 9, so highlight the range D4:D9, and select **1st Y-Series** from the Data menu. Highlight A4:A9, and select **X-Series** from the same menu. Use the CHARTS dialog box to change the name of the chart to Gross Margin. Select

Pie from the Format menu, **View** the chart, and compare it with Figure 7-26.

Before you return to your memo, be sure that you've chosen the same printer in the SELECT CHART PRINTER dialog box as you have chosen in the SELECT TEXT PRINTER dialog box. Now, let's use this chart within your memo.

Figure 7-26 A pie chart of Gross Margin values

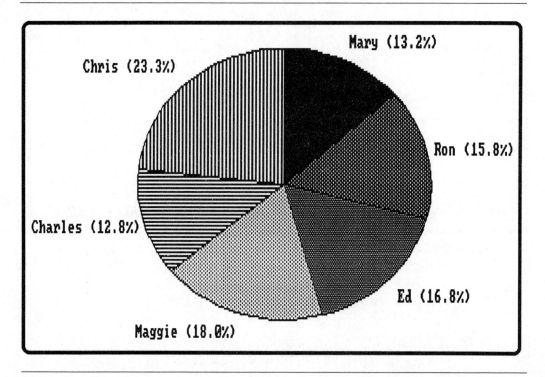

Inserting and Scaling the Pie Chart

Display PEPTALK2.WPS and verify that the cursor is still on the blank line below the "I thought you might be interested" paragraph. Pull down the Edit menu, and select **Insert Chart**. Highlight SALES-COM.WKS in the **Spreadsheets**: list box. Then, press (Alt) + (C) to move the cursor to the **Charts**: list box and highlight the Gross Margin chart. Figure 7-27 shows the INSERT CHART dialog box. Close the dialog box by pressing (Enter).

Figure 7-27   Select the spreadsheet and then the chart

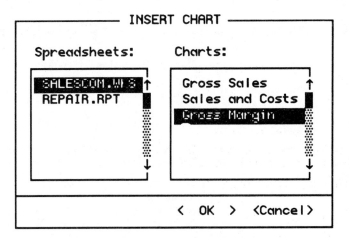

Works inserts a chart Placeholder (Figure 7-28) to mark the location of the chart within your memo. You could print the memo, including the inserted chart, by simply selecting **Print**. But how big will the chart be when it's printed, and what will be its orientation? These features are controlled by the CHART dialog box.

Move the cursor to the chart Placeholder, just under the first asterisk (*), and select **Paragraph** from the Format menu. Instead of the standard PARAGRAPH dialog box, you'll see a special CHART dialog box (Figure 7-29). The options displayed here control the chart's placement, size, and orientation.

Together, the Left and Right Indent values determine the chart's width and horizontal placement. The value you choose for Chart Height determines (as you probably suspected) the height of the chart. You need to be careful when adjusting the chart's height and width, especially for a pie chart, or the chart may be distorted and appear oval instead of round. Space Before and Space After options control the number of blank lines separating, respectively, the top and bottom of the chart from the text in the word processor document.

The two options Portrait and Landscape establish the chart's orientation. Portrait, the default choice, prints the chart so that its top is directly under the text above it. Landscape orientation rotates the chart 90° so that the chart's left side is directly under the text above it. For this example, you can accept all of the CHART dialog box's default choices, and just press (Enter) to close it.

Figure 7-28   *Works* inserts a chart Placeholder

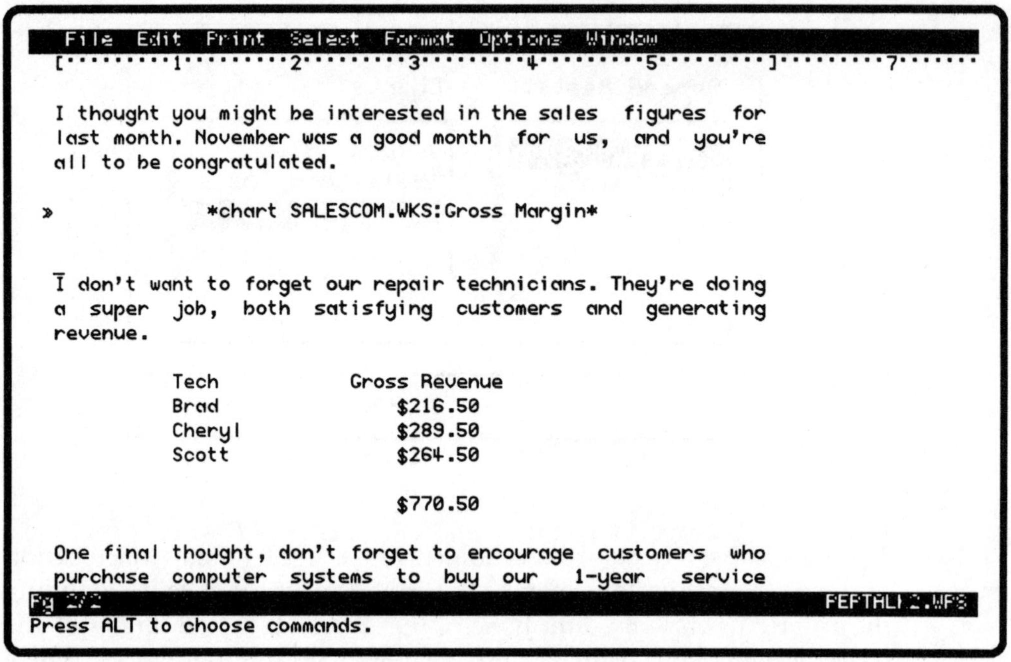

```
 File  Edit  Print  Select  Format  Options  Window
[········1·········2·········3·········4·········5·········]·········7·····

 I thought you might be interested in the sales  figures  for
 last month. November was a good month  for  us,  and  you're
 all to be congratulated.

»           *chart SALESCOM.WKS:Gross Margin*


 I don't want to forget our repair technicians. They're doing
 a  super  job,  both  satisfying  customers  and  generating
 revenue.

        Tech          Gross Revenue
        Brad             $216.50
        Cheryl           $289.50
        Scott            $264.50

                         $770.50

 One final thought, don't forget to encourage  customers  who
 purchase  computer  systems  to  buy  our  1-year  service
Pg 2/2                                            FEFTALI 2.WFS
Press ALT to choose commands.
```

Figure 7-29   The CHART dialog box is used to scale and position the chart within the document

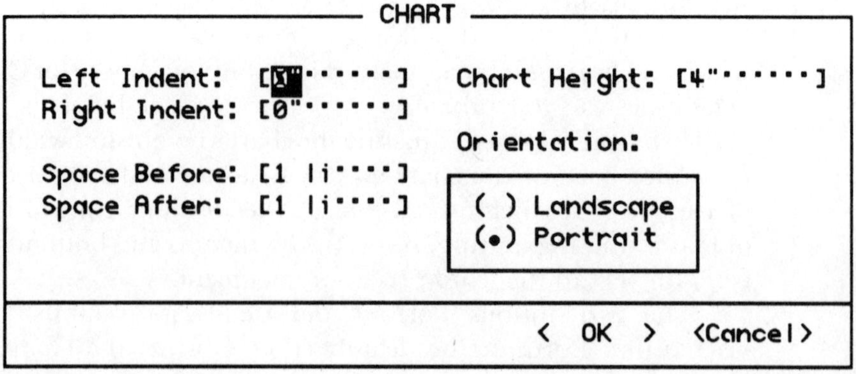

```
───────────── CHART ─────────────

 Left Indent:  [0"······]   Chart Height: [4"······]
 Right Indent: [0"······]
                            Orientation:
 Space Before: [1 li····]
 Space After:  [1 li····]   ( ) Landscape
                            (•) Portrait

                            <  OK  >   <Cancel>
```

Printing the Memo with the Chart

Be sure that the printers selected for text and chart are the same printer. Then, select **Print** and press (Enter). Your memo will begin to print immediately, but when *Works* gets to the chart, it will pause to format. This may take a minute or two, depending on the orientation, the fonts used for Title and Other labels, and the printing quality, so don't get anxious. Figure 7-30 shows page 2 of the memo.

Figure 7-30   The pie chart is inserted at the location of the Placeholder

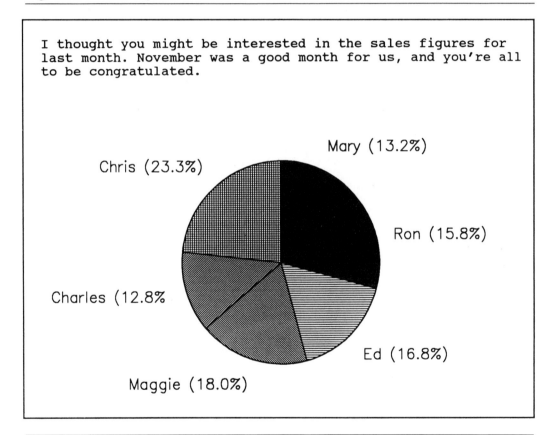

I thought you might be interested in the sales figures for last month. November was a good month for us, and you're all to be congratulated.

If you want to get fancy, you can add a title to the chart, change the font, or draw a border. Anything you add to the chart is entered in the chart window of the spreadsheet. You can use the **View** command to see each effect.

≡ Adding a Bar Chart

Let's insert a bar chart in place of the repair activity table. First, remove the table (highlight it and press ⎡Del⎤).

You're going to create the bar chart from a spreadsheet, using the REPAIR.RPT file you created in Project 13. (*Note*: You'll actually be integrating data from *three* different types of *Works* documents.)

Create the Chart

If REPAIR.RPT hasn't been opened as a spreadsheet document on your *Works* desktop, open it (Figure 7-24). (*Note*: The method for opening this file is discussed in Project 13.)

Change the format of cells B2:B4 to Dollar with 0 decimal places. *Works* uses the format of these cells for the chart's Y-axis labels.

Create the chart with *Works' speed charting* feature. Highlight the range A2:B4, and select **New** from the Chart menu. Display the DATA FORMAT dialog box and change the pattern for the 1st Y-Series to Sparse. Use the OTHER FONT dialog box to change the axes fonts to 12-point Modern B. Select **Show Printer Fonts** from the Options menu. Then, **View** the chart and compare it with Figure 7-31.

This is the chart you want to insert into your memo, so select the **Charts** command, and rename this chart Revenue. If you like, you can add titles and horizontal grid lines to the chart (see Chapter 5 for details on these chart features).

Inserting the Chart into the Memo

OK, let's insert the chart into your memo. Choose **PEPTALK2.WPS** from the Window menu, place the cursor on the blank line below the "I don't want to forget" paragraph, and select **Insert Chart** from the Edit menu. Highlight REPAIR.RPT in the **Spreadsheets:** list box, and Revenue in the **Charts:** list box. Close the dialog box, and see that *Works* has inserted a chart placeholder.

This time, let's change the size of the chart before you print the memo. Select the chart Placeholder by moving the cursor to the first asterisk. Then, choose the **Paragraph** command to display the CHART dialog box. Change both Left and Right Indent values to 1.5", and

Figure 7-31   A bar chart from the Report summary

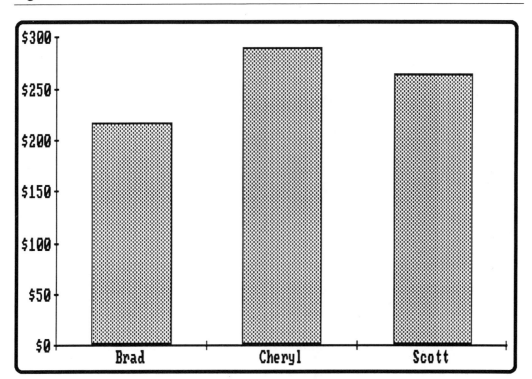

the Chart Height to 2″. These changes will reduce the printed chart to one-quarter of its original size (half the width and half the height).

Close the dialog box, and print the document. Figure 7-32 shows page 3 of the memo.

Finally, save your memo, and print it out. Look closely at the pie chart on page 2 of the printed memo. The pie looked oval on the screen, but it printed round, didn't it? This type of distortion is common when screen images are printed, and *Works* automatically compensates for it.

Figure 7-32 Page 3 of the memo shows the inserted bar chart

I don't want to forget our repair technicians. They're doing a super job, both satisfying customers and generating revenue.

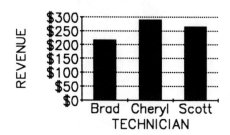

One final thought, don't forget to encourage customers who purchase computer systems to buy our 1-year service contract. These service contracts serve two purposes. They provide protection to our customers against unexpected repair costs, and they generate additional revenue to the store. As an incentive, I am offering a bonus of $10 for each service contract sold this month.

Happy holidays, and remember our motto at the Miracle Computer Store, "If it's a good computer, it's a miracle."

☰ Final Comments

The ability to cut and paste from one word processor document to another, or from one spreadsheet to another, is a useful feature. But it's the ability to construct a document from sections of different kinds of documents (and to do it easily) that sets *Works* apart from virtually any other software package. The more you practice integrating data from one application into another, the more reasons you'll find for using this feature, and the more useful you'll find *Works* to be.

Chapter **8**
TIPS AND TECHNIQUES

General Purpose
Word Processor
Database
Spreadsheet
Data Communications

It's virtually impossible to incorporate every one of *Works'* features into a dozen projects. Inevitably, some commands or procedures are skipped over because they just aren't applicable within the context of the projects. This chapter presents a series of *Works* tips and application techniques that supplement the work you've done in the preceding chapters. Typically, the topics are arranged by application (word processor, database, etc.), but the first group describes general-purpose features that are available in all four *Works* applications.

GENERAL PURPOSE

All of the general-purpose features are found within the File menu.

The Save All Command

Works allows you to open up to eight files on its desktop. These may be eight of the same application type (for example, eight word processor documents), or a mixture of all four application types. I can't emphasize too strongly the need to save your work frequently. But when you're concurrently working on several documents, it's awkward to display each document in order to save it to your data disk.

    Works simplifies the process with the **Save All** command. Selecting this command saves the current version of all open *Works* documents.

Using Subdirectories

DOS, your computer's disk operating system, can create special areas on your disks called *subdirectories* where you may store related files. For example, you might want to store your correspondence grouped by month (all the January letters in one group, the February letters in another group, and so forth). This would necessitate creating twelve subdirectories, one for each month, on your data disk.

    You create a subdirectory with DOS' Make Directory command, MD. Since this is a DOS command, you have to leave *Works*—either by quitting the program or by selecting the **DOS** command (described below) from the File menu. To create a "January" subdirectory, for instance, you would first make sure that the DOS prompt indicated the drive containing your data disk. Then, you would type **MD JAN**. When you press (Enter), DOS creates the subdirectory. (*Note*: Subdirectory names take no extension.)

How do you place files in or retrieve files from a particular subdirectory? By using the **Other Drives & Directories**: list box in, respectively, the SAVE AS and OPEN dialog boxes. Figure 8-1 shows a SAVE AS dialog box after the twelve monthly subdirectories have been created. You can see the first few subdirectories in the **Other Drives & Directories**: list box. Pressing (Alt) + (O) moves the cursor to the list box where you can scroll to see the rest of the list. (*Note*: If you don't see the subdirectories you created, use the list box to select the drive containing your data disk. Look at the **Current Path**: to see to which drive *Works* is set to save.) Once you've selected a subdirectory, *Works* will display your choice in the **Current Path**: indicator. For example, if you select the JAN subdirectory, the **Current Path**: will display A:\JAN. When you press (Enter) to save your file, the document will be placed within the JAN subdirectory.

Before you can select a different subdirectory, you must return to the top level of your data disk. That's the function of the double-dot (..) selection in the list box. This choice is always the top-most

Figure 8-1   Subdirectories appear in alphabetical order

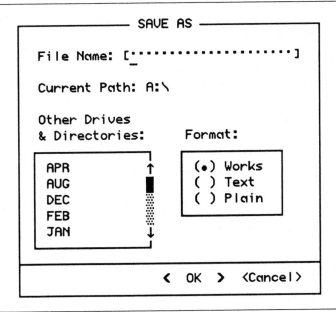

item in the **Other Drives & Directories**: list box. If you don't see it, you're already at the top-level directory.

Opening a document that's been saved in a subdirectory uses the same procedure. The OPEN dialog box has its own **Other Drives & Directories**: list box.

≡ Backup Subdirectory

When you resave a document, *Works* replaces the old version on your data disk with the current version in your PC. But *Works* doesn't throw out the old version. Instead, the old version is placed in a special subdirectory on your data disk, named "BACKUP."

Where did this subdirectory come from? *Works* created it the first time you resaved a document. The BACKUP subdirectory contains previous versions of all *Works* documents that have been resaved. Only a single version (the one immediately preceding the current version) of each file is kept in the BACKUP subdirectory.

These backup files provide protection if the current data file is accidentally destroyed or becomes unusable. To open one of the backup files, just select the BACKUP subdirectory from the **Other Drives & Directories**: list box.

≡ Using DOS from *Works*

There may be times when you want to perform a DOS command while you're in the *Works* program. You might, for instance, want to format a new data disk or create a new subdirectory (see above). Select **DOS** from the File menu, and *Works* will display an alert box (Figure 8-2) reminding you to type "EXIT" to return from DOS to *Works*. Press (Enter), and the *Works* desktop disappears. You're now in DOS and can use any of DOS' commands and utilities.

When you're ready to return to *Works*, just type **EXIT**. You're returned to the same application and file from which you executed the DOS command.

Figure 8-2   Transfer to DOS alert box

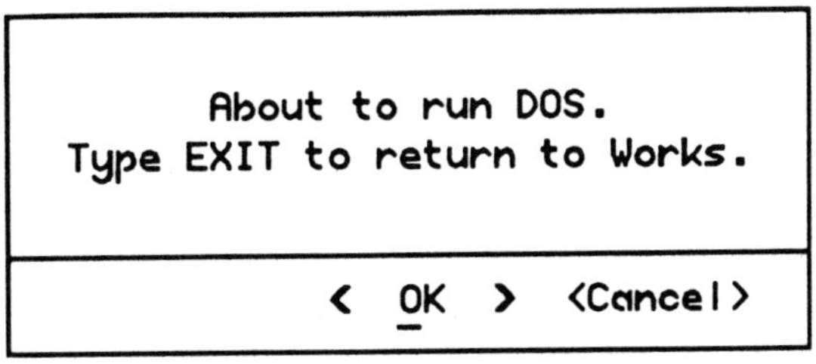

```
┌─────────────────────────────────────┐
│          About to run DOS.          │
│   Type EXIT to return to Works.     │
├─────────────────────────────────────┤
│       < OK >   <Cancel>            │
└─────────────────────────────────────┘
```

WORD PROCESSOR

The word processor application is full of seldom-used but fascinating features. Some of these features, such as the extended character set, stand alone. Others, such as tab leaders and default tabs, are extensions of commands and features you've already used.

Tab Leaders

Suppose you wanted to type a theater program, listing the play's cast of characters. Traditionally, the characters' names are left-aligned while the respective actors' names are right-aligned. Figure 8-3 shows a partial cast listing from a Stratford (Ontario) production of Shakespeare's *King Lear*. The listing doesn't appear to be too difficult to format.

In fact, the alignment consists solely of a right-aligned tab marker at 5 inches. Each line of the cast list contains the name of a character, a (Tab), and the actor's name. But suppose, as is customary with most theater programs, you wanted to fill the space separating the character from the actor with a string of periods (...).

Figure 8-3   The players are right-tabbed to 5 inches

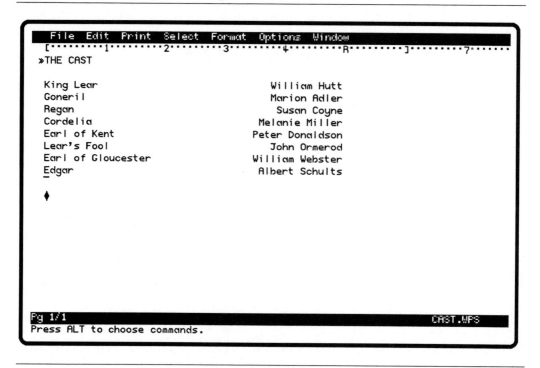

You could type them in yourself, but *Works* can do it for you. In addition to defining tab marker alignment (left, right, center, or decimal), you can specify a tab *leader*. Normally, tab markers are set without leaders. But if you examine the TABS dialog box (Figure 8-4), you'll see a selection of leaders in the Leader list box. I've chosen the dots (...) leader for the right-aligned tab marker at 5 inches.

Works uses the leader character you select to fill in the space between the tab character you type (when you press [Tab]) and the next character that appears on the line. Figure 8-5 shows the same partial cast list you saw in Figure 8-3, but this time the tab marker includes a dots leader.

Notice the dot in front of the "R" tab marker on the ruler. The dot indicates that this tab marker has a dots leader.

Remember, if you want to add a tab leader to each line in the cast list, you must highlight the entire table before you add the leader.

Figure 8-4   Add a dots leader to the 5" tab

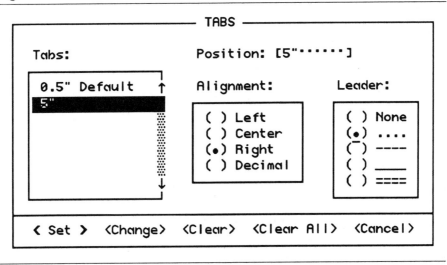

```
┌──────────────────── TABS ────────────────────┐
│                                               │
│  Tabs:              Position: [5"······]      │
│                                               │
│  ┌────────────────┐ Alignment:    Leader:     │
│  │ 0.5" Default  ↑│                            │
│  │ █5"█           │ ┌───────────┐ ┌──────────┐│
│  │              ▓▓│ │ ( ) Left  │ │( ) None  ││
│  │              ▓▓│ │ ( ) Center│ │(•) ....  ││
│  │              ▓▓│ │ (•) Right │ │( ) ----  ││
│  │              ▓▓│ │ ( ) Decimal│ │( ) ____ ││
│  │              ↓│ │           │ │( ) ==== ││
│  └────────────────┘ └───────────┘ └──────────┘│
│                                               │
├───────────────────────────────────────────────┤
│  < Set >  <Change>  <Clear>  <Clear All>  <Cancel>  │
└───────────────────────────────────────────────┘
```

Figure 8-5   The space between tabbed text is filled by the tab leader

```
 File  Edit  Print  Select  Format  Options  Window
[········1········2········3········4······.R·········]·········7········
»THE CAST

King Lear...........................William Hutt
Goneril.............................Marion Adler
Regan...............................Susan Coyne
Cordelia............................Melanie Miller
Earl of Kent........................Peter Donaldson
Lear's Fool.........................John Ormerod
Earl of Gloucester..................William Webster
Edgar...............................Albert Schults

♦

Pg 1/1                                        CAST.WPS
Press ALT to choose commands.
```

☰ Default Tabs

While we're on the subject of tabs, *Works* sets default tab stops every half-inch. You can prove this to yourself by displaying the ruler and repeatedly pressing (Tab). Each time you press (Tab), the cursor advances another half-inch. When you set tab markers in the TABS dialog box, those markers override *Works'* default markers. You can't delete the default tabs, but you can change their value. Display the TABS dialog box. Highlight the 0.5″ (Default) value from the **Tabs:** list box, then press (Alt) + (P) to move the cursor to the **Position:** text box. Type a new value, but *don't* press (Enter). Press (Alt) + (H) instead. Close the dialog box by pressing (Esc).

Unlike the tab markers *you* set, changing the default tab marker affects every paragraph in the document that uses default tabs, not just the one containing the cursor. The change does not, however, affect the value of default tab markers in other documents.

☰ Multiline Headers and Footers

In Project 2, you used options in the LAYOUT dialog box to create single-line Headers and Footers. While a one-line Header or Footer is usually sufficient, there are times when you need a multiple-line Header (or Footer). The **Headers & Footers** command lets you insert Headers and Footers of any length.

Open any word processor document, and select **Headers & Footers** from the Options menu. *Works* places two special one-line paragraphs at the top of your document (Figure 8-6): one marked "H" for Header, the other marked "F" for Footer. The Header paragraph is blank except for the paragraph mark (¶), while the Footer line contains default text to print the document's page number. Both paragraphs have centering tab markers halfway between the left and right margins and right-aligned tab markers at the right margin.

Tip: Set the Left and Right Margin values in the LAYOUT dialog box before you select **Headers & Footers**. Otherwise, the tab markers in the Header and Footer paragraphs won't be properly placed.

Figure 8-6 Using Headers and Footers from the Options menu

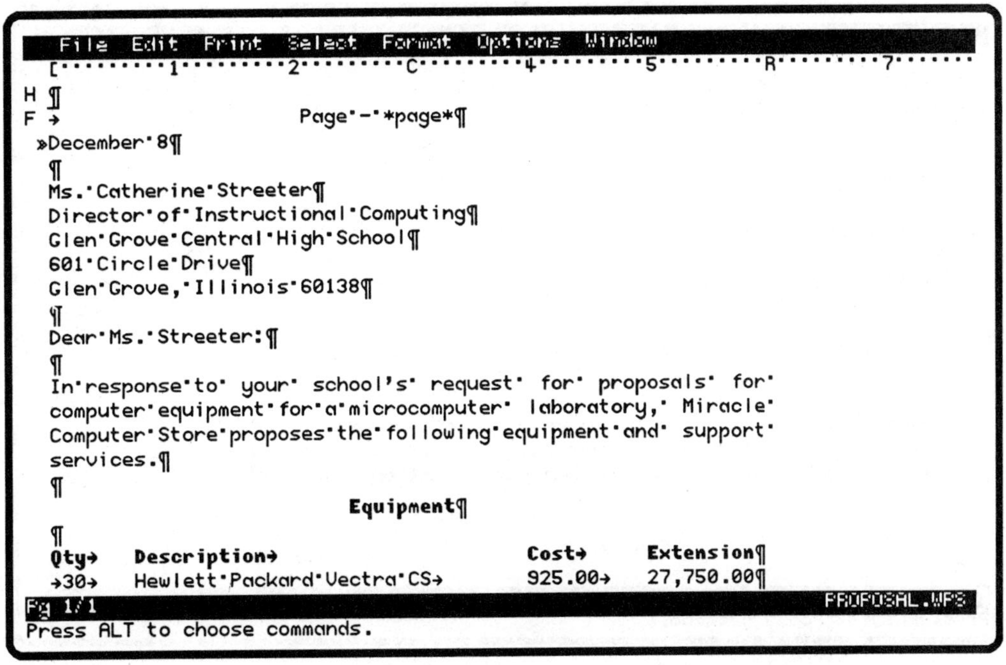

```
 File  Edit  Print  Select  Format  Options  Window
[·········1·········2·········C·········4·········5·········R·········7········
H ¶
F →                        Page·-·*page*¶
»December·8¶
  ¶
 Ms.·Catherine·Streeter¶
 Director·of·Instructional·Computing¶
 Glen·Grove·Central·High·School¶
 601·Circle·Drive¶
 Glen·Grove,·Illinois·60138¶
  ¶
 Dear·Ms.·Streeter:¶
  ¶
 In·response·to· your· school's· request· for· proposals· for·
 computer·equipment·for·a·microcomputer· laboratory,· Miracle·
 Computer·Store·proposes·the·following·equipment·and· support·
 services.¶
  ¶
                       Equipment¶
  ¶
 Qty→  Description→                 Cost→    Extension¶
 →30→  Hewlett·Packard·Vectra·CS→   925.00→  27,750.00¶
Pg 1/1                                            PROPOSAL.WPS
Press ALT to choose commands.
```

Each Header or Footer consists of one paragraph, so *don't* press
(Enter) when you insert text into either paragraph. To create a multiple-
line Header (or Footer), press (Shift) + (Enter) at the end of lines. Pressing (Shift) + (Enter) inserts an end-of-line mark (↓) instead of a paragraph mark. Figure 8-7 shows a three-line Header paragraph. I've used
Show All Characters feature so that you can see the end-of-line and
paragraph symbols.

When you use the **Headers & Footers** option, *Works* ignores the
contents of the Header and Footer text boxes in the LAYOUT dialog
box. But the values for Header Margin and Footer Margin still determine
where on the page the Header starts and the Footer ends. The No
Header (Footer) on 1st Page options control whether the multiple-
line Header (Footer) will appear on the first page of your document.

Figure 8-7   Creating a three-line header

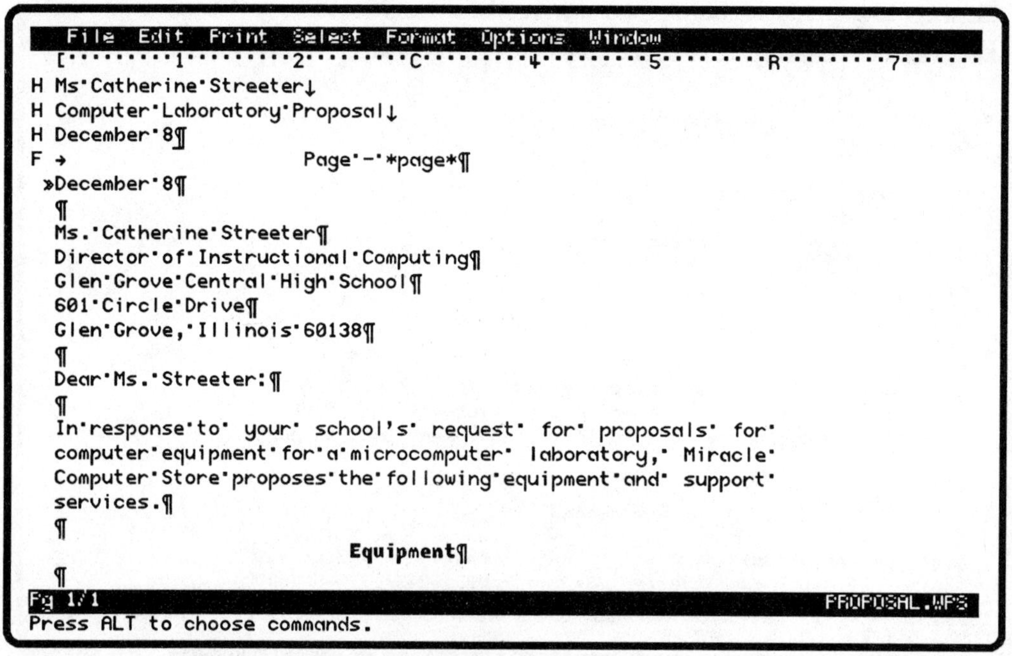

```
 File  Edit  Print  Select  Format  Options  Window
[·········1·········2·········C·········4·········5·········R·········7······
H Ms·Catherine·Streeter↓
H Computer·Laboratory·Proposal↓
H December·8¶
F →                    Page·-·*page*¶
 »December·8¶
  ¶
  Ms.·Catherine·Streeter¶
  Director·of·Instructional·Computing¶
  Glen·Grove·Central·High·School¶
  601·Circle·Drive¶
  Glen·Grove,·Illinois·60138¶
  ¶
  Dear·Ms.·Streeter:¶
  ¶
  In·response·to· your· school's· request· for· proposals· for·
  computer·equipment·for·a·microcomputer· laboratory,· Miracle·
  Computer·Store·proposes·the·following·equipment·and· support·
  services.¶
  ¶
                    Equipment¶
  ¶
Pg 1/1                                              PROPOSAL.WPS
Press ALT to choose commands.
```

If you use a multiple-line Header, you must be sure that there is enough room for the Header on your page. The Header occupies the space between the Header Margin and the Top Margin. *Works'* default values of 0.5 inches and 1 inch, respectively, allow for a maximum of three Header lines. To increase the Header space, increase the Top Margin value. Similarly, to increase Footer space, increase the value for the Bottom Margin.

If you select **Headers & Footers** a second time, the Header and Footer paragraphs will disappear from your document, and *Works* will again use the contents of the Header and Footer text boxes in the LAYOUT dialog box. A bullet (●) next to the **Headers & Footers** command in the Options menu indicates that the command is active.

Tip: If you delete the default Footer text, be careful not to delete the paragraph mark. Use **Show All Characters** to display the paragraph mark before you erase the text.

Your Header or Footer can include one or more special features such as automatic page numbering or automatic date and time stamping. Each of these features is placed into your Header or Footer by inserting the corresponding special character. See the next section in this chapter for a complete description of all of the word processor's special characters.

☰ Inserting Special Characters

The *Works* word processor uses several special characters to perform certain tasks. For example, you can insert optional or nonbreaking hyphens or nonbreaking spaces into your text. Or you can automatically insert the current date or the current time, or print the file name or the page number into a Header or Footer (created with the **Headers & Footers** command).

Figure 8-8 shows the dialog box that *Works* displays when you select the **Insert Special** command from the Edit menu. To choose one of these special features, move the cursor to the one you want, and press ⌷Enter⌷. The special character is inserted into your document at the current cursor location.

Figure 8-8 The INSERT SPECIAL dialog box

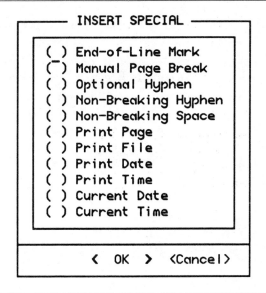

While the INSERT SPECIAL dialog box can be used to insert these special characters, you can type them directly into your document. Table 8-1 lists the keystrokes that correspond to each special character. The following paragraphs describe each special character and how it's used.

Table 8-1   Special characters and their corresponding keystrokes

Special Character	Type
End-of-Line Mark	Shift + Enter
Manual Page Break	Control + Enter
Optional Hyphen	Control + -
Non-Breaking Hyphen	Control + Shift + -
Non-Breaking Space	Control + Shift + Space Bar
Print Page (number)	Control + P
Print File (name)	Control + F
Print Date	Control + D
Print Time	Control + T
Current Date	Control + i
Current Time	Control + Shift + i

The *End-of-Line Mark* moves the cursor to the beginning of the next line without terminating the paragraph. This is useful when you want *Works* to format a series of lines as a single paragraph. The end-of-line mark must be used when you create a multiple-line header or footer (see above). If you invoke **Show All Characters**, the end-of-line mark appears as a ↓ symbol.

Works automatically begins a new page for your document when its length exceeds the available page length (the actual page length minus the top and bottom margins). Often this break occurs in the middle of a paragraph or in the middle of a table that you do not want to divide. You can force *Works* to start a new page at the beginning of the paragraph or table by inserting a *Manual Page Break* character just above the paragraph or table. The page break appears as a row of dots across the screen.

If you type a long word near the end of a line, *Works* will *wrap* the word to the beginning of the next line. If you hyphenate the word and the portion before the hyphen fits on the line above, *Works* will split the word at the hyphen. A problem arises, though, if you edit the paragraph containing the hyphenated word and as a result of the editing the word is no longer at the end of a line. The hyphen will remain, even though the word now fits on a single line. The *Optional Hyphen* solves this problem neatly. Insert this character as you would a normal hyphen. It will normally be invisible, but it will appear if the word can be split between lines. You can see where you've placed optional hyphens with **Show All Characters**.

On the other hand, there are times when you hyphenate words that you *don't* want split between lines. For these situations, use the *Non-Breaking Hyphen*. This character looks exactly like an ordinary hyphen, but *Works* will not split a word on a non-breaking hyphen.

You can keep two (or more) words from being split between lines by inserting a *Non-Breaking Space* instead of a normal space between the words. This is typically used to prevent names from being split. If you were typing a letter to a Mr. Moyer, for example, and used his name within the text of the letter, you wouldn't want "Mr." at the end of one line and "Moyer" at the beginning of the next line. Inserting a non-breaking space between the "." and the "M" would keep the name together regardless of its location on a line.

The remaining special characters are used primarily in Headers and Footers, although they may be inserted anywhere in your document. When you created Headers and Footers in Chapter 2, you used the Header and Footer text boxes in the LAYOUT dialog box. With these one-line Headers and Footers, you indicated automatic page numbering, for instance, by typing "&P." When you use the **Headers & Footers** command, you insert features such as automatic page numbering by typing special characters.

You can add a page number in your Header or Footer by inserting the *Print Page* character. This character appears as "*page*" and *Works* treats it as a Placeholder for the page number. Each time the Header (or Footer) is printed, *Works* notes the current page number and replaces the Placeholder with this value. Your documents do not have to begin with page 1. You can set the first page number (in the LAYOUT dialog box) to any value you wish.

The *Print File* character inserts the Placeholder "*filename*" into your Header or Footer. When you print the document, the document's file name replaces the Placeholder.

Works provides two ways of date stamping your documents. The *Print Date* character inserts a "*date*" Placeholder. When you print the document, *Works* looks at your computer's system clock and replaces the Placeholder with the current date.

The second method of date stamping uses the *Current Date* character. When you insert this special character, *Works* immediately replaces it with the current date from the system clock (e.g., "4/25/89"). This date remains fixed regardless of when the document is printed.

The *Print Time* character inserts a "*time*" Placeholder into your Header or Footer. When you print the document, *Works* replaces the Placeholder with the current time taken from your computer's system clock.

The *Current Time* character inserts the current time (from the system clock) into your document. As with the *Current Date* character, *Current Time* does not change once it's inserted.

☰ Controlling Page Breaks

Inserting a Manual Page Break character is one way to control the beginning of a new page, but *Works* provides two other methods. The options Keep Paragraph Together and Keep With Next Paragraph are both found in the PARAGRAPH dialog box.

When you apply the Keep Paragraph Together option to a paragraph in your document, should a page break occur within that paragraph, the entire paragraph is moved to the next page. If you format all the paragraphs in your document with this option, none of the paragraphs will be split between pages.

The Keep With Next Paragraph option prevents the paragraph formatted with this option from being separated from the one following it. You might use this option to prevent a line of column headings being separated from its table.

☰ The Extended Character Set

You may not know it, but your computer can type 256 different characters. All of the characters are numbered, from 0 to 255. For example, the letter "A" is character number 65 while "a" is character 97. These numerical values are called ASCII values (ASCII, pronounced "as-key," stands for the American Standard Code for Information Interchange).

The first 32 characters (ASCII 0–31) are special symbols used by the *Works* program. For example, the paragraph symbol (¶) that's displayed each time you press Enter is really ASCII 20, and the tab character (→) is really ASCII 26. These characters are reserved for *Works'* use, so you can't display them.

The ASCII characters from 32 to 127 are the letters, numbers, and symbols that you can type directly from your computer's keyboard. But there're an additional 128 characters, including accented characters, graphics, and mathematical symbols, that you can insert into your word processor documents. These characters comprise the extended character set, and you'll find a complete listing of them, including their corresponding ASCII values, in Appendix A.

Your keyboard normally produces ASCII characters 32–127, corresponding to the symbols appearing on the key caps. But you can type any of the extended characters using the following technique. Find the symbol you want to type, using the table in Appendix A. Then, hold down (Alt) while you type the corresponding three-digit ASCII value on the keypad. (*Note*: You *must* type the ASCII value on the keypad. If you use the number keys on upper keyboard row, nothing happens.) Release (Alt), and your character appears.

For example, suppose you wanted to include the French phrase, *déjà vu*, in a letter to a friend. The é in *déjà* takes an acute accent (´) while the à takes a grave accent (`). If you look at Appendix A, the é corresponds to ASCII 130 while the à corresponds to ASCII 133. To type déjà, you would type a "d," hold down (Alt) while you typed "130," type a "j," and hold down (Alt) while you typed "133."

The graphics characters are mostly used to draw borders around text. The paragraph in Figure 8-9 has a double-line border drawn around it. I used the following technique to draw the box. The first line began with an ASCII 201 character, followed by a row of ASCII 205 characters, and ended with an ASCII 187 character. Each line of text began and ended with an ASCII 186. The bottom line began with an ASCII 200, followed by a string of ASCII 205s, and ended with an ASCII 188.

One caution: Your printer must contain and be able to reproduce the same extended character set as your computer. If it doesn't, the printed version won't match the screen.

☰ Importing and Exporting Files

You can transfer files created with Microsoft *Works* to other word processor programs (such as Microsoft *Word*, *WordPerfect*, *WordStar*, etc.). The transfer process is called exporting, and it's very easy to do.

Start by choosing **Save As** from the File menu. Name the document, and use ".TXT" as the extension (e.g., LETTER.TXT). (*Note*: See the discussion of document names in Chapter 2.) The ".TXT" extension identifies this as a text file, and this is the format *Works* uses when it exports a word processor file. Press (Alt) + (T) to select Text from the **Format:** list box. Then, press (Enter).

Figure 8-9 Use graphic symbols from the extended character set to draw borders around paragraphs

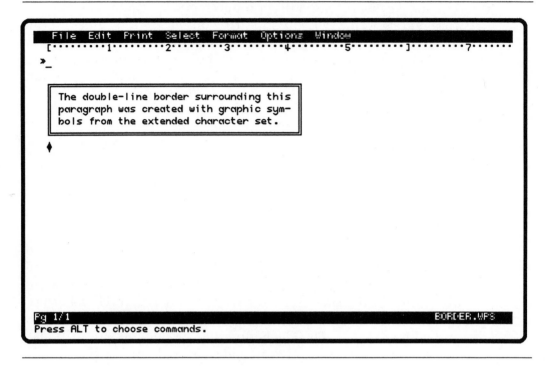

Works will display an alert box asking you whether it's "OK to lose formatting." When you save a document in Text format, only text, tab characters, and the carriage returns at the end of paragraphs are saved. Any formatting you may have applied to characters (bold, underline, italic, etc.) or paragraphs (spacing, etc.) is ignored and is not saved. The alert box asks if you really want to save the file this way. When you export a file, this is exactly how you want it saved, so press (Enter) to complete the exporting procedure.

Virtually all word processor programs will be able to read text files exported from *Works*.

Tip: Be sure to use Text format, rather than Plain format, when you export your word processor documents. Plain format inserts spaces in place of tabs, indents, and left and right margins, and inserts blank lines to fill in the top and bottom margins. Plain format also inserts carriage returns at the end of each line of text (rather than solely at the end of paragraphs).

Importing files into *Works* from other word processor programs is equally easy. Just save the document as a text (or ASCII) file, and use a file extension of ".TXT" as you do when you export a file from *Works*. Select **Open** from the File menu, and type the document's file name (including the extension). When you press ⌜Enter⌟, *Works* will ask what kind of a file this is—word processor, database, or spreadsheet. Select Word Processor, and *Works* will import your file.

DATABASE

Most of the database's commands were demonstrated in the two projects in Chapter 3. This section gives me an opportunity to elaborate on the query feature and introduce some seldom-used formatting commands.

Query

Works' query feature allows you to select and display a portion of the records in your database. Only records that match your selection criteria will be displayed. And if you use this database to produce form letters (see Chapter 7), only displayed records are merged.

What happens to records that don't match the selection criteria? They're not thrown away; they're just *hidden*. You can cancel the query by selecting **Show All Records** from the Query menu. Or you can swap the hidden records for the displayed ones by selecting **Switch Hidden Records**. If, for example, your query had displayed records with last names beginning with letters K through R, selecting **Switch Hidden Records** would hide records with last names beginning with K through R and display records with last names beginning with A through J and S through Z.

You might wonder how to specify a range of values in a query. Let's set up a query for a range of numbers first and then extend the idea to letters. Suppose you wanted to display records of the employees of your company with salaries between $20,000 and $35,000. Another way of saying this is that you want a range of salaries *greater than* or *equal to* 20000 and *less than* 35000.

The first part of the query, salaries greater than or equal to $20,000, translates to the expression = Salary >= 20000. The second part of the query, salaries less than $35,000, translates to the expression = Salary < 35000. You can combine these two queries into a single expression,

= Salary >= 20000 & Salary < 35000.

(*Note*: Spaces within the query definitions are for clarity. *Works* ignores them.)

The & symbol represents a logical "AND" and tells *Works* to display records whose salaries are greater than or equal to (>=) 20000 *and* are less than (<) 35000.

If you enter this query in the Salary field of the Query window, the field name, Salary, is assumed. This means that the above expression can be simplified to

>= 20000 & < 35000

Now let's set up a range of names as a query. *Works* (and all other computer programs) treats letters as if they possessed numerical values. If you've read the above section on the extended character set, you know that each character has an assigned ASCII value—65 for "A," 66 for "B," and so forth. To a computer, "A" is less than "B" because A's ASCII value is less than B's.

This fact allows you to specify a range of names for a query using the same logic as that used for numbers. Suppose you wanted to look at records with Last Name entries beginning with "S." Mathematically, you want last names greater than or equal to "S" *and* less than "T." The query expression is

= Last Name >= "S" & Last Name < "T"

Again, if you enter this query into the Last Name field, the field name is assumed, and the query becomes

>= "S" & < "T"

You can refine the query as much as you want. For example, you can display all of the last names beginning with "S" but excluding "Smith" by adding & <> "Smith".

>= "S" & <"T" & <> "Smith"

Try this query on the CUSTOMER.WDB database and see that only two records are displayed.

When you exit the Query window (by selecting **Exit Query** from the Edit menu), *Works* automatically applies the criteria you defined to the records in your database. Selecting **Show All Records** cancels the query, but the criteria still exist in the Query window. You can invoke the query again without entering the Query window by selecting **Apply Query**. If you want to completely erase all the criteria from the Query window, enter the window and select **Delete** from the Edit menu.

≡ Automatic Date and Time

Both the database and the spreadsheet allow you to enter either the current date or the current time into a cell with a single keystroke. Typing (Control) + (i) inserts the current date, read from the system clock. Typing (Control) + (Shift) + (i) inserts the current time.

Tip: (Control) + (Shift) + (i) inserts the current time in hours and minutes only. If you format the cell for hours, minutes, seconds, the seconds will always be "00."

≡ Copying Entries

You learned how to use **Fill Right** and **Fill Down** in the spreadsheet projects of Chapter 4. These commands are also available in the database, but only in the List window. Here's a situation where **Fill Down** would be useful.

Suppose you had created a database that combined city, state, and zip code data into a single field. After entering several (dozen? hundred?) records, you realize that you should have assigned city, state, and zip code each to its own field. So, you change the name of the original field to "City" and add new fields for "State" and "Zip." While the "City" and "Zip" data cells have to be individually edited, all of the entries are from the same state (at least they are in this example).

Instead of typing the same entry into each of dozens (or hundreds) of "State" cells, you could enter the state into the first record and use **Fill Down** to copy the entry into all of the remaining records. See Chapter 4 if you need help using this command.

Tip: **Fill Down** does not copy data to hidden records, only to the records currently displayed on the screen.

Fill **Down** can also be used to make multiple copies of a single record. To do this, highlight the entire record. Then, extend the highlight to as many rows below as you wish. Select **Fill Down** and the job is done. (*Note*: The rows you're copying *to* should be blank. If they're not, the copied data will replace the existing data.)

Fill **Right** can be used to copy an entire field using the same technique as was used to copy an entire record. Highlight a column, extend the highlight one or more columns to the right, and select **Fill Right**. (*Note*: The columns you're copying to should be blank. If they're not, the copied data will replace the existing data.)

☰ Importing and Exporting

As with word processor files, *Works* allows you to export your database files to other database programs, such as *dBase III*, and to import files from these programs. Text files are used for both importing and exporting.

To export a *Works* database, select **Save As** from the File menu. Name the document, and use ".TXT" as the extension (e.g., DATABASE.TXT). (*Note*: See the discussion of document names in Chapter 2.) The ".TXT" extension identifies this as a text file, and this is the format *Works* uses when it exports a database file. Press ⌨Alt + ⌨T to select Text from the **Format:** list box. Then, press ⌨Enter.

Works saves your database as a pure text (ASCII) file. Text entries are enclosed in quotes, and all entries in a record are separated by commas. Each record ends with a carriage return. This is the standard format used by most database programs for importing and exporting data.

Tip: When you save a database as a text file, all computations, field names and formats, and report forms are ignored. If your database uses computed fields, only their current values are saved, not the formulas.

To import a file from another database program, save the document as a text (or ASCII) file, and use a file extension of ".TXT." Select **Open** from the File menu, and type the document's file name (including the extension). When you press ⌨Enter, *Works* will ask what kind of a file this is—word processor, database, or spreadsheet. Select Database, and *Works* will import your file.

Since *Works* doesn't know the names of the imported data fields, it will use "Field1," "Field2," etc. You can use the **Name** command in the Edit menu to rename the fields.

SPREADSHEET

Chapter 4 gave you a taste of the computational power of a spreadsheet. I couldn't hope to include all of the functions and features contained in *Works'* spreadsheet with just three projects. So, here are some techniques for using the spreadsheet's time and date functions, plus a brief look at *Works'* MS-Key macro generator.

Time and Date Arithmetic

The spreadsheet contains nine time and date functions. Here are some examples of their use. Suppose you wanted to list the names of the months in the year (January, February, etc.). I'll assume you want to list the months in column A, rows 3 through 14 (A3:A14).

First, format the entire range to display only months. Do this by highlighting the range, selecting Time/Date from the Format menu, and choosing Month Only from the dialog box's **Show:** list box.

Type **Jan 1** into cell A3, and press (Enter). Notice that only the month, "Jan," appears in the cell because you chose Month Only format. Highlight cell A4, and enter the formula =**A3 + 31.**

When you press (Enter), "Feb" appears in the cell. *Works* interpreted =A3 + 31 as adding 31 days to the date, Jan 1. This yielded a date in February (Feb 1), but because you formatted the cell for Month Only, only the month was displayed.

Now, highlight the range A4:A14, and use **Fill Down** to copy the formula from A4 into the remaining cells.

Tip: *Works'* date functions will display only the first three letters of the names of the months.

Here's an example of time arithmetic. Suppose you wanted to keep a record of the time you spent working on a client's project. You might set up a spreadsheet similar to the one shown in Figure 8-10.

Figure 8-10 Create a spreadsheet to perform time management

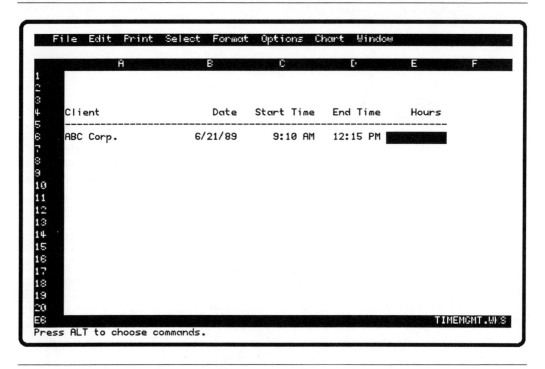

You can insert the current date into the Date cell (B6) by typing ⌃Control + ⓘ (and pressing ⏎Enter). And you can enter the current time into the Start Time cell (C6) by typing ⌃Control + ⇧Shift + ⓘ. Later, when you stop working on the client's project, you can return to the spreadsheet and use ⌃Control + ⇧Shift + ⓘ to enter the current time into the End Time cell (D6).

To compute the difference between the two times in hours, use the following formula:

= HOUR(D6–C6) + MINUTE(D6–C6)/60

The HOUR function computes the number of whole hours in its argument. Note that the function does *not* round to the nearest hour; it truncates. So that if, for example, cell C6 contained the time 8:30 AM, and D6 contained 10:20 AM, =HOUR(D6–C6) would yield a value of 1, not 2. The MINUTE function takes the fraction of the remaining hour and converts this value to whole minutes, so =MINUTE(D6–C6) would return a value of 50, given the above entries for cells C6 and D6. And, of course, dividing this value by 60 converts minutes into a fraction of an hour.

First, before you enter the formula, highlight column E and format it as Fixed with 2 decimal places. Then, type the formula shown above into the Hours cell (E6). *Works* will display time difference to the nearest hundredth of an hour (Figure 8-11). This format simplifies adding individual times for the same client.

Tip: If you're the type of person who works past midnight, modify the above formula to:

$$= \textbf{HOUR(1+D6-C6)} + \textbf{MINUTE(1+D6-C6)}/\textbf{60}$$

This formula will work whether you work past midnight or during "normal" business hours.

Figure 8-11   Use time arithmetic to compute the difference between two times

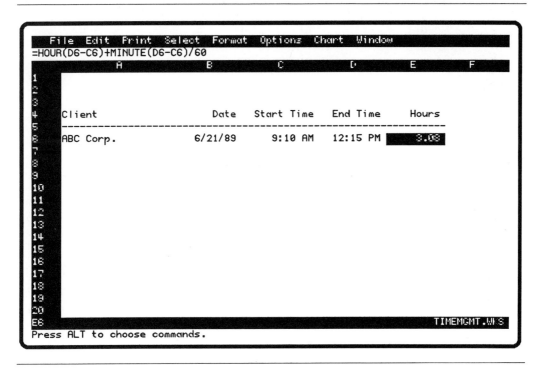

☰ Macros

Microsoft includes a macro generator, called *MS-Key*, with its *Works* package. A macro is a sequence of keystrokes that can be "played" automatically. For example, you could define the keystrokes that type the letters in your name as a macro. Then, by typing a single character, the macro would type your name.

Creating a Text Macro

Let's create a macro to type your name. First, though, be sure you've installed MS-Key on your DOS disk or on your hard disk's root (top level) directory. Also, you must have run the MSKEY.COM program before running *Works*. If you haven't run MSKEY.COM, quit *Works*, switch to your DOS disk or the root directory of your hard disk, and type **MSKEY**. Then, rerun *Works*.

Open a new spreadsheet. While the macro generator can be used in all four *Works* applications, you'll probably use it most often with spreadsheets.

To check that you have MS-Key properly installed, press (Alt) + (/). The spreadsheet's menu bar should change to display three menus: Macro, File, and Options.

Press (M) to pull down the Macro menu. The first menu command is **Record**. Select this command by pressing (Enter). The macro generator asks you to "Press key to record." Each macro you record is associated with a particular key. You could, for instance, assign your name macro to the "N" key. But you probably want to continue using this key to type N's. A better choice is to assign your macro to a key you normally don't use. (Control) + (N) is a good choice. Type (Control) + (N). (*Note*: Pressing (Control) + (Esc) in response to the "Press key to record" prompt aborts the macro recording.)

Once you have assigned a key, everything you type is automatically recorded into the macro. Type your name and press (Enter). Since your name is all you want in this macro, end the recording by pressing (Alt) + (/) to display the MS-Key menu bar, pull down the Macro menu, and select **End**.

That's all there is to recording a macro. If you want to see your macro in action, highlight any cell and press (Control) + (N). By the way, your macro can be used in any of *Works'* applications, not just the spreadsheet.

Creating a Command Macro

A macro is a recorded sequence of keystrokes—any keystrokes. As such, a macro can include menu commands as well as straight text. Let's create another macro to demonstrate this ability. In an earlier section of this chapter, you experimented with date and time arithmetic. Refer to that section, and to Figure 8-11, and duplicate the time management spreadsheet. (*Note*: For this macro demonstration, the spreadsheet should be the only document on the *Works* desktop.)

Begin a second line of data in row 7. Enter any client name into A7, the current date (Control + i) into B7, and a time a few hours earlier than the current time (e.g., if it's now 2:15 PM, enter 11:45 AM) into C7. Move the cursor to cell D7 and leave it there.

Create a new word processor document (select **New** from the File menu) and pretend that you've been working on a client project for the past couple of hours. Let's create a macro that will automatically display the time management spreadsheet, enter the current time in the End Time column, and compute the hours spent on the project.

Press Alt + / to display the MS-Key menu bar, then select **Record** from the Macro menu. Assign this macro to Control + T . Now let's enter the keystrokes that will accomplish the task you want the macro to perform. Try to enter the following keystrokes exactly. If you make a mistake, just correct it. The macro will record both the mistake and its correction.

Tip: Don't use the mouse while you're recording a macro. MS-Key doesn't recognize the location of the mouse or mouse clicks.

Press Alt + W to pull down the Window menu, then press 1 to select the spreadsheet (it should be document 1). The time management spreadsheet will be displayed with the cursor in cell D7, where you left it. Press Control + Shift + i and then Enter to insert the current time into D7. Use the arrow keys to move the cursor to cell E6, the cell with the Hours formula. Hold down the Shift while you press ↓ once to highlight the two cells, E6:E7. Then press Alt + E to pull down the Edit menu, and select the **Fill Down** command. This action copies the formula from E6 into E7. Finally, move the cursor to cell A8.

Press Alt + / , pull down the Macro menu, and select **End**. Your macro has been recorded. Let's see how it works.

Enter another client in cell A8, the current date in B8, and an earlier-than-current time in C8. Move the cursor to cell D8, and display the word processor document. Now for the moment of truth. Press (Control) + (T), and watch your macro in action.

Macro Files

The two macros you created exist only in your computer's memory. If you quit *Works*, they will disappear. You can save your macros (as many as you can find keys to assign to them) to a macro file on your data disk.

To do this, display the MS-Key menu bar, and select **Save** from the File menu. (*Note*: Be sure to use the File menu from the MS-Key menu bar, and not *Works'* File menu.) Use any file name (TIME.MCR, for example), with or without an extension. You can save as many macro files as you like.

Even after you save the macros in a file, they're still available in memory. They'll remain in memory until you delete them or until you quit *Works*.

Loading a macro file is easy. Just select **Open** from the File menu on the MS-Key menu bar, and type the name of the macro file into the dialog box.

You can delete individual macros or erase all macros from your PC's memory. To delete a single macro, display the MS-Key menu bar and select **Delete** from the Macro menu. MS-Key will prompt you for the key assigned to the macro you want to delete ((Control) + (N) , (Control) + (T) , etc.). Press the appropriate macro key, and that macro is erased.

You can erase all macros from memory by selecting **Clear** from the MS-Key menu bar's File menu.

If you'd like to see how your macros were recorded, select **List** from the File menu. You can use (PgUp) and (PgDn) to scroll through all the macros currently in your PC's memory. The feature can also be used if you forget which key corresponds to which macro.

Using macros can increase your productivity and make the integration of data between *Works* applications even easier. MS-Key includes a macro editor so that you can enter and edit macros directly, rather than just recording keystrokes. As with *Works*, itself, the more time you spend with MS-Key, the more useful it will become. I encourage you to share macros you create with other *Works* owners. You can use my *Working with Works* BBS to exchange macros, spreadsheet templates, or anything else you feel might be of interest.

☰ Page Breaks

Because most spreadsheets are too large to print on a single page, *Works* will automatically divide your spreadsheet into page-size portions, both horizontally and vertically, and will never split a column between pages. But you may want to control the location of page breaks.

The **Insert Page Break** command in the Print menu will insert either a row (horizontal) or column (vertical) page break. The page break marker is the >> symbol and appears between the column letters and alongside row numbers.

When *Works* prints your spreadsheet, it starts in the upper-left corner and prints all the rows of the first few columns (A through F, for instance) to the last row containing data, printing as many pages as needed. Then, it returns to the top of the spreadsheet and prints the next few columns from the top row to the last row, and so on until the last column containing data has been printed.

☰ Printing in Different Sizes

Works can print your spreadsheets in your choice of fonts and sizes, depending on your printer. The Epson FX-80, for example, can print in any of six fonts—Pica, PicaD, Elite, EliteD, NLQ (Near Letter Quality), and PS (Proportional Spacing)—and, depending on the font chosen, up to four sizes (8, 12, 14, and 16 points).

Both choices, font and size, are made in the FONT dialog box (Figure 8-12). Display this dialog box by selecting **Font** from the Print menu. Choosing a small type size (8 point, for example) won't change the size of characters on your screen. The FONT dialog box only affects your printer. The smaller the type size, the more rows and columns will fit on a page. *Works* automatically adjusts its page breaks to compensate for different type sizes.

☰ Importing and Exporting

Works' spreadsheet files are created with what is called WKS format. Two major spreadsheet programs, Microsoft *Excel* and *Lotus 1-2-3*, use this format and can read *Works* spreadsheets, including formulas *and* charts.

Figure 8-12 Use the FONT dialog box to change your printer's type font and size

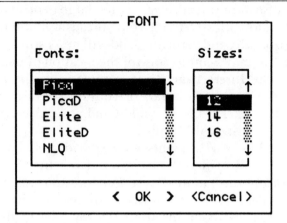

For other spreadsheets that do not use WKS format, you'll have to export using text format. *Works* will save your spreadsheet as a pure text (ASCII) file. Text entries are enclosed in quotes, and all entries in a row are separated by commas. Each row ends with a carriage return. This is the standard format used by most spreadsheet programs for importing and exporting data.

Tip: When you save a spreadsheet as a text file, all formulas, row and column labels, and charts are ignored. Your cell entries are saved exactly as they appear on your screen.

Works can import spreadsheets saved with WKS format or saved as text files. WKS files contain both text and formulas, and may include charts. Both Microsoft *Excel* and *Lotus 1-2-3* can save their files with WKS format. Remember that spreadsheets imported as text files will contain no formulas.

DATA COMMUNICATIONS

There is only one feature that was not discussed in Chapter 6—recording a sign-on procedure. You know that *Works* will dial the telephone number of a computer service or BBS. But if the sign-on procedure (typing your name, a password, etc.) remains constant from one call to the next, *Works* can enter the sign-on sequence for you.

First, you have to teach *Works* how to log on to a computer service or BBS. I'll use my *Working with Works* BBS as an example, and I'll assume that you have already registered with the BBS.

Open a new communications document and, if necessary, change the Baud Rate or the Port in the COMMUNICATION dialog box. All of the other settings are correct for my BBS. Enter the BBS telephone number (1-312-260-9660) in the PHONE dialog box.

Tip: A useful Modem Setup for Hayes-compatible modems is ATM0E1Q0 (the 0's are zeros). "AT" gets the modem's attention. "M0" inhibits the modem's speaker so that you won't hear the modem dialing and connecting. "E1" tells the modem to echo back characters you send to the modem before connection is made. And "Q0" tell the modem to transmit its messages ("Connect 1200," for instance) to your screen.

To begin recording the sign-on sequence, pull down the Connect menu and select **Record Sign-On**. Now, choose **Connect** from the same menu. *Works* will dial the BBS' phone number, and in a few seconds you'll see the modem acknowledging the connection with a "CONNECT 1200" message (or "CONNECT" or "CONNECT 2400"). Press Enter. At the appropriate prompts, type your first name, last name, and password.

When you see the BBS' Main Menu, the sign-on sequence is complete. Select **Record Sign-On** again to stop recording. *Works* now knows how to dial and log on to the BBS automatically.

To test this feature, quit (log-off) the BBS and select **Connect** to go Offline. (*Note*: You must begin the sign-on sequence from the "Offline" state. You should see the word OFFLINE on the status line.) Select **Sign-On** from the Connect menu. *Works* will dial the BBS, wait for the "Connect" message, and automatically type your name and password in response to prompts from the BBS.

You might wonder why *Works* has a special function in the communications section to record a sign-on when the MS-Key macro generator is available. The reason is that a macro executes keystrokes as fast as it can. While you can slow it down by inserting pauses, macros are not designed to respond to prompts. But, by its nature, a sign-on procedure must respond to prompts from a BBS or other computer service. When you record a sign-on sequence, *Works* records everything that appears on the screen—what the BBS transmits *and* what you type. When you play back the recorded sign-on, *Works* waits until it "sees" specific prompting text before it types its responses. If the BBS or computer service changes its sign-on messages, you'll have to re-record the sign-on sequence.

You can change the recorded sign-on at any time by just repeating the entire procedure. The new recorded sequence will replace the old one. When you save the communication document, the recorded sign-on is saved with it.

☰ Final Comments

I thought you might be interested in the hardware and software I used to write this book. My computer is a Macintosh Plus with 2M bytes of RAM and a 40M-byte hard disk drive. I used the Macintosh version of Microsoft *Word,* both to write the manuscript and to produce the index.

The screen shots from *Works* were taken with a Macintosh II computer running *SoftPC* from Insignia Corporation. This program emulates a PC. With it, I was able to run *Works* and use the Mac's screen-shot features to take pictures of the program.

These pictures were edited with Apple Computer's *MacPaint* program and printed on a LaserWriter II printer.

Appendix **A**
EXTENDED CHARACTER SET

Special and Accented Characters

Code	Character	Code	Character	Code	Character
128	Ç	144	É	160	á
129	ü	145	æ	161	í
130	é	146	Æ	162	ó
131	â	147	ô	163	ú
132	ä	148	ö	164	ñ
133	à	149	ò	165	Ñ
134	å	150	û	166	ª
135	ç	151	ù	167	º
136	ê	152	ÿ	168	¿
137	ë	153	Ö	169	⌐
138	è	154	Ü	170	¬
139	ï	155	¢	171	½
140	î	156	£	172	¼
141	ì	157	¥	173	¡
142	Ä	158	Pt	174	«
143	Å	159	ƒ	175	»

Graphics Characters

Code	Character	Code	Character	Code	Character
176	░	192	└	208	╨
177	▒	193	┴	209	╤
178	▓	194	┬	210	╥
179	│	195	├	211	╙
180	┤	196	─	212	╘
181	╡	197	┼	213	╒
182	╢	198	╞	214	╓
183	╖	199	╟	215	╫
184	╕	200	╚	216	╪
185	╣	201	╔	217	┘
186	║	202	╩	218	┌
187	╗	203	╦	219	█
188	╝	204	╠	220	▄
189	╜	205	═	221	▌
190	╛	206	╬	222	▐
191	┐	207	╧	223	▀

Mathematical Symbols

Code	Character	Code	Character	Code	Character
224	α	235	δ	246	$\div$
225	β	236	∞	247	$\approx$
226	Γ	237	$\varnothing$	248	$\circ$
227	π	238	ϵ	249	$\bullet$
228	Σ	239	$\cap$	250	$\cdot$
229	σ	240	$\equiv$	251	$\sqrt{}$
230	μ	241	$\pm$	252	n
231	τ	242	$\geq$	253	2
232	Φ	243	$\leq$	254	■
233	Θ	244	$\lceil$	255	(reserved)
234	Ω	245	$\rfloor$		

Appendix **B**
MANUFACTURER'S LIST

Apple Computer, Inc
20525 Mariani Ave.
Cupertino, CA 95014
408-996-1010

Ashton-Tate
20101 Hamilton Ave.
Torrance, CA 90502-1319
213-329-8000

CompuServe Information
  Services
P.O. Box 20212
5000 Arlington Centre Blvd.
Columbus, OH 43220
800-848-8199

Dataviz Inc.
16 Winfield Street
Norwalk, CT 06855
203-866-4944

Dow Jones & Company, Inc.
P.O. Box 300
Princeton, NJ 08543-0300
609-452-1511

The FreeSoft Company
150 Hickory Drive
Beaver Falls, PA 15010
412-846-2700

General Electric Information
  Services Company, USA
401 N. Washington Street
Rockville, MD 20850
800-638-9636

General Videotex Corporation
3 Blackstone Street
Cambridge, MA 02139
800-544-4005

Hayes Microcomputer
  Products, Inc.
P.O. Box 105203
Atlanta, GA 30348
404-449-8791

Insignia Solutions, Inc.
1255 Post Street, Suite 625
San Francisco, CA 94109
415-885-4455

International Business
  Machines Corporation
P.O.Box 1328-W
Boca Raton, FL 33429-1328

Lotus Development Corp.
55 Cambridge Parkway
Cambridge, MA 02142
617-5778500

MicroPro International
  Corporation
33 San Pablo Ave.
San Rafael, CA 94903
415-499-1200

Microsoft Corporation
16011 NE 36th Way
Box 97017
Redmond, WA 96073-9717
206-882-8080

Source Telecomputing
  Corporation
1616 Anderson Road
McLean, VA 22102
800-336-3366

WordPerfect Corporation
1555 N. Technology Way
Orem, UT 84057
801-225-5000

INDEX

CM, Communications; DB, Database; SS, Spreadsheet; WP, Word Processor

NOTES

NOTES

NOTES